P9-AOY-232

Inside the Fashion Business

Text and Readings

Inside the Fashion Business

Text and Readings

Jeannette A. Jarnow
Edwin Goodman Professor
Chairman of Fashion Buying and Merchandising Department
Fashion Institute of Technology

Beatrice Judelle
Research Consultant

John Wiley and Sons, Inc., New York · London · Sydney

Library of Congress Catalog Card Number: 65-25855
Printed in the United States of America

Dedicated to our two husbands

Foreword

A hundred, perhaps even fifty years ago, "fashion" was directed toward the few—a leisured few to be elegantly adorned in the moments of tranquility which the calm pace of life afforded. Today we move in a larger world, and a faster one, and the fashion industry has become as complex as that world itself. The eloquent but mild postures of Poiret have given way to the lively, study-in-motion clothes of current American and European designers. For fashion is simply the most attractive front to the spirit of the times; and if experiment, change, and motion are the characteristics of our times, then they, too, are the ingredients of fashion.

With this change in the speed of life there has come an equally enormous change in the scale and scope of the fashion industry. Fashion for the few was ordained, cultivated, and handled by the few, in small shop operations. Yet the business that began as an enterprise of small shops now caters to millions of people, accepts a great diversity of talents, and offers a multitudinous array of products. The fashion industry is, on the one hand, the pleasant air of a Fifth Avenue salon, presenting a carefully edited collection of high-priced originals; and, on the other, it is factories that dispatch "blue jeans" in endless dozens to seaports, cities, and prairie towns across America. It is at one time the custom fitting room *and* the mail-order warehouse: a curious and exciting contrast.

More vast than the sheer size of the industry is the number of human resources that it calls into play. The citizens of the fashion world are designers and salesmen, seamstresses and accountants, merchandisers and markers, models and publicity experts. Together, they represent a wealth of contrary and complementary talents, feeding and fostering each other. In their cooperative endeavors fashion employs an incredible number of technical skills, a great deal of financial acumen, remarkable inventiveness, and occasionally a touch of what we can only call "genius." It is always astonishing, for example, to consider the demands that we put upon our fashion creators. In a society that expects from its authors and playwrights one or two great works in a lifetime, we take it in stride when a designer does a magnificent collection each season. And no less astonishing are the skill and enterprise that can adapt, promote, and sell these collections to meet the fast-changing demands of women throughout the world.

Of course there is glamour in the fashion industry and amazing vitality, which make it intriguing to the romantic and to the ambitious. But between the sketches in the margin of a schoolgirl's notebook and the order blank in a New York showroom—between the first imaginative interest and the real business of fashion—lies a vast terrain. And the young pioneer who sets out to chart this territory will need more than imagination, although that is a prerequisite, and more than ambition, although that is essential.

The troika of speed, scale, and scope has made the fashion industry a formidable subject for study. New tools are needed to bridge the gap between simple theories and the complex world of fashion that exists today. Providing some of these tools is the task that Jeannette Jarnow and Beatrice Judelle have set for themselves in this book. Professor Jarnow, as the Edwin Goodman Professor of the Fashion Institute of Technology, directs the Fashion Buying and Merchandising program under the Edwin Goodman Chair, which was established in 1955 in my father's memory. Prior to joining FIT, she had a long and successful merchandising career in fashion retailing. Miss Judelle has been associated with a variety of publications and the National Retail Merchants Association as a writer and a research specialist. From their collective experience they have compiled a book that will introduce the fashion aspirant to the many facets of our worlds, its insights and intrigues, its colorful personalities, and its calculated costs. This comprehensive survey set before the newcomer can only make the challenge of that world even more intriguing.

ANDREW GOODMAN
President, Bergdorf Goodman Company

Preface

This book is for those who have a particular interest in what is called the "fashion business"—that complex of enterprises that is concerned with the design, production, and distribution of women's apparel. Our objectives are twofold: to develop an understanding of the workings of an industry that is an important segment of our economy, and to expose the newcomer to the viewpoints of people who are actively engaged in the fashion business.

Fashion, in its broadest sense, touches nearly every business today. However, we have limited ourselves to women's clothing and to the industries and services that make and sell it.

The best way to learn what makes the wheels turn in the fashion business is to consult those who have achieved success and recognition as leaders in that business. From them come some of the most vivid analyses and some of the most penetrating insights into this fascinating field. These people usually express themselves in articles appearing in business periodicals that have a limited life and circulation or in speeches before groups of business people. A collection of some of the most illuminating, diverse, and provocative material of this kind is presented in this book.

The plan that we have followed is simple. After an introduction on the nature of fashion, there are different sections, each dealing with one particular aspect of the fashion business. These sections are divided into two parts. First comes an introductory text, designed to give an organized body of facts and principles. Next comes a collection of readings, chosen to complement, supplement, and illustrate the subject matter of the text. There are suggested questions for review and discussion at the end of each section. Within this framework, the newcomer should be better able to understand the industry, its workings, and its people, and should be helped to crystallize his objective and reach his own specific goal in fashion.

We are most grateful to the many publications, writers, organizations, and business leaders who so generously gave us permission to reprint. Also our thanks must go to the faculty members and students of the Fashion Institute of Technology for their continued support and suggestions, and to so many friends in the academic and fashion worlds, who gave advice and counsel, and helped us shape this book.

JEANNETTE A. JARNOW
BEATRICE JUDELLE

New York, New York, 1965

Contents

SECTION

I

Understanding Fashion

Fashion, in its most general sense, evidences itself not only in what people wear but in what they do, how they live, and the things they use. Its influence is felt in all categories of business today. Embodying more aspects of fashion than any other single rallying point is that group of industries dedicated to the design, construction, production, distribution, and promotion of fashion in women's apparel. It is a business community which has even been caricatured as "suffering from a form of schizophrenia because it manufactures clothing but it really doesn't sell clothing. What it sells is fashion." [1]

What is fashion? Where does it originate? Who controls it? In this section we attempt to explain fashion in terms of generally accepted definitions and concepts, and to suggest some of their implications for the business of women's clothing. We also introduce the reader to the scope and economic importance of the fashion business. The readings in this section present the fashion philosophies of successful professionals in the world of fashion.

What Is Fashion?

Few words in any language have as many different implications as does the one word "fashion." To the layman, it implies a mysterious force that makes a particular style of dress or behavior acceptable in one year but quite the reverse in another. Economists see it as an element of artificial obsolescence that impels people to replace articles which still retain much of their original usefulness even though the new ones may not greatly differ from the old. To sociologists it represents an expression of status seeking; [2] psychiatrists find indications of sex

[1] "The Rag Business: 7th Avenue Goes to Wall Street," *Forbes Magazine,* July 1, 1964, pp. 24–29.
[2] See Bernard Barber and Lyle Lobel, "Fashion in Women's Clothes and the American Social System," *Social Forces,* December 1952. Also see R.K. Merton, *Social Theory and Social Structure,* Glencoe, Ill., The Free Press, 1949, Ch. 1.

impulses in patterns of dress.[3] But whatever fashion may mean to others, it represents billions of dollars in sales to the group of enterprises concerned with the production and distribution of women's clothing. As one fashion student put it, "Everything that matters, everything that gives their trade its nature and place in the world must be ascribed to fashion." [4]

Terminology of Fashion. Among the countless definitions of fashion, the following from *Webster's Third New International Dictionary* comes very close to what professionals in the fashion business mean when they use the word: "The prevailing or accepted style or group of styles in dress or personal decoration established or adopted during a particular time or season." A widely recognized and often quoted fashion economist, Dr. Paul H. Nystrom, defined fashion in very similar words as being "nothing more nor less than the prevailing style at any given time." [5]

Frequently the word *fashion* is used interchangeably with the word *style*, and people will say, "Isn't it stylish?" when what they really mean is "Isn't it fashionable?" A *style* of clothing is considered to mean a type of product with specific characteristics which distinguish it from another type of the same product. For example, all full-skirted styles, even though they may differ in trimming, cut, or fabric, have a common characteristic which makes them different from straight-skirted garments. A full-skirted style, however, can have many individual variations in materials and details of line and decoration; these are called *designs*. To offer an example: The fashion may be for full-skirted silhouettes; the most popular type or style may be pleated skirts; the individual designs might be for box-pleated, pin-pleated, or pleated in other ways.

A few other key words should be explained at this point to facilitate further discussion of fashion principles. A *fashion trend* refers to the direction in which fashion is moving; the styles which are gaining in favor is the trend. A *fad* describes a style whose life is usually short, characterized by a sudden sweep of popularity and followed by an abrupt descent into limbo. *High fashion*, a term in common use, has a number of meanings, all of which imply a fashion of limited appeal. Some styles are high fashion because their high cost keeps them permanently out of reach of all but those in top income brackets, owing to expensive materials, intricate design, elaborate workmanship, and so on. Other styles are high fashion and remain so because they are too sophisticated to be in tune with the needs of the average woman, or too extreme for the woman who has to wear last year's coat with this year's new hat or dress. Still others are high fashion only temporarily, until the newness wears off or the price drops, and they become acceptable to people in general. High price alone does not make a garment high fashion, but it can keep an otherwise widely acceptable fashion from reaching all the people who would enjoy it. Because high fashions are so well publicized, one is likely to lose sight of the fact that they account for only a small portion of the total fashion business.

---

[3] See Dr. Edmund Bergler, *Fashion and the Unconscious*, New York, R. Brunner, 1953, for a provocative work based on his psychoanalysis of many persons connected with the fashion industry.

[4] Dwight E. Robinson, "The Economics of Fashion Demand," *Quarterly Journal of Economics*, Vol. LXXV, August 1961, p. 377.

[5] Paul H. Nystrom, *Economics of Fashion*, New York, Ronald Press, 1928, p. 4.

Fashion Means Acceptance. Although fashion feeds on new designs and styles, it is not the producers or designers of these styles who determine fashion. Fashions are not business creations; they are essentially social in their origin. No style or group of styles, no manner of dress can be considered to be a fashion unless it is accepted—that is, bought—by a substantial portion of the public. This element of public acceptance of a style is the very essence of fashion, and of the many styles that are created only those that are followed by sufficient numbers of people can be called fashions. Designers who acquire a reputation for "creating" fashion are simply those who have been outstandingly successful in giving tangible expression to the shapes, colors, lines, or looks wanted by the general public.

Fashion Means Change. Also to be considered in the concept of fashion is its changeable nature; fashion is not static. The preceding definitions recognize the changeability factor by using such words as a "given" or "particular" time. They do not, however, stress that fashion is also a force or movement that causes people to prefer one style more than another at certain times and places. Thorstein Veblen, writing at the turn of the century, made this clear in his *Theory of the Leisure Class*. He pointed out that:

> We readily and for the most part with utter sincerity find those things pleasing that are in vogue. Shaggy dress-stuffs and pronounced color effects, for instance, offend us at times when the vogue is goods of a high, glossy finish and neutral colors. A fancy bonnet of this year's model unquestionably appeals to our sensibilities today more forcibly than an equally fancy bonnet of the model of last year; although when viewed in the perspective of a quarter of a century, it would, I apprehend, be a matter of the utmost difficulty to award the palm for intrinsic beauty to one rather than to the other.[6]

These changes are not purposeful nor are they dictated by one or even a handful of designers. They are a result of altering socioeconomic conditions that affect the public's needs, wants, and receptivity to styles.

Fashion Involves Places and People. Consider also the element of places and people. Obviously, what may be considered fashionable in the Orient or in the Australian bush may be simply outlandish on a New York street, and what New York women wear is very often unacceptable in parts of the United States which have markedly different climate, terrain, or mores.

Finally, consider the group of people by whom a style or manner of dress must be accepted before we may call it a fashion. What is adopted by those who are venturesome or who seek distinction may be anything but acceptable to those of more conservative tastes. Furthermore, what is used by a particular age or occupational group may not be appropriate for those of a different age or occupational group.

Definition of Fashion. Our concept of fashion, then, emerges as a continuing *process of change in the styles of dress* (or behavior, if one is interested in the broadest aspects of the term) *that are accepted or followed by substantial groups of people at any given time and place.* "A fashion," however, would be the particular style that is popular at a specific time.

---

[6] Thorstein Veblen, *The Theory of the Leisure Class,* Mentor Edition, New American Library of World Literature, Inc., New York, 1963, p. 97.

How Fashion Moves

Fashions Change Gradually. Styles shift constantly, and minor innovations appear every season, but a full-scale changeover is never completed at any one time. Fashions usually evolve gradually unless some momentous event induces an abrupt switch. There was one such dramatic change in 1947 when the government curbs on the use of fabric during the Second World War were rescinded and the much publicized "New Look" by Dior was launched. The natural shoulder line, cinched-in waist, and full, long skirts changed the look of fashion almost overnight and made up in one season for the many years of wartime "freezing" of fashions. Had there been no war to require fabric economies, there probably would have been a gradual rather than dramatic abandonment of the skimpy short skirts and padded shoulders that had endured for most of the decade.

Trends do reverse themselves eventually, of course. Fashions usually move so steadily in one direction that revulsion seems to set in and the trend begins to move in an opposite direction. It is only in retrospect that changes in fashion seem sudden and drastic; actually they are cumulative and come about as a result of a series of gradual shifts over a period of time. When women's skirts began inching up from mid-calf, for example, or when men's trousers began to narrow, the change was not particularly noticed at first. It was not until skirts finally reached the knees, and trousers became very tight, that people took notice of their extreme length and width. They seemed to mistake their belated recognition of the gradual changes for a sudden, dramatic change in the fashions.

Fashion Cycles. Academically minded students of fashion have described the rise, peak, and eventual decline of accepted styles as the fashion cycle.[7] Some have even sought to chart the ups and downs of fashions in an effort to determine the length of time a fashion movement takes to run its course. The time intervals, however, elude measurement. The spread of fashion, as of every new idea, is a complicated social phenomenon. The public's needs and interests, which affect its receptivity to new styles or its boredom with an old one, do not change by clockwork.

[7] Nystrom, *op. cit.* p. 19.

Hemlines rise gradually.

The problem of applying the stopwatch technique to an analysis of fashion movements is also complicated by the fact that price differentials, which at one time tended to mark the different stages of style acceptance, have virtually disappeared. Furthermore, it is rare nowadays for a single style to dominate the scene at any particular time. While some cycles are in their peaks, their successors are already in the growing stage. Many new fashions often reach full growth without ever entirely displacing those that preceded them. A further complicating factor is that owing to the evolutionary nature of changes, clearly definable shifts in fashion do not occur at a given time, and it is impossible to pinpoint the exact beginning or end of a specific fashion.

The more one studies fashion, in theory and in practice, the more apparent it becomes that the term "fashion cycle" is a misleading concept. The very word "cycle" implies a repetitive rise and fall, as if a wheel had turned and the fashions that were "in" had to go "out" for a time and then reappear at predictable intervals. There are revivals of styles from time to time but the fashions of another day never quite come back in their entirety; neither history nor fashion ever plays itself back to us unchanged.

Fashions are cyclical, however, to the extent that they do go through stages of increasing and decreasing popularity. They also vary in duration and in degree of acceptance. As an overall rule, broad, general trends have the longest life: for example, the fashion of casual clothes. Those that are narrow and more specific, such as particular styles of casual apparel, are usually of shorter duration. Occasionally an individual style so satisfies a basic need that it remains in fashion almost indefinitely; this is called a *classic*. Typical are simple cardigan sweaters for women and white shirts with button down collars for men.

Dr. Paul Nystrom, enunciating his theory on the life cycles of fashions, noted that cycles in accessory fashions such as scarfs, handbags, costume jewelry, and the like tend to run for a season, whereas fashions in color, design, and materials usually require a year, and silhouette cycles tend to run much longer.[8]

A reading in this section has aptly compared the rise and decline of a particular fashion to the rise and fall of waves in the surf.[9] No mathematical formula governs their formation, cresting and breaking, but the experienced swimmer learns to study them and to time the individual waves that concern him. So it is in the fashion business. Like experienced swimmers and navigators, fashion firms evaluate the rise and fall in the popularity of styles by their own curve of sales and develop a fairly good idea of where their particular organization stands in relation to fashion movements.

What Makes Fashions

It is far easier to recognize what is fashionable than to say why or how it became a fashion. When we search for the influences that bring forth fashions such as the crinolines of the past or the silhouettes of the present, we are confronted with a complex question indeed. One thing we do know: esthetic appeal does not produce a fashion. Veblen made this point when he observed that there

---

[8] *Ibid.*, 29.

[9] See Kenneth Collins, "Fashion Cycles," included in this volume on page 15.

is no intrinsic difference between the gloss of a patent leather shoe and the shine of a threadbare garment. People, he observed, are ready to find beauty in what is in vogue; therefore the shine on the shoe is beautiful and the garment's shine is repulsive.[10]

Imitation Makes Fashions. Styles can become fashions through a simple follow-the-leader process. Widespread imitation of the styles worn by admired individuals or groups result in the development of a fashion.[11] A great fashion designer, Coco Chanel, said this very clearly: "If there is no copying, how are you going to have fashion?"[12]

Centuries ago, the leaders and setters of fashion were royalty. The nobility copied royalty and was copied in turn by those of the middle class who had the means. The lower classes, of course, had neither the means nor the temerity to copy. In time, royalty themselves went out of fashion in many countries and their position as fashion leaders was assumed by outstanding individuals at the top of the economic and social ladder. Many such people made it their business to dress well, and their activities and appearance were highly publicized and reported. The large majority of the public, with more restricted social activities and more limited budgets, were necessarily cautious in their spending and, in fashion, this caution expressed itself in imitating what "they" wore and in avoiding experimentation.

Today, however, fashion is not a matter of imitating any particular social or economic class. Fashions seem to emerge spontaneously; if style offerings are appropriate and acceptable, they need not wait for the approval of an elite in order to become the fashion. It is true, of course, that there are always people that other people will copy—a movie star, a big man on campus, a public figure who captures the imagination. But the choice of models is no longer limited to those with glittering genealogy or fabulous wealth. People choose their own heroes and heroines in fashion today, as in anything else.

New Technical Developments Make Fashions. Some fashions also seem to have their origins in the development of new fibers and fabrics, new processes for utilizing familiar ones, and other fruits of the chemist's genius—plus, perhaps, a waiting need for the new or a weariness with the old. For example, the synthetic fibers which made wash-and-wear fabrics possible, and which in turn influenced fashion, might not have received such a rousing welcome if they had come upon the scene at a time when domestic help was plentiful and when the stiffly starched, beautifully ironed garment was a symbol of the well-run household. More recently, the development of stretch fabrics has had a great impact upon trends in fashion.

The "Times" Make Fashions. A glance at the past makes it apparent that fashions also grow out of the interaction of many factors which serve as sources of inspiration and appear to trigger both the trends and their acceptance by the public. During this century, for example, fashion has been influenced by two world wars and by the social and economic currents that caused and, in turn, were stimulated by the exodus to the suburbs. Casual clothes, for instance, which

---

[10] Thorstein Veblen, *op. cit.*, p. 97.

[11] See Melvin T. Copeland, *Principles of Advertising*, New York, A. W. Shaw Co., 1926, p. 163, for a discussion of emulation in fashion.

[12] *Women's Wear Daily*, November 16, 1964, p. 1.

had not yet won wide acceptance when the Second World War began, swept into importance on the tide of relaxed suburban living.

Fashions have been made by major events and outstanding personalities in the worlds of science, entertainment, politics, art, and sports. To cite some examples: Egyptian motives inspired by the discovery of the tomb of King Tut-Ankh-Amen; Hawaiian prints gaining impetus when the territory became a state; the fashion for ballet slippers, pony tails, and other ballerina influences inspired by the popularity of the Russian ballet; colors and print designs that sprang from modern paintings; the growing enthusiasm for boating and the resultant popularity of sailing denims for city wear; the impact of a young and lovely First Lady like Jacqueline Kennedy upon hair and dress styles.

Creative designers are alert to such stimuli. People and events in the news suggest to them new silhouettes, new fabric textures, new colors, new accessories. If the designer is successful in translating the outside happenings into styles that reflect the public's own enthusiasm for the person or place concerned, then a new fashion is "created."

Even though it may seem that the fashion grows out of the news, actually the news is only the catalyst. A fashion must be ready to be born, just as soil must be fertile if seed is to grow. No one factor alone—people, places, events, inventions, or creative designer—can make a fashion. Each influences the other, but in the final analysis it is the customer's acceptance or rejection that makes or breaks a fashion idea.

The Business of Fashion

The more familiar one is with the fashion business, the more obvious it becomes that fashion is not imposed upon the public by the industry, but rather it is a phenomenon that must be analyzed and interpreted into the shapes and looks of clothes. Thousands of styles and designs are created and produced each year by designers and manufacturers of fabrics and apparel.[13] Those that are purchased by the retail distributors and, in turn, by a substantial group of ultimate consumers are considered to be a fashion. The fact that a new style may be highly publicized as a new fashion does not make it so; neither is a style a fashion because it is worn by one or a few individuals, no matter who they may be. Fashion is not a matter of opinion but is determined by actual count.

One of America's most successful designers has made this same point. In a reading in this book ("He's a fashion purist with the golden touch"), Norman Norell is quoted as saying, "I'm more interested in launching a fashion than in creating beautiful things. Fashion is what is accepted and worn by the general public. When it reaches that point, you know the design is a good one."

Fashion is Big Business. Fashion plays an important role in our economy. Americans spend over $33 billion a year on clothing, shoes, and accessories; this amounts to nearly one out of every ten dollars spent.[14] Millions of people are

[13] The ILGWU once estimated that the dress division of the New York market annually produced over 50,000 different designs ("Picture of a Union," a special supplement in the *New York Times,* May 17, 1959).

[14] Personal consumption expenditures for 1964, as estimated by the Bureau of the Census, U.S. Department of Commerce, and published in *Survey of Current Business,* March 1965, p. S–2.

employed in producing the apparel and accessories, and in staffing the retail stores which sell this merchandise. Of the nearly 18 million people employed in manufacturing industries in the United States in 1964, one in every eight was employed either in the industries that produce apparel for men, women, and children, or in the textile and other industries that produce the materials from which clothing and accessories are made.[15] Apparel manufacturing employs more people than the automotive industry, more people than the entire printing and publishing field, more people than the chemical and drug industries. Its payroll of nearly $5 billion a year is almost one-twentieth of the total payroll for all manufacturing industries in the United States.[16]

The women's branch of this huge industry is important. The classification known as women's, misses, and junior outerwear (blouses, dresses, coats, suits, and skirts) alone represents 40 per cent of the value of apparel production, having factory shipments of nearly $4 billion.[17] This one branch of the fashion business uses more factories and employes more people than, for example, the household-furniture industry or the tobacco industry. Among department stores, at least one-third of the over $18 billion total sales volume is produced by the departments devoted to feminine apparel and accessories.[18] This means that over $6 billion a year of the money currently being spent in department stores is for such fashion merchandise. An additional $5.6 billion or more is spent in stores specializing in women's apparel and accessories.[19] When we add what women spend for themselves in shoe stores, family clothing stores, and in purchases from mail-order catalogues, the total comes to $16.5 billion a year spent to outfit women of all ages.[20]

Complexity of the Fashion Industry. Unlike industries such as tobacco or automobile manufacturing, the fashion industry is not a clearly defined entity. It is a complex of many different industries, not all of which appear to have anything of fashion among their products.

Plainly recognizable as part of the fashion business are those industries devoted to the making of dresses, coats, suits, skirts and similar articles of women's apparel, as well as the millinery industry, the makers of scarfs, lingerie, foundation garments, costume jewelry, handbags, and other accessories of feminine dress. Also part of the fashion business are producers whose output is partly for women and partly for men or children. In this category are makers of gloves, shoes, sweaters, hosiery, and other knitwear.

When one moves back to an earlier stage of production, to the fabrics, leathers, and plastics from which the finished products are made, the line between what is and what is not the fashion business becomes even harder to draw. Some

[15] Monthly Report on the Labor Force, December 1964, U. S. Department of Labor, Washington, D.C., p. 36.
[16] *Ibid.*
[17] 1964 *Preliminary Apparel Survey,* Current Industrial Reports, Series M23H (64), Bureau of Census, Industry Division, Apparel Section.
[18] Annual reports of the Board of Governors of the Federal Reserve Board, Washington, D.C., "Department Store Trade, United States, Distribution of Annual Sales by Departments," and Department of Commerce estimates of department store sales, both for 1964.
[19] Monthly Current Retail Trade Report, U.S. Department of Commerce, for 1964.
[20] Research Department, ILGWU, "Conditions in the Women's Garment Industry," September 1964, p. 18.

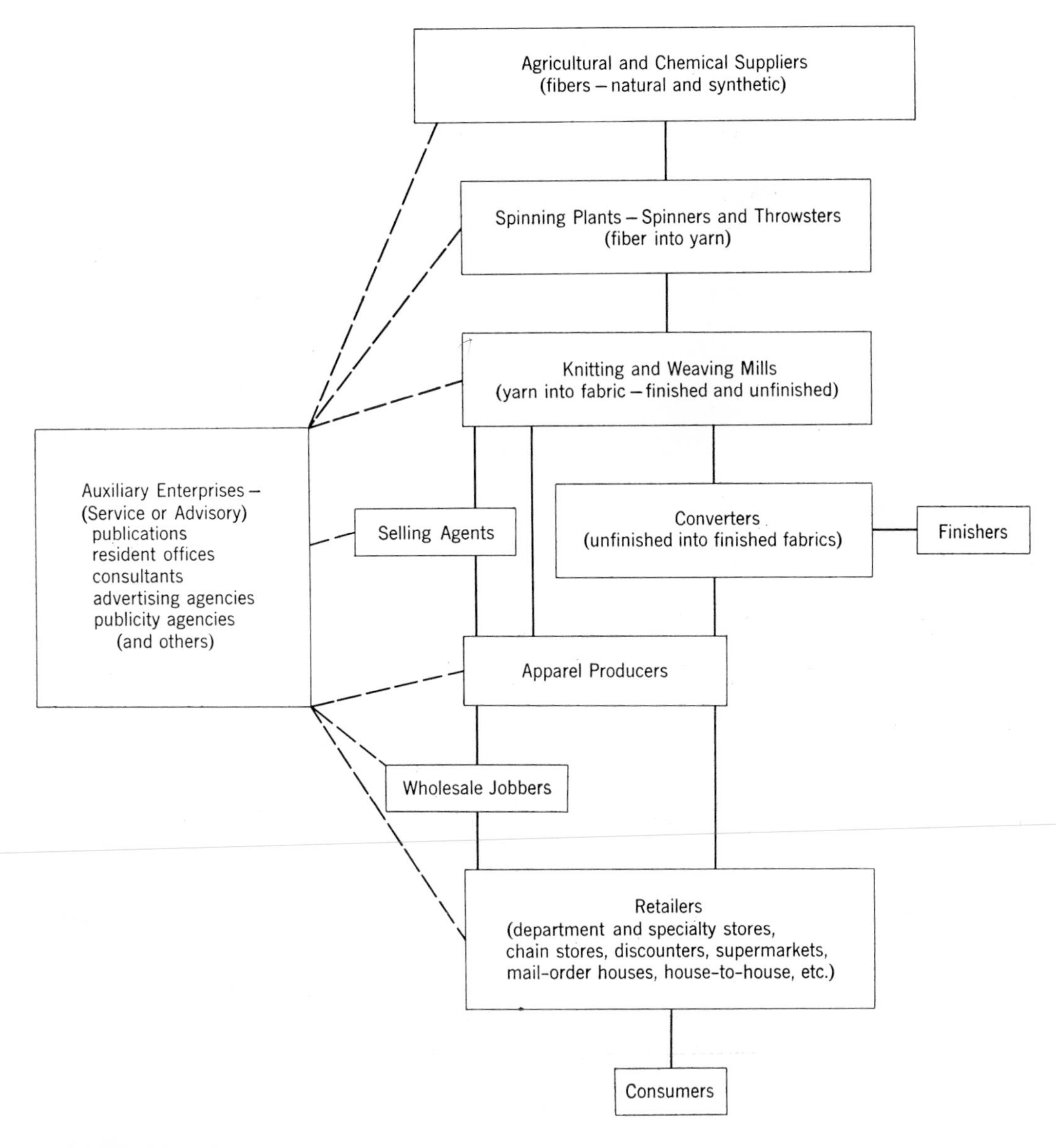

textile mills that produce dress and coat fabrics also produce bed sheets, carpets, or industrial fabrics. Some chemical companies that produce fibers which eventually are spun and woven and cut to make women's garments are also producers of explosives, fertilizers, and photographic film. Some factories mold rubber and synthetic foam into shapes for various household and industrial uses, and then, when the foundation business requires bust pads, or the coat and suit trade needs shoulder pads, find themselves with a foot in the fashion business.

The fashion business includes the stores that sell apparel and accessories, and the mail-order catalogues from which many consumer purchases are made. It also includes businesses that neither produce nor sell merchandise, but which are as much a part of the fashion business as enterprises that do.

In this last category are consumer publications that disseminate news of fashion, ranging from the women's page of the daily newspaper to magazines devoted primarily to that one subject, such as *Vogue* or *Harper's Bazaar.* Also included in this category are trade periodicals which carry news of fashion and information on production and distribution techniques to retailers, apparel manufacturers, and textile mills. It includes also publicists and advertising specialists, fashion consultants, and buying offices that represent retail stores in the vast wholesale centers.

All these and more are part of the business—farms and mills and factories, union labor and white-collar workers, business tycoons and creative artists. All play their parts in the business of women's fashions.

Readings

The readings in this section present the fashion philosophy of professionals who have achieved success and recognition in their respective specialties—a fashion consultant, the head of a great store, a brilliant retailer turned columnist, a design consultant, a well-known fashion historian, and a business economist. Notice that their viewpoints are not based on any flashes of intuition. Each, in his own way, stresses the essential point that fashion is nothing more or less than what the public accepts.

Notice also their emphasis on the interrelation of fashion and socioeconomic developments. This relationship is illustrated in the concluding reading which highlights the fashions of the first fifty years of this century.

What Is Fashion?

by Tobé Coller Davis

When I talk about fashion I'm talking about a *force which is an integral part of every business that caters to people at every economic level* and in every social station. I'm talking about this motivating force in cars and homes, furniture and appliances, and food and drink—and of course, apparel for every one—man, woman, or child. When I emphasize the fashion element of life and especially the multibillion dollar fashion and beauty industry, I am most emphatically not just talking about surface design or the little gimmicks and gadgets by which manufacturers vary their models from day to day or season to season. This is only the fringe on the surrey—it isn't the carriage itself.

Basically fashion is something much more solid and substantial. It is the reflection of the lives we lead and the way we live them, expressed every day. Fashion is like a mirror that reflects the feeling, the pace, the activities—and most of all the needs of our daily lives. *Therefore, the business of fashion is the business of making goods best suited to our times and our lives.*

Where does this fashion come from? I can assure you it is not from the "bright ideas" of a few master designers. No one—and I really mean no one—can make or create fashion arbitrarily. Fashion "makers"—and I put that word in quotes—are really people who realize and express in terms of style and design the way of life of the communities they serve.

Then what does make fashion, if the so-called fashion "makers" don't?

First, economics. Fashion follows the wealth line, for in serving the needs of the community, it must cater to the class in the community that commands the biggest purchasing power. Once again, let me emphasize that I'm not just talking about fancy clothes, but about all goods which reflect daily life. Over the history of fashion, since the early days of the Egyptians—it has been the wealthy class, the patrons of the arts, to which fashion has responded or which has inspired it. Hence, as the wealth line

Excerpted and reprinted with permission from a presentation at the Harvard Graduate School of Business Administration, April 25, 1957. Before her death in 1962, Mrs. Davis was generally considered to be the leading fashion consultant in the business.

changes, fashion changes too. It once reflected the lives of the courts of Venice and France. Another time the church, still another the nobility or the bourgeoisie.

Secondly, sociology affects and influences fashion. The structure and organization of society dictate what fashion must be. A society dedicated to courtly ceremony, such as that of France in the 1700's, must inevitably have had an entirely different kind of fashion than a society dedicated to the business of making money, as was nineteenth century America.

Third, art and taste inspire fashion. Fashion is, after all, essentially a matter of esthetics. It must reflect not only the wealth and the functions of a society, but its ideas of what is beautiful. Much as art swings between realism and abstraction, so in apparel too, the pendulum swings in cycles between "naturalism" and "abstraction"—between revealing the human figure and concealing it.

Let me illustrate by pointing to some current fashion sources. Economics, for example. I'm sure I don't have to spell out for you the great economic revolution of our time—the shift in the economic center of gravity of our nation. Little more than three generations ago the wealth of our country, like the cream in a bottle of milk, lay concentrated at the narrow upper neck of the bottle. In 1939, for instance, the top 1 per cent of America controlled 20 per cent of the nation's spending power. That bottle has had a vigorous shaking and today the cream and the milk are almost homogenized. The wealth of the nation no longer lies at the top. The neck of the economic bottle now has less than half the cream—that is, the income—that it had twenty-five years ago. Instead, the cream is distributed in the upper two-thirds to three-quarters of the bottle. It is distributed to the six out of ten American families with incomes between $3000 and $10,000. Furthermore, our economic bottle is still being shaken: Within another decade or two, probably seven or eight out of every ten families will comprise this great new category of the "poor rich." By 1980, if our present economic trends continue, the average family income will be $8000 at today's prices. By the year 2000—when our children are well grown up—it will be $15,000.

This economic homogenizing of American wealth has affected fashion more profoundly than all the stupendous piles of publicity releases from New York, Paris, and Hollywood put together. For as I have pointed out, where wealth is, there fashion goes—and wealth, as we have seen, is now a diffuse, rather than a concentrated phenomenon. Hence fashion today caters to the gigantic diffuse middle-income, middle-class market. It is not, as I have often said, Mrs. Chauncey Gotbucks and her four hundred who set the pace today, but plain Mrs. Tom Jones and the sixty million like her. Of course, there is still a tiny percentage of very rich Americans to whom fashion caters, but this is no longer, as it once was, the most important part of the fashion business.

It isn't the Cadillac and Lincoln that reflect the basic fashion of our country but the Chevrolet, Buick, and the Ford. It isn't Newport or Southampton mansions that reflect the fashion in housing, but simple Southern California ranch-type houses. It isn't Steinway grand pianos, but spinets; it isn't grand opera but TV. In a word, the focus of fashion today is aimed squarely at the middle of our economy, rather than at the diminishing top for the simple reason that the middle is where the money is.

Now let me mention a sociological change that has affected present-day fashions very drastically. Unlike the intangible economic change, this great revolution is laid right out where we can see it—although you have to fly in an airplane to appreciate the view. It reflects a new kind of living environment for America—no longer the small town, which once so accurately reflected our way of life—neither is it the great metropolis which we mistakenly think of as the typical American habitat. The new truly representative environment is the belt-city—the strip-city—the road city. You can see it, stretching along the superhighways which serve as its "streets." They string along in almost unbroken continuity from Boston to Washington and all over the rest of our land. It's not city and it's not country—it's in between and part of both. It is, in fact, an utterly new living environment.

We call it suburbia or exurbia, sometimes with a condescending smile. But the long-range planners aren't smiling. This is where 90 per cent of the 50 million increase in population will take place over the next twenty years. Hence the belt-city will pose tremendous problems for the future—new economic, political, and social problems. Crossing state lines and county lines with a fine disregard, the new strip-city will require new concepts of government and social planning too.

Already—and this is the point that interests us here—it poses new fashion demands. For suburbia is not just a new location for the average American. It is a new kind of life which requires new kinds of living equipment. Look at the boom in station wagons, in small cars, in the need for two cars. Look at the stupendous rise in do-it-yourself equipment! Look at the trend of magazine content toward suburban family living. *McCall's* "togetherness" slogan is probably the single most successful advertising concept of the past decade because it mirrors so well the feeling as well as the fact of this new communal life-setting.

So far I've tried to show how economic and sociological trends have vastly influenced the design of daily living and its goods.

Now let me talk about art, culture, and taste for a moment. We have today the greatest dissemination of culture and art of any civilization in history. Our hunger for culture is stupendous—unsatisfied! The part that *Life* magazine alone has played in bringing to millions the great masterpieces of the past and present is simply without any precedent. It is just one of many other efforts of similar impact.

As a result American taste is enormously sensitive to currents in arts. The very business man who says that he doesn't "care for" modern art is probably sitting in a Knoll chair behind a Henry Miller desk. He looks out of a window of a building designed by Mies Van der Rohe. He may drive a car designed by Henry Dreyfus or by Chrysler's Virgil Exner. Modern art simply surrounds us and we insist on the modern artist and his talent in the products we use in daily life. From appliances and furniture, to fabrics and colors—the imprint of the modern artist is unmistakable—bold but simple shapes, new colors, dramatic contrast. In great abundance this new art surrounds us daily.

Fashion—Integral Part of Life

What I've been talking about so far is the meaning of fashion to each of us in all walks of life. I wonder if you have noticed that I haven't even mentioned clothes—I avoided it for a very good reason. I wanted to drive home the fact that fashion is an integral part of living—not merely a fancy "addition" to our lives. Fashion is the basic pattern not a meaningless set of decorative doodles scribbled on the pattern of life.

Nature of Fashion

by Alfred H. Daniels

Nature of Fashion

This is a field where the only good place to begin is with a definition of the subject. Much of the mystery of fashion merchandising is simply a matter of not knowing what fashion is.

There are a host of definitions, many by erudite men and women. For instance, Ambrose Bierce has said that "fashion is a despot whom the wise ridicule—and obey." And according to Thoreau, "Every generation laughs at the old fashions but follows religiously the new." In Oscar Wilde's opinion, "Fashion is a form of ugliness so intolerable that we have to alter it every six months." Shakespeare philosophized that "the fashion wears out more apparel than the man."

In each of these observations—and there are countless others equally appropriate—there is something germane. But the definition which best seems to sum up the essential characteristics of fashion is a much more mundane one: "Fashion is a conception of what is currently appropriate." The report from which this quotation is taken goes on to say:

Excerpted and reprinted with permission from "Fashion Merchandising," *Harvard Business Review*, May, 1951. Mr. Daniels, President of Burdine's, Inc., Miama, Fla, was Vice-President of Abraham and Straus, Brooklyn, N. Y. when he wrote this article.

> Fashion influences human activities and shapes the forms of our possessions. It affects the things we do, the things we say, the things we wear, and the things we use. Times and conditions largely affect fashion and may be looked upon as a subtle reflection of our composite feelings and reactions to life at any given period. Fashion is not necessarily high fashion, the latter being the expression of a limited number of people with above-normal means or taste to enjoy it. Mass fashions are the most widely accepted versions of high fashion trends.[1]

Definition. Our definition of fashion as a conception of "what is currently appropriate" means, in simpler language, a conception of what the customer wants. This idea will be popping up again and again in the subsequent discussion. Once the concept is well understood, it will be seen that the fashion merchant need only look at the facts and rarely at the reasons behind the facts. If he can jump this hurdle, he is over the hurdle of inferiority complex in his business. Since this point is such a vital one, let me break it down into its four essential components.

(1) There are psychological and biological drives involved in fashion, and these drives remain pretty constant. Hence, what is wanted is constant: glamour and a sense of belonging or security; the desire to keep up with the Joneses, on the one hand, and the attempt to become Mrs. Jones on the other.

(2) *General* fashions change slowly. For instance, emancipation of women had to be reflected in women's clothes, but that was a long, historical process. Suburban and casual living has increased the importance of sportswear, but that too did not happen overnight. The increasing number of working women has brought about many new fashions, including the basic dress that can change its look at 7:00 P.M. by the addition of an accessory, but this has not been a quick development either. The fact is that *general* fashions change slowly. The specific causes of a general fashion change are not necessarily of concern to the fashion merchant. For example, there is an Oriental influence taking place in women's apparel. The fashion merchant will know this—he cannot escape it—but he does not need to know how it came about. If he is curious, he can call up some fashion expert, who may tell him that it is the result of pressure by Mongolian idiots or of the decision of women in Bali finally to dress themselves. He would find this very fascinating and proceed about his business, reassured that the development was going to stay on for a while.

(3) Fashion no longer refers to price. Students of marketing used to talk about the fashion cycle as having three phases—a conveniently divided Tinkers-to-Evers-to-Chance sort of affair—with different price characteristics for each phase. By contrast, the fact today is that the fashion cycle moves so quickly that it is a blur. Almost everyone instantaneously wants the same thing. The differential price characteristic has virtually disappeared. Radio, TV, the theater, and the press can be thanked for this.

(4) If fashion in the broad sense changes slowly, specific manifestations of fashion can and do change quickly—very quickly. This point is a crucial one. To make the distinction, some people have called general fashion merely "fashion," and specific fashion "style," or vice versa.

Let me illustrate the distinction by an example previously referred to: the growing importance of sportswear. This is a general fashion trend, and its course will not be altered except in the space of a long period. At the moment, however, within sportswear there can be a demand for white sweaters. Tomorrow this demand may change to purple skirts; the next day, to something else. These are the changes involved in Professor Melvin T. Copeland's fashion cycle theory, where emulation becomes the pivotal drive. The nub of the whole thing is right here. William Hazlett's definition, "Fashion is gentility running away from vulgarity and afraid of being overtaken," is just another way of stating Copeland's thesis that there are "distinctive," "emulation," and "mass emulation" stages (however momentary) of every specific fashion.

Going back to our illustration, certain social leaders, a distinguished campus, or the "international set" will decide to wear white sweaters. Why is unimportant. Then other persons in the

[1] Associated Merchandising Corporation Committee Report on "The Significance of Fashion Leadership to Our Stores."

next social stratum down begin to emulate—and there we go. It should be clear, though, that the distinguished group, no matter how distinguished, cannot bring about a fundamental change in fashion. The roots have to be deeper than that. Given a general fashion trend, what the distinguished group does is to try to be different within it. That is all. As has been indicated, because of improved methods of communication and because of economic competition on the part of manufacturers, this difference remains momentary. So the process to gain prestige starts again. It is like perpetual motion.

Let me summarize the foregoing points about fashion, now, very briefly:

(1) Women buy fashion to look pretty and glamorous and to be "in the swing" or to belong.

(2) Long-range fashions change slowly.

(3) Fashion does not refer to price.

(4) Specific fashions or styles change quickly because certain people want to look unique within the general fashion trend.

Fashion Cycles

by Kenneth Collins

A young woman writes: "From your experience, is there any way to foresee the beginning of a new fashion? How does one estimate or guess its duration? What are the signs that it is about to die?"

I shall, of course, not attempt to answer these questions. They go far beyond my knowledge. But they do give me an excuse to present an analogy between ocean waves and style trends that has been in my mind so many years. I should like to air it even if only to have it laughed at. Please bear with me.

If you have ever sat idly watching the surf, you must have noted that each wave rolls in with a curve, a crest, and a crash. To me, this general pattern seems identical to that of fashions which certainly curve, crest, and crash.

But the similarity appears to go much further. Some waves race headlong for a shallow beach, swell rapidly to a tremendous foaming top, then drop abruptly with a thud. Is this not precisely what happens with fads? But other waves move gradually upwards, curl over in a quiet, leisurely way, then break with little or no force. Is this not precisely the movement of sane, properly conceived style cycles? They are slow to develop, hold their own for a time, then subside rather than collapse.

You may now say: Your analogy is amusing and is no doubt a useful way to describe the emergence and disappearance of fashions. But that is all it is—a bit of description.

Probably so. But people who have done much swimming or boat handling in the surf might see more to the comparison than something merely pictorial. They know it is great fun to time a wave and to ride over it. They also know it is a very different matter to miss one's timing and to get caught just as the crest topples. That can be annoying. And in some circumstances it can be exceedingly dangerous—just as dangerous, for example, as taking disastrous markdowns after badly miscalculating the appeal of a freak style.

Oh well, I must not go on with the analogy. It may simply be a pleasant conceit on my part. But if it does not make at least a little sense, I wish someone would tell me why.

Reprinted by permission of *Women's Wear Daily*, June 19, 1957. Copyright 1957, Fairchild Publications, Inc. Upon retirement from a long and distinguished retailing career, Mr. Collins became a feature columnist for *Women's Wear Daily*.

Are There Really Fashion Cycles?

by John Robert Riley

If only there were such convenient timetables as "fashion cycles," life and merchandising would be infinitely happier and more profitable. Our cyclical alarm clock would alert us to creped yarns, lengthened hems, lowered heels, and close-cropped hair. Buying and selling, designing and manufacturing, would be as automated as the electronic skills of IBM could make them.

The punch cards of automation can be very useful to the fashion industry. . . . But the shape of the ultimate product must rely on the aberrations of the human mind and the experiments of the human hand.

One of the truths of fashion is deceit. We make our shoulders look broader, our waists slimmer, our feet shorter, or, as we wish, we accomplish just the opposite effect. The one achievement we will never consider is to show ourselves as we really are.

This shifting illusion of dressing requires endless expensive experiment and an adventurous clientele to wear it. For us, the workrooms of the French couture are the laboratory and their customers the guinea pigs. But why should we practice such legerdemain upon ourselves? The answers are infinitely complex, for we are dealing with a whole series of connecting economic, political, and cultural factors which constitute the life of a time. All of these factors mixed together are the catalyst for change in fashion, for change in the way we wish to appear to one another.

We are educated on many truisms which eventually reveal themselves as simple untruths. One of the foremost of these is "History repeats itself." It is mathematically improbable and historically impossible for all those complicated economic, political, and cultural factors to rearrange themselves in the same way twice.

Those who explore the past to find the future are chasing ghosts. The past is dead and we cannot revive it. That is why all so-called fashion "revivals" are doomed to failure. But even as the ideas of those before us live on, so do we build on ideas of the past to create the new. For this creative process there is no mathematical or mechanical formula. No machine can extrude nor die-press out a new idea. Here we rely on that unique and precious individual, the creative designer. His radar is more finely tuned than others. He senses the thousands of facts of the future. These he translates, molds, makes real for us. Without his vision we would not have the reality of our vast industrial production.

Abridged and reprinted by permission of *Boot and Shoe Recorder*, September 15, 1961. Mr. Riley is a design consultant and curator of the Design Institute of the Brooklyn Museum, Brooklyn, New York.

Fashion:

A Detective Story

by James Laver

As soon as fashion crops up, some hard-headed fellow who takes pride in having no illusions is sure to say: "It's all a romp. Half a dozen men in Paris get together and decide to change the fashion. They want to sell their goods. It's as simple as that."

Reprinted with permission from *Vogue*, January 1959. Copyright © 1958 by the Conde Nast Publications, Inc. James Laver, noted fashion historian was Keeper of Prints and Drawings of the Victoria and Albert Museum, London, England for almost forty years.

It is not as simple as that, for if it were, fashion would be arbitrary and meaningless. But that is just what fashion never is, and one can see this quite plainly when looking at the fashions of the past. Every style seems completely appropriate to its epoch. We can not imagine Madame de Pompadour, or the Empress Josephine, or the early Victorian lady in anything but the clothes she actually wore. Each represents completely the ideals of her time: elegant artificiality, or post-Revolutionary morals, or the prudery of the rising middle class. When seen in retrospect fashions seem to express their era. Although it is more difficult to draw conclusions from contemporary clothes, the same principles which hold for the clothes of the past must hold for clothes of the present and the future.

I am a social historian, if I may call myself that, a museum official, and my interest in fashion began in a round-about way. At the Victoria and Albert Museum, we have, I suppose, the largest collection of miniatures in the world, and people are constantly bringing in their family heirlooms for an opinion. "This is my great-, great-aunt Augusta who danced at the Waterloo Ball," one might say. I would reply, with growing confidence as the years went by, "I'm afraid there must be something wrong with the family records. This portrait represents a woman of about twenty wearing the clothes of 1840. She couldn't have danced at the Waterloo Ball in 1815."

For this purely utilitarian purpose I began to assemble a file of fashion. I found that I could date any picture to within a year in the nineteenth century, to within two years in the eighteenth century, to within ten years in the seventeenth. I could, that is, if there was a fashionable woman in the picture.

Men won't do, for men's clothes perpetually formalize themselves and do not follow the principle of fashion. Peasants won't do, because peasant, or regional costume as it is properly called, changes by place and not by time. Until the fourteenth century, that was how all fashion changed. During the greater part of human history, if you stayed where you were nothing altered. If you went into the next village, however, everything was different. Today, if you travel the world, everything is the same. If you stay in one spot for a year, however, practically all the women change their hats. We have exchanged the tyranny of place for the tyranny of time. We have the Time Disease.

When I had assembled my file of fashion, I began to make such curious discoveries as the strange relationship which seems to exist between clothes, especially women's clothes, and architecture. It is generally agreed, for example, that the dominant architectural shape of the Middle Ages was the sharply pointed lancet arch. Sharpened still further, it is the pinnacle or the steeple on a church. Similarly, in the fifteenth century, men's shoes were so long they sometimes had to be turned back and tied to the knees. The female headdress, the hennin, was correspondingly steeple-shaped. By 1500 the lancet arch was blunted, and became what we call the Tudor Arch. When Henry VIII came to the throne in 1509, his shoes were not sharp and pointed like those of his father Henry VII, but blunted. The headdress of his wife, Catherine of Aragon, was blunted too—just like the Tudor Arch.

In the eighteenth century, the dominant architectural motif of the period the French call Louis Seize and the English, Adam Brothers, was the neoclassical pilaster. One can see the same motif as it was interpreted in fashion, in the costumes of the Empress Josephine. Simple, straight, her dress is typical of what I call the post-crisis style. After a great social upheaval like the French Revolution women have a burst of emancipation, sometimes only momentary. When about ten years have elapsed and fashion settles down into a post-crisis style, women's clothes become "little girl" clothes. They are subconsciously designed to "do down" the older woman.

If we take the dress of 1925, another post-crisis period, we find that, different as the dresses of 1800 and 1925 are, they have certain things in common. The lines are as straight as nature will allow, or even straighter; the waist is in the wrong place: very high in 1800, very low in 1925. In both years, the hair was worn short. It seemed to me that in the next post-crisis epoch we would see something similar and therefore, after World War II, I predicted that in approximately ten years we would have a dress with straight lines and a wandering waist. Just about that time Dior introduced his H-line and his A-line. I think it fair to say that this style, with the chemises that followed, had a definite resemblance to the clothes of 1800 and 1925.

In violent contrast to these post-crisis styles was the full-skirted dress of the relatively placid mid-nineteenth century. The skirt was swelled by what might be called a machine age triumph, a steel hoop that substituted for a prodigious number of petticoats. Its size said: "This is an age of male domination, expanding population, social stability, and 'hard' money," just as the skimpy clothes of 1800 and 1925 said, "This is an age of female emancipation, declining birthrate, social instability, and inflation." (Incidentally, the frame of the hoop bore a curious resemblance to the butt-end of the Crystal Palace, which was erected in 1851.) The hoop was hollow and if you are looking for a symbol of mid-Victorian hypocrisy you could hardly find a better. The hoop seemed to say, "You cannot come near enough to touch my hand," and yet it swayed in every wind. It was also uncontrollable, and a deplorable number of young women were burned to death when their clothes caught in open fires.

Nothing is more revealing of an age than its hypocrisies and perhaps analysing them can help us to understand how fashion works. There seem to me to be three principles: The hierarchical principle, or dressing for class. The seduction principle, or dressing to attract the opposite sex. The utility principle, or dressing for warmth, et cetera.

Women's clothes follow, on the whole, the seduction principle (slightly modified by the utility principle) because men largely select their wives by their attractiveness as women. The object of women's clothes is, therefore, to make their wearers attractive to men. Many women say, "I dress to please myself," or even, "I dress to displease other women." Perhaps this is the formula: Women dress, in competition with other women, to please themselves by attracting men.

Women, on the other hand, select their husbands with the hope that they will be able to support a family. Men's clothes, therefore, are essentially hierarchical, or class-conscious. Compared to the constant mutations of women's dress, men's fashions are like fossils.

The psychologists have invented something they call "the shifting erogenous zone." In other words, woman as a whole is a desirable object, but the mind of man is too weak to take it all in at once. He must be persuaded to concentrate on one bit of that object, and it is the function of fashion to emphasize and exaggerate that little bit until the whole thing becomes a bore causing the erogenous zone to shift. In 1925 I wrote in my diary that I found the newly exposed legs of women rather exciting. By 1930 legs were a bore, and attention had to be directed elsewhere. In 1915, however, a woman in 1925 clothes would have been arrested for indecent exposure. This is the game which seduction plays with prudery. Prudery in fact might be called a necessary psychological device for keeping up the temperature of eroticism in cold climates.

We can therefore draw up a chart and say:

The same dress is indecent ten years before its time; daring one year before its time; chic (contemporarily seductive) in its time; dowdy five years after its time; hideous twenty years after its time; amusing thirty years after its time; romantic one hundred years after its time; beautiful one hundred and fifty years after its time. It would have been quite impossible to revive the fashions of the mid-twenties until thirty years had elapsed. Thirty years elapsed and behold! Those fashions or modes very like them, came back again.

If we could understand the full significance of a woman's hat we could prophesy her clothes for the next year, the interior decoration of the next to years, the architecture of the next ten years, and we would have a fairly accurate notion of the pressures, political, economic, religious, that go to make the shape of an age. Properly evaluated, fashion is never a frivolity.

The Meaning of Fashion

by Dwight E. Robinson

The behavioral complex underlying all stylistic innovation—by this I mean all changes in design which are not purely the results of engineering advances—can conveniently be summed up under the single word *fashion*. And fashion, defined in its most general sense, is the pursuit of novelty for its own sake. Every market into which the consumer's fashion sense has insinuated itself is, by that very token, subject to this common, compelling need for unceasing change in the styling of its goods.

The reason for this is that the stimuli of fashion derive solely from the *comparisons* that consumers draw between new designs and the old designs they replace. No single style of design, no matter how brilliantly it is conceived, can claim any independent fashion significance at all, nor can it possess more than a fugitive lease on life.

Rule of Excess

Paul Poiret, the top Paris couturier of the 1920's, once summed up his credo by declaring "All fashions end in excess"—a principle which is the beginning of wisdom for all who are concerned with style policy. He was aware that the overriding responsibility of the designer in a fashion market is the unending provision of novelty. Implicitly he recognized that one of the most exacting problems the stylist ever faces is that of deciding what to do when he has exhausted the possibilities of a current direction in styling emphasis. What does he do, for example, when the waistline, hemline, or any other line has been carried as far as it will go? It is here that the couturier must exercise to the utmost every ounce of his insight into the meaning of fashion.

Excerpted by permission from "Fashion Theory and Product Design" *Harvard Business Review*, November-December, 1958, Vol. 36, No. 6. Professor Robinson is widely recognized as one of the few business historians who has done research in the field of fashion.

As a couturier Poiret knew that the appetite for novelty, arising from the twofold insistence of the lady of fashion on preserving her inimitability from the onslaught of the vulgar and on demonstrating her affluence through unrelenting expenditure on newly cut costumes, is never satisfied with any one mode of presenting the figure. Fashions in dress design subsist on measures to transform or to distort, whether through exaggeration or minimization, the shape and features of the human figure. To illustrate:

> The hoop skirts of the eighteenth century and the crinoline of the nineteenth ballooned to diameters of eight feet. As the hip line was exaggerated beyond the point of simply imperiling navigation to the point of making it literally impossible, the waistline was tightened to the point of suffocation and interference with digestion.
>
> In the interim, in the Directoire and Empire periods around 1800, a contrary tendency toward undress was exploited. *La Parisienne's* test of the suitability of a pseudoclassical gown of transparent silk was to see whether she could easily draw it through a ring taken from her little finger. The last resort of modesty was flesh-colored tights.
>
> The flapper of the Jazz Age, though she was in her turn the despair of her late-Victorian parents, never dashed about in quite the dishabille of Mme. Récamier, but what she missed in transparency she made up for with leg display.

Whether, at a given time, the particular form of emphasis is toward padding out or constricting, toward concealment or exposure, once such a movement is launched it must be intensified each season, ensuring that the ultrafashionable will be able to disport themselves in more of a good thing than their less-favored contemporaries. Indeed, this recurrent pattern can be traced back to even earlier centuries. The style of European costume associated with the

French Regency (1715–1730) emphasized delicacy and restraint. Its graceful, free-flowing costume is best remembered in the airy, idyllic scenes depicted in the paintings of Watteau. Yet it fell between the ornate periods of the stately Baroque and the frivolously extravagant Rococo.

Corollary of Reversal

The most important corollary of Poiret's axiom is this: a fashion can never retreat gradually and in good order. Like a dictator it must always expand its aggressions—or collapse. Old fashions never just fade away; they die suddenly and arbitrarily.

The reason for this is simple and logically inescapable. The one thing fashion cannot stand is to repeat the recently outmoded style, the *passé*. Better for the lady of fashion to look like a freak than to be mistaken for her grocer's wife dolled up in a cheap version of something she herself sported a year or two ago. For instance:

> The hoop skirts of the French court and the crinoline of a century later did not gradually contract: they both exploded in a fragmentation of trains, loops, and bustles.
>
> Within a decade after court ladies found it necessary to crouch on the floor of their coaches so as to accommodate their soaring headdresses, Lady Hamilton (Nelson's Emma) was enthralling the court of Naples and eminent visitors such as Goethe with her "classical attitudes," for which her main props were no more than her own silky curls, a few yards of gauze, and a pet dove or two. And it was not long before thousands of less notorious ladies were taking her cue.
>
> Again, a couple of generations later, after such devices as the bustle and the leg-of-mutton sleeve exhausted the expansionist tendencies of late-Victorian days, the shirt-waist and hobble skirt were suddenly introduced, clearing the way for the boyish skimpiness of the 1920's. . . .

Classic Compromise

What lies behind these swift and extreme changes? If functional criteria could be more precisely defined, the game of fashion change might be interpreted as a series of departures from, and returns to, the norm of function. Unfortunately, this is not the case. Function is permissive. Even nature's experiments in animals —on land, in the sea, and in the air—reveal that the laws of locomotion or mechanics permit a kaleidoscopic variety of anatomical forms.

The designer has learned that the usefulness of a garment—together with all the functional criteria surrounding utility—is a consideration of only incidental relevance to his purposes. Naturally, he is more than willing to play up the merits of a new design by claiming that it permits greater freedom of movement, better accentuates the feminine figure, or is more suitable to modern living. But he does this with tongue in cheek. He is only too aware that, judging by results, the aims of feminine coquetry have been as well served by the dress designs of one era as by those of another.

The safest thing that can be said of costume variation is that it veers between extremes of overdressing and underdressing, although there are many other variables. Perusal of the fashion journals suggests that when one of these extremes has been reached, the recourse that has typically proved most successful is swift return to a form of compromise, or golden mean, which lies about halfway between overdress and underdress. Such norms are somewhat loosely referred to as "classical" styles in the dress trade. In turn, they serve as points of departure toward an alternative extreme.

The couturier is then likely to visit the art galleries or museums to seek inspiration from the designs of past eras. (The Metropolitan Museum of Art in New York, for instance, maintains a Costume Institute, where thousands of dresses going back several centuries are carefully preserved, catalogued, and made available for inspection by qualified visitors from the garment district.) He will also, of course, give careful heed to technological advances in the form of new materials or new mechanical dressmaking aids, as well as to arising needs of contemporary living, in shaping his patterns to present-day conditions.

As Christian Dior puts it, "There is room for audacity in the framework of tradition." It is an arresting thought that relics of the past, together with fruits of industrial progress, so frequently form the chief supports of the game of novelty which is fashion. . . .

Conclusion

My aim has been to provide a springboard to a better understanding of a fascinating but perplexing area of decision making. I have sought to point out that fashion—the impulse underlying the dynamics of style—is both a less mystifying and a more profound force in social behavior than is commonly supposed. Most authorities on fashion consider it an evolutionary process. In this I join them. Yet evolution relies on sudden mutations as much as, if not more than, small changes. For this reason, I have emphasized the sharply pronounced reactions which always seem to follow the extremes of styling.

Of course, I do not intend to put forward a formula or nostrum for the automatic prediction of style trends. History does not repeat itself any more neatly and prettily in styles than it does in any other sphere—business fluctuations, for example. My objective has been only to present a systematic exposition of a few of the insights that have long been the guideposts of fashion's most adept practitioners.

Nobody's crystal ball can show up the fashion future in complete detail. If it could, a lot of brain power would be unemployed; a lot of fun would go out of life. But this much is certain: the fact that an industry invests billions of dollars in equipment is no guarantee of a continued market for its products. Fashion is absolutely and callously indifferent to any monumental achievements in manufacturing proficiency. If anything, she take capricious delight in nullifying man's industry—or pretenses to rationality. All of the fame and bulk of a leading textile, appliance, construction, or automobile company will not save it from fashion's dustbin if she so wills. She, and not the so-called fashion dictator—as Paul Poiret always professed—is the true autocrat; and only in a totalitarian state, where the consumer's taste is legislated by government edict, does she meet her match.

What Were They Wearing? 1910–1960

1910–1920

The Gibson girl was departing, even as *Women's Wear Daily* was making its entry on the 1910 scene. The dress silhouette was changing: Skirts were straighter, narrower at the hem, sometimes draped and crossed at front (see sketch). Clothes generally had a more sophisticated look. *Ensembles* were tremendously significant. There were many elaborate dresses with matching coats, for all seasons. The simple tailored suit, often bound with silk braid and worn with ruffled white blouse, became generally popular about 1913, and on. This same year was known for the exaggerated dressmaker suit which simulated a dress. . . . About this

1910–1920

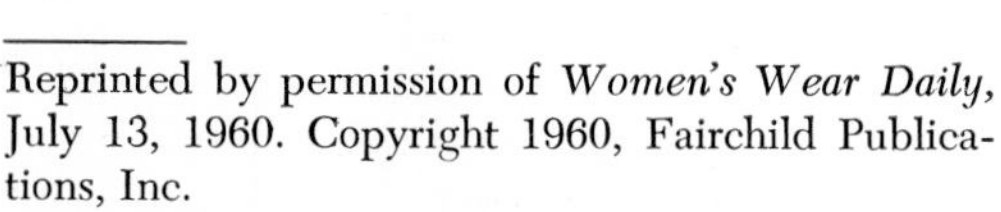

Reprinted by permission of *Women's Wear Daily*, July 13, 1960.

This capsule review of 50 years of fashion change has been digested from material in the Fairchild Costume Library. Nucleus of the library is a collection of books on the history of costume and textiles, considered one of the finest in the country. Supplementing this are more than 2000 scrapbooks of current material, which keep references up to date.

time the first *fur-lined coats* were introduced, usually lined with squirrel and with large fur collar. By 1915 coat silhouettes had changed and fur bands now accented voluminous, swirling hemlines. Within four years, design interest had again shifted: Bulk was at the top, capes in all lengths were important, as was the dolman coat. By 1919 Paris was striving for shorter skirts, but most Americans still clung to lower hems. The *large fur muff* worn with single fox scarf or long stole came into its own about 1912. White fox was among the long-haired furs immensely popular then. This decade in furs also produced the long, fitted black pony-skin coat, frequently with black lynx collar. Older women favored black caracul coats. . . . It was in 1912 that *the toque* was launched by milliners, a then radical departure from the large merry widow or lacy lingerie hats of earlier years. By 1919, wide brimmed trimmed models with smallish flat crowns were an important adjunct to the many soft dressy afternoon costumes. . . . Women had been going down to the sea in heavy wool serge sailor-dress bathing styles, and when at the turn of the century Annette Kellerman popularized the one-piece knit suit it was as much of a shocker as today's bikini, although it provided neck-to-toe coverage. . . . The average city women spent $64 for her wardrobe in 1917.

1920–1930

The 20's brought in a new era in dress designing. The Poiret-inspired, unlined, uncorseted dress of soft Oriental contour was generally adopted early in the decade. Lanvin's ageless robe de style was introduced in the early 20's, was still going strong at the start of World War II. Chanel first launched her two-piece jerseys and untrimmed chiffon evening gowns in this period. By 1926, skirts were knee high for the first time in the twentieth century. For evening, the beaded sheath credited to Callot had won wide popularity. When World War I badly damaged France's cotton and woolen mills, a radical change in style resulted as the couture turned to the ensemble, popularized the little straight wool coat which could be worn over several silk dresses. It was the great era of silk crepe de chine, flat crepe and satin dresses for all ages. Suits, as such, all but disappeared, instead taking on the characteristics of the dominant ensemble: Soft skirt plus dressy overblouse, jacket lined to match (see sketch). . . . The luxurious 20's brought in the sumptuous long *wraparound fur coat,* and by 1926 the short ermine evening wrap, bulky at top. This was also the start of the mink coat as known today. 1926 furs for people of modest income included natural muskrat, often in three-quarter length, the pelts seamed without being worked into strips. The affinity of the 1920's coed for the casual raccoon coat hardly bears repetition here. . . . Hats were untrimmed and *the cloche* became a uniform, varying only in material used and manipulation. Growing interest in spectator sports led to development of simple felt or straw hats, shielding the eyes and turned up in back. Berets appeared in great variety. . . . The 20's witnessed the *birth of sportswear.* Stars like Suzanne Lenglen and Helen Wills popularized knee-length tennis dresses. Riding skirts were abandoned for breeches, worn with long jacket and high boots. Long trousers and knickers, combined with heavy sweater and high socks on the ski slopes. Covered legs persisted even with the slim above-knee bathing dress of 1924. . . . Average wardrobe expenditure in 1929 was $76.

1920–1930

1930–1940

Longer skirts and bias cuts came in with the 30's, as Patou succeeded in bringing the hem down again. Vionnet was still doing the dress depending entirely on bias cut for its appeal, devoid of trim and needing no fastenings, which was a hallmark of the 1930's (see sketch of 1932 model). Coats capitalized on the overwhelming fashion for *silver fox* bringing in full length fitted wool coats with large face-framing fox collars extending to the waistline. In mid-decade, Schiaparelli did a collarless dressmaker coat accenting large sleeves, very different from the later simpler coat cuts associated with the collarless neckline. The 30's also revived simple suits with longer skirts, the short jacket often in contrasting color. In 1937, Schiaparelli was the first to use *padding* in suit shoulders, borrowing her idea from the London Guardsman's uniform. . . . Subtle tailoring in furs came in by 1934 with the fitted broadtail full-length coat. This was also the year of the *collarless fox jacket,* beloved of women for both day and evening wear. The 30's were famous, too, for the many black and gray persian lamb coats, which continued significantly into the 40's. . . . The manipulated hat body offered many unusual hat shapes at the start of the decade. In 1931 *the bonnet* associated with Sally Victor appeared. By 1934, off-face types were popular. Suzanne Talbot created for the Duchess of Windsor the Pompadour hat whose wide appeal continued right through World War II. 1936 brought the pointed clown hat of Schiaparelli, and 1938 her "doll" hat. . . . The divided skirt, or *culotte,* returned to favor in 1936. The riding habit of this decade was jodhpurs and tweed jacket. On the ski slopes, the snow suit with full trousers and matching jacket dominated. On the beach, the dressmaker suit shared honors with the sleek *one-piece maillot* made popular with the invention of elasticized yarns. . . . The city woman in 1939 spent an average of $55 for her wardrobe.

1930–1940

1940–1950

World War II brought restrictions to the fashion industries, chiefly L-85 which fixed the outside measurements of garments. The influence of the shirtwaist dress was very strong in the war period. Along about 1942 came a tendency toward severity in dress which produced many masculine coat styles, including the officer's coat and the *Chesterfield* (see sketch). Adrian's square-shouldered, long-jacketed suit clicked with the general public, and women for a long time after resisted the many serious attempts to woo them from heavily padded shoulders. Suits were often topped with simple tailored coats, including the fur-lined model of 1943, popular for the first time in over 25 years. *The short coat* of 1945, sometimes belted, had a long life, toward the end of this decade becoming the shortie or topper, so adaptable with sportswear. Style curbs finally disappeared, opening the gate to the *new look* which made up in one deluge for all wartime fabric pinching, with its nipped waist, padded hips, long full skirts, and over all the voluminous tent coat. In 1945 Balenciaga had shown a suit with padded hips and tiny waist but with a short skirt. However, it was Dior's long-skirted 1947 version which caught on in America. . . . Even before the war's end the first French influence to filter across the seas was the large, elaborate *"more hat"* which few people wore but which tended to restore more trimming on millinery. . . . The 40's also witnessed the introduction of informal western riding rigs made up of levi, cotton shirt, and casual jacket. Skiers adopted

1940–1950

the more practical slope fashion of slim tapered trouser and separate jacket. Bare midriff swimsuits made an appearance followed by the two-piece bra and shorts. The strapless top of the late 40's extended corsetiere techniques of wiring and boning to swimwear. . . . In 1949, the average woman spent $136 on apparel.

1950–1960

Casual and relaxed were key words in the 1950s, when sportswear truly came into its own, in part reflecting the new emphasis on suburban living, in part, the maturing of this comparatively young industry. It was helped by Chanel's decision to reactivate her design career, and the warm reception of her styles by a new generation of Americans. Italian designers, taking a leaf from California's book, found their niche in this branch of style, contributing much to knitwear and to color palettes, and pioneering the *tight tapered pants* which many women gradually adopted for everything from beach to street wear (see sketch). In this decade, Bohemia's beatnik added a new word and new look to the fashion lexicon. Coats and suits decided to compete with sportswear on its suburban battlefield, where the uniform was largely the camel boycoat or classic tweeds. With a TV set in every ranch house and apartment, *at-home clothes* flourished, as did teen fashions which were nurtured by a fashion-conscious crop of former war babies. Dress designers, bored with the pretty-doll aspect of many styles, launched a drive toward a looser silhouette which, had it followed the logical sequence of "filtering down" from couture to basement levels, might have made progress. But in this quick-copying period, there were immediately *sacks on the racks* in cheaply made versions which diverted what might have been a new style direction into an abortive fiasco. Immediate aftermath was a sharp swing to classics, although some influential designers are still much attuned to eased, unwaisted styles, a possible augury for the future. There was but one story in furs: *mink*. Many deplored this lopsided development and sparked a move to revive non-mink furs in youthful styles, going outside the industry for the design talent to blueprint the revival. This was the decade that spawned "togetherness," but milliners and hairdressers somehow missed the cue and embarked on separate paths signpointed to the spread of hatlessness as the widely copied Hepburn shingle, Italian boycut, and Bardot scrambled coiffure defied the milliners' best efforts. Another imponderable: The acceptance of dyed hair, women's pleasure with their new locks, and reluctance to cover their handiwork. . . . The average woman budgeted $169 for wardrobe needs in 1959.

1950–1960

Questions for Review and Discussion

1. Some people claim it is wasteful to urge customers to buy new fashions in clothing when plenty of wear remains in their present clothing. They criticize the emphasis on fashion in the marketing of apparel as a social and economic waste. Discuss.
2. How many industries, other than clothing, can you name that are directly or indirectly affected by the apparel business? How?
3. After analyzing the "definitions" of a fashion, style, fad, fashion-trend, design, and high-fashion, give a current example of each in men's and/or women's apparel. Explain your selection.
4. Why do fashions change? Do you agree that fashion changes are evolutionary in nature? Cite current examples to prove your answer.
5. What events and "personalities" in today's news are influencing current fashions? How do these things influence fashions?
6. Is it correct to say that designers create fashion? Why?
7. Study the fashions in the reading "*What Were They Wearing 1910–1960?*" and explain how they reflected their "times."
8. When the average person thinks of style and fashion, he probably relates it to wearing apparel. What other products are produced and sold with the fashion element in mind? Explain?
9. Dorothy Shaver who was President of Lord and Taylor in New York, once stated that "Fashions go their own way regardless of the efforts of business people to regulate or direct them. Fashions cannot be promoted artificially." Do you agree? Why?
10. Do you agree that fashion does not refer to price? Defend your answer by citing examples.

SECTION II

The Materials of Fashion

Fashion is a serious business, and its makings form the basis of a highly complex, multibillion dollar, many-faceted manufacturing industry. Its producers, of which there are many thousands, divide into two broad categories: (1) the primary markets that provide the raw materials of fashion, such as fibers, fabrics, and leathers; and (2) the cutting-up or needle trades that manufacture the finished articles of apparel.

This section discusses the primary fashion markets, whose designs and colors frequently pace a new fashion trend and provide apparel designers with the stuff that gives substance to their ideas. Using the textile industry, which is the largest segment of the primary markets, as an example, the text will discuss its history and development, and the influence upon one another of fashion and the primary industries. The readings which follow the text have been selected to illustrate and amplify points made in the discussion.

The Textile Industry

Size and Scope. The textile industry is made up of several thousand widely scattered heterogenous companies engaged in one or more steps in the processing of materials known as textile fibers. Because of its size and scope, the industry plays a vital role in the economy of the United States. The manufacturing of fabrics alone—exclusive of the agricultural and chemical suppliers—gives employment to nearly one million workers, and enjoys annual sales in excess of $15 billion.[1] Although the bulk of the manufacturing facilities is in the South and in New England, some phase of textile activity is carried on in nearly every state of the union. Styling and design activities are centered in New York City, and the sales and merchandising operations reach into almost every other major city. The output is used in such diverse products as missile nose cones, industrial filters, artificial arteries, and fashion apparel.

[1] 1963 Census of Manufacturers, General Statistics for Industry Groups and Industries, MC63(P)-3, November 1964, U.S. Bureau of the Census, Washington, D.C., p. 4.

TEXTILE PRODUCTION IN UNITED STATES

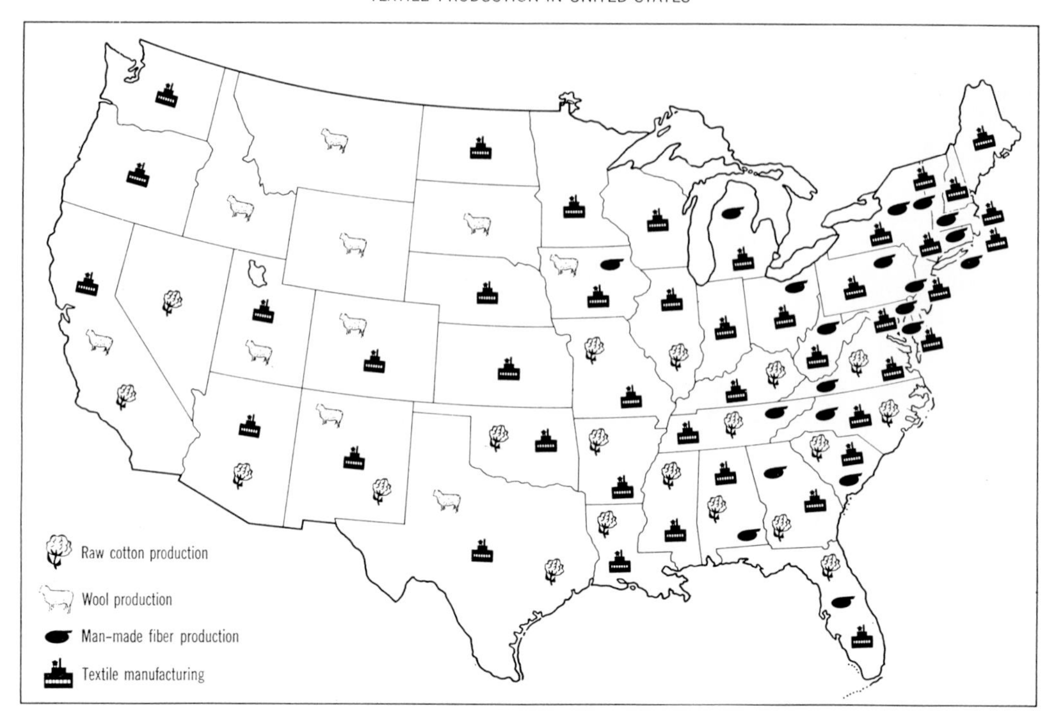

Courtesy of American Textile Manufacturers Institute, Charlotte, N.C.

In the fashion business, which absorbs much of their output, the basic responsibility of the textile industry is the conversion of raw fibers into finished fabrics. At one end of the industry spectrum are some 8000 mills [2] which perform one or more of the three major processes involved in the manufacture of textiles: the spinning of natural or synthetic fibers into yarn, the weaving or knitting of yarn into fabric, and the finishing of fabric to impart color, texture, pattern, ease-of-care, and other characteristics. At the other end are the sales offices, which market the finished cloth to the cutting-up trades. Some of these sales offices are owned by the mills; others own their own mills; still others are independent selling agents who represent several mills and receive a commission for their services.

History and Development. Although the United States textile industry is today the largest in the world, textile manufacturing had its industrial beginnings in Europe during the seventeenth century, and was well established in the Old World when the New was discovered. Production in America began in the cabins of the early settlers, where, from home-grown fibers, the spinning, weaving, dyeing, cutting, and sewing were the responsibility of the housewife; her husband supervised the tanning of leathers, made the shoes, and cured such furs as were to be used. The prosperous settlers found imported fabrics more attrac-

[2] "Textiles—An Industry, A Science, An Art," American Textile Manufacturers Institute, Charlotte, N.C., p. 2.

tive than the crude homespuns produced by these early household industries, and purchased them from Europe.

The transition from handicraft to factory production of textiles had its start when the first textile mill was built in 1790 at Pawtucket, Rhode Island, by Samuel Slater.[3] Slater had migrated from England where he had served a six-year apprenticeship in a textile-manufacturing plant. His mill was not only the first successful manufacturing plant in this country, but it was also considered the forerunner of mass production in the United States. Its contribution to the industrialization of this country was later recognized by President Andrew Jackson, who called Slater "The Father of American Manufacture." [4] For the first twenty years, the growth of the industry was quite slow, due largely to the competition from the more attractive imports, and in 1808, there were only fifteen more-or-less-isolated little mills scattered about New England.[5] The War of 1812, however, led to a rapid expansion when blockades and embargoes cut off imports from abroad, and the United States was forced to satisfy its needs from domestic textile sources. More mills came into being and, protected by the tariffs imposed when the war was over, the industry was able to exploit the growing domestic market and maintain a high rate of expansion. By the close of the year 1815, there were reported to be, "according to a memorial presented to the United States Congress, 99 mills in Rhode Island, 57 in Massachusetts, and 14 in Connecticut, making a total of 170 mills." [6]

The years preceding the Civil War saw a period of great development and manufacturing activity. The country was growing rapidly, and the continuing improvement of factory machines and methods now made it increasingly economical to produce textiles, leathers, and furs outside the home. More and more factories were built to supply the needs of a growing nation. By 1831 there were 795 textile mills throughout New England, and in that year they produced 230,000,000 yards of fabric.[7]

American textile producers were not yet in a position, however, to compete with the better grade textile products that were available from European sources, notably England and France. In 1858 broadcloth and other fine fabrics were entirely supplied from Europe, and the New York Chamber of Commerce reported "that American wool, when used alone, cannot produce cloth of equal quality and finish as that made of foreign wools." [8] The Civil War gave additional impetus to the further development of the industry. The great demands upon American mills for fabrics for soldiers' uniforms were added to normal requirements and by the end of the war the industry was firmly established and well on its way toward mass production of quality fabrics.

---

[3] Frederick Lewton, "Samuel Slater and the Oldest Cotton Machinery in America," Smithsonian Report for 1926. (Authors' note: The old Slater mill in Pawtucket is now a textile museum.)

[4] "Textiles—An Industry, A Science, An Art," p. 15 (cited in footnote 2).

[5] Frank Walton, *Tomahawks to Textiles*, New York, Appleton-Century Crofts, Inc., 1953, p. 98.

[6] F. Lewton, *op. cit.*

[7] "The Dress Industry," Market Planning Service of National Credit Office, New York, March 1948.

[8] Herbert Heaton, "Benjamin Gott and the Anglo-American Cloth Trade," *Journal of Economics and Business History*, Vol. II, November, 1929, p. 147.

Throughout the nineteenth century, the geographic development of the industry was confined almost entirely to the North, principally New England. Toward the end of the century, however, as Southern states began to recover from the turmoil of the Civil War, a rapid expansion of cotton textile manufacturing occurred in the South. Southern leaders, concerned by the lack of industrialization in their states, offered special inducements, such as low taxes and utility rates, to textile companies to build plants in the South. By 1920 over half of the cotton spinning and weaving capacity of cotton textile manufacturing was to be found in the South.[9]

Parallelling the production changes in the industry were the changes that occurred in the selling and distribution of textiles. Merchants who had originally started as importers handling the products of European mills gradually changed to selling agents for the domestic mills, or bought their products outright for resale. The expansion of domestic output after the Civil War stimulated the establishment of a textile center in downtown Manhattan on and near Worth Street, which became the heart of the textile trade. The name, Worth Street, became synonymous with textile merchants upon whom American mills depended for their orders, and often for their financing.

From Fiber to Fabric. In the beginning, the industry was highly specialized, and much of the fabric produced, other than wool, passed through the hands of many small individual manufacturers and selling agents before it reached the garment producers. Some mills would spin the raw cotton or other fibers into yarn, and then sell it to other mills, who would weave it into *greige* goods, or unfinished cloth. At this point, a selling agent took over, and sold the greige goods to a converter. This converter, in turn, would then have the processing and finishing done according to his specifications, by contracting it out to still other specialized finishing, dyeing, or printing plants. Many of these converters were small operators "carrying their business in a hat," while others were "big names" in the industry, such as Everfast, Cohn-Hall-Marx, M. Lowenstein, and the like. The converters devoted much of their attention to contact with the apparel manufacturers, and would have the greige goods finished in the colors, patterns, and finishes that they could readily sell. Since they entered the process of production in its late stages, converters could work quite closely to the time of need and adjust quickly to any changes in demand. Some converters were keen students of fashion, studied trends, and anticipated demand. Others simply kept close to the cutting-up trades and had goods finished according to what the garment manufacturers were buying.

The converter, described as a "person who changes the form of a basic textile product by varied techniques and distributes it," [10] did not play an important role in the production of woolen fabrics, however. Woolen mills were usually completely integrated with respect to the spinning, weaving, and finishing processes. That is because styling and color starts very early in the life of a woolen or worsted fabric, where the dyeing and pattern is often woven into the yarn. The mills, therefore, could not divorce themselves from the styling function or wait for the last-minute demands of garment producers or converters.

---

[9] Walter Adams, *Structure of American Industry,* revised edition, New York, The Macmillan Co., 1957, Chapter 2.

[10] Paper presented at December 5, 1962, meeting of the New York Chapter of the American Association for Textile Technology in New York, by Jerome Blum, Vice President, Cohn-Hall-Marx Co.

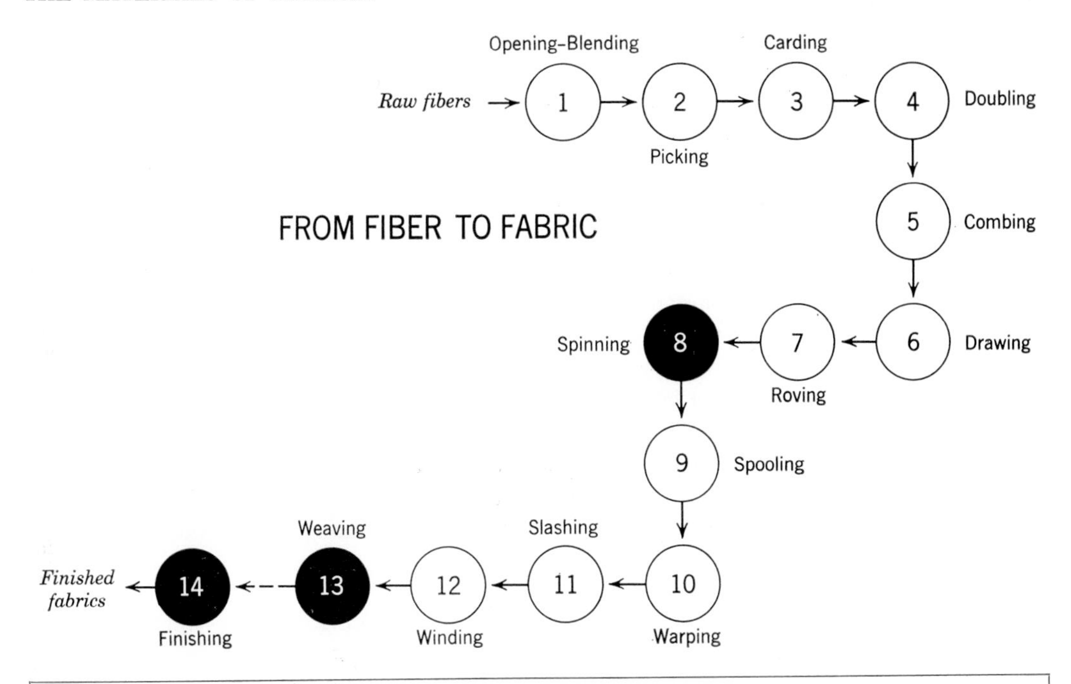

Many processes are required to transform raw fibers into yarn and yarn into fabric. They begin in the opening room where staple from many different bales of cotton are blended or where blends of natural and man-made fiber staple are made. In the picking room, the fiber is cleaned and foreign matter removed.

The carding and doubling processes further clean and begin to parallel the fibers. Through the combing, drawing and roving processes, the short fibers are removed and the remaining fibers are drawn out or lengthened, given a slight twist for strength, and readied for the spinning frames where the ropelike strands of loose fiber are spun into yarn.

From the spinning frame, the yarn is wound first onto "cheeses," then onto large warp beams. Slashing adds a starchlike substance called sizing to strengthen the yarn. In the winding process, the filling or crosswise yarns are transferred to bobbins which feed the yarn to the loom shuttle. The back-and-forth motion of the shuttle "weaves" the filling or "woof" yarn into the warp or vertical yarns to form the fabric.

The finishing process bleaches the fabric, and then adds color, texture, pattern, and, depending on the type of fabric, chemical and other finishes to impart ease-of-care characteristics to the finished fabric.

[Courtesy of American Textile Manufacturing Institute, Charlotte, N.C.]

Giants by Mergers and Acquisitions. In the period between the two World Wars, man-made fibers entered the textile picture and produced many changes in the pattern of the industry's operation. The increasing use and popularity of these fibers took a large proportion of fiber production out of the hands of agriculture and placed it in the hands of giant chemical corporations, such as E. I. du Pont de Nemours and Company, Inc. and the Celanese Corporation of America. Also, many textile plants which had formerly specialized in a single natural fiber became major producers of synthetic and/or blended fabrics, thus obliterating the traditional boundary lines between the heretofore specialized divisions of the industry.

During and immediately after the Second World War, problems of scarcity and price made the prewar marketing procedures of the textile industry unfeasible. The industry began to integrate and diversify itself. In some cases, mills ceased to rely upon independent converters and selling agents, and set up their own converting plants and sales organizations. An example of a textile mill that extended its operations to include later stages in the industry by acquiring interests in converting facilities, selling organizations, and in some instances undertaking the production of finished consumer goods, is Burlington Industries. In other cases, converting firms like Cohn-Hall-Marx bought mills in order to be sure of having fabrics to sell. In still others, sales agents acquired textile mills and absorbed them into their corporate set-up. A notable example of this latter method of expansion was J. P. Stevens and Co., then a leading selling house in the cotton and rayon goods field, which in 1946 united its selling house and its mill company with eight other companies.[11]

The process of integration speeded up in the 1950's and is still continuing.[12] The textile industry today includes giant corporations whose operations encompass the many steps in the production of fabrics, from the purchase of natural and man-made fibers to the sale of the finished cloth. There is also an increasing tendency to diversify the products that they produce. Although the various operations may take place in different plants, each in a different location, all are under one ownership.

Mergers and acquisitions have given impetus to both trends, and have helped to create publicly owned giant enterprises which dominate the textile industry. The largest of the giants is Burlington Industries, Inc., which began in 1923 as a small mill in North Carolina and which by 1958 ranked fifty-fourth in sales and twenty-eighth in number of employees in *Fortune's* survey of the five hundred largest corporations in the United States.[13] Today, its thirty-one divisions produce and sell fabric from many fibers; make and sell yarn; sell greige goods to independent converters; finish greige goods for other textile firms; produce ribbons, hosiery, and vinyl-coated fabrics; act as selling agents; and are publicly owned. Financial reports show that their annual sales passed the $1 billion mark by 1962. The second largest is J. P. Stevens Co., Inc., which celebrated its one hundred-fiftieth anniversary in 1963. Highlights of their history and development are to be found in the readings in this section.

The rapid pace of individual growth in the industry is reflected in published sales figures of leading textile firms (see Table 1).

Table 1

	Net Sales		
Company	1939	1948	1964
Burlington Industries	$39,171,000	$288,162,000	$1,206,000,000
J. P. Stevens & Co., Inc.	71,064,000	287,258,000	684,660,000
United Merchants & Manufacturers	35,360,000	211,538,000	522,650,000
Cannon Mills Co.	44,532,000	153,999,000	271,296,000
Cone Mills Corp.	16,999,000	120,438,000	237,387,000
M. Lowenstein & Sons, Inc.	31,474,000	120,118,000	277,093,000
Dan River Mills, Inc.	22,914,000	103,604,000	185,722,000

[11] See reading, "The Durable Threads of J. P. Stevens."

[12] "The Merger Movement in the Textile Industry," U. S. House of Representatives, Committee on the Judiciary, January, 1955, p. 14, and *Women's Wear Daily,* April 14, 1965, p. 1, report of study by Dr. John M. Blair, chief economist, Senate Judiciary Subcommittee on anti-trust.

[13] "This is Burlington Industries," company booklet of Burlington Industries.

Emergence of Brand Names. A natural development of the trend to bigness in the textile industry has been the growing emphasis on brand names in fibers and in fabrics. The giant producers of man-made fibers have been extremely aggressive in building their brand names and promoting their fibers. This is not merely to give their own nylon or acrylic or rayon fiber an edge over similar fibers from other producers, but also to make the public familiar with the brand name so that, when the next new fiber emerges from the laboratory, that familiarity will help pave the way toward its acceptance.

To accomplish these ends the great chemical companies that produce man-made fibers advertise in consumer magazines and other public media in their own names, or in conjunction with fabric or finished-product sources. They also seek to publicize fashion products, in which their fibers are involved, by educational programs that include talks to women's clubs as well as educational talks to salespeople. Frequently, they arrange elaborate fashion showings with retail stores which feature fashion merchandise made of fabric in which their fibers are used. The impact of their publicity and advertising gives wide exposure not only to their brand names but also to the fashions with which their fibers are associated.

Likewise, the giant textile firms—sometimes on their own, and sometimes in cooperation with fiber sources—will advertise their names and/or subsidize advertisements by garment makers in consumer fashion magazines and fashion sections of newspapers. In a typical Sunday magazine section of *The New York Times,* for instance, it is not unusual to see many advertisements for dresses, coats, and suits which feature not only the name of the fabric source, but also the name of the garment maker or designer, and often the fiber source as well. With such financial assistance from sources of supply, a dress or coat manufacturer can advertise more widely to the public than he could dream of doing on his own.

In the process of promoting their brand names, fiber and fabric sources have used promotional methods undreamed of in the days when a mill's responsibility ended with the sale of the cloth. As recently as the 1940's, it was most unusual to find any name but that of the retail store on a garment. Today, promotions of the various brand names reach all the way down to the consumer in the form of hangtags on garments which carry the name of the garment manufacturer, the fabric source, the fiber source, and even the special finish which has been applied to the fabric.

There is keen competition, too, among the suppliers of natural fibers, and this competition also gives impetus to the flow of fabric information to the consumer. Each fiber—wool, cotton, linen, silk—has an industry association that makes itself a source of information about fibers, fabrics, and fashions in general, and keeps directing the public's attention to the desirable qualities of its own fiber. Typical is the Maid of Cotton program of the cotton industry. Each year an attractive young woman is selected as the Maid. She travels widely in a wardrobe of cotton fabrics styled by well-known designers. In the course of her travels and the attendant publicity, designers, garment producers, and the consuming public are reminded of the practical and fashionable virtues of cotton. The effort to hold the public's attention is unremitting.

The net effect upon the consumer is that she is more conscious of brand names in fibers and fabrics, and is exposed to infinitely more advertising and articles about fabrics than ever before.[14] The more money these fiber and fabric makers pour into making the consumer aware of their brand names and virtues of their products, the more closely must these companies study the consumer in order to understand her preferences and response to their efforts.

Fashion's Impact on Textiles

Until well into the twentieth century, the elements of style and fashion did not play an important part in the production of textiles. Today it is estimated that well over 50 per cent of its output is subject to the dictates of fashion.[15] The public's appetite for things which are new and different has encouraged the industry to search for new fibers and fabrics. In turn, new textile developments have influenced style trends. The result is that fabric and apparel styling not only complement each other—each acts as a spur to the other.

Importance of Variety and Change. Before the First World War, about 80 per cent of the output of the American textile industry consisted of extremely staple fabrics, weaves, and colors.[16] Those were the days when the blue serge suit was the uniform of the white-collar male, and the good black gabardine was his lady's Sunday best. Those were the days, too, when fashion was the prerogative of the wealthy Four Hundred, who bought much of their wardrobe abroad. The woman at the opposite end of the income scale had very little to spend on anything but bare necessities. The ready-to-wear industry was still in its infancy, and such apparel producers as there were bought those fabrics that the mills offered, and sought to make attractive, acceptable styles from them. With such a market for their output, mills could afford to pay little attention to design and produce relatively few fabrics, each of which could look forward to a fairly long if unexciting fashion life. Even the seasonal factor which shifts demand from light to heavyweight fabrics and back again was not as important as it is today. In that age of long underwear, multiple petticoats, and shawls, a woman did not have to change her outer garments to adjust to colder weather; she simply added layers.

During the period between and after the two World Wars, the buying power of middle- and lower-income families grew,[17] and so did the ready-to-wear industry. Fashion and seasonal changes became elements for the textile industry to reckon with, and fabric producers found that they could not afford to separate the idea of cloth from the conception of fashion. Operations had to be adjusted, not only to the most economical procedures, but also to those that would permit quick response to the demands of both the growing garment in-

---

[14] Authors' note: *Advertising Age,* September 6, 1964, p. 5, reported advertising expenditures of $55 million in 1963 by fiber producers alone.

[15] E. B. Alderfer and H. E. Michl, *Economics of American Industry,* third edition, New York, McGraw-Hill Book Company, Inc., 1957, p. 329.

[16] *Ibid.,* p. 329.

[17] Studies of the U.S. Department of Commerce, Office of Business Economics, show that in 1935–1936, 45.4% of families had annual incomes under $2000; in 1941, only 27.9% had less than $2000; in 1963, 10.6% had less than $2000. Annual figures are reported by the Bureau of the Census in its reports, Series P–60, Consumer Income; earlier figures are summarized in the Statistical Abstract of the United States.

dustry and consumer for greater variety in fabric offerings. At the same time that variety in designs, colors, and textures did much to stimulate the sales of the industry, the increasing importance of fashion also made their operations more difficult. As one industry observer put it, the difficulties are numerous, but they arise from one cause: uncertainty as to what styles the consumers will accept, and how long they will continue to accept them.

Fashion Planning and Promotion. Because they must be ready with their offerings long before the apparel and accessory designers work on their lines, every branch of the industry must develop its own early opinion of what colors, textures, patterns, weaves, or weights are likely to enjoy consumer acceptance. Each works far ahead in its study of fashion trends, and each tries to influence fashions by the information it disseminates and by what it makes available to the cutting-up trades.

The planning that goes into a fiber selection, a fabric promotion, a style event in a store, and an advertising campaign was detailed by an executive of the Celanese Corporation of America as follows:

> Long and patient hours, stretching into days and months and years, go into planning by such a concern as Celanese of what it expects to be popular—which weight, thickness, and finish; which colors and which combinations will catch the popular fancy; and which designs will be accepted and re-ordered. With it all goes promotional planning, checking, surveys of stores and individual consumers, market testing, and trade advertising, long before consumer copy appears in newspapers and magazines and on television and radio. Our task is to work out new uses for fabrics. That means we must decide at least a year ahead what the trend is going to be, in terms of color, construction, and appearance. Then we take trade advertising to spread the news of what is going to be advertised and what stores will have. . . . All the steps in the selling chain—from the yarn producer to the mill, to the converter, to the cutter, to the retailer, to the consumer—were as nothing, unless the consumer is sold.[18]

Fashion Activities and Style Specialists. The rise of giant textile firms has also provided important new sources of fashion information and new influences upon fashion. For one thing, to guide their own complex organizations, they need much longer-range fashion thinking than a plant which is concerned only with one of the many steps from fiber to fabric. For another, they are so dominant that their decisions as to what fabrics are to be made available may have a good deal to do with the course that fashions will take. All these huge companies have their own fashion staffs who research and report on trends. Their recommendations guide the production of the company's various units, and also provide advice for the industry's customers, the garment trades. So sound is the fashion research of leaders in the industry that apparel manufacturers look to them for advice on coming trends.

Many companies have design departments and technical staffs to show their customers how best to work with their fibers or fabrics. Some maintain "fashion libraries" for the convenience and use of manufacturers and retailers alike. Some also stage clinics or fashion shows for the trade at the beginning of the seasons

[18] Paul H. White, general merchandise manager of the Celanese textile division in "News of the Advertising and Marketing Fields," *New York Times,* November 4, 1956.

to present their new fabrics made up into garments.[19] Occasionally mills, designers of apparel, and retail buyers will work together to create designs for a particular promotion. Usually, however, the fabrics that are needed to give substance to an apparel designer's ideas are ready and waiting.

Some of the many activities and job titles of fashion specialists working within the textile industry have been described in an article in *Mademoiselle* as follows:

> A really first-rate stylist must rely on a good bit more than what may be her own impeccable taste. She must be thoroughly familiar with fabric firms and their customers, the manufacturers. She must know the best end uses for fabrics—this for a daytime dress, that for a man's sport shirt. What will a shopper buy if she has $10.95 to spend on a blouse? Or $39.95? What print styles, inspired by French or Italian couture, can survive a descent to mass usage? . . .
>
> An experienced woman named Billy Gordon, who works for the Brewster Finishing Company, which does the printing for Loomskill Fabrics (a converting firm), will spot a trend-print with a Persian motif, say, and will feed her ideas to a design studio for execution. Or she may bring a Pucci blouse back from a trip to Europe. . . . The blouse has an interesting arrangement of male figures marching through the pattern. Knowing that the average woman who buys a medium-priced blouse made of Loomskill fabric "wouldn't be caught dead wearing men," Miss Gordon works out with design studio artists a pattern substituting seashells for the men. . .
>
> The firm names of the average-sized fabric house, like Loomskill, are probably little known to those outside the fashion business. But even the fashion-ignorant know the big ones—big by virtue of their connections, since they are the finishing divisions of mills that produce gray goods. Galey and Lord, for example, is a well-known converting division of Burlington Industries. J. P. Stevens is another such giant mill-fabric house: two of its well-known fabric divisions are Forstmann and Worumbo.
>
> Within such fabric houses as these, you will find, besides stylists and staff designers, a woman fashion coordinator or director. Her responsibilities are indirectly concerned with getting the fabric sold to customers: manufacturers and their designers, and buyers of piece goods. (Store buyers of apparel must also be sold, in a sense, since they often get a manufacturer to use something they like.)
>
> The fabric-firm coordinator, whose salary can get to fifteen thousand dollars or more, organizes fashion shows to impress clients and the influentials—buyers and the press. The coordinator is in touch with manufacturers and their designers every day, too, and makes sure in this way that she knows which manufacturer has bought what fabrics—and how he intends to use them. She can make herself invaluable to these customers by telling them, "Don't use this stuff for swimsuits—Joe Blow's already bought it for that." Her knowledge is helpful, also, when she works with the fabric firm's advertising manager and the outside ad agency involved in plotting the resource to be used for an ad.
>
> "I case the market," says Mary Ellen Fannon, fashion coordinator of Galey and Lord, "to find a designer like Trigère or Ben Reig whose high-quality product—using our fabric—will work into an ad. The ad's snob appeal hooks the volume market into buying our merchandise."
>
> Fabric coordinators also work closely with editors on fashion magazines, showing them swatches of new materials, and keeping them posted on resources.[20]

---

[19] The Deering Milliken Fabric Comany is noted in the trade for their annual musical fashion show which is presented daily for a one-week period. Their 1964 show was reported in the *New York Times* of May 26 to have drawn 25,000 business executives.

[20] "Are You Cut Out for Seventh Avenue?" *Mademoiselle,* March 1962, pp. 118–119. Reprinted by permission.

Change of Location. A significant indicator of fashion's impact upon the textile industry and its closer relationship to the cutting-up trades is found in the geography of the textile market in New York. Before the Second World War, only the major woolen and silk textile firms had sales offices in the vicinity of Seventh Avenue—the general region south of Times Square in which most of the women's garment makers have their offices. Worth Street was the heart of most of the textile trade, a community in itself, with its own charities, its luncheon clubs, its opportunities for textile men to talk textiles.

After the Second World War, as fashion's full impact hit the industry, the showrooms began moving uptown. There are still great textile names in Worth Street, but they are likely to be represented only by sheets, blankets, and towels, not by fashion fabrics. Between Seventh Avenue and the Avenue of the Americas, between 42nd Street and 38th Street, right on the doorstep of the women's garment industries, one can find virtually all of the fashion fabric "greats." The textile industries have indeed woven themselves right into the fashion world.

Other Primary Fashion Markets

Much of what has been happening in the textile industry during the past few decades has been paralleled by similar developments in other primary markets as they learned first to anticipate fashion trends and then to make themselves into fashion influences.

The 30 to 35 million or so hides tanned in the course of a year are processed by nearly six hundred tanning and finishing establishments in the leather industry.[21] Some plants are completely integrated; they start with the hides and the chemicals and turn out completely processed leathers. Others are simply contract tanneries, owning the tools of production, but not the leather on which they work. The leather is owned by a converter who has the processing done to his order, but is primarily concerned with the marketing. In both operations, the need for early decisions on color and textures is great. In fact, each season the leather people are among the first in the fashion field to research and anticipate trends, and produce accordingly—and their decisions, in turn, influence directions in the textile industry and later stages of garment design and production.

Apparel leathers can be dyed in perhaps five hundred colors, in a variety of finishes. To decide which ones are important for a given season, the industry must do its research and make its decisions about fashion trends much earlier than the textile markets. The quickening pace of fashion has made leather fashion planning vital at as early a stage as the purchase of raw skins. For each end-use, the colors, finishes, and kinds of leather expected to win acceptance may be quite different.

One season handbags and shoes may be color match-ups, or may even be matched in design and kind of leather. If that is expected to be the case, the industry will dye leathers for both purposes in identical colors. In another season, these two accessories may go their separate ways, and the color spectrum for bag leathers will be quite different from that offered for shoes.

Along with its study of the colors and finishes most likely to be important in

[21] Census of Manufacturers 1958, U.S. Department of Commerce and Tanners Council of America.

the fashion picture for a given season, the industry also has to consider the availability and price for each type or grade of leather needed to express a promising trend. If the leathers needed to implement an incoming trend are scarce and prohibitively high in price, the trend may never get expression—at least in leather.

Since they must work so far ahead of actual wearing time, leaders in all the primary industries are necessarily sensitive to change, and must be quick to catch hints of incoming trends. Manufacturers, retailers, and fashion reporters have learned to watch the primary markets closely, sounding out the most creative individuals in each field and exchanging opinions with them. They are the great clearing houses for early and basic information about what is happening in the fashion business.

Readings

The articles that follow illustrate points made in the preceding part of this section. The first reading, from the pages of *Fortune Magazine*, describes the events that sparked the growth of J. P. Stevens & Company, a publicly owned giant textile corporation, founded more than 150 years ago. The next three readings describe the fashion activities of three different kinds of specialists in the textile industry—a fabric designer, a color stylist for a yarn company, and a fabric editor. Each specialist expresses, in his own words, the alertness to fashion which characterizes every branch of the textile industry that is in any way concerned with producing the raw materials of fashion apparel. The concluding reading summarizes the major fabric innovations of the past fifty years.

The Durable Threads of J. P. Stevens

by Richard J. Whalen

In the whole history of United States business there has never been anything quite like Stevens. Its uniqueness goes beyond being the world's oldest diversified textile company. Over the century and a half, the management of the firm has passed from father to son in a direct line (even the du Ponts had to rely on an occasional son-in-law) from the founder, Captain Nathaniel Stevens, who began it all by weaving woolen broadcloth in a converted gristmill in North Andover, Massachusetts. Among some one hundred families who started woolen mills in the United States in the years 1800 to 1815, the Stevenses are the sole survivors.

Last year the company's 1,200,000 spindles and nearly 30,000 looms poured out more than 800 million linear yards of fabric, which almost defy classification by end use. A billowing ocean of cloth, this output included luxurious woolens (at $6 a yard), lightweight cotton muslins (at 17¼ cents a yard), sheer dress fabrics of 65 per cent Dacron and 35 per cent cotton, fiberglass to be laminated and machined into missile nose cones and other components, snowy damask tablecloths and flower-bedecked printed sheets, and a synthetic fabric for tents that will be pitched on the roof of the world this year, if the American climbers conquer Mount Everest. Also, Stevens sold 150 million yards of fabric for outside mills.

Handling nearly a billion yards of goods implies unusual size and scope in an industry commonly described as "fragmented" among some 5500 small companies. Stevens is big. In eight states from Maine to Georgia, the company employs some 35,000 workers in fifty-five plants. (The word "mill" is passing out of fashion among modern textile men.) With record sales of $586 million in fiscal 1962, the company boosted volume 18 per cent over 1961. Stevens is the second-largest textile company in the United States (and the world), surpassed only by Burlington Industries, which last year became the first billion-dollar textile company. With a diversified base dating from before and immediately after World War II, Stevens has

---

Excerpted and reprinted with permission from *Fortune*, April, 1963. J.P. Stevens & Company is one of America's oldest and most respected textile firms as well as the second largest fabric organization in the country.

been on the leading edge of a glacial trend toward ever larger textile entities: there were fourteen $100-million textile companies in 1962, compared to ten a decade earlier. Large companies like Stevens, by transforming themselves, are gradually transforming the industry.

The Uses of Diversity

Stevens has propelled itself light-years away from the one-mill, one-fiber textile business because it meant to stay in the game. The old business of supplying staple goods to huge markets was production-obsessed; the new business lives by merchandising. "We're continually fitting equipment to fabric," says Harry Carter, a vice president of the synthetics division. "It's not the business it was ten years ago, when we ran crepes for five years in one mill. Now it's a style and merchandising business." Eighty-four Stevens selling departments in the New York City headquarters tailor the mills' output to the specialized wants of hundreds of distinct markets. An enormous 73 per cent of Stevens' production goes into the volatile apparel trade, which rips apart the familiar pattern every season.

A newcomer might lose his head (not to say his business) in the swings. In 1961 and 1962, Stevens' cotton and synthetics divisions each provided about two-fifths of the company's total volume, and the woolen and worsted division the remaining one-fifth. But consider the relative profitability of fibers in these years: in 1961 the cotton division was the leading money-maker, contributing 44 per cent of company profits, followed by synthetics (29 per cent) and woolens (27 per cent). In 1962, however, synthetics, especially spun rayons and blends of natural and man-made fibers, made a strong comeback, and the synthetics division contributed 47 per cent of company profits. Meanwhile, the cotton and woolen divisions tailed off, contributing 32 per cent and 21 per cent of profits, respectively. The ups and downs from year to year, even quarter to quarter, are extreme. Since 1950, for example, the synthetics division has made as much as 75 cents of each dollar of company profit in a year—and as little as 18 cents. Despite the swing, 1962 was a good year for Stevens: the company's volume of $586 million produced a net income of $16 million.

Quiet, mild-mannered Chairman Stevens, the former Secretary of the Army under Eisenhower who did battle with the late Senator McCarthy before a television audience of millions, is frankly sentimental about the company founded by his great-grandfather. He is unsentimental about how his company spins a profit. "We go to the marketplace and attempt to find out what the public wants. If the public wants straw, we'll weave straw. We're not wedded to any particular product or fiber."

That philosophy has an oddly radical ring in an industry still composed largely of "cotton men," "wool men," and the like. Indeed, so deep is the attachment to a fiber (and so difficult the adjustment to new ones) that a Stevens executive, lecturing not long ago at Manhattan's Fashion Institute of Technology, was hissed by "silk men" in the audience after what they took to be a slur against their true love. But Nathaniel Stevens was nothing if not adaptable, and he would approve the trait in his heirs and their company.

The Bride Could Wait

Nathaniel Stevens, known familiarly as "Captain Nat" in recognition of his rank in the Massachusetts militia, was typical of the early Yankee entrepreneurs. One of fourteen children of a farmer who fought the British at Concord and Lexington, Nathaniel shipped out at twenty-one on a merchant vessel, returned to clerk in a general store, and showed a talent for trading. War with Great Britain in 1812 decided young Nathaniel on his career. With the westward push of population, United States markets for cloth were expanding, and imports would be cut off for the duration. Borrowing money from his father, Nathaniel, with two friends as partners, took over the gristmill and converted it to woolens. Family lore provides an illustration of his diligence. On his wedding day, in 1815, while his bride-to-be waited at the church, Captain Nat was discovered in his mill, absorbed in dyeing a piece of cloth.

Postwar resumption of imports drove many infant mills out of business and posed an early test of Captain Nat's flexibility. He converted from broadcloth to flannels, a daring diversification: up to then no one had successfully produced flannel in the United States. Captain Nat succeeded, and reinvested the profits. However, a Boston importer, Abbot Lawrence, advised

Captain Nat to "shut down your mill and save what you have, for we can bring goods in here and sell them for less than it costs you to manufacture them." Unconvinced, Captain Nat chose instead to whip the invader.

He parted company with one partner and bought out the other to become sole proprietor, served a term in the Massachusetts legislature, and sired nine children. He kept on improving the mill. The Panic of 1837 hit New England hard and every mill closed down for a spell, except the one at North Andover, which kept running and was even expanded as Captain Nat took advantage of the scare to steal a march on the competition. He drove himself and his help through a six-day, seventy-six-hour week, for which he paid above-average wages: $4.50 a week, plus board of $2.

One of his sons, Moses Tyler, became a partner in 1850; his help was needed. For the Stevenses soon acquired a mill in Haverhill, Massachusetts, and became the first family owning more than one flannel mill. Sons were a blessing in the growing business. Captain Nat sent a second son, George, to Haverhill, summoning a third, Horace, from his studies at Harvard to assist Moses at North Andover. When the Civil War broke out, the mills worked overtime, under flickering whale-oil lamps, to supply the Union Army with blankets.

Captain Nat died a month before Lee's surrender, and Moses was his natural successor among the three sons who had become partners. Like their resourceful father, they were willing to experiment. They bought a bale of cotton and proceeded to whip up a blended fabric, an indigo-dyed mixture of 60 per cent wool and 40 per cent cotton. The blend sold well, and the Stevenses were in a position to ride out the collapse of the postwar boom in 1873. They acquired two mills. The deaths of Horace and George left Moses alone but, once again, there was a son on hand. On the day the name of the firm was changed—from Nathaniel Stevens & Sons to M. T. Stevens—another Nathaniel Stevens, son of Moses, quit school and went to work for his father.

A Salesman in the Family

However, one young Stevens, John P., the son of Horace, did *not* enter the family business, at least not in the usual way. Instead, he went (at a salary of $150 a year) into the commission house that handled the goods from the Stevens mills. He learned to sell and to sniff out a poor credit risk. A blood tie with a commission house being thus established, expansion from manufacturing into merchandising soon seemed an obvious move, so the family created its own selling house. On August 1, 1899, J. P. Stevens & Company, with capital of $25,000 and twenty-one employees, opened its doors on Thomas Street in lower Manhattan's textile district. True to the time-honored script, the day before it opened John P. had occasion to wire cousin Nathaniel in North Andover, announcing the arrival of a "new office boy," later christened Robert Ten Broeck.

While the selling house was gaining its feet, the mill company prospered. Like his father, Moses admitted his three sons to partnership early, and served in the state legislature and Congress, where he was pointed out as the largest individual woolen manufacturer in the country. But the Stevenses were also reaching out for cotton. John P. crisscrossed the rapidly developing South, lining up cotton mills for the selling house and investing in likely ones. When Moses died, in 1907, after sixty-four years in the business, the family already had laid the foundation of diversification.

By World War I, J. P. Stevens & Company from its New York office was selling the output of nine cotton mills and was doing the bulk of its business in that fiber. The usual bust after the war boom found the Stevenses shopping as usual; they acquired five mills. Experiments with the new-fangled synthetic, rayon, were begun in the Twenties. John P.'s son Robert served an apprenticeship in the mills, and got a start in his father's firm selling the handkerchief trade. He assumed command in the selling house when J.P. died two days before the crash in 1929. Over the next decade Bob and his older brother, John P. Jr., hustled the house to a volume of better than $100 million.

As a result of acquisitions and investments, the Stevens textile interests sprawled in all directions. The explosive expansion of World War II, and a death in the family, produced a crisis. Moses' son Nathaniel, "Mr. Nat," who had run the mill company since 1907, died in 1946 at the age of eighty-eight. His estate needed to sell stock to settle with the tax collector. The selling house, which now dwarfed the family's mill operations, needed access to the capital markets to continue growing. Everything pointed to the wisdom and necessity of going public.

In September 1946, after months of negotiations, a merger was arranged, uniting the Stevens selling house and mill company with eight other companies. J. P. Stevens & Company, Inc., with Bob Stevens as chairman and J. P. Stevens Jr. as president, was listed on the New York Stock Exchange, the ninth-oldest company on the big board. Within two years the family sold 375,000 shares. Going public brought only a passing twinge. "I think the change was a good thing," reflects Chairman Stevens. "The discipline of public ownership is a stimulus to management to do a better job. We wouldn't retrace our steps."

While J. P. Stevens was about rebuilding, it built a different kind of business, integrating such operations as finishing, which had formerly been done by outsiders. A cotton-finishing plant at Wallace, South Carolina, built in 1950, has been automated and expanded to five times its original size. In synthetics, Stevens used to sell its entire output of tricot as gray goods; now it finishes most of its tricot, and has seen sales grow from $10 million to $30 million. Vertical integration is profitable, but mainly it shortens the channel of trade between manufacturing a yard of goods and the final sale at the retail counter. This long channel, in which goods pass through the hands of the converter, the jobber, the cutter, the wholesaler, and other specialists, has been the grave of many a primary producer. For the message signaling the turn of the retail market from one product to another travels slowly along this complex network, usually not reaching the manufacturer until he is buried in unwanted inventory. Stevens wants to control its goods through as many processes as are profitable, with the aim of getting closer to the consumer.

Fashion Is a Form of Divorce

Whatever Captain Nat might think of computers, he would doubtless applaud, and marvel at, his great-grandson's attention to style and fashion. With almost three-fourths of its yardage going into apparel markets, J. P. Stevens is goaded by the generally accepted estimate that half of the apparel fabrics in use in 1970 will be constructions now unknown. The firm employs 140 stylists. Some of their ideas are exuberant—e.g., the decision a few years ago to splash bright colors through the lingerie line. ("Fashion is the desire to change," says a stylist. "For a woman, it's a mild form of divorcing her husband.") Other style ideas are coldly practical, such as the application of a relatively underpriced fiber to an emerging trend. "We caught the market unaware on the development of mohair fabrics in the fashion cycle of luxury and style," says a Stevens man. "We bought mohair near the beginning of a rise from $1.50 to $2 a pound, and had a good thing going for a year and a half."

In today's textile markets, size, once it is under skilled management control, tends to attract sizable customers. In 1952, Stevens had about fifty million-dollar-plus accounts. Last year it had twice as many, and the ninety-nine largest among its 17,000 customers accounted for 40 per cent of Stevens' total volume. Large retailers, apparel manufacturers, and other customers, witnessing wholesale liquidation of primary textile producers, have given new weight to the continuity of supply offered by a large company, and relatively less to the lower price sometimes offered by a small company that may go under. The trend toward lean inventories in U.S. industry also favors the larger, more efficient supplier. Stevens' transportation fleet of 450 units, with headquarters at Greensboro, can make delivery to warehouses on the West Coast within seventy-two hours. In Kenosha, Wisconsin, American Motors operates on a three-day supply of auto carpets, depending on Stevens to deliver every fourth day. The interaction of large customers and large producers is an important force affecting the structure of the textile industry. Bigness breeds bigness.

Still, the more things change at Stevens, the more they remain the same, in at least one respect. When John P. Stevens Jr. retired a year ago, he turned the chairmanship over to brother Bob. But the role he had loved best was being chief woolen and worsted merchant for the company. Both John and Bob were particularly careful about filling that vacancy. Now selling a tough line in a tough business is thirty-six-year-old Whitney Stevens, one of Bob's four sons. And in the generation right behind are more sons, whose job it may be to stretch the durable Stevens threads from North Andover around the world.

A Fabric Designer's Philosophy

by Pola Stout

The credo on which I was nurtured was beautifully expressed by an old friend in Vienna, who said, "The artist must learn only one thing in order to be creative—not resist himself, but to resist without exception, everything else that prevents him from being himself." More and more often during the past year I have been asked: "Is design fabrics an art? If you call designing an art, how do you define art?" To me art is perfectly defined when you say that it is intuition plus hard work. It is largely a matter of original concepts; no amount of training and education—necessary though they are—can substitute for the spontaneous expression of individuality of the creative worker. . . .

Another way to state an important aspect of my philosophy is to say that I never give up the search for *quality* in *quantity* production. My feeling about this is even stronger than it was at the time I designed the Botany Perennials. More than ever at this period of history, fashion cuts across all lines of economic status, and is gradually becoming part of the heritage of the whole world. . . .

Creative Designing Versus Styling. The *designer* starts from scratch, evolving new concepts out of her own creative ability and experience. To be sure, it can be said that there is nothing new under the sun, but there are new ways and genuinely creative ways of reexpressing basic esthetic principles. The designer might be said to be an artist; the stylist an artisan. *Styling* might be said to be the fashion equivalent of editing in the literary field. The good stylist has a grounding in the history of art, the principles of design, and a knowledge of fibers and construction, so that she can "edit" fabrics, that is, change proportions, colors, checks, stripes, weights, etc., in adapting a design. But she starts with a fabric already completed by one or another designer. . . .

When people ask me how I design, I have to say that I approach design analytically and logically. I have to develop my ideas on a logical basis—but I also trust in intuition (which really can be defined as logic that operates more quickly.) As time goes on, one's work acquires greater and greater technical proficiency, and the creative person is liberated for a far greater range of creation when he has technical knowledge in his fingertips. . . .

It is also essential that the fabric designer be thoroughly familiar with the kind of clothes with which the apparel designer is identified, and then the designer of fabrics must search for the colors and weights and textures that would be most appropriate in styling these specific garments. The designer needs to have a solid understanding of the commercial side of her job; to have a general love for creative expression in textiles; to study merchandising problems; to constantly experiment with original design and to constantly strive for newer and clearer solutions to the problems that exist in the manufacturing field. The textile designer needs to develop fundamental ideals and principles to stand up for those principles. And in order to achieve competence in self-expression, she must have a basic knowledge of the graphic arts. She must learn to be flexible, to adapt herself to economic and production necessities without permitting her designs to suffer as a result of changes, when changes are necessary. She must be a craftsman—that is, a patient, disciplined, concentrated worker in the field she has chosen because she loves it. She must have a sixth sense about the needs and tastes of living people—not only in terms of fashion, but in terms of the problems of the individual. She should take time to familiarize herself thoroughly with the intricacies of various styles—in a world-wide range, since this is in truth one world. . . .

It is regrettable but true that the consumer,

Excerpted and reprinted with author's permission from presentations at the Workshops of Color and Design of Textiles for Apparel, College of Household Arts and Sciences, Texas Woman's University (July 20–25, 1959; July 11–16, 1960, July 17–22, 1961). Pola Stout is particularly noted for her designs for woven fabrics.

by and large, is completely unaware of the contribution to the finished garment that has been made by the designer of fabrics. Consumers may be familiar with certain trade names attached to fabrics, such as Forstmann, Hockanum, Stroock and so forth; some may have heard of the late European fabric designer, Paul Rodier—but this is the exception that proves the rule. Actually, whether the consumer knows it or not, her acceptance or rejection of the designer's concepts is a decisive factor in gauging the public taste; and I believe it would be desirable to educate the public in the understanding of the designs and what has inspired the designer's concepts. . . .

The Color Styling of Dixie Yarn Company

by Mabel Nolan

Dixie offers a color service to its customers which they graciously tell us they find helpful. What is the special ingredient that makes this color service helpful?

We believe it is the timing . . . because we make our colors available early enough for maximum effectiveness.

Stated simply, it sounds simple . . . but let me explain the mechanism of our timing, and you'll agree it is not that simple. Picture, if you will, a juggling team tossing several balls into the air at almost the same time. Each ball must be received by the juggler at just the right time or the act is a disastrous fiasco. Just so with fashion color and timing. Split-second timing is of the essence.

First, let us consider just who are Dixie's customers. We sell mercerized cotton and chemical-fiber yarns to weavers, knitters, and other specialty fabricators. In the case of knitters, they may only knit the fabric . . . and then sell it to manufacturers to make up into garments . . . which means they have to work early. They have to allow plenty of time for their own creative thinking . . . they need time to sell the finished fabric. In turn, their customers need time to dream up and create fashions from this knitted fabric. Or, the knitters may knit the fabric, as well as manufacture the end product. The same may well apply to weavers. And what are the products to be made of the yarn knitted or woven of Dixie Yarns? Apparel of all kinds for women, men, children . . . upholstery fabrics . . . rugs and carpeting. As you see, the gamut is wide and varied. And so the individual calendars or timetables are equally varied.

Now, to tell you how Dixie juggles the seasons and calendar to serve its varied customers and their various needs. For example, we are now working on our Fall 1961 colors. By this, we mean the colors that will reach the consumer in the Fall season of 1961 . . . in some cases, the end products planned for the ultimate consumer will be in retail stores by July or August 1961. We have been developing these colors for several months, and we will finally crystallize our thinking early in June . . . June 1960 . . . and in July, we will send Dixie's Fall 1961 Color Projection to our customers in the form of a brochure. This mailing-piece reproduces the colors as faithfully and accurately as four-color process printing can achieve. It will be similar to those which we have mailed in previous seasons . . . and which I should be happy to have you look at more closely at the end of our meeting here today. Please note . . . we will mail this in July 1960 . . . a year before Mr. and Mrs. Average Consumer will see the finished products in these colors in retail stores.

However, in the interim, we work with many of the other colorists in various and allied industries . . . comparing notes, sharing our thinking, passing along our predictions. Also, we show the beginnings of our Fall 1961 colors . . . the embryo . . . to those of our customers who may want to start their thinking early for the forthcoming season that is actually eighteen months hence.

Mabel Nolan, color stylist for Dixie Yarn Co., a major yarn producer, delivered this address at the Marketing Forum for Foreign Textile Executives, May 20, 1960 at the Hotel Edison, N. Y. Reprint permission granted.

The timing for the Fall 1961 season is no different than for seasons in the past. For instance, Dixie Spring 1961 Color Projections got under way in October 1959, and the colors were released in January 1960 . . . to be shown at the retail level early in 1961. Proverbially, in America, the retail selling season for Spring starts in January-February of the year, and the Fall selling season starts in July-August, depending on the stores' position in the fashion cycle.

Interestingly enough and coincidentally, sometimes we juggle two similar seasons at one time. For instance, while working on Spring 1961 colors, we developed a group of colors . . . lovely and provocative . . . but yet they did not seem right for 1961 . . . a bit too *avant-garde* . . . but we do see them for Spring 1962 . . . and so our Spring 1962 Color Projection began simultaneously with that of Spring 1961.

The Dixie Color Service is always at work . . . analyzing trends . . . examining color acceptances and color directions . . . projecting our thinking even beyond the season in which we are working, as I have just explained.

What fashions our color thinking? What is meaningful to the colorist?

I can only speak for Dixie . . . and to us, the very world and the times we live in are grist for our mill: current events . . . world happenings . . . vacation spots . . . museums . . . the whole world of art . . . maybe a village craftsman's rug loom . . . perhaps a jaunt to far-off lands . . . a ballet . . . an opera. Everything looked at with the colorist's eye, ever on the alert for the newest nuance of color and tonality . . . offers fresh fields for fashion and inspiration.

But let me say that, while we are always responsive to new sources of inspiration, we also pay strict heed and mind to the historical color patterns of selling and consumer acceptance with relation to a specific product. Color changes cannot always be sudden and startling at the consumer level, and acceptance may take several seasons.

We have discussed Dixie timing . . . now let us consider the aids or tools by which Dixie implements its color service. Believing that nothing describes or tells about color like color itself, we mail our customers, as we have mentioned, printed seasonal color projections. These show, in printed color, the colors . . . by families . . . which we consider to be of fashion significance. The range is wide. That is because we sell to knitters, weavers, and manufacturers, who in turn create and sell men's, women's, and children's hosiery . . . underwear . . . outerwear . . . swimwear . . . sportswear . . . evening wear . . . also, rugs, carpeting, upholstery, and drapery fabrics . . . as well as Leavers laces and Schiffli embroideries . . . and I shall return to this point a bit later.

While the printed seasonal color projection gives a fairly accurate idea of the colors, we, at Dixie, believe that the yarn itself in color is the best color tool we can provide for our customers . . . and so we provide them with what we call the Dixie Library of Colors . . . consisting of small cards, 3 by 5 inches in size, each swatched with yarn. . . . The card gives the name and ordering number of the color . . . a description . . . and the alternate types of dyeing that we recommend. For example . . . Petal Pink, No. 207 . . . was vat dyed; but it is also available in direct dyeing "with relative colorfastness properties," whereas . . . Carib Blue, No. 775 . . . is reactive dyed, and, for color fastness, is recommended in this type of dyeing only.

Currently, the Dixie Library of Colors consists of 254 colors. We started with 75 color cards in 1957 when we inaugurated this new accelerated system. We supplied our customers with wooden file boxes to store color cards and keep them handy for quick and easy reference. Periodically . . . but not necessarily seasonally . . . we add more colors, and these are sent, when ready, to those of our customers who use this service. The color cards have worked out very well in actual use . . . they are easy to handle and are effective in showing how colors look in combination and in blends.

When we mail out the seasonal color projections, it is quite possible that some of the colors projected are already in the Dixie Library of Colors. A new season brings with it new thinking about colors already in existence, often when used with new colors in fresh-to-the-eye combinations. However, new colors are always appearing on the horizon, and are being developed in our extensive laboratory at the Chattanooga plant . . . sparked by the Dixie Color Service that operates out of the New York office.

Another working aid for designers and manufacturers offered by Dixie is a color blanket. It is woven of 60/2 ply mercerized cotton on a

64-inch box loom. This is a rather intricate and expensive operation, in that each filling change has to be done by hand in the proper sequence of color as arranged by us in advance to give a good blend. The warp contains thirty colors, including black and white, and these same thirty colors are in the filling, so that every color crosses every other color and itself . . . producing the rather staggering total of 900 different blends or color effects. Weavers find it very helpful in predetermining the exact shade a warp of one color and a filling of another will produce.

Because Dixie maintains this color service, it does not follow that customers are limited to Dixie colors only. On the contrary . . . we dye almost as many special colors for customers to their own specifications. The advantage in using Dixie Colors is, however, a matter of time . . . always that matter of timing! . . . for Dixie Colors have been fashion-authenticated, and the formulas are ready . . . where, with a special color, it takes time to develop the formula to arrive at an exact match.

Because of the many sizes and types of yarn Dixie works with, and the diversity of color, we do not carry dyed yarn stocks. All colors are dyed to order to meet customer requirements as needed.

If you recall, I mentioned that our color range is so wide because we sell to customers who have such a wide variety of end uses. Naturally, therefore, this wide color range must be edited down to meet each customer's particular needs. In many instances, where customers employ stylists, they—the stylists—edit the colors to fit their company's needs. Many stylists bring their choice to us for discussion and confirmation. Sometimes we are able to suggest new additions that would be desirable for their product, but not appropriate for our general release.

Then, there are customers who ask us to select a group of colors from which they can select color for their own clientele, and we supply them with groupings of our color cards in one of these folders. This card represents toddler's swimwear colors for Spring 1960—and swimsuits of some of these very colors may well be in stores in New York right now. It so happens that this card was prepared in July of the year 1959.

How Color Comes to Life in Fashion

by Margaret Ingersoll

I will first talk on the subject of color itself, a subject which is an unknown quantity . . . a subject that is air, a subject which is not factual, and yet has the greatest influence in fashion today. Cecil Beaton said, "Perhaps no element making up the total fashion image is as important as color." Color is emotional . . . one cannot pinpoint it. There is not any one formula in determining color . . . but sensitivity, deduction, and timing are three factors important in arriving at color selections each season. Let us examine these factors further.

Sensitivity. One must be sensitive to every new trend—yet expert in analyzing, appraising, selecting, and discarding.

Deduction. Before looking for the new, I subtract those colors which have become accepted each season and have now become staples. Red, for instance, is in everyone's wardrobe each season. Blue now is becoming an all-season color. Also, I subtract colors which have overstayed their welcome—colors of which we are weary. The eye becomes tired of certain colors after a length of time. Then, I start thinking about colors that look fresh, new, rare. I might add here that many colors which we tire of can several seasons later be new colors again and important.

Timing. This is the most sensitive factor of all. Usually there is a need for certain colors—for instance, if a season has been a troubled one, you might say a season depressed in the

---

Abridged and reprinted with permission from an address delivered at the Metropolitan Section's Ladies Night Meeting, April 13, 1962 (North Jersey Country Club, New Jersey). Margaret Ingersoll is Fabrics Editor of *Vogue Magazine.*

large sense, the next season will have a natural appetite for more color—for a lift—a sparkle. Colors are created to fill this need. On the other hand, a color that appeals to the emotions at the time for no obvious or accountable reason can make a place for itself. But let's look deeper into this. Is it really unaccountable? Here, I would suggest that one should expose oneself to creative minds, to different parts of the world, to all sections of this country, by talking to people, seeing how they live, observing their needs. This must be our guide, no matter what field we are in. We cannot sit behind a desk, in a mill, or our showroom, and predict color and fabric developments without contact with the constant change that is going on in the world today. As color and fabric in fashion go hand in hand let's see what is happening in the fabric world. There is a revolution going on in fabrics, and not without reason, there has to be or should be a reason for everything. So, our reason: There is a revolution in our way of life. Movement is the trend. Women are in motion all the time; therefore, their clothes cannot be restricted and fabrics cannot be restricted.

Knits have become more important than any passing fashion. They are appearing in every fiber. Stretch fabrics in wovens are in their infancy and will revolutionize our clothes. They have been in sportswear and now are appearing in daytime and evening fashions. I feel there is a great future in this fabric.

Women will never want to return to heavy, bogged-down fabrics. When mohair appeared several years ago, it was the beginning of revolutionary fabrics. One could have that wonderful bulky look, yet weightless. Mohair is continuing in different forms and structures in fabrics. It influenced the open leno weaves. For warmth without weight, weightless linings are being created; therefore, the woman can have her wonderful old loves such as meltons, heavy broadcloths, duvetyns, in coats without weight.

Crepes returned with great impact due to the fluid, animated skirt trend. Certain fabrics are made before the fashions; therefore the fabric must have an influence on the fashions. Fabric today is more influential in fashion than ever before. However, there is a meeting of the minds of both fashion interests as both are sensitive to the new movement. Now, all of this emotion, sensitivity, and feeling must be organized, emphasized, and brought into focus. How is this done? Color starts in fabric; other markets must be related; one does not stand alone. This is how we work at *Vogue* each season with the fashion markets: about ten months before the ready-to-wear showings, I, as the fabric editor, draw from my experience, sensitivity, and deduction to formulate my thinking in color and fabric trend forecasting for the next season. I start pinning up snips of colors which might be drawn from my fabric line, start pinning up snips of colors which might look promising for the coming season. These can be snippets from the previous French collections, or a color from a fabric of the dark ages, but it gives me something to show myself; gives me a device for reacting to color freshly. The delight of colors and the fashion news that they contain are transmitted better through the eyes than through the ears. Many people call me on the telephone to ask what the colors are for the coming season. I will never discuss color over the telephone. One must see color to know it. Usually the first who come in to discuss color are the yarn people. At the same time they discuss design, pattern, and texture of fabric. In exchanging ideas, and discussing trends with the various fabric manufacturers who come to get our thinking, one is reminded of Ping-Pong —batting the ball back and forth—the decision is not made by one person, but through an exchange of ideas among creative minds. Many old fabric favorites are transformed into new fashions through the inspiration of new colorings. It is color that inspires and vitalizes the new as well as the old in fabrics today, and, as I said before, fabric today is more influential in fashion than ever before and color is more influential in fabric than ever before—one cannot be a success without the other. Various fashion market people come to the *Vogue* fabric room to get color and fabric information, and to make selections for their lines, or to relate their fashions to the fabric colors. I'd like to explain this further. The jewelry people come to coordinate their jewelry colors with the ready-to-wear colors for the next season. The shoe people, the hosiery, the glove, hat, sweater, and cosmetic people. We even have fountain-pen companies, ribbon houses for tying packages, automobile people, button people—just to show you that the world and everyone in it is color conscious today.

Finally the designers take a stand, and color,

fabric, and silhouette become established for the new season, dramatized by the magazines and executed through the stores to the consumer . . . the two units in this vast fashion industry that go directly to the consumer.

Now I would like to show you how color comes to life in fashion—to show you the follow-through from a swatch to the consumer. On *Vogue's* fabric chart, which was mailed out October 1960 predicting colors for spring and summer 1961, this mauvy pink swatch, which was on the chart, started the phenomenal success of pink. It started in a suit by Ben Zuckerman, which appeared in the January 1, 1961 issue of *Vogue*. This is how it was born . . . I selected the color for *Vogue's* fabric chart. Our editors saw it in *Vogue's* fabric room before the chart was completed. They found it new and exciting. We took it to Miss Daves, our editor-in-chief, who agreed. We had Mr. Zuckerman make it up and it was the success of the season. In this case, certainly the color helped sell the fabric and the suit. From the success of this suit, pink became the color of the season. Another success story in color started in a much different way. The Northup King Seed Company came to us with a new zinnia color—a new red never before in a zinnia, which they named Polynesian Red. They wanted to advertise and promote it . . . we thought it was a beautiful new and unusual zinnia color and said that we would like to introduce it. First we asked a jewelry manufacturer if he would like to reproduce the exact zinnia in a pin—the result was the pin by Trifari shown editorially by *Vogue* September 15, 1961. In the meantime, we contacted Everfast Cottons and asked if they would like to join in a promotion with B. Altman and Everfast to make the zinnia prints for both ready-to-wear and home furnishings. They were as enthusiastic as we were, and one year from the time the Northup King Seed people contacted us, the zinnia promotion was in full bloom in *Vogue* and B. Altman—January 1, 1962. The B. Altman windows and every department on every floor had merchandise made of the zinnia print.

Fifty Landmark Years for Fabrics

1910–1920

The United States already had flourishing mass production mills (whose styling ideas were European) but much fabric and 90 per cent of all dyes were imported, mostly from Germany. National textile unions versus existing craft and company unions came into being, did away with child labor, improved wages.

When World War I that started in Europe in 1914 embroiled U.S.A. in 1917 and 1918, development of a national dye industry began. Silk hosiery then was $3.65 per pair for service types plus tax. Today nylons hose runs 99c to $1.95.

Vol. 1 No. 1 WWD quoted cotton gray goods 64x64 at 4c and 39-inch 68x72 (returned to popularity today as a base for wash-wear finished goods) at 5¾ c. It was news that American Printing Co. (now vanished) had reduced prints from 6c to 5½ c.

During 1910 the first rayon fiber mill was started in Marcus Hook, Pa., a beginning of a new era in fabrics that did not ripen until the late twenties when mills learned to concoct the popular crepes of the period and dye them properly. It was not until the thirties that the cheaper prices of rayon and acetate goods gave rayon mills a boom period during what was depression time for all other textile markets.

1920–1930

Historically "mad." Soaring stock market after brief depression in 1921 and 1924. Sharp changes in women's fashions, behavior, and lives.

The Flapper, shingled heads, the Charleston, boyish form, dieting, waistlines dropped to the hips, knee-length skirts, corsets abandoned, (leading to a big flurry in rubber reducers in the

---

Reprinted by permission of *Women's Wear Daily*, July 13, 1960. Copyright 1960, Fairchild Publications, Inc.

mid-twenties), sports for women, more women in business, demands for sports, and career girl clothes.

Big spurt in ready-to-wear and fabrics that would "cut," beginning of the eclipse of the private dressmaker. But Macy's carried French handmade and ready-to-wear at less than $50. Stenographers wore "from Paris hats" or a $15 Fortnum & Mason British cloche.

There were crazes . . . sunbathing, tennis, golf, nightclub life, cruises in the winter, all with special fabric requirements. Every European and Asian fabric-producing nation had branches in New York. American firms expanded to meet the demand for silks, Kaska (invented by French Rodier), white flannels, plushy coatings topped by long-haired furs that framed shingled heads concealed by cloches.

Rayon and acetate trade was plodding, came up with transparent velvet, later crepe, and Schiaparelli serpentine crepe.

Some of the crazes that made special fabric demands were not only crepes, prints, and embroideries, but "King Tut" motifs (following the discovery of King Tutankhamen's tomb in Egypt).

Rodier's discovery of the United States Southwest Indian art which he translated into cottons, woolens, and silks, and Vionnet's bias cuts that made a fashion for "balance" crepes.

Loads of beads, spangles, and Chanel-inspired costume jewelry came into being, influenced the fabrics styled for fashion trades, built a demand for glittering metal brocades (now having a renascence). Poiret's introduction of effete harem pants were the forerunners of the shorts, beach pajamas, and playsuits of the thirties, "Rosie the Riveter" garb and jump suits in war-time forties, skin-fitting "crazy" pants, suburbanite dungarees, and the bifurcated skirts for street wear introduced by American designer, Norell, for this fall.

1930–1940

Financially depressed years all over the world. Stock market crashes in 1929 and 1930, failures of banks and insurance companies, declines in tourist business and cruises, apple sellers on corners in cities, bread lines, soup kitchens, overproduction of unpurchaseable edibles . . . importers folded and many mills faded. The National Recovery Act began to operate to stem the unnecessary devastation in a growing country.

It was opportunity time for the rayon and acetate fabricators. With a lot to gain (from investments in previous decades), fiber companies such as Du Pont, Celanese, American Viscose, and Eastman floated mills and converters who would play. Silk had gyrated in price so much that mills were afraid of it.

When everyone buckled down to work, some of the prettiest, most becoming clothes in years succeeded the short straight lines of the twenties—floor-length evening dresses, coordinated sheers and heavy fabrics, revivals of matelasses, satins, taffetas, and laces, all contributing to the growth of rayons and acetates. Toward the end of the decade, war had begun in Europe and the first sensational nylon hosiery and lace had been introduced.

1940–1950

World War II removed France as a fashion source, removed silk and nylon from civilian uses, imposed restrictions on uses of cottons and woolens, on lengths and widths of skirts, cuts of sleeves and the composition of play clothes. As women moved into war work, pants became the daily uniform and sequin-trimmed rayon afternoon dresses the thing for the relaxed hours and the business girl.

Preoccupied with producing fabrics for the services and war uses, mills reduced their civilian output to a minimum number of quick weaving fabrics made of rayons and acetates. Cottons became so scarce that many retail stores closed down counters where cotton yardage, sheets, pillowcases, and towels had been sold. This went on for two years after the war ended while world-wide needs for American cottons were being served.

During this period with a war-depleted staff, *Women's Wear Daily* followed and interpreted all the many government regulations on fabric uses and pricing, and the rationing of goods into the most needed channels.

Meanwhile, the cotton industry had become aware of the threat of highly washable nylon and pushed war-built research departments into intensified efforts to develop the wash-wear cottons that have become basic in sales.

1950–1960

A ten-year period of mergers, big fabric firms growing bigger, diversifying into metals, plastics, chemicals. The shift of mill locations from North to South intensified, Government control of cotton and wool, establishment of a minimum wage law, appearance of strong, machine-washable rayons, Federal Trade Commission recognition of acetates as separate from rayons, legislation barring flammable fabrics, a wealth of new trademarked fibers, and a sharp rise in imports marked the years.

There are now sixteen separate generic classes of man-made fibers, including stretch, rubber, glass, and metal types, fibers with new molecular structures, expensive fibers, cheap fibers, processes that protect against flame, mildew, moths, stain and water spotting, germs. Finishes that make fabrics crush-resistant and wash-wear and whiter-than-white are taken for granted, so are fast colors.

Big mills' research departments are headed toward more improvements in a big way. Coming are wash-wear woolens, and possibly silks.

Techniques in handling yarns to make pleasant textures advanced notably in the fifties. Stretch yarns, for example, have given rise to a new type of ski-pants cloth, a market for half-leotards, and new lightweight corsetry. Fluffed-up man-made fibers invaded the sweater field, and compete strongly with woven woolen goods.

Meanwhile, mills have gone "on steam" in buildings, machinery, and merchandising, reaching through all manufacturing and retailing levels.

During the last five years controversies between textile producers and government have sharpened. Japan is on a self-imposed quota of cotton goods and cotton articles to export to the United States. The whole wool-supplying world tries to get in on the quota of goods that may be imported into United States at a low rate of duty. Makers of velveteen and silks are vocal about foreign competition and cotton goods manufacturers (although Japan has been curbed) are complaining about rises in exports by Hong Kong and India, both countries that have such low-cost production that the higher-geared American economy cannot hope to compete with it, as is. However, they are already taking steps in cost cutting through more efficient machinery, development of perfection in quality for the masses, on-time deliveries, and creation of goods and merchandising especially suited to the American public—all things in which foreign countries lag more or less.

Questions for Review and Discussion

1. What is the major function of the textile markets in the business of fashion?
2. Are fabric "names" or brands important to consumers when they buy clothing? Why? How many fabric brands can you name and by what textile firms are they promoted?
3. Find five "giant" textile firms listed on the New York Stock Exchange. What does this "listing" mean in terms of ownership? What is the current price of their stock?
4. From current advertisements, cite or show examples of "tie-ins" or cooperative advertising by textile and apparel producers.
5. J. P. Stevens is an example of a vertically integrated textile firm. What does this mean? Do vertically integrated firms have an advantage? Why?
6. Do you believe that the consumer's acceptance or rejection of a designer's concepts should be the "decisive factor" that Pola Stout claims it is? (See "A Fabric Designer's Philosophy.") Considering that professional designers are more qualified to judge "good design" than the average customer, do you think that this is "fair" to designers? Why?
7. In what products, other than apparel, do fabrics play a "fashion role?" Cite examples.
8. The reading "Fifty Landmark Years for

Fabrics" suggests that apparel styles and fabric developments influence each other. Cite several examples from the past or present to prove or disprove.

9. Discuss the social and economic events in the history of this nation that influenced the development of the textile industry. Explain when, how, and why. What current factors, if any, are affecting the industry?
10. If you were employed as a "fashion specialist" in a fabric or leather firm, how could you contribute to its success?

SECTION

III

Apparel Producers — U. S. A.

Although the idea of ready-to-wear did not originate in the United States, this country has brought mass production of fashionable clothing to its highest development, and leads the world in the quality, quantity, and variety of its output. The apparel industry is relatively young in the industrial history of America, but its growth has been rapid. A little more than a century ago there were fewer than one-hundred manufacturers of women's wear whose combined output amounted to a scant two and a quarter million dollars' worth of cloaks and mantillas.[1] Today, the output of fashionable ready-to-wear garments for women in all walks of life is the heartbeat of a big, dynamic, machine-producing, ferociously competitive, billion-dollar industry. Known by many names, such as the apparel industry, the garment trades, the cutting-up trades, the needle trades, the "rag" business, and even characterized as the "Wild West of United States industrial society," [2] the production of women's apparel is a sizeable force in our nation's economy. The 1963 factory value of shipments of major apparel items for women's and children's garments amounted to over 6 billion dollars, which places it high in terms of total sales among United States manufacturing classifications.[3] Employment in the garment trades for 1963 was estimated at some 622,200 workers in all parts of the country, close to 4 per cent of all manufacturing employment.[4] Not only is the apparel industry of considerable size in and of itself, but its activities have great influence on many other business areas. In addition, it is an industry which has changed "fashion" from the privilege of the Four Hundred to something within reach of all but the most deprived women in this country.

It is with the development, operations, and economics of the American

[1] "Fifty years of Women's Fashion Industries," *Women's Wear Daily*, August 28, 1950, p. 2.

[2] S. Freedgood in "$100 Million in Rags," *Fortune*, May 1963, p. 151.

[3] Apparel Survey, Current Industrial Reports, Series M23A(63)–1, June 24, 1964, Bureau of the Census, Industry Division, Apparel Section.

[4] Research Department, International Ladies Garment Workers Union, "Conditions in the Women's Garment Industry," March 17, 1964, pp. 18–19.

apparel industry that this section is concerned. The selected readings which are included aim to give the reader a deeper insight into the unique nature of one of this country's major industries.

History and Development

Less than a century ago, when fashionable clothing was something that few could afford, the needs of these few were imported, usually from England and France, or were supplied by the hand labor of a small number of custom tailors and dressmakers working at home or in small craft shops—generally using imported European fabrics. The majority of the early American colonists wore clothes dictated by what they could afford, and they had to make their own. Every home of modest circumstances was its own clothing factory, a loom and a spinning wheel. Ready-made clothing was virtually nonexistent, and what little was available was of the poorest quality and completely lacking in design. Home dressmaking continued to prevail into the early twentieth century and it was not until well into the 1900's that the term "store clothes" was used in other than a derogatory manner.

Menswear First. The development of the garment industry started with men's ready-to-wear. It was born in the early 1880's in the port cities of New England, almost half a century before the women's apparel industry had its beginnings. A few enterprising merchants, notably Brooks Brothers,[5] conceived the idea of producing and selling cheap ready-to-wear trousers and shirts for sailors who needed to replenish their wardrobes inexpensively and quickly during their brief stays in port. The market for ready-made clothing soon expanded to serve bachelors who had no one at home to sew clothing for them, and to fill orders for cheap clothing for plantation slaves. Other merchants followed suit, and established men's clothing plants in Chicago and St. Louis in response to the demand generated by the Gold Rush. Apparel manufacturing had begun in earnest and in a way typical of American frontier life—with work clothes for laborers. The clothes were poorly made and sewn by hand. They certainly were not fashionable. The designing—such as it was—and the cutting of this early ready-to-wear clothing was done in the dealer's shops; the garments were "put out" to local women for hand sewing.

Two events in the mid-nineteenth century opened the way to expanded production. The first was the perfection of the sewing machine by Elias Howe in 1846. This invention revolutionized clothes making in America by making possible volume production in machine-powered factories. The second was the Civil War, which created an unprecedented demand for ready-made Army clothing and hastened the change from homemade, hand-sewn garments. A further development was the standardization of sizes, developed by the government for military uniforms. After the war, these sizes were converted to civilian needs, and helped to place the men's ready-to-wear trade on a firm basis.

Women's Wear in 1860. Meantime, the production of women's ready-to-wear

[5] Brooks Brothers company booklet, "Established 1818." Also see Egal Feldman, "FIT for Men," for the history and development of the men's clothing industry (Washington, D.C., Public Affairs Press, 1960).

was also developing, but more slowly. The first official report of a women's clothing industry appeared in the U.S. Census of 1860, covering products such as hoop skirts, cloaks, and mantillas. Once started, the industry grew rapidly. From 1860 to 1880, the wholesale volume of production increased from 2 million to 32 million dollars; the number of manufacturers from 96 to 562, and the number of employees from 5739 to 25,192.[6] Factory production, however, though stimulated by the invention of the sewing machine, was still in its infancy. Between 1890 and 1910, the pace of the industry's growth received additional impetus from the influx to America of immigrants from Central and Eastern Europe, many of whom brought with them traditional tailoring skills and a capacity for hard work. By 1900, the women's clothing industry reported 2070 manufacturers, employing 96,000 workers, with sales exceeding 150 million dollars and surpassing the combined efforts of all the custom tailors and dressmakers in America.[7]

The early decades of the twentieth century saw many technological improvements in production methods, such as powered cutting machines which could cut many garments simultaneously. The First World War helped the industry come of age. Factories and offices, stripped of male help, turned to women and, as more and more of them entered business, the demand for the ready-made garments grew. The variety of the industry's output multiplied many times and sales jumped from 168 million dollars in 1914 to over 400 million dollars in 1921.[8] The manufacturing of women's wear had not only caught up with the men's clothing industry, but had forged ahead of it.

Growth of Unions. No history of the industry would be complete without mention of its union and its unique contribution to its development. In the early days of the industry, working conditions were, as in so many industries of the period, extremely bad. Factory conditions were primitive and unhealthy; work

[6] "The Dress Industry," Market Planning Service of the National Credit Office (a division of Dun & Bradstreet), March 1948.
[7] *Ibid.*
[8] *Ibid.*

GROWTH OF THE INDUSTRY

Wholesale volume of business
1900 $174,000,000
1963
$6,300,000,000

Source of data: National Credit Office and Research Department, ILGWU.

was also carried on in tenements; hours were long; wages were low. Some workers provided their own machines, paid for thread and needles, for the water they drank, and sometimes even for the "privilege" of working in the shops. Sleeping overnight in the shop to gain an extra hour or two of working time was not unknown.

It was in this atmosphere that the ILGWU (International Ladies' Garment Workers' Union) was founded in 1900, with 2000 members, after a desperate struggle dating back to the 1880's. After two years of bitter conflict in an effort to achieve better working conditions and higher pay levels, industry and labor made common cause with one another. Since the 1920s, industry-wide strikes and lockouts have been all but nonexistent. Today, labor-management relations are characterized by cooperation in research, education, and industry development, and the apparel industry pattern is held up as a model for others to follow.

Geographical Centers

Concentration in New York. It is not entirely an accident that New York City is the unquestioned fashion capital of the country, and, insofar as mass production of women's and children's apparel is concerned, of the entire world.

When Elias Howe first perfected his sewing machine, the mass manufacturing of garments took to no city in particular. But then came outside events that ensured New York's dominance in women's fashions. From 1880 to 1910, as a result of Jewish persecutions throughout Eastern Europe, a great wave of immigrant Jews arrived at the port of New York. Since tailoring had been a Jewish occupation in Europe, many of these immigrants were skilled tailors, and they entered the then fledgling, ready-to-wear industry.[9] Others who were not skilled, but eager to find work in the city where they landed, were absorbed into the infant garment industry. It was also during this period that the ready-to-wear concept was catching on; American women were putting away their thimbles, needles, and patterns, and buying the "store-made" apparel. The coincidence of a bottomless pool of immigrant labor at hand and the upsurge in American consumer demand was the circumstance that permitted New York City to leave all its rivals far behind in the production of apparel.

New York had the further advantage of being close to the woolen mills of New England and the cotton mills of the South. It was also the market to which retail buyers came for almost every kind of merchandise carried in their shops. Once New York had gained dominance, it became a magnet, attracting such auxiliary businesses as embroidery, pleating, stitching, trimmings, and the like. With these advantages, plus its traditional position as the nation's largest city and center of fashionable society, the city became, and still remains, the hub of the fashion industries. It presently accounts for about 60 per cent of the wholesale sales of all women's and children's garments in the United States,[10] and is the largest industry in New York City and in New York State.

---

[9] Florence S. Richards, "The Ready-to-Wear Industry, 1900–1950," New York, 1951, p. 7.

[10] National Credit Office, "The Apparel Manufacturing Industry," 1964, p. 30.

THE GARMENT CENTER IN NEW YORK CITY
Names of garments show heavy concentrations of manufacturers and jobbers

Seventh Avenue. So much of New York City's garment business is done within a distance of one block east or west of Seventh Avenue, from 40th Street south into the low 30's, that the term "Seventh Avenue" has become synonymous with the women's fashion industry, and particularly with that part of it concerned with the large-scale production of women's outerwear. There are other centers elsewhere in the country, and even in other parts of New York City, where women's garments are produced, but to those in the fashion business, no other industrial center has the color, tension, or drama of Seventh Avenue.

Originally, all the manufacturing operations of a garment firm took place under one roof. Today, many concerns locate their cutting, and, to a larger extent, the actual sewing processes, elsewhere. But the nerve center of their operations—the showrooms, designing, and shipping—remains quartered on "Seventh Avenue." New York's vast supply of skilled labor and the availability of many supporting industries make it a desirable headquarters for fashion manufacturers. Equally important is the availability of designing talent and production know-how, plus the opportunity to exchange ideas with others. To creative people, this last element is usually vital.

Paris-born designed Pauline Trigère, has been quoted as saying: "With the possible exception of Paris, New York is the only city in the world in which I could work . . . I need the tempo of New York to create clothes for the women of the world: sensitive, elegant, practical clothes. In New York, my mind never stays still. Inspiration comes from within, and New York feeds the 'within' constantly." [11]

Secondary Fashion Centers. There are other fashion centers outside New York,

[11] Jack Alexander, "New York's New Queen of Fashion" *Saturday Evening Post*, April 8, 1961, p. 30 *ff*.

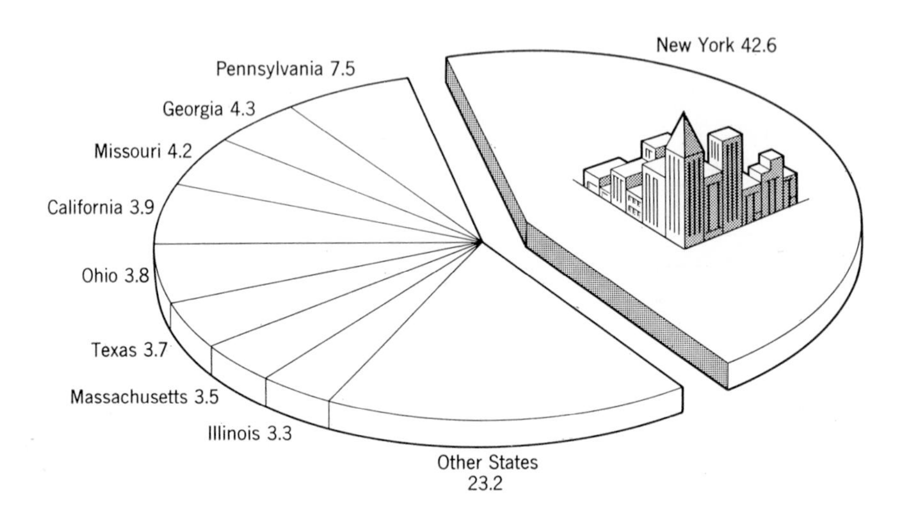

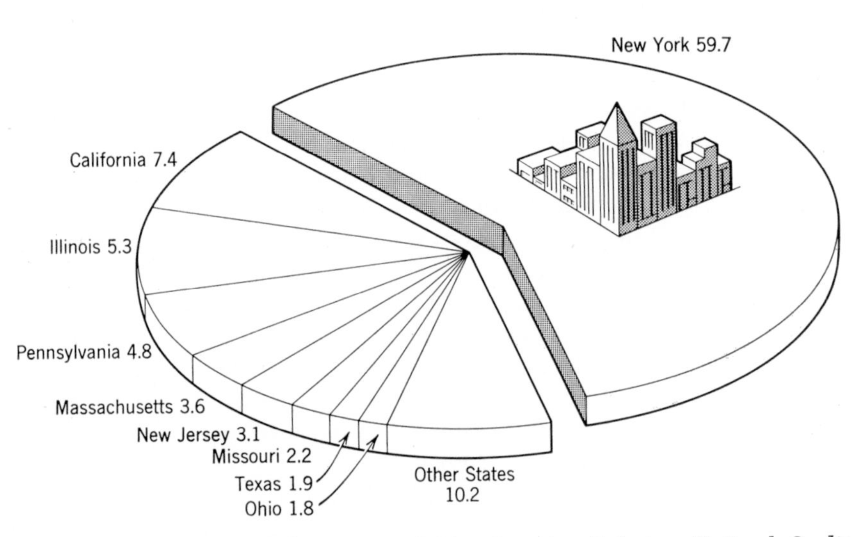

Data for 1963. Source of data: Apparel Manufacturing Industry, National Credit Office, 1964.

although none can compare with New York in the variety or quantity of its output. These are known in the trade as "markets," and they tend to be fairly specialized as to the types and price ranges of their products—Los Angeles for sportswear, for example, and St. Louis for junior dresses. Or, in men's wear, Rochester for quality men's tailoring.

A detailed description of these regional fashion markets is found in a reading in this section. The accompanying pie charts show the sales percentage enjoyed by the leading secondary markets, compared to New York; a similar chart for men's wear is inserted for comparison.

Characteristics of the Industry

"Outside" Contractors and "Inside" Shops. There are several different types of manufacturing plants in the industry. Some firms, referred to in the trade as "inside" shops, produce in factories of their own; others plants, called "outside" shops, farm out the sewing, and sometimes the cutting, to contracting shops. These contracting shops, which are often independently owned, employ the operators and produce to the specifications of those who hire them.

The contracting system evolved during the early history of the industry. Prior to 1880, the manufacturing of women's apparel was generally completely integrated. During the expansion of the industry between 1880 and 1890, the manufacturers turned to contractors because of the many advantages they offered—the burden of seasonal idleness and the responsibility of dealing directly with labor could be shifted to the contractors, as could the problem of increasing or reducing productive capacity. Today the industry remains a combination of the old and the new. Some firms have both "inside" production facilities and also hire independent contractors for extra capacity in busy periods; other firms subsidize or own contracting plants; some still employ outside contractors exclusively. The U.S. Census of Manufacturers classifies the industry's plants into three different categories according to their production activities: manufacturers, jobbers, and contractors. The manufacturer produces the garment from beginning to end; the jobber handles everything but the actual sewing, which is done by outside shops; the sewing shops are classified as contractors. The contractors never take title to any of the goods, but merely return them in finished form to the jobbers (if one uses Census terminology) who hire them. Common trade usage, however, does not ordinarily make the distinction between jobbers and manufacturers that the Census does; any firm that buys fabric, designs and cuts their own garments, and maintains a showroom to sell the finished product to retail buyers is generally referred to as a manufacturer, irrespective of who does the sewing.

A Stronghold of Small Business. The apparel industry is unique among major manufacturing industries because it is still a stronghold of small business. Unlike other major industries, such as steel, automobiles, chemicals, petroleum, and the like, where the giants control and are numbered in the dozens, the garment industry numbers thousands of highly competitive small shops still operated along craft lines. Not only is the field one of many small concerns, but no single company, or group of companies, controls more than a small percentage of the total output. Until after the Second World War, only a few companies had attained a 1 million dollar annual sales figure. Of the 4530 concerns now in the field, 60 per cent still average less than $400,000 annually.[12] There are comparatively few larger companies; less than five companies out of every hundred have an annual sales volume in excess of 5 million dollars and only one company in every hundred does over 10 million dollars.[13] The relative distribution of large and small firms differs somewhat among the different branches of the industry. Nonetheless, there is a similarity of comparative smallness, whatever the branch of the industry.

The smallness of the individual manufacturers (and jobbers) makes it inevitable that the average factory in the industry will also be small. Figures cited by the ILGWU indicated that "only 2.1 per cent of the concerns employed 250 workers or more, while 72.2 per cent had fewer than 50 employees." [14]

Because it takes comparatively little capital to open a shop, an enterprising person with a flair for fashion can set up in business and hope to prosper. Basic equipment consists of a cutter, two sewing machines, and the operators to run them. As one producer put it: "What do you need to open up shop? One month's deposit on a loft. You sell on 30-day terms, buy on 60-day terms, and you're in business. Fly-by-night manufacturers come into the industry with nothing and pull out in a couple of seasons with a million—or with nothing." [15] The key to success is ingenuity in producing styles which can find customer acceptance; in that, the small firm has an equal chance with the larger one. In fact, a sudden style shift can often be more quickly exploited by a small manufacturer, since he has greater flexibility in production. On the other hand, a single poor season can wipe out a small, undercapitalized producer—and often does. There is a high failure rate in the industry, and some two to three hundred firms go under annually.[16] Nevertheless, for every firm forced out of business, another takes its place.

Highly Specialized. Although the industry as a whole covers the widest range of types, price lines, and qualities, there is a high degree of specialization by individual firms. A typical manufacturer will specialize in a particular size range, such as juniors, as well as on a particular type of garment, such as cocktail dresses, within a narrow range of prices. Once he has built his reputation for distinct types and prices, he has difficulty in winning acceptance for other types or price lines. A maker of coats at $16.75 to $22.75, wholesale, for example, could not readily switch to $29.75 to $39.75. He would be out of reach of his former customers, and would have to make a fresh start among those who could patronize the new price lines. The effect would be about the same as going out of business and starting all over again.

Style Piracy Prevalent. Design and styling are such important competitive weapons in the fashion industries that style piracy, against which our laws provide no protection, is considered a "way of life" in the garment trades.

[12] Source of data: "The Apparel Manufacturing Industry," cited in reference 10.
[13] *Ibid.*
[14] Report of the General Executive Board, ILGWU, May 12, 1965, page 104.
[15] From "The Garment Center," one of a series of articles in the *New York Post*, October 14, 1962.
[16] From press release of the Credit Clearing House, a division of Dun & Bradstreet, Inc., on commercial failures (dated January 29, 1964).

Copying the work of creative designers is standard operating procedure for many firms, especially the smaller ones and those dealing in cheaper lines. There are several reasons for this copying practice. Plunging into a fast-selling style, regardless of whose design it was originally, is one way to make a modest capital work to the limit. Another reason why style piracy is rife arises from the highly specialized nature of the firms themselves. If, for example, a dress intended to retail at $100 has features that would make it a fast seller at a lower price, the originator of the style is in no position to produce or market the inexpensive versions. On the other hand, a maker specializing in garments to retail at $30 quite definitely is. And, if the style can be copied still lower down the price scale, to perhaps $8 retail, a maker specializing in that level steps in.

Occasionally, the copying process is reversed, and a style that originates in the lower-price lines will have features that make it desirable for higher-priced manufacturers to adapt. Normally, however, the procedure is for a style that originally retailed for hundreds of dollars to be "knocked off" at successively lower prices, if it shows signs of popular acceptance by customers. So common is style pirating that the industry even has a special term for a style produced by many different manufacturers at many different prices: they refer to it as a "ford."

Patterns of Operation

Seasons and Lines. Seasonal factors and the periodic presentation of new lines, or collections of new styles, are fundamental in the operating pattern of the fashion industries. Although the number of seasonal showings varies from one branch to another, at the very minimum a firm must invest in fabric and present a new "line" twice yearly. In the women's apparel industry, three to five new collections are customary. A dress firm, for example, will bring out a spring, fall, summer, holiday, and often a special resort line. In addition to revising their lines seasonally, many firms continue to revise their offerings as the season progresses. Styles that win consumer acceptance may be produced in a wider range of fabrics than originally planned; new "hot" styles may come into demand; those that prove to have little or no consumer appeal may be dropped altogether.

The showing of a new line is only the beginning: the reaction of the professional retail buyers must be measured before styles are put into production, and those that do not win acceptance must be eliminated to avoid costly markdowns or "closeouts."

Market Weeks. During periods known to the trade as "market weeks," buyers from retail stores all over the country converge on manufacturers' showrooms to shop and compare the different collections in preparation for placing their orders.

The method of presenting new lines to buyers varies. Some firms present elaborate fashion shows on live models to open their collections; others simply have the garments ready for inspection on racks in their showrooms. Some firms stage previews of their new collections, to which they invite reporters from fashion magazines and newspapers, in order to get publicity; others do not. But, although the method of showing may vary, the timing for a particular branch of the industry is fairly standardized. Customary business practices dictate the week or weeks of the year in which the largest number of buyers is likely to be in the market; the maker who is conspicuously early or late risks ringing up the curtain on an empty house.

From Design to Finished Product. In order to be ready with their lines for the normal market weeks of their industries, apparel manufacturers must start working on their collections at least two or three months prior to the showings—or about six months before the consumer herself is ready to buy. In some branches of the fashion business, even longer preparation is required. For example, large producers of sportswear coordinates may work as much as a full year ahead to assemble the many kinds of materials they need for mix-and-match sweaters, blouses, slacks, skirts, and jackets. The farther ahead the maker works, the more intensely must he anticipate trends in fashion and study the customers in order to foresee their needs and tastes with sufficient accuracy.

First of the many steps in the production of apparel is the designing process for the coming season. Weeks or months before the openings, the firm's designer, or team of designers, is busy working up the styles that will fit into the price range and type of merchandise in which the firm specializes. Among the fashion leaders in the industry, the designs originate on the drawing board or in the muslin, but for many less-original manufacturers, a style will often start life in the form of someone else's merchandise which has been sketched or purchased for copying purposes. In many instances, because fashion is basically an evolutionary process, many of the "new" designs will be repeats, or merely slightly revised versions, of the previous season's best sellers.

Once the design has crystallized, the next step is to execute an actual garment. This is generally done by an assistant, working closely with the designer and making revisions until a satisfactory sample emerges. For these early trials, some firms work in muslin; others, in the fabric of the garment. Next, company executives check the style for costs, availability of materials, potential salability, and the possibility of profit. Some styles may be changed at this point; others may be discarded entirely.

If a style is to become part of a line, it is given a number, and a highly skilled patternmaker makes a production pattern for it—in one size only, whatever size the firm uses for its samples. From this pattern, one garment at a time is made for testing and for a possible correction of the pattern. When the pattern is right, as many samples are made as are needed to show the line.

Large confident producers decide at once which numbers they will produce. Innovators and those less sure of themselves await retail reaction before putting any number into production. From an initial collection of 200 samples, perhaps one third will be eliminated after they are shown; of the remainder, it may be that only about a dozen will develop into "runners" or reorder styles. The number of orders received or realistically anticipated that are sufficient to warrant production varies with each firm's needs and price levels. One manufacturer of dresses that retail at $150 upward explains his criteria regarding fabrics that have to be cut in volume: "We don't consider a piece for cutting unless it sells over a hundred. Of course, in our $1250 retail numbers, we'll cut a few, a dozen or two. These pieces are cut individually. At that price, you'd expect them to be."[17]

After it has been decided to produce a style in quantity the pattern for it is graded. This means that the pattern's various parts are "sloped" up and down to adjust for each size that is to be produced. The process can be done more or less mechanically by adding or subtracting the appropriate fraction of an inch; or it may be done with care, skill, and constant checking to insure excellent fit.

Next, after grading, comes the marker. This is a long paper guide that shows all of the various pieces and sizes of the pattern, as they should be laid out in order to cut the cloth economically and with bias and straight where each is needed. For the actual cutting, layers of fabric are rolled out on long tables. The marker is placed on top. Guided by the marker, the cutters use electrically powered knives that cut through a very substantial depth with speed and accuracy. The number of garments cut at one time varies with the thickness of the fabric, the cutter's skill, the price of the garment, the number of orders, and so forth. As many as 6000 garments of a style can be cut on a long table in one operation.

The cut parts of the garments are then collected, identified, and "bundled," to be passed along for the sewing operation. This may be done in the firm's own plant if it is an "inside" shop; more commonly, the bundles go by truck to a contractor's plant for the sewing. In some instances, contractors do the cutting, working from the marker and continuing from that point.

In many sections of the apparel industries, piecework prevails among the sewing operators. This requires a preview of the garment by an industry-union committee, which determines the precise price to be paid for each step in the sewing.

In some plants, a single operator does all of the machine sewing on a garment. This is the tailor system, still followed for better garments (notably coats and suits), and it requires highly skilled workers. More often, team or section work prevails, and each operator does just one part. Where different machines or different adjustments of one machine are needed for the various elements of the garment, the team system makes for speed. Any hand sewing that is required comes under the heading of trimming, and is done by operators other than those who put together the main body of the garment.

Garments are then inspected, pressed, and readied for return from the contractor (if one is involved) to the original establishment where they are finally inspected and distributed to the stores that bought them.

The period beween design and delivery of a dress is a long one that the ultimate consumer knows little about. Yet the important decisions on what type of merchandise customers will find in the stocks of their favorite stores are made during this period.

Concentration on Best Sellers. The manufacturer's concern with the acceptance of his styles is not ended once the garment has been delivered to the retailer. Initial orders and production of a style often do not cover the costs of manufacturing, distribution, and overhead, and frequently, the margin of profit is

---

[17] Marie Shapiro, Publicity Director of Hannah Troy Inc., in the *New York Post*, October 10, 1962, p. 53.

dependent upon the degree to which the firm receives reorders and can recut styles in large quantities. Manufacturers must keep abreast of changing fashion trends because outmoded styles can be sold only at disastrous prices—if indeed they can be sold at all. The typical manufacturer continues to recut only those styles on which retailers continue to place relatively sizable orders; slower-selling styles are discarded. As the season progresses, production is further narrowed down to a handful of the most reordered "hot" styles. By increasingly greater concentration, as the season progresses, upon fewer and fewer fast-selling numbers, producers can reduce some of the many risks inherent in the manufacturing of fashion merchandise.

Importance of Speed. The production and distribution of fashion in the United States is distinguished by the rapidity with which accepted styles are manufactured and marketed. In a business which must keep up with changing fashion, time and distance factors tend to be surmounted by its speed of action and productive flexibility. Fortunes can be made if the right style is marketed at precisely the right moment; they can be lost if the style is too early or too late. Timing is of paramount importance. As previously explained, designs for a coming season are prepared from six weeks to three months prior to openings. Once orders are received, the production process at the beginning of each season will take anywhere from three weeks to two months on the new styles. The retailers start their selling season with broad style assortments, but with relatively limited quantities of individual numbers, so that they may reorder quickly and in quantity those items that get good reception from their customers. To be able to fill these reorders while demand is at its peak, the manufacturer must have speed and maneuverability. No matter how early the industry starts preparing its lines, and no matter how early the retailers stock them, production becomes a race with the clock once the consumer has entered the picture. Once the season gets under way, the productive process is speeded up, and reorders take approximately one to three weeks for delivery.

This is not entirely true of the more basic items of fashion merchandise, such as classic shirts, shirtwaist dresses, plain pumps, etc. Such items generally have predictably long fashion lives, and manufacturer and retailer alike can anticipate demand with minimum risk. But even among the classics, an occasional color, fabric, or detail of design may enjoy a sudden vogue, and thus bring the beat-the-clock element into the picture. No branch of the fashion business—men's and children's, as well as women's—is immune to the need for speed.

Marketing Activities

Distribution Policies. Distribution in the fashion industries is generally directly from manufacturer to retailer, without wholesalers or other types of middlemen. Only in such staple items as hosiery, underwear, and some children's wear, does the wholesaler distribute appreciable amounts of merchandise. Since most fashions are relatively short-lived, there is little time for the middleman to inject himself into the picture.

Distribution policies vary from firm to firm. Some manufacturers will sell to retailers of any type or size; others prefer to limit their distribution to one or a few stores in each trading area. Deciding factors in the distribution policy of an individual firm relate, for example, to its price lines, its productive capacity, and the potential consumer market for its products.

It is not common for a women's fashion manufacturer to own his own retail outlets, although there are a few manufacturer-owned retail outlets in the shoe field and in the men's clothing field. In general, a fashion manufacturer needs all the time, energy, and capital he has for his own part of the job; he hasn't enough of any of these for forays into retailing. A potent deterrent, too, is the reaction he can expect from his present retail outlets if they find him in competition with them for the consumer's trade. His retail customers are quite likely to drop him completely.

Reliance upon Salesmen. By and large, apparel producers rely upon their own salesmen to bring their products to the attention of the retail trade. Most firms maintain selling staffs in their showrooms to wait on retailers who come to the markets and build up a following among professional buyers. The majority of firms employ "road" salesmen who travel with samples and whose duty it is to call upon retail prospects in assigned territories. For the manufacturers who do not choose to develop sales staffs of their own, or who seek continuous representation in areas not covered by their own salesmen, there are independent selling organizations which maintain permanent showrooms and represent several noncompetitive lines. Examples are to be found among many out-of-town producers who are represented in the New York area and among the New York producers who hire manufacturers' representatives in major fashion centers such as Los Angeles.

Advertising and Promotion. The emphasis on personal selling, however, does not stop the fashion manufacturer from advertising nationally to the consumer if he can afford it, or from seeking publicity in consumer publications. Some manufacturers invite representatives of the fashion press to their openings each season, and follow through with a barrage of press releases about their lines and their activities. Many of the photographs and stories about fashion that appear on the women's pages of newspapers actually originate in a press "hand-out" from the publicity department of a manufacturer.

Other promotional techniques include providing the retailer with selling aids, like counter cards, display materials, customer mailing pieces, newspaper advertising mats, and photographs for use in the store's ads. Still others are training talks to the store's salespeople, and help in staging fashion shows for the store's customers, by supplying scripts and sometimes commentators. Widespread use is made of cooperative advertising, an arrangement under which manufacturer and retailer share the cost of newspaper advertising run in the store's name to promote the manufacturer's goods. The retailer enjoys more advertising space than he pays for out of his own pocket; the manufacturer enjoys advertising that is run in conjunction with the name of a locally known and respected retail store, and that is usually backed up by the store with a substantial stock of that maker's goods.

In addition to efforts made to reach the customer directly or through the retailer, fashion manufacturers also use trade publications to advertise their merchandise to the retailer. The small, often highly specialized circulation of these publications brings their advertising rates far below those of consumer magazines, and a fashion manufacturer does not have to be very large to make good use of them.

Current Trends in the Apparel Industry

Since the end of the 1950's, there have been some notable changes in the traditional patterns of the apparel industry: the rise of publicly owned giant concerns; the emergence of nationally advertised apparel brands; an increasing diversification of output; developments of automated production devices; and decentralization of production facilities—these developments are beginning to change the shape and face of the garment trades. These patterns have been characteristic of the American economy, but they are relatively young in the apparel fields. The "new look" in the industry has been stimulated by the rise in living standards, the development of new production and marketing techniques, and the emergence of national fashion markets, coupled with a degree of fashion stability resulting from the increased popularity of classic sportswear.

Rise of Publicly Owned Giants. One of the most marked changes has been the rise of publicly held giant apparel firms. Mergers, acquisitions, and internal expansion have created a cluster of large corporate set-ups whose annual sales range from 10 to 100 million dollars, and who have "gone public"—converted a partnership or privately owned corporation into a publicly owned one, listed on the stock exchange and inviting investment capital from the public. Nevertheless, this trend to bigness has not yet produced concerns that compare in size or leadership with the dominant U.S. Steels or General Motors of other major industries, or even firms large enough to represent a substantial percentage of the garment industry's output.[18] In the dress industry, for example, the combined output of the four largest firms still does not amount to more than 4 per cent of the industry's total. By way of comparison, the output of the four largest makers in the automotive field amounted to 75 per cent of the total.[19]

Table 1 The Rise of Fashion Giants: Growth Pattern of Five Publicly Owned Apparel Firms (Sales in Millions of Dollars)

Firm	Major Products	1960	1962	1964
Kayser-Roth	Men's, women's and children's lingerie and accessories	121	154	215
Jonathan Logan	Dresses, sportswear, knitwear	48	77	138
Bobbie Brooks	Junior sportswear	53	76	88
Colonial Corp.	Men's, women's and children's apparel	20	56	83
Russ Togs	Sportswear	16	21	32

Source: Annual Reports of Companies.

For the most part, the industry is still dominated by thousands of small manufacturing partnerships, who consider themselves fortunate whenever a few "runners" bring their annual dollar sales up to 1 million dollars. What the future will bring remains to be seen, but today, small reputable manufacturers and

[18] In December 1964, the National Credit Office listed 68 firms whose sales were in excess of 10 million dollars. These 68 consisted of 22 sportswear firms, 18 dress firms, 11 lingerie firms, 12 corset firms, and 5 children's wear firms.

[19] Statistical Abstract of the United States, 1962 edition, pp. 785–797.

outstanding designers, with virtually handicraft operations, still continue to set the fashion pace for the industry in the high fashion and higher priced fields. It is the firm conviction of a noted industry analyst that "while big ready-to-wear and accessory manufacturers will grow bigger, and others will appear on the scene, theirs is not the wave of the future . . . On the whole, the industry will continue largely the domain of the little man." [20]

Increase in Brand Identification. The emergence of manufacturer's brand names and national advertising programs in consumer media are also relatively new in the apparel industries. Before the Second World War, the names of American designers and garment manufacturers were not generally well known to consumers; apparel was purchased by a combination of approval of a garment's appearance and confidence in the retail seller. The source of a dress or coat was considered the retailer's trade secret.

There are several reasons for the increased emphasis on brand names and national advertising. One was the shortage of merchandise during the Second World War, which made the retailers willing to go along with the idea of featuring the maker's name if that was how he wanted it. Later, when merchandise was again plentiful, other advantages demonstrated themselves: opportunities for free advertising and promotional tie-ins with fabric and fiber sources; editorial mentions of producers' names which were offered to makers by consumer magazines; opportunities for giant concerns to cultivate nation-wide markets for their name products by means of national advertising which they could now afford.

The amount of brand-name advertising done by apparel makers today is impressive in comparison with the almost nonexistent advertising done by the industry twenty years ago, but it is still small in comparison with what is spent by other major industries, such as automobiles, drugs, cigarettes, and foods. David Schwartz, who heads the largest dress corporation in the world—Jonathan Logan, Inc.—believes that "In the fashion industry, it may be dangerous to over-advertise. If a particular design is seen too much, the woman who wants to be different will not buy it." [21] Another reason may be that the average woman is much more concerned with style and becomingness of garments than with the name that appears on them.

This last element, especially, gives a newcomer to the fashion business as good a chance to succeed as a more widely advertised maker, if he is able to offer a better styled line. The premium is still on ingenuity in producing clothes that find consumer acceptance.

Diversification of Products. A further industry development to be noted is the trend away from traditional specializations and toward a greater diversification of output. A major reason for this trend has been the acquisitions by large companies of concerns which produce types of apparel products other than those of the parent company. Nowadays there are dress concerns in control of sportswear plants; sportswear firms that own coat and suit factories; blouse companies with lingerie divisions; menswear firms that produce and market women's apparel.

---

[20] Sam Feinberg, "Rise of the Giants," *Women's Wear Daily*, November 11, 1960.

[21] "Big Business Comes to the Fashion Industry," in *Challenge*, the Magazine of Economic Affairs, April, 1962.

Automation on the Increase. Improved production methods have also begun to give the industry a new look. There are now some plants employing hundreds of workers, where automation is increasingly taking over. Although automation has taken hold in the garment industry only within the past five years, it is expected to increase rapidly for some segments of the industry (such as staple items) faster than for others. Whether automated machines can produce styled garments such as suits, coats, and dresses as well as skilled individuals still remains to be seen. As of today, however, the industry stands unique among the major industries of this country. Its output is still controlled by thousands of operators working at thousands of sewing machines. Automation plays a minor role in its productivity.

Decentralization of Production Facilities. New York remains the headquarters for the designing and merchandising activities of the city's manufacturers, but a number of New York firms have begun to produce their goods in areas outside of New York. Jonathan Logan, Inc., for example, operates several factories in different parts of the country, and shuttles raw and finished materials among these plants by means of a company owned airplane. So far, this trend toward decentralized operations has been more evident for the sewing stages of the cheaper and more standardized apparel operations. It remains to be seen, however, whether the production process of highly styled garments can be successfully separated from their design and marketing operations.

Fashion Design and Creativity

The creative expression of the designer or stylist is still the foundation of any garment company, but the economics of mass production imposes tremendous pressures on the creative process. Whether the designer be the employer or an employee, he must be practical and know what his firm is capable of and willing to produce. He must know what the customer has accepted in the past and will accept in the future. He must be original, notwithstanding the fact that it is a great struggle to get huge textile concerns to produce, in small yardage, new textures or colors with which to experiment. His new style creations must be acceptable to many retail buyers, or they will never be produced.

The development of American designers was inhibited considerably by the undisputed position long held by Paris couturiers as fashion originators. Not until France fell to the Germans in the 1940's, and America was cut off from the French influence, did our own country's designers receive their long overdue recognition. Today, American designers include among their number many who are trend setters in their own right. Theirs is the responsibility of keeping abreast of the changing tastes and demands of the American public, and bringing out styles that represent their own interpretations of current and coming fashions. Fashion designing is an art, but in the final analysis, fashion is a business. No matter how creative the designer, no matter how much advertising his firm does, no matter how many salesmen it has, if the styles do not please the customer, there is no sale.

Readings

In the readings offered in this section, the editors have selected articles and talks by observers close to the scene and with the perspective to assess each new development in the light of conditions that influenced it. The first two readings—one by a noted fashion editor and the other about a well-known American designer—deal with the creative design aspects of the apparel manufacturing field. Three readings follow which concentrate on the business operations of the industry. A general information calendar and a statistical picture of the industry are also included in order to familiarize the reader with timing and output.

The Development of American Creativity in Fashion

by Virginia Pope

You've often heard the expression "from rags to riches." Creativity, as applied to the garment industry, might well be referred to as "from the tailored skirt to billions." It has all happened in a comparatively short space of time, as human events go. It has taken about three-quarters of a century to move from the cutting table to the design room and the most beautiful and luxurious of creations by highly trained artists.

In the late 1800's, there existed only men's suit factories and makers of underwear. The former graduated into the making of ladies' skirts, the latter produced shirtwaists. Such was the market in those days. Fine ladies were costumed by dressmakers. Women went out and sewed by the day; small dressmaking houses had plates as their guides. Then there were the extravagant salons where costly costumes were confectioned. I question that the word designer was used, certainly not with frequency. The caterers to the wealthy went to Paris for their fashions.

You will find it hard to believe, when I tell you that it was not until 1908 that some bright fellow had the brilliant idea of joining a bodice to a skirt and calling it a dress. Out of this marriage grew the house dress. Houses manufacturing them were later to become well known in better brackets.

It was just before World War I that manufacturers became aware of Paris. They learned that the Miss Carrolls, Thurns, Farquahrson & Wheelock, and similar houses, went to Paris and brought back fabulous clothes for their private clientele. Awesome names were Worth, Paquin, Cheruit, and Callot. These were creators in a real sense. The boys got wise: they hopped on fast French liners, taking a showroom girl or model with them. Off they went to the races—it was at Longchamps that they saw the styles worn by the flashing demi-mondaines who set the pace. They went, they saw, they bought. From the costumes they brought back they learned the intricacies of French cut. They were apt at translating them to their need, and applying their technique to their purpose.

Creators of fashion were in the making. Some

As fashion editor of the *New York Times* for twenty-five years, Miss Pope "eye-witnessed" and also influenced many developments in the apparel industry. She delivered this address to a Retail Workshop in Fashion Merchandising on February 3, 1964, at the Fashion Institute of Technology, New York, N.Y.

of the young women pioneers were later to grow famous in their own right. Outstanding was Louise Barnes Gallagher, designer and manufacturer of suits. She was perhaps best known for a fabric she developed, Gallagher mesh, forerunner of our present-day knitted fabrics. Another smart gal was Jo Copeland, whose name is known from coast to coast for her high-style fashions.

Merchants caught the Paris fever. In the summer of 1914, John Wanamaker sent his top buyer and stylist, Mary Walls (her name is legend), to bring back a collection. The Germans were advancing on Compiègne. In the course of being shipped out, her trunks were lost. Nothing daunted, Irish Mary dashed behind the lines, the atmosphere blue around her (she could swear like the best of troopers), and found her treasures. She returned to New York triumphant. Mr. Wanamaker turned on the works. He notified Mr. Hearst, of journalistic fame; the papers carried banner headlines; and crowds rushed into the store. Paris fashions had their first volley of publicity.

The couture furore spread. Fabric houses found a means of bringing Paris to the manufacturers. They bought sizeable groups of originals, and invited the cutters to see and copy them, provided they signed a guaranty to purchase $250 worth of fabrics with which to manufacture them.

The industry was struggling to its feet. Embryonic creators were getting their first experience. A new element was entering the scene. The leaders had been tailors. Edwin Goodman, Eddy Meyer, and Harry Frechtel knew the intricacies of cutting and fitting, bringing perfection to their trade. Young designers, artists in the matter of coloring and detail, added embellishments to the severity of the tailored costume.

In 1918, the wholesale price of a dress ranged from $16 to $39. The $10 dress was born over the weekend in the May 1919 depression. The bottom fell out of the fabric market: raw silk dropped from $20 to $7; silk fell from $2.75 a yard to $1.50. John Wanamaker jumped into the situation, and marked down his prices by 25 per cent. With such a drop in values, the manufacturer could afford to cheapen his product. By the end of 1919, the $10 dress was firmly established, and has held its own ever since.

Unions were few and far between in those days, and lacked organization. Price adjustments were easily made. It was all week work: those who were paid $12 then receive $125 now. Bundles went to the factories, dresses were individually draped. Mass production was in full sway.

Let us remember that, immediately after the war, fabric types were limited. Dresses were of cotton, wool, or silk. Textures were not known as they are today. Among the woolens. broadcloth was high style; gabardine and serge were utilitarian. Designers had less to work with. It was not until some time later that nubby fabrics came into being. Textures and weights changed. Man-made fibers were soon to revolutionize the fabric field. Creativity was at work in chemistry, as well as in fashion.

The art of fashion was beginning to bloom when the industry moved uptown into the garment center. Young women who had been trained in the skills of French dressmaking used their ability to devise the soft suit. In Paris, they had outstanding leaders: Chanel and Molyneux were revolutionary. The severely tailored suit yielded its place to the newcomer. Jane Derby is mentioned as one of the first to skilfully adopt the theme. From her dressmaking establishment on upper Broadway came Nettie Rosenstein, whose little black dresses made fashion history. Another name in the twenties and thirties was Anna Smithlein, sister of Adele Simpson. Not only were these women able designers, they were, and still are, successful business executives.

It was about this time that creativity in fashion branched out in another direction. A new and exciting influence came out of Hollywood and the movies. The pictures called forth talent —American talent. The most brilliant was Adrian: he influenced a generation. I hear young designers speak of him with baited breath. Other men who dressed the stars were Travis Banton and Omar Kyam. The glamorous actresses whose charms they enhanced cast their aura over the country; in every hamlet, women aimed to copy them.

In the thirties, we had good designers in New York, but so great was the enthusiasm over Paris that they went unsung. Their names were rarely mentioned in the press or by the stores. It took another war to bring about a change in creativity. Complying with the limitations on the use of materials imposed by the government, the designers performed brilliantly. With Paris blacked out and no couturiers to play up, we discovered our own. A great woman and an outstanding merchant, Dorothy Shaver (later president of Lord & Taylor), recognized America's young designers and brought them to the fore. She promoted and advertised them, gave shows, and invited press and public. Among them were: Elizabeth Hawes, Helen Cookman, Clare Potter, Claire McCardell, and Vera Maxwell. What an incentive to creativity!

Fashion was reaching out in many directions. The urge of youth was strong. Ours is a country of sport-loving people; nature offers us vast playgrounds. Responding, young talents turned to sportswear. They created brilliantly with freedom and color. Once again, California, with its enthusiasm for open-air fun, came to the fore. Throughout the world, America took the lead in playclothes. An enormous market was developed.

American democracy and know-how gave creativity another opportunity to show its ingenuity and strength. Ready-to-wear opened a broad vista—clothes for everybody, short and tall, thick and thin, young and old. Sizing and styling for age groups were the next steps. In the "dark ages," there had been 10's to 14's and mamma house dresses (32, 34, 36, 38, 40). Children's clothes were very simple. A whole army of young things was crying out for styles of their own. Along came Jack Horwitz with the gayest of junior togs, styled by college-age kids who understood their own needs. Emily Wilkens took teenagers out of the little-girl class and offered them sophistication. There followed designers for subteens. Soon, tiny tots' clothes were inspired by Paris.

Then statistics forced on makers the fact that 75 per cent of the women in the country were 5′4″ and under. Designers faced another challenge. Came fashions for the short-waisted, the petites, the "Troy" figure—everyone has a different name for them.

With each new phase, there was fresh talent to meet its call. The young element was better equipped than its forerunners had been. Far-thinking spirits in industry and education recognized the need for training young people eager to enter the fashion world. Schools and colleges started courses in design and merchandising. Three great institutions were founded in New York—Pratt, Parsons, and the Fashion Institute of Technology, the last-named the outgrowth of the Needle Trades High School.

All of this puts us on the threshold of a fabulous era, for as in the other arts such as science and industry, fashion is living up to the American tradition of productivity and progress. But, it is not all whipped cream. Our artists face many stumbling blocks, and they are not easy to hurdle. This Niagara of talent that we have in our midst is sometimes dammed—I use the word without the "n." It is restrained because of the constrictions and restrictions of the business world.

Once again, I look back to earlier days when New York's stores were under the guidance of giant merchants, men of authority and individual taste. They had a personal interest in all that went into their businesses. Such were John Wanamaker, Paul Bonwit, Franklin Simon, Edwin Goodman. They were in close contact with their buyers, they knew the manufacturers and their products, and they were well informed about the customers who came into their stores. An amazing example was S. Klein of 14th Street, who invited the most fashionable social registerites to luncheon at Sherry's. Mr. Edwin Goodman, I am told, was a frequent visitor to the garment center houses from whom he bought. He checked fabrics, and made certain that production came up to standard. He was often seen throughout the store. No one was a better judge of furs. Owner-controlled shops were more individual in their buying. Men of the type I refer to gave wide latitude to their buyers, who were the Napoleons of their departments.

True, business was not conducted on the same volume basis as it has been in the last quarter of a century. Management and policies have changed. In 1963, figures count—we are in the impersonal IBM stage. The mechanical mind, rather than individual thinking, is in control. Banks are at the helm. Statistical information is the guiding power of the chain-store empire. The buyer is no longer as close to the customer. She is directly responsible to her merchandise manager. The bugbear of her existence is the markdown. With corporation control, banks care more about figures than style and individuality.

Buyers, prone to stick with the best sellers of last season, resist experimental new styles—a dampening effect on creativity. The manufacturer, seeing a bold innovation on the part of his designer, removes it from the line or never cuts it. Young designers, and older ones as well, who aim to put America abreast if not ahead of Paris, are discouraged by these hindrances. . . .

My friends in the market, who have lived through several decades of expanding creativity, point out other changes. For example, in the twenties and thirties, it was not the custom to show large collections. Limited groups were presented for not more than six or seven weeks. Buyers came to the showrooms frequently, and placed their orders promptly. All of this has altered. Collections are larger and more comprehensive, ranging from daytime to cocktail and evening dresses. As about 50 per cent of the average collection is put into production, it is almost impossible for the manufacturer to place the orders for his fabrics far in advance. Deliveries are frequently from eight to ten weeks.

The designer has greater stature. Much more is demanded of him. The scope of his creativity has broadened. The dress house makes suits, the suit house makes dresses. Contrary to the practices of yesterday, the designer's name is promoted by stores and press; his clothes carry his signature as unmistakably as a canvas does a painter's. The customer, aware of this identity, seeks the creations of a favorite. The manufacturer, on his part, has developed customers with whose buying habits he is familiar, and which he is partially responsible for molding.

He's a Fashion Purist with the Golden Touch

Norman Norell, Rival of Paris as Arbiter of U.S. Fashion, Reaches New Sales Peak by Offering Simplicity of Design, Top Quality—at Seventh Avenue's Highest Prices

At 64, Norman Norell of Norman Norell, Inc. is going stronger than ever. His sales this year are expected—conservatively—to reach a record $2.5 million. His fall-winter line, now reaching the eighty specialty and department stores (one hundred twenty outlets, counting branches) that carry it, drew rave notices as "the greatest ever" when buyers got their look at it at the showings in June.

Paris Rival. The credo itself doesn't explain how Indiana-born Norell got to the top of his profession. It doesn't explain why American women will pay from $300 to $4000 for one of his garments. But as this bundle of controlled energy expounds his ideas—a tough combination of idealism and practicality—it becomes plain how his single-mindedness of purpose has made the Norell look a rival even of Paris in determining what American women will wear.

Strictly speaking, Norell does not belong to the world of "haute couture." The couturier is primarily a dressmaker, who designs a collection from which an individual woman chooses. He sells her choice direct to her, tailor-made for her. In the United States, Mainbocher ranks tops in this tiny world; the custom departments of Bergdorf Goodman and Saks Fifth Avenue are other key examples. It's the costliest way a woman has to fill her wardrobe.

The great European couture houses, of course, also follow another path to the United States market. They sell rights to copy their originals to United States stores and manufacturers.

Meticulous Ready-to-wear. Designers such as Norell and James Galanos, the young Los Angeles star and the only other noncustom United States designer in Norell's price league, classify themselves as ready-to-wear manufacturers. They sell at wholesale to their select retail clientele.

At their level, the line between couture and ready-to-wear becomes blurred. The meticulous

---

Excerpted and reprinted from the September 12, 1964 issue of *Business Week* by special permission. Copyright 1964 by the McGraw Hill Co., Inc., p. 64 *ff*.

"making" that goes into each of the 7000 to 10,000 units turned out yearly in Norell's own factory and in that of George Oliva, who manufactures only for Norell, has become a byword in the trade. "I think," says Norell with characteristic restraint, "my clothes look fairly well in Europe, in the quality of the fabric and in the making."

Fashion editors and retailers would put it much more strongly. A Saks Fifth Avenue executive calls the Norell craft "An appreciation of what hands can do over machines." Mrs. Evelyn Byrnes, whose Park Avenue shop is an important Norell customer, has never had to return one garment for faulty quality or workmanship.

Norell and The Look

This doesn't diminish his job. "It's far more difficult to design now. Simplicity is hard to make distinctive enough so that women will pay for it." Even though originality for its own sake is "out," women still want "something—not crazy, but something. A designer must have a look." If he doesn't have one, a store doesn't need to carry his products. On business details, Norell tends to vagueness. Ask him his title in his corporation—a tightly held concern in which he owns controlling stock—and he ponders. "Why, I don't know. I'm the president, I guess. I must be the president."

But the vagueness disappears when he gets talking about fashion. For a starter: "I just want women to look as marvelous as they can." This means dressing very simply by day, very glamorously at night.

High Goal. He aims way beyond his immediate clientele. "I'm more interested in launching a fashion than in creating beautiful things. Fashion is what is accepted and worn by the general public. When it reaches that point, you know the design is a good one."

So he designs for no special group. "I strive for a young look, but older women can wear my clothes." A shop owner amplifies: "He designs for a figure, not an age. You won't look silly in a Norell if you're 40 or 60 or 70 if you have the figure."

Norell makes sure you have the figure by the simple expedient of making no garment in a size larger than 16, and very few of those. "We decide," he says firmly, "what dresses we will make in 16. Buyers will do terrible things. They'll squeeze a 20 into a 16. Horrible."

But aesthetics alone won't win the general public, Norell qualifies: "Women must look as marvelous as is practicable at the moment." That means comfort. "They won't wear uncomfortable clothes."

He chides the fashion magazines for playing up the sensational design or showing styles in outlandish poses. "The editors get carried away with gimmicks. I'm against all the crazy photographs they do." Editors, for their part, lament that he is adamant on how his own line shall be photographed in their pages.

It's a final ingredient of his creed that a look should last. "I never design to obsolete the past."

It's a Business

Convictions such as his wind up with a high price tag. For he insists on the best with a fanatic zeal.

In his one-designer shop, he's the boss. "I throw out designs they tell me will go great guns, if I don't like them." He has the courage of his convictions, adds Andrew Goodman, president of Bergdorf Goodman. "If he believes in a design, he'll use it twenty-five different ways." If it doesn't take one season, he'll try it again later on.

Fabrics First . . . Norell's working season, though, starts with buying, not designing. Last month, he roamed France and Italy, buying samples of choice brocades and other fabrics for his spring collection, to be shown in December. Since he had not then put a single design on paper, he was buying blind—hence expensively. "I buy material for 500 cuttings," he says, "and at most I may use 150."

. . . then the designs. Back in New York this month, he starts grinding out the designs. Ideas come from anywhere—from Paris, say the Paris couturiers bitterly, and he freely admits it. The fabric itself gives him some ideas. He starts slowly, picks up steam as the deadline nears. "The fabric comes late, the ideas come late, and it's horrible," he says. As a result, his shop never sees the final collection put together—some 150 to 175 designs—till the gala opening day. "It's a terrible way to do," he grants cheerfully.

Constant Supervision. Production starts before the collection is shown. Max Bernegger, textile engineer, the "Swiss hardhead," as he calls himself, who is the manager of the company, has already laid in a load of stocks—staple fabrics that Norell is sure to need. Norell hovers over each production step like a hen mothering chicks. "A designer can't design and then go away for two months," he says. "The production man would like that. He'd like to cut a skirt narrower here, take out a bit of fullness there, to make it easy and less expensive. A designer has to follow the dress right through."

Meanwhile, the factory is going full steam and overtime from September till November, the shipment deadline for the winter season. But it's laborious going. A fast girl can make three dresses a week. A tailor may take half a week to make a jacket—not counting time for lining and finishing. Counting fabric, labor, accessories, the cost of the collection alone runs to some $250,000. When it shifts to regular production, the factory turns out perhaps 300 chemises all season; for a fancier dress, it may make 100. When it gets to the top of the price scale, it may cut only 10 to 20 of a given model.

Microscopic though such output would seem compared with the big, mass-produced houses, things get pretty hectic. But thanks to Norell's easy rapport with his staff, Bernegger observes, "There are probably fewer neuroses around here than at most high-fashion houses."

Year-round Production. Bernegger has managed to up production some 40 to 45 per cent in the year and a half since he joined Norell. He persuaded Norell to bring out "little" lines of Norell staples—the straight jersey dress, for example, to keep the factory going in the normally dead months of December and January, June and July. As a result, says Bernegger, "We're probably the only Seventh Avenue factory going twelve months a year."

For Norell, this is plenty and then some. "I'd like to shrink production a little. Bernegger probably wouldn't like it, but I'd like it."

Though delivery schedules have improved, stores fret because shipments come in dribs and drabs—one reason, explains Mrs. Edna Sullivan, who runs the showroom selling, that a few privileged Norell customers, who habitually want a whole Norell wardrobe, get invited to see the line. But they must come with a retailer, buy from him.

Choosey Seller. With supply unequal to demand—"We're overbooked on orders right now," according to Bernegger—Norell can be picky in choosing accounts. He also can insist that they buy a "representative line." That might mean twenty items some years; other years it might mean ten. "We threw out a $25,000 account last year because it included no suits," Bernegger says. In a few cases, stores' orders run to $100,000 and more.

Norell himself is aghast at the prices his clothes add up to, once the factory has taken an admittedly "nice" profit and the store has added its markup. "But he never thinks about price when he's buying," says Bernegger. "We had a suit last year that had $80 worth of buttons on it—wholesale. Norell never asked the price. He just wanted that button."

Bernegger's business instincts may rebel, but he—like everyone else on the staff—feels an immense pride in his perfectionist boss. "He couldn't do any other way, not Norell," Bernegger says.

Putting the Line Over. The collection itself is the main selling expense. Then there are the press opening and two showings for buyers. Norell cooperates with stores on fashion shows, advertises perhaps once a year in *Vogue* and *Harper's Bazaar.* Otherwise, the editorial attention he gets is promotion enough.

The system works, for the Norell concept of fashion has some commercial pluses.

Because of the line's simplicity, "Many, many women can wear it," fashion editors say. Its staying power in style appeals to the consumer's pocketbook. Even the well-heeled woman boggles at paying $1,000 for a suit she wears only one season.

Few Markdowns. For the retailer, the Norell line has another powerful lure. A high-priced, high-fashion line represents a major risk; heavy end-of-season markdowns can eat up profits. More than one retailer testifies that in Norell's case, the markdown hazard is minimal.

Norell could reach the "general public" he sets his sights on by going the European route of selling designs for copying. He won't do this. "It would cheapen the line. It's fine for Paris and good for fashion in this country. The European woman doesn't care that women in the United States are wearing cheaper copies of her original. Here, it would be too close to home."

Knock-offs. Seventh Avenue, of course, has its own time-honored solution. It imitates—"knocks off"—his designs. Norell takes this practice philosophically. "I don't mind if the knock-off houses give me a season with my dress. What I mind is if they bring out their copies faster than I get my own dresses to the stores."

He has known since he was 13, when his name was still Norman Levinson, that he wanted to be a designer. He started in theatrical costumes, got his first big break working for Hattie Carnegie. After fourteen years, in 1940, he went to Traina-Norell; he learned from Traina, "a magnificent maker," the practical end of the game. On Traina's death, he set up his own shop, in 1960. Long since, he had become Norell—"Nor" for Norman, "ell" for the L in Levinson.

New Talent. Though he knows he is running against strong currents in United States thinking, Norell has faith in his customers, and his industry.

Women aren't quite the sheep they used to be in following the latest mode. The young, especially, are developing their own independent tastes ("good, bad, or horrible"). To cater to them, young houses with their own designers have sprung up in recent years, who are doing "wonderful things." To Norell, this spells the end some day of the cutthroat competition of the knock-off. "Houses will exist because there is an artistic force behind them, and the industry will be much more what it is in Europe."

Till then, enough women see eye to eye with him to keep him in business. "I'll probably never retire till the young designers push me out," he says. Meanwhile, he has made himself what he wants to be, a force in the public market. David Schwartz of big Jonathan Logan, Inc., pays him Seventh Avenue's ultimate accolade. "Norell has the best reputation for fashion in the United States—as good as Paris."

A Look at Today's Apparel Markets

This Survey of America's Apparel Marketplaces Shows a Continuation of the Trend which Has Seen Younger and Smaller Apparel Centers Growing at the Expense of the Older and Larger Ones. The Greatest Gains Have Been Made by the Secondary Markets

New York

The largest industry in the world's largest city continues to give New York overwhelming importance as an apparel marketplace.

The city is in a class by itself in the creation of garment and textile styles. Countless thousands of apparel lines that are produced and distributed in other cities—as well as in other countries—are styled, merchandised and sold here.

Buyers are attracted to New York for a variety of reasons, but the big one is that the greatest assortment of merchandise classifications, as well as the most thorough representation of lines within each classification, may be sampled within a few square miles on Manhattan Island.

A total of 70,000 buyers were counted as they visited the city last year. No one knows exactly how many more buyers slipped into town unrecorded.

While the number of apparel buyers coming to New York appears to be decreasing bit by bit as other markets become popular, New York remains the focal marketplace.

In the New York metropolitan area, the U.S. Department of Commerce reports there was a 14 per cent gain in apparel production between 1954 and 1957. This was figured on the basis of value added by manufacture; the New York area total was $2.36 billion—almost double that of the next fourteen largest apparel production centers combined.

Reprinted from *Apparel Manufacturer,* August 1961. Permission granted.

Philadelphia

Long an established center for the manufacturing of men's, women's, and children's apparel, with an annual product value of $446,962,400, according to recent figures, Philadelphia is at long last asserting itself as a fashion leader.

Philadelphia's diversified industry matches the pattern of the apparel industry's variety of production. Latest annual figures show that 122 manufacturers of men's and boys' suits and coats did a volume of $180,000,000. This category employs 15,083 persons.

Some 126 other manufacturers of men's and boys' sport shirts, nightwear, ties, dress and sport trousers, hats and caps and other clothing had an annual volume of $59,000,000.

Women's and misses' outerwear, including suits, blouses, dresses, and skirts, accounted for an annual volume of approximately $68,000,000. Millinery was listed at $4,000,000 and women's and children's undergarments and nightwear totaled $5,000,000. Girls', children's and infants' dresses, blouses and skirts accounted for $20,000,000; children's and infants' outerwear—$9,000,000.

West Coast

Los Angeles-Long Beach. In the south, the Los Angeles-Long Beach metropolitan area ranks a strong third behind New York and Philadelphia in terms of value added by manufacture. The latest available figures from the Department of Commerce (for 1957) put that total at $264 million. More recent indications are that the Southern California market is growing at an accelerated rate.

The Associated Merchandising Corporation held its Spring meeting in Los Angeles in 1960 for the first time since 1953, and its top executives noted that AMC considers California one of its prime markets. All of the buying group's member stores send their buyers to the West Coast market, and the number of buying trips have been increasing as the "made in California" label reclaims its glamor as a merchandising aid.

San Francisco-Oakland. To the north, the San Francisco apparel market continues its steady pace. It ranks tenth among garment production centers.

According to the San Francisco Fashion Industries, the Bay Area has approximately 123 apparel manufacturers. Forty of these produce women's sportswear, 25 turn out men's wear, 15 offer women's coats and suits, and another 15 are in the dress business. The balance of the firms produce girls' wear, infants' wear, women's accessories, millinery, intimate apparel, etc.

A trend towards more women's sportswear manufacturers has been noted.

Hawaii. Traveling a bit further west, the nation's fiftieth state gives signs of becoming an important marketer of apparel. Hawaii's status as a source of specialized styling has long been recognized. A whole class of men's and boys' sport shirts and other sportswear items have been rendered in Hawaiian motifs. These were done almost exclusively by producers on the mainland, particularly in California. Now Hawaii itself is offering more authentic styling that may become representative of Pacific and Far Eastern fashion impulses.

A spokesman for the Hawaiian apparel industry recently noted that it has grown from $5 million in wholesale volume and 900 employees in 1954, to around $15 million and 5000 employees in 1959.

Chicago

The Windy City still holds a prominent position among the apparel markets of America, and continues to serve as the major marketing center for thousands of retailers in the great midwestern and south central areas of the country. It is estimated to have turned out over $90 million worth of clothing and $13 million in men's and boys' outerwear in 1958.

There's buying and selling in progress the year around in the giant concentration of nationally known men's, women's and children's apparel lines in Chicago's Merchandise Mart. Two complete floors totaling over 430,000 square feet are devoted exclusively to the permanent showrooms of apparel firms from all over the country.

Occupying the entire eighth floor and a portion of the ninth are over 350 men's and boys' wear manufacturers.

Occupying virtually the entire ninth floor of

the Mart are over 800 infants', children's, and women's apparel lines. Children's wear lines comprise the largest such concentration under one roof in the world.

Boston

Rainwear has kept the Boston men's apparel market afloat. The switch in consumer taste from formalized, traditional topcoats to raincoats for use in all weather has been responsible for some startling transformations.

Today nearly every clothing and outerwear producer in the Boston area, including some trouser manufacturers as well, offer raincoats, according to one trade observer.

It should be remembered, however, that a good deal of the apparel marketed in Boston is produced in neighboring localities in New England, where the manufacture of garments in many categories has undergone a revival during the past half-decade.

Baltimore

The stable Baltimore apparel market, particularly that part of it devoted to the production of men's and boys' wear, easily retains its sixth ranking position among metropolitan areas in the manufacture of garments. In men's clothing, the Maryland city is the fourth largest market behind New York, Philadelphia, and Chicago.

According to the Baltimore Association of Commerce, unpublished data collected by the Maryland Department of Employment Security for the month of September 1959 showed 217 apparel firms reporting. Of these, 79 were engaged in the production of male clothing, employing over 6800 persons. Separate trousers for men, youths, and boys accounted for the next largest subdivision, with 27 firms.

St. Louis

The special flavor of the St. Louis apparel market is epitomized by the junior dress.

Fashions for young women—in dresses as well as suits and coats, sportswear, lingerie, and millinery—have been the heart of the area's garment business since the early thirties, when these styles were first introduced.

Men's clothing contributes a sizeable share of volume to the St. Louis apparel market, as do men's raincoats, millinery, and footwear. According to the latest available statistics from the Department of Commerce, the Mound City is seventh among apparel production centers in terms of value added by manufacture ($80 million).

Dallas

One of the fastest growing apparel markets in the country, Texas as a whole ranks tenth among the states in its number of garment workers, eleventh in terms of value added by manufacture.

Over half of this volume is done by firms in the Dallas-Ft. Worth area, with Dallas by far the larger market.

Long considered a local market, Dallas has stretched its influence in the apparel world far beyond the boundaries of the Southwest. Market registration lists show that its quarterly apparel market weeks attracts buyers from more than thirty states and Mexico. Its sportswear fashions and work and play garments for all members of the family have given this market an authentic regional stamp that has developed ever-widening sales appeal throughout the nation.

Minnesota

A wide range of apparel is manufactured in this Northwest market—coats, suits, and dresses for misses, women, and half-sizes; maternity dresses and sportswear, sportswear for men, women, misses, and children, lingerie, infants' and children's clothes, and millinery and outerwear for the whole family.

Stability is characteristic of the Minnesota market and of the member firms. More than 75 per cent have been in business longer than twenty-five years.

Minnesota styling has been inspired by its country and its climate. Some of the designs created in Minnesota, such as the storm coat, the parka, quilted underwear, and the goal coat, have influenced styles worn throughout the country.

Secondary Markets

Atlanta. This regional market serving the southeastern part of the country has taken great strides recently, along with the economic advance of the South in general.

Atlanta enjoyed the greatest percentage increase among the top fifteen apparel-producing metropolitan areas between 1954 and 1957.

Cincinnati. The number two apparel city in Ohio (which ranks high among states as an apparel producer), Cincinnati has always been a specialist in the tailor-to-the-trade clothing business. With a steadily shrinking demand for custom-tailored clothing, however, the city's specialty houses have begun to concentrate on uniforms. These garments require specific tailoring techniques for which the Cincinnati trade is admirably qualified, and which would present problems for the average producer of ready-made clothing.

Cleveland. Home of several large tailored clothing and women's sportswear producers, this Ohio city ranks eleventh in terms of value added by manufacture, with $54 million recorded for 1957. Much of its output is sold on the road or in other marketing centers, however.

Kansas City. Work clothes, boys' wear, and women's dozen-priced dresses are important elements in the Kansas City market. It is on the move as a production center, having increased its dollar volume over 30 per cent between 1954 and 1957, and is a sizeable wholesale market for retailers in the midwest and south central regions.

Miami. Some ninety dress and sportswear houses specializing in summer and cruise wear lines for women are now operating in the Miami area, demonstrating remarkable growth for an industry that only got started thirty years ago.

Informed estimates put the city's wholesale apparel output at over $70 million in 1960.

Rochester. Traditionally strong in men's clothing, Rochester features a handful of very large producers.

"Going Public". . .

New Fashion in Financing for the Fashion Industry

by Henry Bach

For several years now, a significant new trend has been apparent in the apparel industry: the fashion world seems to be moving into the securities market. During 1959 and 1960 a number of sportswear issues enjoyed the popularity of the market. And now another wave of new apparel issues appears to be readying itself for sale to investors.

Such group movements are phenomena long noted and studied by securities analysts. Issues do have a tendency to rise and fall in industry groups, as seen in electronics, missiles, optics, fiberglass boats, bowling, aircraft, printing and publishing, and discount stores. The vogue for a particular business sets off a chain reaction which, in turn, is stimulated by the feverish search by stock analysts for issues of a popular industry which have not risen with their peers. This searching out and recommending of overlooked issues in itself serves to heighten the tendency of industry groups to advance "by the numbers."

Participating in the excellent market which characterized most of 1959–1960, a number of relatively recent apparel issues have given admirable accounts of themselves. Some scored spectacular gains. Bobbie Brooks common stock ranged from a low of 5¾ in 1959 to a high of 50⅞. The Majestic Specialties Inc. issue jumped from an 11½ low in 1960 to 44¼. Colonial Corporation rose from an 8⅛ low in 1959 to a high of 44. Some of the more seasoned apparel equities which have been on the market for many years also turned in excellent

---

Reprinted from *Apparel Manufacturer,* October 1961. Permission granted. Henry Bach heads Henry Bach Associates, Inc., a leading advertising and public relations agency, with offices at 245 Fifth Avenue, New York City.

records during this period. Hart, Schaffner and Marx common, for example, ranged from a low of 17 to a 33½ high. Munsingwear rose from 12⅜ to 27, Reliance Manufacturing from 16⅜ to 47, and so on.

Why Go Public?

Why do companies go public? Why do businessmen who are doing well on their own go out of their way to take on a few hundred partners?

Undoubtedly, the biggest bull market in the history of this country has proven to be an irresistible lure. This attraction has been highlighted by the vigor of the new-issue market. Constantly repeated oversubscription of new issues by the investing public has made "going public" seem easy.

But what are the advantages of a public issue? There are a number, and they are compelling—if you measure up.

1. To Raise Capital. This may be required to enable the company to launch a new sales program, to produce a new product, or just for working capital purposes. Some have sought to escape the factor's relatively high rates by resorting to public funds. Needless to say, if this is the company's sole reason for going public, caution is wise counsel. A thorough study should be undertaken to determine the urgency of the need for new money. And, equally important, the availability of alternate sources should be explored.

2. To Become Liquid. Often, having spent most of his adult life building a business, the entrepreneur finds himself tied to his company. It becomes virtually impossible to convert the years of sweat, worry, and creativity into ready cash. A public issue is the simplest and best way of withdrawing cash while retaining control. While most responsible underwriters will cast a jaundiced eye on a "bail-out" for insiders, liquidity may be attained in a number of ways. Some stock may be sold by the insiders at the public offering. In addition, a small amount may be sold every six months without resort to expensive registration procedures. Eventually, if the issue flourishes, a sizeable secondary issue may be floated in which the principals can sell a substantial part of their holdings to the public.

3. To Expand. Businesses these days must grow or perish. Utilization of internal capital resources for expansion purposes is a long, slow and difficult process. The fastest way to expand is to acquire companies in allied fields, with needed sales coverage or other desirable features. However, selling out for cash presents many tax and other problems. By far the most preferable way, for most companies, is through the exchange of stock, with perhaps some cash involved. There is little inducement to accept the shares of a privately owned company. The lure is great, however, if the purchasing firm's stock is traded publicly.

Further, in many fields of activity it becomes necessary to attract outside talent in order to grow. Really competent personnel look for stock options rather than salary as an inducement to make a change.

4. To Improve Public Relations. The publicity which going public imparts to a company can be important. Aside from hundreds or thousands of new stockholders who become company boosters, repeated references to a company in the financial pages of newspapers or investment journals offer priceless opportunities for free publicity. Often the glamour which may surround an issue favored by the stock market carries over to the products manufactured or sold by that company.

5. To Minimize Inheritance Litigation. The successful businessman is naturally concerned about his family's future. He may be adequately insured; his children may even have their own incomes; his wife may be well provided for. But his most important earthly possession is the business he leaves behind him. If the company is sizeable, the estate may be tied up for years in negotiation and litigation with the Internal Revenue Service while the true value of the business for tax purposes is determined. In a publicly owned company this problem does not exist. Market price determines the value.

But, before You Rush to the Underwriters . . .

Going public requires a good deal more than a company's mere desire to take this step. A company must justify this move by meeting certain criteria of suitability. Accounting and profitability requirements aside, there must be an intrinsic quality about the company and its products which would make its shares an attractive investment. There must be a combination of factors present which serve to excite the imagination and interest.

In this age of electronics, space flight, matter and anti-matter, an out-of-this-world product list or program serves as the only vital ingredient for many investors. A prospectus needs something to embellish it. Obviously, no matter how hard the imagination is worked, it is no simple matter to find "Buck Rogers" products or talents in the apparel industry; even space suits have been pre-empted by the rubber and electronics companies.

It is possible, however, for an apparel company to justify its public status the old-fashioned way—by being a well-run, profitable business. A five-year history of rising sales helps. Good earnings, of course, are the real clincher. Rising sales and earnings curves on the charts provide the sex appeal to which Wall Street responds.

Such a record, maintained over a period of time and with some indication that it will continue in the future, carries with it the designation, "growth company." This is the "open sesame" to successful financing in today's market. Of course, it also helps if the balance sheet shows substantial stockholder equity.

Then, there is the question of leadership. Management, as a factor in underwriting, is seldom underestimated. Investment bankers pay particular attention to the qualities of top company management. They also look for second-echelon understudies to provide depth of leadership. Unless you can take the underwriter to your leaders, they will probably not take to you.

Remember, there are literally thousands of stock issues traded on the various exchanges and over-the-counter. Among these are a large number of apparel issues, some with years of seasoning behind them. It is a humbling experience to ask yourself what your company has to offer an investor which cannot be found in one or a number of equities already in the market. If the answer is not a record of above-average growth or the possibility of a superior, safe return on investment, perhaps "going public" may not be the answer to your problems.

Marketing: Latest Thing in Fashions

Why Do New Clothing Styles Catch On? The Fashion Industry, No Longer Content with the Delightful Mystery of It All, Is Taking Doses of Good, Solid Marketing to Add Predictability to Its Sales Methods

by Ann R. Lyon

The fashion industry wears many hats:

In the movies it's a world of "Think pink." Broadway calls it "I can get it for your wholesale." On record albums it's "Jump down, spin around, pick a dress of cotton."

To those who work in it, it's a lot like having a seat on a roller coaster—when you're on top, you're flying; when you're down, it seems you'll never get up to the top again, and the distance between the ascent and the plunge can be covered awfully quickly.

To those on the outside looking in, it's a world lined with glamour, laced with excitement. An existence dominated by a few eccentrics out of whose antics and achievements have grown a folklore, a singular set of customs.

But to marketing men, whether in or out, the women's fashion (or ready-to-wear apparel) industry is a venerable $15-billion-a-year business in the midst of an advertising and marketing revolution that is giving it a streamlined shape, a new look.

Excerpted and reprinted with permission from *Printers' Ink*, April 26, 1963. Copyright 1963 by Printers' Ink Publishing Corp.

I. New-Style Marketing

Traditionally backward in many of the distribution, selling, and promotion techniques that have sparked the phenomenal growth of the consumer packaged-goods industries, apparel makers, spurred by the recent advent of marketing-minded executive staffs within apparel companies, are beginning to catch on to new methods.

Fashion has long been a highly appealing enigma to the marketing minded in other industries. Though slow to pick up modern selling methods, purveyors of fashion goods have been puzzlingly successful in subtly disseminating an influence, a way of looking at things which is uniquely their own. There is a certain cachet about the very word "fashion," and the image and aura its use conjures up.

II. Who's in Fashion?

Prime mover in the marketing push now surging through all phases of apparel making is the appearance on the scene of *giants,* in a business long one of the last strongholds of the small businessman.

The giants are of two types: those companies that started small and grew big within fashion, and those that were already big in other fields before they became active in fashion to develop healthy markets for their own products.

Within fashion, Jonathan Logan (New York) and Bobbie Brooks (Cleveland) have come to the top as sales leaders. Their annual retail volumes are variously estimated at $70–$80 million. In addition a handful of companies in the over $10-million category—considered big by apparel-industry standards—have grown primarily through acquisition and merger, both in and out of the industry. Today, the corporate structure of a major apparel firm, in fact, is often a complex of subsidiaries, divisions, or wholly owned companies that are diversified at least to the extent that the parent company makes blouses, one subsidiary makes slacks, another dresses, etc.

But the diversification may be more complete. Some apparel enterprises are corporations making everything from Bermuda shorts to missiles, plywood, cement, or food and wines.

Although the number of the big firms in relation to the one-man shops is still small in terms of the industry as a whole (only 1.1 per cent of the 3000 jobbers and manufacturers in apparel have annual sales volumes of over $10 million), they are universally considered the wave of the future in the business.

Moving into apparel from outside the industry have been fiber manufacturers of the size of Du Pont, Chemstrand, and Celanese. Their interest in the industry is an elemental one. By making their marketing talent and experience, plus their substantial promotion dollars, available to ready-to-wear manufacturers to build their sales potential, they are at the same time strengthening their own market for man-made fibers.

What has been the marketing significance of this post-war move to bigness? A quickly apparent effect has been the emergence of planned and budgeted-ahead ad and merchandising campaigns on a national scale.

These campaigns have sprouted not only because there is more money to spend on them and a more progressive attitude about them, but because of changes in traditional distribution and selling patterns. Big firms, like Logan and Brooks, Aileen and Westbury and Puritan, have led the way. Not only are they replacing the two- or three-man commission sales system with large staffs of salaried salesmen, but in their eagerness to achieve national distribution, many firms are supplementing their sales task forces with regional sales offices around the country, to provide better service to retail buyers. This regional selling system is old hat in most major industries. In fashion, it is recent and revolutionary.

III. What's in a Name?

The achievement of national distribution by big fashion firms opened the door for national advertising. In the past five to ten years, this once-rare advertising spread has become not only possible but commonplace. And the reasons are simple. A big one is that a strong brand name is an effective stopper for any kind of retail pressure that might be put on the manufacturer by a department store for excessive co-op funds. If the brand name is strong and in demand, it forces a line's distribution.

David Altman of the Altman, Stoller, Chalk agency, which does a considerable amount of fashion advertising, explained another advantage accruing from brand-name identification: "In this business there is an old adage: 'You're only as good as last season's line.' A good brand name gives a manufacturer a longer time to be wrong and stay in business if his last line flopped."

David Schwartz, industry pioneer and founder of Jonathan Logan, which Schwartz hopes to build into the first ready-to-wear house to do an annual retail sales volume of $100 million, feels that "Supporting a large sales force requires brand names. National advertising helped Jonathan Logan achieve brand-name identification, aiding both retailer and manufacturer."

How? Schwartz explained further: "The retail customer enters the shop with a mental image of the dress she has seen advertised, and asks for it by name. By helping retailers sell nationally advertised merchandise, the manufacturer benefits from increased orders and consumer demand for his line."

Bernard Goodman, marketing director of Gilbert Advertising, seconds this opinion: "While the consumer still responds primarily to 'eye appeal' in the purchase of apparel, advertising and brand names give impetus to buying and add confidence to the purchase. The consumer is a little more convinced her choice of color and style is right if she recognizes the brand of the maker."

The cultivation of brand-name awareness among shoppers is subtly switching some of the emphasis of apparel advertising away from the trade and to the public. Even in consumer-oriented media, many of the ready-to-wear houses once slanted their ads to the trade. Much of this intra-industry promotion still goes on, but the buying public is now, at the same time, more assiduously courted.

All signs indicate the cultivation of brand-name consciousness among consumers will continue to be the hallmark of the industry's ad efforts during the '60s. The marketing director of Bobbie Brooks, E. L. Kalberg, believes this emphasis will have an effect in other fashion-marketing areas: "Big makers involved in developing their own national brands," he said recently, "will become more involved in sales training and better service to retailers, in helping them move the merchandise to the consumers. This trend is likely to parallel the developments of the past thirty years in food products sold through supermarkets."

IV. Problems of Co-op . . .

With the maturity in advertising outlook that has come into fashion, has come some grown-up problems too. One current trouble spot is co-op advertising.

Co-op arrangements between retailers and ladies'-garment manufacturers have long been a very powerful weapon for big retailers, who often can make "either-or" demands of garment houses that depend upon them for distribution. For the small manufacturer, though, also concerned with distribution but more concerned with capital, the co-op system has been the best possible means of stretching meager ad dollars.

Last year, the Federal Trade Commission, alarmed over what it considered discriminatory co-op practices within the industry, began a campaign to get many of the apparel manufacturers to sign consent decrees voluntarily abandoning certain co-op practices. And in January of this year, the FTC said 153 apparel manufacturers had agreed to stop giving discriminatory advertising and promotional allowances to their customers. Another 95 producers refused to sign similar consent agreements, and the FTC said it would consider their cases individually.

V. Enter Fiber Makers

In the last several years many apparel makers were heard to lament what they considered the absence of frequent-enough style changes to make last year's dress passé. They felt that many millions of dollars in potential sales had been lost a result of too little obsolescense.

But to a large extent, the lack of radical new departures in fashion has been compensated for by the introduction, in the last ten to fifteen years, of many new synthetic fabrics. Tremendous strides made by chemical industries have transformed old synthetics, like rayon and nylon, into virtually new substances. And new names, like Acrilan, Verel, Fortrel, Teflon, Vicara, Dacron, Carolan and a host of others, have become and are becoming as familiar to consumers as wool, silk, and cotton.

Also, new finishes, which make material crease-resistant, washable, drip-dry, dirt- and wrinkle-resistant, have added dimensions to the role of fabrics in garment styling.

The revolution in materials continues. Materials as yet not extensively used include paper and other nonweaves, which could go into the production of garments to be worn only once and then discarded, and plastic sheeting with the porous qualities of fabrics. For all of these items, the dependence of fashion firms upon the fiber manufacturers is complete. Carl Rosen, president of fast-growing Puritan Fashions, expressed the importance of new fabrics when he described them as "the lifeblood of our industry."

Fiber makers have contributed to fashion in another way, too, by helping to introduce into the industry an awareness of what Olive Plunkett of BBDO's Du Pont fashion account referred to as "the total marketing concept." And many of the fiber makers themselves exemplify this kind of service to the stores.

Celanese has a staff of women who visit department stores and spur the sale of Celanese-made garments through sales-training programs and other in-store promotion and publicity aids. The sales-training programs are much appreciated by the clothing manufacturers, according to Benita Wald of the Celanese ad department, since they look upon training as one of the weakest links in their selling chain.

Fiber makers also give their apparel-manufacturer customers a big boost by tying them into national ad programs and giving them exposure—especially on seldom-used TV—they would not be able to afford otherwise. If a company wants to introduce a new fabric and a clothing manufacturer agrees to include it in his line, the new fabric and garments made with it are frequently tied together in ads.

Also, the fiber makers, and to a certain degree, firms in other areas of apparel making, like finishers, will frequently give a push via national advertising to areas of manufacturing that are momentarily flagging. Celanese has field reporters who pass on the word to the home-office ad department if a certain market, like sportswear or children's garments, needs an ad push and where possible, they get it.

VI. Research for What?

Fashion-market research, unheard of until a couple of years ago, has been encouraged by fiber makers. They have been joined in this venture by the women's and fashion magazines, and teen magazines, which have undertaken comprehensive and valuable studies to measure the women's-apparel market for characteristics and preferences.

In the past, fashion firms generally depended upon department stores to tell them who their customers were and what kind of things were selling or might be marketable. Now they are exploring these areas on their own, defining their own markets, and most significantly, looking for neglected ones, like children's wear, to cultivate. Meanwhile the fiber firms are doing research for the industry to uncover new uses for existing fibers as well as to develop new ones. Chemstrand, according to its fashion ad director, Arthur la Hines, is currently looking into areas into which popular stretch-type fabrics can be expanded beyond use in sports wear.

Celanese, said Benita Wald, has also researched selling patterns of consumers to add to ready-to-wear manufacturers' knowledge on the vital subject of retail timing—to find when, for example, the most blouses or slacks are sold. These data are essential to the effective planning of promotional campaigns.

VII. Problems and Promises

What about the future? Apparel makers and their colleagues, the fiber makers, will have to hustle as never before to sell against mounting pressures and competition from all sides. But the opportunities for progress are there to be grasped.

On one hand is the exciting prospect that the female population of the groups that purchase the most clothing will soar by 1970. The 21 million in the junior-age group from 16–24 today represents less than 20 per cent of the United States population; but they still purchase nearly 35 per cent of all clothing. The U.S. Census Bureau predicts that this age group will increase to 22 or 23 million by the mid-1960's.

And on the other hand, as these groups' income mounts, so, too, will their participation in activities, from skiing to boating to at-home hobbies. And they will be eager customers for apparel tailored specifically to these activities.

Other industries have given apparel a big boost by promoting the notion that activities like bowling, or even automobile riding, are more enjoyable if the participant has a special outfit to go along. They have added another dimension to the old "dress-for-the-occasion" adage.

Thus the women to be sold will be plentiful —if they can be reached. For other interests will be after them in a big way, too, and there is the unpleasant fact that, although sales have increased steadily and comfortably since the end of World War II, from $9.7 billion in 1946 to $15 billion in 1961, women's apparel's share of the discretionary spending dollar has been diminishing. In the postwar period, it has dropped from 6.6 per cent to 4.5 per cent.

A giant new market remains to be tapped by the fashion industry if its old insularity, called "arrogance" by one fashion publicist, doesn't get in the way. That is, the opportunity afforded by exporting women's ready-to-wear fashions to the Common Market, whose wage earners now are eager buyers of goods of all kinds.

As they continue the emphasis on brand-name advertising and promotion in the 1960s, many of the apparel makers will, ironically, be nagged by the dilemma of what to do about the threat unbranded merchandise poses. Discount operations, moving more and more into soft goods, are a real challenge to the only-lately-established brand-name concept. There is a feeling expressed by several of the clothiers that "since we can't lick them, we'll sell to them." What this whole area of discounting and price slashing will do to traditional modes of apparel retailing is a puzzle currently begging for solution.

Fashion does indeed wear many hats. But its preference now, as it goes to market dressed in its selling best, is for a topping that labels it three important things: modern, progressive and, hopefully, lady-liked.

General Information Calendar

January

Cutters usually sample imported Fall woolens. Buy Spring and Summer fabrics in bulk for immediate and later deliveries.

Knock-off cutters may begin their offerings of Spring and Summer specials—usually based on bargain fabrics. In some years, these offerings continue from January into June.

Retailers in general conclude their buying for pre-Easter period.

February

Converters usually begin looking at resort, Spring, and Summer gray goods and print designs for the following year—cottons, rayons, acetates, synthetics.

Cutters buy Summer fabric in bulk. Buy additional Spring goods to *copy Paris* models. Begin opening Summer lines, if any.

Cutters begin sampling corduroys, velveteens, velvets, domestics, woolens, and flannelettes.

Retailers begin to concentrate on Spring selling and final Winter clearances are sometimes in the market for "mid-season specials."

Paris openings—reproductions at popular price level—end of February and early March.

March

Converters and mills continue to buy fabric designs and gray goods for the next resort, Spring, and Summer season.

Cutters sample Fall cottons and rayons and woolens.

Cutters continue buying of Summer fabrics.

Retailers' Spring selling season at peak in most areas.

Women's Wear Daily, "Calendar of the Women's and Children's Textile and Apparel Industries," p. 2 *ff*. Reprinted by permission of *Women's Wear Daily*.

April

Converters continue to buy gray goods and fabric designs for the following year; yarn-dye cotton mills open resort, Spring lines.

Cutters conclude buying of Summer fabrics; clean up "buy" in end-of-season goods in fabric market.

Cutters continue to sample Fall goods with Emphasis switched to holiday types.

Retailers generally conclude spring selling.

Retailers generally begin Summer selling.

May

Better converters usually have resort, Spring, and Summer fabrics ready for showing last week of month. Yarn-dye cotton mills continue resort, advance Spring. Buying of fabric designs concluded.

Cutters high-style sample resort and Spring fabrics late in month. High-style Fall lines open mid-May.

Cutters open Fall back-to-school lines and begin buying Fall fabrics in quantity as orders are confirmed. 1954: This spotted May 10 was a trial—one month earlier than previous years.

Cutters on West Coast and out-of-town markets open bulk of regular Fall ready-to-wear lines mid-May and continue to sample resort lines.

June

Knock-off Cutters close their offerings of "Summer specials."

Retailers conclude their full-price Summer selling—sell transition dresses.

Retailers buy back-to-school merchandise and Fall merchandise.

July

Converters bulk of cotton, man-made fiber fabrics lines for Spring open.

Cutters of West Coast and out-of-town markets continue to sample holiday and resort lines; reorder Fall goods.

Retailers may begin selling back-to-school merchandise the week after July 4th—advance Fall dresses, coats.

Many in trade leave in middle of the month for Italian and Paris openings for Spring.

Mills, fabric finishers usually have one to two weeks shutdown vacation first of month.

August

Cutters sample resort lines in earnest.

Wool mills show Spring goods.

September

Mills and converters—push Spring goods.

Cutters conclude sampling of resort lines.

Cutters, beginning of month, open resort lines.

Retailers, toward end of month, buy first resort merchandise. (*Note:* New York cutters usually show their holiday and resort lines at the same time.) Promote Paris import copies—popular price level.

October

Cutters continue to open resort and Spring lines and buy fabrics as confirmed orders are received. High-style Spring lines open mid-October.

November

Converters show late Spring and Summer fabric lines.

Cutters buy Spring fabrics; show Spring lines from first week of month.

Retailers usually begin resort cruise promotions about November 15th; plus holiday merchandise.

December

Converters continue to show Summer fabric lines; importers show next Fall and Winter lines.

Cutters begin to sample imported British and Scottish woolens for the following Fall.

A Statistical Picture of the Women's Wear Industry

A selection of statistical data follows, in order to provide an indication of the variations in size and output within the fashion industry. Table 2 shows the extent to which production in women's outerwear concentrates in the lower-price ranges. Other sets of figures (Tables 1 and 3) give the volume of shipments in certain branches of the trade. A final compilation classifies makers by size of annual output (Table 4). Note how few are in the larger categories.

Table 1 Apparel Manufacturers' Summary—by Trade

Type of Apparel	Factory Value of 1963 Sales [a] (Add 000)
WOMEN'S WEAR	
Dresses	$1,655,584
Coat and suit	681,016
Blouse and sportswear	1,733,977
Girls and Children's wear	768,967
Housedresses, uniforms, and service apparel	317,055
Lingerie	675,208
Corset and bra	533,358
Total women's wear	$6,365,165

Type of Apparel	Factory Value of 1963 Sales [a] (Add 000)
MEN'S WEAR	
Suits, topcoats, and overcoats	$1,112,710
Dress and sport shirts	841,170
Boys and children's wear	538,210
Pajamas, underwear, and robes	224,395
Sportswear	418,099
Outerwear	385,152
Rainwear	192,404
Slacks	335,283
Work clothing and leisure wear	810,173
Uniforms and formal wear	86,285
Total men's wear	$4,915,881

Source: National Credit Office, "The Apparel Manufacturing Industry," copyright 1964 Dun and Bradstreet, Inc. This report covered manufacturers of men's, women's, and children's apparel who purchase fabric. Knitting mills that produce apparel are excluded except where they purchase fabrics in addition to their yarn requirements. For a more detailed breakdown by products, see latest Apparel Survey, Series M23A, Bureau of the Census, Industry Division, Apparel Section.

[a] Retail value, allowing for transportation and markup, would be roughly 1.6 times the value of shipments.

Table 2 1964 Production of Selected Women's Apparel by Wholesale Price Ranges and Units [a]

Product	Total Units (Add 000)	Price Ranges	Percentage of Total Units
Untrimmed coats	20,223	Under $16.00 per unit	50.5
		$16.00–$38.99	36.6
		$39.00 and over	12.9
Fur-trimmed coats	3,806	Under $39.00 per unit	50.0
		$39.00–$75.99	35.4
		$76.00 and over	14.6
Suits	9,676	Under $16.00 per unit	48.2
		$16.00–$38.99	33.6
		$39.00 and over	18.2
Dresses, unit-priced	152,991	Under $6.00 per unit	41.0
		$6.00–$15.99	47.5
		$16.00 and over	11.5
Dresses, dozen-priced	8,131 dozen	Under $23.00 per dozen	13.3
		$23.00–$45.99	67.8
		$46.00 and over	18.9
Skirts, dozen-priced	7,871 dozen	Under $39.00 per dozen	53.3
		$39.00–$75.99	30.5
		$76.00 and over	16.2
Blouses (other than knit)	16,438 dozen	Under $23.00 per dozen	51.6
		$23.00–$38.99	33.5
		$39.00 and over	14.9

Source: Report of the General Executive Board, ILGWU, May 12, 1965, page 96.
[a] Includes women's, misses' and juniors'.

Table 3 Annual Factory Shipments of Shoes and Selected Accessory Items

Product	Factory Value of 1963 Sales [a] (Add 000)	Product	Factory Value of 1963 Sales [a] (Add 000)
Shoes [b]	$2272	Millinery	162
Jewelry, precious metal [b]	484	Furs	331
Jewelry, costume [b]	285	Apparel belts	103
Handbags, billfolds, and small leather goods [b]	424	Artificial flowers	59
		Umbrellas, parasols, canes	37

Source: (except where otherwise noted) Bureau of the Census, preliminary reports from the 1963 Census of Manufacturers, and 1963 Current Industrial Reports.
[a] Retail values, allowing for transportation and markup, would be roughly 1.6 times the value of shipments.
[b] Includes men's, women's, and children's.

Table 4 Manufacturers and Jobbers, Women's Garment Industry, Classified by Annual Sales Volume, 1963

Womens, Misses, Juniors	Under $1,000,000	$1,000,000– $2,500,000	$2,500,000– $5,000,000	$5,000,000– $10,000,000	$10,000,000 Over
Blouses and sportswear	740	231	84	33	22
Unit-priced dresses	843	293	115	32	13
Coats and suits	344	138	49	21	—
Housedresses, uniforms and service apparel	132	52	17	9	5
Lingerie	310	112	38	17	11
Corsets and bras	131	41	22	14	12
Children's wear					
Outer apparel	375	112	52	15	5
Lingerie	70	14	4	3	—

Source: National Credit Office, compiled from "The Apparel Manufacturing Industry," Copyright 1964, Dun and Bradstreet, Inc.

Questions for Review and Discussion

1. Discuss the major factors contributing to the growth of the men's and women's apparel industry. Explain when, how, and why the industry developed.
2. The apparel industry has been described as one of the "last refuges of the small independent manufacturer." Do you agree? Cite facts and figures to prove your answer.
3. The statement was once made that "Although competition in other major United States industries is an after-dinner boast, it is a reality in the women's apparel industry." Do you agree? Why?
4. The president of one of the industry's giant firms stated that "There will always be many small concerns in the apparel industry. Probably none of us will ever see the day when any one or two apparel manufacturers will do as much as 5 per cent of the total apparel business." Do you agree? Defend your opinion.
5. Name the three most important apparel production centers in the United States. For what are each of these particularly noted?
6. How does an "inside shop" differ from an "outside shop?"
7. Does "style piracy" help or hurt the industry as a whole? Why?
8. Why should apparel producers have to "wait" for buyers' reactions before putting their new styles into production? Why shouldn't their designers have the final say about what designs should or should not be produced?
9. Compare the sales volume of the garment "giants" with the sales volume of the largest firms in other major United States industries. How can you explain the difference?
10. Are manufacturers' brand names as meaningful to customers when they are buying apparel as they are to the same customers when they buy foods, cosmetics, or appliances? Why?
11. Do you agree with Norman Norell that "When styles reach the point where they are accepted and worn by the general public, you know the design is a good one"? Explain.
12. How many apparel firms can you find listed on the New York Stock Exchange? When did they "go public" and why might they have gone public?
13. An article in the July 1, 1964, issue of *Forbes Magazine* characterized the apparel industry as "suffering from a form of schizophrenia" because although it manufactures clothing, it doesn't sell clothing. "What it sells is fashion." Discuss.

SECTION
IV

The "Couture" of Fashion

Since importing, copying, and adapting European styles is a multimillion dollar activity of the American fashion business, no book about United States fashion industries can omit a discussion of foreign producers in general, and Paris in particular.

Paris is the center of an industrial area, in many ways the most remarkable in the world, devoted to the production of textiles, apparel, and accessories for women. Why is Paris considered to be fashion's capital?

This section of text and readings aims to introduce the reader to the reasons for Paris' fashion leadership; the workings of the Haute Couture; and the increasing variety and volume in European ready-to-wear imports by the United States.

Paris

The influence of Paris on this country's fashion business dates back to Colonial days, when the wealthier ladies copied the latest French fashions with the help of seamstresses. From the early years of our own fashion industry, manufacturers have looked to Paris to set the styles. An exhibit of French dress models at the Chicago World's Fair of 1893 furthered popular interest in French styles, and a number of American stores began to send their buyers regularly to Paris to buy original creations for resale or copying purposes. The emergence and growth of fashion publications, such as *Vogue's* and *Harper's Bazaar,* which did much to publicize Paris fashions, kept France in the forefront as the authority on fashion. When many French design houses were forced to close down during World War I, and again during World War II, the American fashion industries had to look closer to home for design inspiration. Nonetheless, Paris returned to favor stronger than ever following both wars.

Reasons for French Fashion Leadership. The primacy of Paris as a source of fashion creativity is often ascribed by the disciples of French fashion to something intangible in the air of Paris which is conducive to originality and creativity. The reasons, however, are much more mundane, and derive from a complex blend of history and economics.

Brilliance in fashion designing is not exclusively a French talent; in fact, many of the great houses have been headed by people of other nationalities who were drawn there by the advantages that the city offers for fashion designers: for example, we have Balenciaga, a Spaniard, Schiaparelli, an Italian, Molyneux, an Englishman, and Mainbocher, who was born in Chicago. A major attraction for talented designers is the availability of skilled seamstresses, which makes it possible to indulge in the tremendous amount of experimentation that is essential to the development of new clothing ideas. These dedicated perfectionists, to whom designers can safely entrust the steps from drawing-board to finished garment, are the spiritual, and possibly even the physical, descendants of those who stitched garments for the French nobility hundreds of years ago. In Paris, moreover, designers have a magnificent French textile industry upon which to draw, and, of equal importance, an international market of wealthy customers who have the money, leisure, and desire to buy expensive, made-to-order clothes. Another great help to designers is the presence of auxiliary industries that use hand labor to produce materials and trimmings on a small scale. Almost anything that the designer needs to carry out his idea for a sample garment can be found for him. A further factor is the existence of French laws which protect the work of creative designers from unauthorized copying of their creations, and which do much to encourage originality. In the United States, efforts to protect original apparel styles, by contrast, have generally fallen afoul of our antitrust laws.

Of major importance in the development of the French fashion industry has been the historic encouragement and support of the French government; this dates back as long ago as the fifteenth century, when the silk industry in France came under the direct patronage of its kings. Jean Baptiste Colbert, who was an adviser to Louis XIV in the seventeenth century, believed that "French fashions are to France what the mines of Peru are to Spain," and supported them accordingly.[1] Top-ranking designers have long been recognized by the French government as artists and important contributors to the national economy. For example, Rose Bertin, who was Marie Antoinette's dressmaker, was given the title "Minister of Fashion" for services rendered to this unfortunate French queen; it was also not too many years ago that Christian Dior was awarded the Legion of Honor for designing the *New Look*.

A noted American designer explained what it was like to work in Paris:

> Everything is arranged for *couturiers* in Paris . . . when you design in Paris, you know that everyone understands what you are trying to do, and wants to help. . . . The handicraft background provides hand weavers as well as hand sewers. . . . Machines could do it, yes; but no machine can work out the first bit of a new design. . . . Any time you want a special buckle in France, someone will run it up for you. They don't have to make a die and cast a thousand of them.[2]

So many important style trends have been born in Paris that it sometimes looks to the outsider as if nothing more is needed to start a fashion than a Paris address and a designer's caprice. Actually, the meaning behind an expression

[1] Anny Latour, *Kings of Fashion,* New York, Coward McCann Inc., 1958, p. 63.
[2] Elizabeth Hawes, *Fashion Is Spinach,* New York, Random House, 1938, p. 16.

such as "Paris decrees" is simply that, with so many inspired and encouraged talents at work there, coupled with its historic prestige, Paris has become synonymous with fashion.

Paris Haute Couture

The focal point of the French fashion industry is a small group of creative couturiers (the French word for dressmaker) whose dressmaking establishments are known in the trade as Haute Couture houses. The term *haute couture,* literally translated, means the finest needlework, but as used in the fashion business it describes a firm whose designer periodically creates sample collections of original styles which are then reproduced individually on a custom-made basis. To qualify as an Haute Couture house, a concern must: present two collections a year which express the designer's own ideas (rather than executing styles specified by customers); show a minimum of fifty models on living mannequins; show original styles, created by the firm's own designer without recourse to designs bought from outsiders; and produce the samples and the made-to-order reproductions in its own custom workrooms.[3]

There are hundreds of dressmakers in Paris but there are less than thirty who merit the title of haute couturier and whose establishments are considered to be *couture creation* houses.[4] Of these, there are only about ten who have a world-wide fashion reputation at any one time. Among the best known are Balenciaga, Chanel, Dior, Cardin, Givenchy, Jacques Heim, and St. Laurent.

The couture approach to the fashion business is very different from the American.[5] Ours is based upon quantity production by factory methods of fashionable apparel for the many; theirs is predicated upon evolving individually measured and made-to-order garments for the few. Most of our output is at relatively modest prices; theirs is very costly. Our garments are produced to standardized sizes and cut from uniform measurements; theirs are measured and made on live models. Our producers cut and sew thousands of one style at the same time; their workrooms cut and sew one at a time. Their garment production involves endless fittings on living models; ours are measured on dress forms.

Other major differences are the dominant role played by the head designers of the French houses, and the practice of selling their original designs to professional buyers for copying purposes. Apparel designers in our industry do not sell their designs for copying purposes; neither do they, with very few ex-

[3] Press Attachée, English Speaking Countries, Chambre Syndicale de la Couture Parisienne, Paris, France, November 24, 1964. Also, see Celia Bertin, *Paris à la Mode,* translated from the French by Marjorie Deans, New York, Harper, 1957, pp. 76–77.
[4] "Calendrier des Collections Automne-Hiver," 1964, Chambre Syndicale de la Couture Parisienne, listed 26 couture creation houses and 17 lesser couture houses.
[5] Authors' note: There is a group of American high-priced ready-to-wear producers who call themselves the New York Couture Group, but who do not produce custom-made clothes as do the French couture houses. The American operations most similar to French couture are the few concerns who have custom-making workrooms such as Bergdorf Goodman and Saks-Fifth Avenue in New York.

ceptions, head the concerns for which they design. They are more often than not hired employees.[6]

Founded by Charles Worth. The founder of the modern Haute Couture is reputed to be Charles Frederick Worth, who was a brilliant young English designer with a flair for business. In 1854, just about the time that Elias Howe was perfecting his sewing machine, Worth was busy putting Paris "high fashion" on the map. After working in Paris as a draper in a retail shop, he opened his own business with the idea of designing luxurious custom-made clothing for wealthy patrons. He soon attracted the attention of the Empress Eugènie, and was appointed Dressmaker to the Queen and other great ladies of the time.

Worth is credited with being the first dressmaker to show collections of made-up samples of his own designs, rather than working to the specifications of individual customers. He is further given credit for conceiving the idea of showing collections of garments on living models. Prior to his time, dressmakers had usually suggested new styles to customers by means of sketches accompanied by bolts of materials; if a complete dress was produced, it was shown on a wooden dummy, not a live woman. Some dressmakers would occasionally dispatch to American customers, or the courts of Europe, fashion dolls or "fashion babies," as they were then called, which were dressed in the latest Paris styles.

Worth further instituted the practice of selling to foreign trade buyers, along with his private clients, and began the wholesale relationship between France and the United States. At the height of his career, Worth employed as many as 1200 people, a big fashion business even by today's standards.[7]

Organization and Operation of a Couture House. The working organization and operation of typical couture firms are fairly uniform. Each firm is known as a house, for the simple reason that their operations are housed in a residential type of dwelling, rather than in a commercial factory. Their houses, generally elegant old homes or palaces which have been renovated to suit their purposes, are usually found in good residential neighborhoods.

The head of the house is generally the chief designer, who will have several personal assistants, such as a fabric specialist and a sketching specialist (who interprets and sketches the designer's ideas). There will be a number of production workrooms, depending on the size of the house, each headed up by a *première* who is responsible for reproducing the work of the designing department. The *premières* are in charge of the *midinettes* who do the sewing and stitching. For example, Chanel, as long ago as 1930, had as many as twenty-six workrooms, and employed over 2000 people.[8] The live mannequins on whom the original samples are made and shown are supervised by a house *directrice,* who is also in charge of the selling showrooms and the saleswomen, called *vendeuses.* The largest couture house of them all, the House of Dior, also has a complex business office, which includes a public-relations department, a publicity department, and the like.

Although there are exceptions, the name of a couture house is generally that

[6] Authors' note: There are relatively few designer-owned apparel firms in the United States. Some notable examples are the firms owned by Pauline Trigère and Adele Simpson.

[7] Madge Garland, *Fashion,* Penguin Books Ltd., Middlesex, England, 1962, p. 40. Also see Edith Saunders, *The Age of Worth,* Bloomington, Indiana University Press, 1955, for a detailed story on the House of Worth.

[8] *Ibid.*

of its head designer, and its reputation is essentially a one-man or one-woman affair. Occasionally, however, as in the case of the House of Dior, a well-known name is retained after the founder's death, with a hired designer or changing series of designers. As in America, different houses earn their reputation for different things: some, like St. Laurent, become known for their originality as trend setters; others, like Balenciaga, for their outstanding workmanship; some, like Chanel, for their suits; still others, for their dresses.

The couturiers prepare major collections of new designs twice a year for showings which customarily take place in the latter parts of January and July. These collections are first shown to American and European manufacturers and store buyers, who buy styles with the express license to reproduce them in their own countries. A few weeks later the French designers show their collections to their private clientèle, for whom they make garments to measure. At most houses, trade buyers are charged a deposit or minimum purchase fee, which ranges from $300 to $500 for a retail store and from $500 to $1000 for a manufacturer.[9] This must be guaranteed before they can enter a couture house. This deposit, which is called a "caution fee," is then deducted from any purchases they make. If they do not purchase any models, it is considered an admission fee and is not refundable.

The trade buyer who purchases a garment for copying purposes pays typically $650 to $900 for a dress, $600 to $1000 for a suit, and $700 to $1000 for a coat. The price, naturally, varies with the garment and the house concerned, but it is generally higher than would be paid for the same garment if a private customer bought it for her own use. The higher price is explained in part by the fact that the commercial customer is also buying copying rights to the model, partly by an attitude expressed well by Christian Dior himself, who said that the commercial buyer has a photographic eye, and, when he buys one model, he carries ten more home in his head.[10]

Dollar sales figures are not publicly reported but it is generally estimated that sales of Haute Couture models are about evenly distributed between commercial buyers and wealthy private clients. Some authorities say that leading couturiers could not financially survive on private customers alone. The preparation of each new collection is a very costly affair and as one leading couturier himself stated: "We must depend on commercial buyers to recoup our initial outlays. Private customers cannot do so." [11] The trade sales are more profitable than those to private clientele because of the higher prices paid, and also because there is none of the fittings and fuss that is necessary with private customers. On the other hand, couturiers believe that "For the houses of haute couture to be creative, continuing contact with the fashionable women of the world is essential to the creation of collections. We cannot afford to have the prices for our private customers go so high that we will lose them." [12]

[9] Caution-fees are announced twice a year in *Women's Wear Daily*. These were listed on January 8, 1963, p. 30.
[10] Christian Dior, as told to Elie Rabourdin and Alice Chavane, translated by Eugenia Sheppard, *Talking about Fashion*, New York, G. P. Putnam's Sons, 1954, p. 84.
[11] Pierre Cardin speaking in "Paris, A Story of High Fashion," presented on NBC-TV, New York, February 16, 1964.
[12] Robert Ricci, President of the House of Nina Ricci, in an interview reported in the *New York Times,* June 5, 1962, p. 46. ("French See Revolution in Couture.")

Table 1 The Price of Paris: Prices to the Trade and Caution Fees of Representative Houses, as Announced in the Trade Press in Advance of the Paris Openings

	Minimum Prices of Garments			Caution Fee, Manufacturers or Stores
	Dress	Suit	Coat	
Balmain	$ 700	$ 800	$ 750	1 model
Cardin	1000	1000	1000	$550
Carven	500	600	600	——
Courrèges	600	600	600	1 model
DeRauch	500	600	600	1 model
Dessès	150	300	250	$200
Dior	900	1000	900	Manufacturer: $1,000—2 persons Store: $450—1 person
Esterel	400	400	400	$400
Goma	600	650	650	1 model
Gres	650	650	650	1 model
Griffe	600	700	700	1 model or 2 toiles
Heim	700	700	700	None
Lanvin Castillo	750	850	850	1 model or 2 toiles
Laroche	700	800	800	$700
Patou	600	700	650	Mfrs.—1 model Stores—$300
Ricci	750	850	800	1 model
Rouff	600	700	700	1 model or 2 toiles
Simonetta-Fabiani	600	600	600	$360, 1 toile, or 2 paper patterns
Venet	600	650	700	1 model

Source: As announced in *Women's Wear Daily*, January 8, 1963

Couture Openings. The content of every major collection is a closely guarded secret, representing weeks and months of preparation and creative work. There is intense rivalry between the couturiers, and their creations are as jealously guarded until opening day as are the new automobiles in this country. Although the designers do have mutual agreements as to dates of openings and deliveries, there is no collusion amongst members to agree on a color or new silhouette. It will often happen, however, that when one designer develops a new line that meets with the approbation of both his private clients and the foreign copyists, many of the other designers will pick up that trend for the next collection, and may develop it even further.

Before showing collections to trade buyers, it has been the custom to hold press previews for fashion reporters who come to Paris from all over the world to cover and report on the openings. The press, however, must pledge not to publish sketches or photos before a specified release date—approximately six weeks after the collections are first presented. This time lag gives the professional buyers time to copy the costly garments they have purchased before all and sundry can see what has been shown.

Opinion among the couturiers is divided as to the value and importance of press showings. Pierre Cardin, for example, has been quoted as saying that a press showing is "A day that may mean fabulous success or failure . . . for it is through the eyes of these reporters that women of the world see the couturiers' offerings. It is the fashion reporters who pick things to be photographed that they think are right . . . who edit the collections and report on styles they like." [13] Others, however, hold fashion reporters less highly in regard. Balenciaga, for example, who has closed his doors to the press, has expressed himself publicly as "fed up with fashion editors who know nothing about fashions, telling buyers what and where to buy." [14]

The atmosphere of a couture house prior to the openings has often been compared to that of a theatre during rehearsals; like any premiere, it is not until the collection is shown and the orders placed that the principals know whether they have been successful. In addition, success in any one season is ephemeral, and, six months later, the couturier will have to prove himself all over again.

Sources of Income Other than Apparel. Most leading houses have sources of income, other than apparel, which are often more profitable than couture itself:

1. **SALES OF OTHER PRODUCTS.** In addition to apparel, many houses market other products, of which perfumes bearing the name of the house are perhaps the best known and most profitable. For example, in 1960 the couture sales of the House of Balenciaga were estimated to be $1.5 million, with added perfume sales upping the total volume to $2.3 million.[15] Many houses also run boutique shops on the ground floor of their establishments in which they sell jewelry, lingerie, handbags, and other accessories, along with some ready-to-wear.

2. **FRANCHISES.** Some designers, rather than market other products themselves, franchise the use of their well-known names on merchandise ranging from hosiery to social stationery; this merchandise is manufactured and marketed by other more specialized producers, who, of course, pay for the use of the names.

3. **SUBSIDIES.** From 1950 until 1963 couture houses received a yearly subsidy from the French government.[16] These subsidies, ranging in total from $300,000 to $600,000, came from a tax levied against French fabric firms. To qualify for its share of them, a couture house would agree to use approximately 80 per cent of their fabrics from those of French textile producers. The portion received by individual houses depended on how much fabric was actually used.

4. **"OUTSIDE" FINANCIAL BACKING.** Some leading houses are financially backed by outside firms who support the houses for various reasons. Some do it for their prestige value, others for other business reasons. For example, the collections of a couturier can serve as the "display windows" of large textile interests. An illustration of this type of arrangement would be the House of Dior which was deliberately launched by the Cotton Industry Board headed by Marcel Boussac as a means of stimulating demand for French fabrics.[17] Couturiers and their textile suppliers are mutually dependent allies so it is understandable that wool and

---

[13] Cardin, *op. cit.*

[14] "The State of the Paris Couture Today," *Women's Wear Daily,* June 29, 1960.

[15] *Ibid.*

[16] Jacques Heim, President of the Chambre Syndicale, "Letters to the Editor," *Women's Wear Daily,* January 12, 1962, p. 2.

[17] Dwight E. Robinson, "The Importance of Fashions in Taste to Business History," *The Business History Review,* Vol. XXXVII, Spring/Summer 1963, p. 30.

textile magnates should finance individual houses. In many instances, fabric producers will also supply, free of charge, the sample dress lengths from which the first samples are made, and carry, without advance payment, the stock that is necessary for the made-to-order reproductions.

Chambre Syndicale de la Couture Parisienne. Most Haute Couture houses are represented by an association known as the Chambre Syndicale de la Couture Parisienne.[18] This is a trade association which was founded in 1868 to represent the different branches of the French fashion industries and to deal with the administrative and labor problems of its membership. Its major activities on behalf of the couture are to perform the following duties.

1. COORDINATE THE OPENING SCHEDULES. Days, dates, and hours during the week of openings are coordinated so that trade buyers and reporters may be able to see the work of several houses in one day.

2. REGULATE SHIPPING AND RELEASE DATES. All orders placed by professional buyers during opening week are shipped on a uniform date, approximately thirty days after the initial showings. The release date for publication of press photographs or sketches is set for approximately six weeks after showings. This press release date is arranged so that buyers of expensive models will have time to get copies made before all and sundry can see what has been shown.

3. REGULATE CONDITIONS FOR COPYING. The right to offer copies is granted to a purchaser only in his own country, and only in fabrics; the making of paper patterns for resale purposes is forbidden. Manufacturers are also asked to sign an agreement not to sell or sublet the model to an unauthorized producer. These rules for copying are legally unenforceable in the United States, and there have been many violations, as well as some lawsuits; any person or firm suspected of infringing on these regulations, however, is never again allowed in an Haute Couture house.

4. REGISTER NEW DESIGNS OF ITS MEMBERS. If an unauthorized copy of a registered design is found in France, the style pirate is subject to prosecution under French law.

5. ISSUE PRESS CARDS FOR THE OPENINGS. Press representatives can obtain the *cartes d'entrée* to the collections only through the Chambre.

The Chambre also represents its members in its relations with the French government, arbitrates disputes, regulates uniform wage arrangements and working hours, and sponsors a school for the education of apprentices. There is also a Chambre Syndicale des Paruriers which represents accessory firms, and other different divisions represent milliners, ready-to-wear manufacturers, and the like.

The Business of Couture. Parisian haute couture is more than its talented designers, original creations and glamorous mannequins. It is also a business, and one which is of major importance to the economy of France. It may not be large in comparison with the American industry but it does provide employment for many thousands of French workers. The top twenty houses alone are said to employ about 8000 workers at the peak of a season.[19] Equally important is the great prestige that Parisian couture lends to other French fashion products and thereby gives their makers enormous advantages in world markets.

---

[18] Authors' note: Balenciaga and Givenchy withdrew their membership several years ago because of policy differences pertaining to press showings.

[19] Source: Chambre Syndicale de la Couture Parisienne, *loc. cit.*

Figures on the sales of individual houses or on the industry as a whole are not publicly reported; neither are authoritative statistics available. Various trade sources [20] have estimated the export volume of all French fashion products, including such items as ready-to-wear apparel, perfumes, jewelry, cosmetics, handbags, and the like, to be in the neighborhood of some $375 million. Total sales approximations of "couture creation" houses alone, exclusive of perfumes and ready-to-wear, range from $13 to $20 million annually. American professional buyers, according to trade calculations, spend about $1.5 million yearly on couture models for copying purposes, a sum which is matched or slightly surpassed by trade buyers from other countries. Germany is reputed to be the leading nation in terms of purchases of couture models. The House of Dior is generally reported to have the largest sales volume of any of the couture houses and has been listed among the top 300 French exporters.

Haute Couture houses are in good shape creatively but have been facing many financial and operational problems. Custom-made clothes, despite their high selling prices, are not very profitable, owing to the steadily increasing costs of labor, material, and taxes. On one $750 dress in a Dior collection, the following cost breakdown was cited:

> $150 for materials, $250 for labor, $135 for taxes, $45 for sales commissions and nearly $140 for overhead. That adds up to $720, leaving only $30 for profit. Even this profit margin was bigger than in many other Dior originals because Dior repeated the number forty-two times. On garments reproduced only three or four times, the house sometimes winds up in the red.[21]

Despite the low profit margins on custom-made original models, couture houses cannot afford to raise their prices so high that customers would withdraw their patronage. Pierre Cardin explained it this way: "The dresses we make are like sails on a sailboat. They help to sail the boat, but all fishing goes on from the boat itself." [22] Even Dior, the General Motors of the Paris fashion houses, depends on its couture prestige to help sell perfumes, boutique items, licensing arrangements, and so on.

Some people, including the couturiers themselves, see only a downtrend ahead for custom-made clothing. The reasons are economic and are worldwide rather than exclusively Parisian. Emilio Pucci, a leading Italian designer, explained them in the following manner:

> The couturier works with three ingredients—fabrics, labor, and imagination. Formerly, all three cost the couturier practically nothing. Fabrics were given by the manufacturers; workroom personnel were paid negligible wages; and, of course, imagination is free. . . .
>
> Today, all that has changed. Fabric manufacturers are becoming more interested in selling large ready-to-wear customers than in giving their materials to couturiers. . . . I know of one instance last season where a fabric producer actually delivered material to a ready-to-wear house before it was

[20] Authors' note: All dollar figures cited in this section have been compiled from the following sources: "High Fashion Yields Paris Great Prestige But Scanty Profits," *Wall Street Journal,* July 21, 1964; "Couture of Paris Is Big Business," *New York Times,* June 9, 1963, Business Section, p. 10; and Cardin, *op. cit.*

[21] *Wall Street Journal, loc. cit.*

[22] Cardin, *op. cit.*

shown in the collection of a leading couturier. When the couturier complained, he was told that the volume orders from the garment house were preferred to the few pieces taken up by the couture house.

I need not dwell on the enormous increase in labor and other operating costs, including taxation. All the couturier has left today that is free is imagination. Under the old system, a couturier could do as many dresses for a collection as he wanted to do. Today, the couturier must figure out how to make the little suit or coat that will sell commercially at a high profit because of the label, in order to pay for the cost of making all the expensive dresses that we sell. . . .

The ready-to-wear trade is going to nibble away at the couture until there is nothing left. . . . It is exactly what has happened in every other field. For example, custom-made furniture is a thing of the past. Fashion is the . . . only field in which so much effort is devoted to producing one unit. In every other field, mass production has taken over, from automobile to home furnishings. . . .[23]

From Couture to Ready-To-Wear. Many couturiers have long had boutiques on their premises in which they sold less expensive, ready-made versions of their custom designs. More and more of them, however, have been extending this idea and going into the ready-to-wear business on a larger scale. Not too long ago about a dozen leading couturiers, among them Jacques Heim, Guy Laroche, Jean Desses, and Jeanne Lanvin, arranged to design and manufacture collections of *prêt-à-porter* (the French term for ready-to-wear) which are produced for them by Maria Carine, a manufacturer specializing in ready-made garments.[24] These collections are shown together but bear the labels of the individual couturiers. Mendes, another manufacturer, produces ready-to-wear collections for Castillo, Madeleine De Rauch, and Philippe Venet.[25] Some couturiers have established their own wholesale divisions in France and in other countries; Dior, for example has a manufacturing firm right in the heart of Seventh Avenue. Couturiers are now designing exclusive ready-to-wear lines for manufacturers and pattern companies in the United States and other countries as well as for retail stores which, in turn, have them produced by manufacturers. An example of this latter arrangement in our own country is to be found in the styles designed in Paris and featured by Montgomery Ward and Company, Inc.[26] In a few instances, leading couture houses are selling their ready-to-wear boutique clothes to Paris department stores—a practice that would have been unthinkable not too long ago. The development of a sizeable ready-to-wear business is coming along slowly, but the possibilities it offers to creative couturiers to capitalize on their fashion talents is becoming increasingly attractive to them.

American Copies and Adaptations of Haute Couture

The American fashion industries look to the Paris couture for a variety of reasons: one is prestige. Another is for new ideas and trends in silhouettes, trim-

---

[23] An interview with Fairchild News Service reported in *Women's Wear Daily*, October 25, 1960.

[24] Chambre Syndicale de la Couture Parisienne, *loc. cit.*

[25] *Ibid.*

[26] Authors' note: These are usually featured in their fall mail-order catalogues and bear the labels of prominent French and Italian couturiers of whom Jacques Heim and Emilio Pucci are but two examples.

mings, fabrics, and other style details. Many use couturier styles for the purpose of making and promoting exact "line-for-line" copies, a semi-annual business activity for many firms in the United States. This copying is legitimate, and is not to be confused with style piracy, the *stealing* of designs. It must be remembered that French and other European couturiers sell their designs for this express purpose, and trade buyers pay well for this privilege.

The copying operations begin with the January and July showings in Paris, which are attended by two major categories of professional buyers: those who represent the manufacturers, and those who represent and buy for retail stores. In many cases, store buyers and manufacturers work together; the retail buyers will select the styles to be carried and share the cost of the original garments with the manufacturers who make the copies for them. Even though many professionals purchase only a few models, the new ideas that they see are often more valuable than those that they buy.

There is a great variation among the professional buyers in the number of houses that they shop, the number of styles that they buy, and the factors that influence their selection. The tastes of the clientèle to whom their particular firm caters must be taken into consideration, as well as the prices at which they plan to sell the garments. Another important consideration is their advertising and promotion plans. Some styles will be purchased for prestige purposes; others for their volume possibilities; and still others for their newness and trend-setting aspects. A few retailers, such as a Bergdorf-Goodman, will select models that they can reproduce on a made-to-order basis in their own custom workrooms. Other firms, whose copies and adaptations are geared to a volume ready-to-wear market, must consider the practicality of reproducing certain cuts and details by mass-production methods, in which hundreds of garments must be cut at one time. All buyers, however, look for styles that will create fashion news and stimulate customer interest. Indeed, some retailers admit that they buy Paris models to copy purely for prestige purposes. They have no expectation of profiting from the sale of copies, even expensive ones, but they do hope that some of the Paris glamour will rub off on their other ready-to-wear lines.

Since the garments shown in the collections are for sample purposes only, each buyer can specify the color and size of the reproduction that will be made up to his order. French models, despite their high price tags, are not sold on an exclusive basis and, unless there is a special understanding, the couture house will take as many orders as it can get on a given number. It frequently happens, therefore, that the same styles will be sold to many buyers, each one representing a different type of firm, and each copying or adapting them to sell at different prices.

All orders placed during the initial showings are delivered on a uniform date, approximately four weeks after the opening. Although the actual copying or adapting process must wait until models are received, preliminary work on the copies begins as soon as the buyers return. Most firms try to have their line-for-line copies ready for sale two to three weeks after the "originals" arrive in the States. This means that much preparatory work must be done prior to the arrival of their orders. Appropriate fabrics and trimmings must be selected and readied for quick production; store buyers must make arrangements with manufacturers to whom they will give the models to be copied; advertising, window displays, fashion shows, and other promotional devices must be preplanned and scheduled. Since speed is vital, many people wonder why it is necessary to wait for the actual garment itself. The reason is that, for good copies, the manufacturers must be able to examine the original, inch by inch, to determine exactly how it is made in order to make a pattern. This is the only way to be sure that its shape and fit will be what its creator intended.

Since the majority of Paris designs are purchased simply for copying or adapting, buyers have no permanent use for the original models. The garments, therefore, are generally brought into the United States under bond. This is an import arrangement with the United States Customs, which means that American firms have agreed not to resell the original garments within the confines of the United States, and therefore do not have to pay duty (which could amount to almost half as much again as the original cost of the garments). After one year, the United States importer must dispose of the original; many firms often sell the "used" sample to Canadian firms who specialize in the buying and selling of second-hand Paris models.

The majority of buyers deal through foreign commissionaires, for whose services they pay a fee. The commissionaire handles language barriers; translates prices into United States dollar values; follows up on shipping, packing, and customs arrangements; and also acts as the banker, adviser, and buyer's representative until the merchandise is shipped and received.

The actual extent of the influence exerted by the Paris couture on the American fashion industries is indeed debatable. Since couture creations are as noteworthy for their exquisite workmanship and fit as their styling, if not more so, there is a question of how much Paris can be injected into the mass-produced apparel of this country. Furthermore, in recent years, the growing prestige of American designers and the emergence of couturiers in other countries have loosened the hold of Paris to some extent, but its *dicta* are still respected by the American manufacturers and designers. The long history of Paris as the capital city of fashion has developed such a habit of thinking and snob appeal among American trade buyers that many have been accused of buying styles to which they would not have given a moment's notice if they had come from any other city in the world. Although American buying of Paris originals has not increased in recent years, there is still much fanfare about, and borrowing of, French conceptions.

Other Foreign Markets

One of the interesting developments of the postwar years has been the growth of fashion markets in foreign countries other than France. Even more interesting is the manner in which these regional fashion centers have been encouraged and supported by their own governments. Although they have never matched the importance of Paris, cities such as London,[27] Berlin, Rome, and Florence have had long-standing couturier traditions of their own. Recently, however, couture designers and ready-to-wear manufacturers have been given help to develop their ideas and businesses. In England, for example, the Board of Trade has been characterized by one English observer as the "fairy godmother

[27] Incorporated Society of London Fashion Designers, 315 Regent Street, London W.1, England, has ten member houses.

to whom is due the survival of their couture and the rapid development of their now large and excellent ready-to-wear trade."[28] In Italy, the government furnished two historically famous palaces in Florence for their ready-to-wear openings—the Pitti Palace as a showroom, and the Strozzi as a meeting place where the actual selling is done. More recently, a Center for Promotion of Italian Fashions and Textiles has been established at Milan's Mitam (the seasonal textile show mart) with government funds. As one of their ventures, the Center is spending money to back eighteen Italian couturiers by buying six models from each couturier at a cost of about $800 each; the models are being promoted by the Center in Italy, and in other countries. Promotion costs—which include showings, press photos, and an official magazine—are also being financed by state monies. In addition, the Center is giving outstanding couturiers who work in Florence an expense contribution of some $5000 each.[29] Even Hong Kong has become important in the foreign fashion picture.

The key word in all foreign countries is "export" and, even though methods of government support vary, fashion designers are being given every opportunity to develop their ideas, provided they utilize the natural resources of their respective countries. Although European apparel manufacturers are not yet geared for a sizeable mass-produced ready-to-wear industry, there is every indication that history in fashionable ready-made clothing is taking shape today, all over the world. Reports for 1963 by the organization for Economic Cooperation and Development cited Italian exports of ready-to-wear women's and children's clothing of $225 million, West German shipments of $75 million, and, for France, $125 million.[30]

American Imports of Foreign Ready-To-Wear

Until 1950, almost all ready-to-wear garments worn by American women and children were supplied by our domestic industry. Since then, tariff reductions and the activity of American importers have brought about a rising volume of imports. The names of foreign ready-to-wear manufacturers are becoming more familiar in this country; imported apparel is featured by many great retail stores; American producers, in some instances have work done for them abroad; domestic wholesale sources feature imported lines. As yet the amounts are small for women's apparel but they have been steadily increasing. A study by the Bureau of Census showed that, in 1961–1962, for most fashion categories, only 1 to 2 per cent of the total American consumption was imported; in dresses and blouses, for example, the imports in 1962 represented only 1 per cent of that year's supply.[31] A later study, however, reported that between 1961 and 1963, the value of imported shipments of women's apparel items "rose by an additional 44 per cent despite the International Cotton Textile arrangements and a

[28] Garland, *op. cit.* p. 73.
[29] *Women's Wear Daily*, January 5, 1965, p. 50.
[30] *Wall Street Journal, loc. cit.*
[31] "U.S. Commodity Exports and Imports as Related to Output, 1962 and 1961," U.S. Bureau of the Census, Washington, D.C., 1964, p. 21.

number of bilateral agreements with foreign countries."[32] It also showed a continuing upward trend with imports for the first half of 1964 being 13 per cent ahead of the first half of 1963.

The rising tide of imports poses an economic problem for this country. When ideas are imported for copying purposes, we import the inspiration that keeps our own industries working. When we import ready-to-wear clothing for resale, we are providing work for labor in countries other than our own. High tariffs imposed by European countries make our own garments almost prohibitive in price within their borders. United States tariffs on imported apparel are fairly

Table 2 U.S. Apparel Imports: Import Pattern for Selected Women's and Children's Garments (in Thousands of Units)

	1961	1962	1963
Coats and suits, wool	161.9	389.8	477.5
Dresses, cotton	2,703.2	4,821.9	6,199.6
Synthetic	—[a]	28.4	310.6
Blouses, cotton	28,525.6	40,085.5	41,722.0
Synthetic	—	612.4	716.4
Skirts, cotton	—	507.5	273.1
Wool	174.4	894.8	456.2
Sweaters, wool	—	8,657.3	14,811.2
Slacks and shorts, cotton	28,282.4	41,075.7	45,409.8
Wool	—	4,532.2	5,375.0

Source: "Conditions in the Women's Garment Industry," Research Department, ILGWU, September 22, 1964.
[a] The dashes indicate that data are not available.

Table 3 Exports and Imports of Women's Apparel[a] (in Millions of Dollars)

Product Groupings	1947	1958	1959	1960	1961
Imports					
Wearing apparel[b]	5.6	89.1	140.8	153.1	131.3
Knit wearing apparel	3.2	29.4	41.9	57.7	60.8
Corsets and brassieres	.2	5.3	7.0	6.3	7.6
Exports					
Dresses	15.8	12.0	12.1	12.6	11.6
Underwear and nightwear	12.3	13.8	14.7	18.0	16.1
Corsets and brassieres	5.7	8.4	9.5	10.0	10.5
Knit outerwear	11.4	10.4	12.2	14.7	12.7
Other apparel	2.4	5.6	5.9	6.7	6.5

Source: "Trends and Prospects Women's Garment Industry 1959–1962," ILGWU.
[a] Made of woven fabrics.
[b] These figures include some items of men's wear.

low in comparison—about 29 per cent of wholesale value on woolen garments, 20 per cent on cottons, 27 per cent on those made from synthetics.

[32] "Conditions In the Women's Garment Industry," Research Department, ILGWU, September 22, 1964, p. 16.

The ILGWU has gone on record against the increase in imports, but, thus far, its actions have not progressed beyond the resolution stage. The union, however, will undoubtedly protest any attempt to lower existing American tariffs or increase quotas for exporting countries that have unilateral agreements. As the study, quoted above, stated: "The continued high levels of imports of foreign-made apparel do have an effect on the levels of domestic production. . . . This is a relatively novel phenomenon for the United States, but one that is causing much concern in and out of the industry." [33]

---

[33] *Ibid.*

Readings

Famous Paris designers have been the subject of innumerable books which are to be found in most good libraries. In selecting readings for this chapter, therefore, the authors have avoided this aspect of their subject and concentrated instead on material that keeps the business aspects of the matter in focus.

In the first two readings—"What Makes Paris Fashion's Capital" and "Backstage at Paris' Fashion Drama"—two observers on the French scene describe the social and economic climate of Paris fashion, and the twice-yearly excitement generated by the openings. Readings which follow emphasize the use made of foreign markets in the United States and the efforts being made by other countries to woo our dollars via the fashion route. Note particularly Mr. Collins' point that copying activities may be of more help than harm to the French couture. The concluding reading contains a roster of famous fashion designers and analyzes their contributions to fashion's history. The list includes three Americans, Adrian, Claire McCardell, and Norman Norell. The reader has met Mr. Norell in a previous reading in this book.

What Makes Paris Fashion's Capital

Above All, It Is the French Tradition that Frivolity, Taken Seriously, Can Be an Art

by P. E. Schneider

Every half year, at exactly the same moment, the wife of a Brazilian coffee planter, the daughter of a Johannesburg mineowner, the fiancée of a haberdasher in Milwaukee, and the sister of a diplomat in Tokyo hear a call from Paris as imperious as the migratory instinct. The threat of divorce, of ruin, of ridicule—nothing will stop them from obeying that injunction. If the men in their lives have barely accustomed themselves to dresses that cling like paint to the ladies' figures, no matter; now the same bodies disappear inside gauze rocket ships or silk pyramids. Why? Because the distant, mysterious Power has so decreed. And decree what it may—that women be billowed out into the shape of a cupola or stiffened into the silhouette of an arrow, drowned in crinolines or denuded to the kneecaps—they will obey.

Tomorrow, 2000 visitors will be convened in Paris from every corner of the globe to observe the fresh decrees at firsthand: the buyers, the priestesses of the fashion press, the magnates of America's ready-made clothing trade—all those who make a semi-annual pilgrimage to the openings of the Paris dressmaker collections. "People come to Paris to get a message," one of these pilgrims has succinctly explained. On that elusive message, Paris has built an in-

Reprinted from the July 27, 1958, issue of *The New York Times Magazine* by permission of *The New York Times*.

dustry that ranks second on France's list of exports.

About sixty *couture* establishments of various magnitudes account for a total income of nearly 7,000,000,000 francs. They employ some 6000 people and, indirectly, provide work for some 200,000 more. They create approximately 10,000 fashion designs a year, some of which cost as much as $1000—and some even more.

So great an investment in so flimsy a bauble as fashion may seem the maddest extravagance; but extravagance is one of the basic ingredients of fashion at the outset. The life span of a fashion encompasses the time it takes to assimilate it, to rationalize it, to functionalize it—in short, to water it down all the way from the zenith of *haute couture* to the nadir of ready-made. This period, though it generally does not exceed twenty months, is amply long enough (in the words of Yves St. Laurent, the young incumbent at the house of Dior) "for the dreams in our studios to turn into nightmares on the streets."

Thus, the unceasing battle against the routine, the normal, the already accepted, is the essence of Paris' tyrannical power. A characteristic of such power is that it be vested in individuals, and in this case the power is vested in the *couturiers;* for it is the *couturiers* who set fashion today—not queens, princesses, actresses or *grandes courtisanes,* as in other eras. The *couturier's* caprice is law—though, of course, one may choose among them. If you want to look like a church starkly outlined against a Spanish sky, you may go to Balenciaga. If you wish to feel like a willow bending over a romantic lake, there is Dior; for that outer-spatial baroque touch, Givenchy; if you are a believer in tradition, there is Chanel, who is to Balenciaga what an omelet is to *crêpes suzette* (though, as gourmets will tell you, an omelet is the hardest dish to make well).

But if it is true that it is the *couturiers* who formulate and issue the decrees, why cannot these potentates work in some other place? Not one of the major fashion creators of today was born in France's capital; several are foreigners. So, why Paris, only Paris? What makes the Place Vendôme, the Rue du Faubourg St.-Honoré, or the Avenue Montaigne their ultimate refuge? The reply that comes to everyone's lips is hardly illuminating: "It's a mystery," you are invariably told, by the salesgirl, the elegant Parisian woman, even the *couturier* himself.

To be sure; but the ingredients of that mystery can at least be listed. Like any plant, the delicate blossom of fashion needs not only a seed—the *couturier's* talent, probably innate but usually developed in the *atelier* of an older colleague—but also proper climate and soil.

The climate is this city's atmosphere—*l'air de Paris,* in the classic phrase of its incurable addicts. Many things contribute to that atmosphere. "The thing that counts," an elegant Parisian says, "is that we're playing to a wonderful audience here." And the fact is, *la mode* cannot live without proper appreciation of women by men. This commodity is not so easily available as one might think. Countries like Italy or Spain, for instance, where women are still regarded as man's possessions, are not really countries of fashion, for fashion demands freedom; prisoners always wear the same uniform. America suffers from the opposite extreme—there it is the man who is in a position of inferiority. "In France," a Frenchwoman now living in New York told me, "it's the men who look at women in the street; in America, only women look at each other."

Then, too, a certain worldliness is required. Fashion demands that men be interested in women, but not too much; wolves have no patience with the sheep's clothing. That also is why fashion is incompatible with too much beauty. The Venus de Milo could never get a job as an *haute couture* model. "When a woman is too beautiful, one doesn't feel like dressing her," remarks a witty expert on the subject, Mme. Marie-Louise Bousquet, who has been one of Paris' favorite hostesses for many decades and the representative of *Harper's Bazaar* for the past one. (Yves St. Laurent, echoing her, has said that he would rather dress Mme. Bousquet, who no longer claims to be even "a certain age," than Brigitte Bardot.) One of the chief reasons for the elegance of Parisian women is their relative physical imperfection. Flaws stimulate the intelligence.

The *élegante* of Paris also knows that the cult of womankind is one which man likes to celebrate in the plural; she satisfies his polygamous drive by appearing new as often as possible. And the Frenchman shares her wisdom.

He is aware that her freshness lies in her appearance, that beneath it she remains the same, and that he must therefore refrain from pushing too impetuously beyond the exquisite, newly created mask.

In fact, the *Parisienne*—who may be a native of Buenos Aires, Cairo, or Baltimore—is herself a vital part of the Parisian climate. Fashion is what the *couturier* makes for a woman; elegance is what she makes of it. The true *Parisienne* tempers fashion's extravagance with her own private brand of tastefulness. She can make the newest model look as good as old—and in this she is unrivaled. The *couturiers* realize that the ladies of the Paris *gratin,* or high society, are their best publicity; that is why it is common practice to lend them fabulous dresses for an evening at the theatre or a ball.

Few countries in history have attached so much importance to changing form as opposed to stable content, to what people seem as opposed to what they are. France has long been the land of manners, and fashions in dress are the manners of the body. There are ancient reasons behind this French regard for manners.

The country's early and rigorous centralization under an absolute monarchy encouraged the emergence of an *élite* who set the tone, both in the arts and in dress. When Louis XIV deprived the French nobility of its political prerogatives, he left it nothing to busy itself with but frivolity. (The problem that obsessed the Count of Saint-Simon throughout his life, as his memoirs attest, was to prevent the King's bastards and their wives from being allowed to sit down at royal gatherings; in a striking parallel, seating protocol presents hair-raising problems even today at the *couturiers'* showings.) Fashion in art, letters, or dress, in the drawing rooms and in the cafes, is the expression of this concern with manners. In France, Racine noted three centuries ago, "everything is fashion."

To the rest of the world, this may seem ridiculous. But it is well that fashion does not seem so in Paris, for fear of ridicule strangles the creative urge. "You need only look at frivolities," wrote the late poet, Léon-Paul Fargue, "to realize that they, too, have their profundity." French writers, from Balzac to Mallarmé, have said this again and again; French painters—Constantin Guys, Degas, Renoir, Vuillard, Dufy, to name a few of the many—have testified by their canvases to the prestige of fashion. But no one has paid a finer tribute to it than Baudelaire, who wrote: "Fashion is a sublime distortion of nature, or rather a constantly repeated attempt to reform nature."

This climate, in which what elsewhere is laughed at receives due credit, is eminently favorable to the *couturier's* work. It enables him to believe that what he creates has dignity, that like an object of art it is valuable and necessary. Indeed, the *couturiers'* ties with art are as tangible as they are numerous; the father of Jacques Fath was a student of Corot, Dior was an art dealer before turning to dress designing, Balmain studied architecture, Poiret lavishly played host to Diaghilev's Ballet Russe, Cocteau read his poetry to Chanel, and Dali decorated the show cases of Schiaparelli's *boutique.* In this congenial atmosphere, the *couturier's* gift can prosper freely.

There may be healthier or more serene atmospheres, but none so exciting, so filled with a thousand fleeting perfumes, thoughts, and visions. The *couturier* is immersed in it, and it feeds his creation at root-level. The latest book, a ballet, a film, an exhibition of Mexican art, a play about the Etruscans, a film star or dancer who becomes the *cri,* a walk in the Tuileries gardens, the old and the new—all these things and a hundred more make up *l'air de Paris.* The *couturier's* hypersensitive sketch pencil reacts to its variations as finely as a seismograph's needle reacts to the tremors in the earth. The new fashion is in the air of Paris; the *couturier's* drawing brings it down to earth.

Yet, as one of them assured me, "there's a long distance between the drawing and the dress." Fashion needs not only a proper climate but a good soil. Paris provides that, too—a vigorous tradition of craftsmanship.

It is the invisible force of countless artisans that turns talent into reality. Into a breathtaking evening dress may go seventy hours of modest, attentive work. The designer would be paralyzed without the help of the virtuoso seamstresses who instinctively catch his barely hinted intention, and sometimes even improve on it. "Their hands literally talk," the director of a dressmaker's workroom commented admiringly.

Indeed, one might say that France is the

home of fashion because its women still know how to sew. It must be remembered that, even now, 60 per cent of them still make their own dresses or have them made by a little dressmaker. This explains why machines are as rare in *couture* establishments as oil wells on Fifth Avenue. The *couturier* can count on the same kind of superb cooperation from button, bead, and ribbon makers, from the textile artisans who turn out fabrics of incredible intricacy and lavishness—sometimes at the rate of a few yards a day. In no other city in the world can one find such a wonderful array of craftsmanship, all designers declare.

For perfection such as this, there must also be a cult of quality. You can tell from the pained smile that comes over your cleaning woman's face when you offer her a ready-made dress from America that the cult of quality is still strongly active in all walks of French life. It breeds dedication; where else would a cook commit suicide, as Vatel did, because the fish didn't arrive in time when the King came to dinner?

Without going to such spectacular extremes, the little seamstress who spends almost as much time as a physician to learn her calling, yet earns less than an unskilled laborer in an automobile plant, proves her own dedication. Why does she consent to it? "Because I like it"—*it* meaning quality, which she worships and is willing to serve. For she senses that she is as indispensable to the exquisite products of fashion as the designer, the patron, the flashy model, and the air of Paris.

To sum up, fashion, that fragile bit of brilliance which as soon as it is born, conquers the world, reminds me of the pretty young girl who smiles down at a circus audience from the top of a human pyramid. It is she we applaud, yet if a single member of the team supporting her were to default, the entire edifice would collapse. That is why there is no real threat to Paris' fashion supremacy from other cities in the world. They may possess one, or even several, of the elements necessary to build the flimsy scaffolding of *la mode,* but they could not possibly provide them all, and so they must remain earthbound.

The real threat to *haute couture* does not come from rivals in the field, but from the general complexion of the modern world. This luxury trade is as much a freak in the present-day economic scheme as a Roman chariot would be in Times Square traffic. But the enemy is not, as many people think, ready-made styles—at least not directly. On the contrary, the ready-to-wear industry depends on the creative fantasy of the *couturiers* to make its wheels turn. In fact, the more creative talent becomes the exclusive privilege of a few artists, the more industry will depend on them.

"Seventh Avenue needs us," says Mme. Bousquet. "What they buy is not just a dress, but a dozen ideas." *Haute couture,* you might say, is to the ready-made what the research laboratory is to the pharmaceutical factory, or what the monstrous prototypes racing at Monza or Le Mans are to the cars produced by the assembly line.

Indirectly, however, mass production is a grave danger. It discourages personal invention on the part of women. Before the war, only a few well-to-do ladies could adopt the "new line" right away; today, every American secretary can wear it within a few weeks. The press, the women's magazines insidiously force designers to stress sensational innovation, often at the expense of true elegance. They turn fashion's flower into a bomb. Many of the dresses one sees today look good only in photographs. "They are all front and no profile," a dress designer put it. The sense of quality tends to be spoiled, too, by the proliferation of synthetic materials. When all you need to do in order to prepare a meal is to open a couple of cans, you end by forgetting how to cook.

Fashion may die eventually, not for lack of creative talent but because climate and soil will no longer be favorable to it. But that demise, I predict, is a long way off. "*Haute couture* is an anachronism that can survive only by dint of acrobatics," an official of the Paris designers' *Chambre Syndicale* sighed. But fashion has always thrived on acrobatics, and it is to be expected that it will manage even this triple somersault.

Backstage at Paris' Fashion Drama

If Women Await the Spring Modes Breathlessly, the Designers Are Pretty Out of Breath, Too

by Françoise Giroud

The invitations are printed. The chairs have been rented. The new clothes are almost completed. France's couturiers are ready for the opening of the greatest show on earth tomorrow —the show they put on twice a year, now and in August, at which they launch some 2000 new designs in six hectic days.

Naturally, just before the opening, Christian Dior will contemplate suicide. Cristobal Balenciaga will murmur about entering holy orders. Hubert de Givenchy will sob. Coco Chanel will cry, "Why did I ever get back into this ridiculous business!"—and destroy twenty costumes out of forty. But when has there ever been a great spectacle without stars, or a star without majestic opening-night temperament? It's all part of the show, like the chronic outrage of the London press, which biannually proclaims, "We are *not* going to get ourselves up according to Monsieur Dior's dictates."

The fact is, this Monsieur Dior—51 years old, shy, bald, a roly-poly trencherman—has in the last ten years busily transformed women into tulips, cupolas, H's, A's, string beans and arrows; and, moreover, without the slightest serious resistance.*

Dior himself, who sets the best table in Paris, fats up. But his mannequins get thinner and thinner, straighter and straighter, flatter and flatter—except when it occurs to one of them to have a baby. At the first Dior collection in 1947, the one that was to revolutionize fashion, the mannequin Tania fainted twice. "It's emotion," people said. It was, in fact, a baby, protesting the New Look in its own way.

Men, however, were the ones to protest the Flat Look, three years back. Women accepted it almost unanimously. Christian Dior is a man who does nothing without consulting his fortune-teller.

At 40 he was a well-bred, penniless member of the middle class with no discernible future, demurely designing clothes. Today he reigns over an empire that includes Dior branches in London and Caracas, Christian Dior-New York, a wholesale dress operation, and a perfume business. His house in Paris has twenty workrooms and 1200 employes, who make and sell 8000 garments a year—the cheapest of which costs 120,000 francs, or three times a secretary's weekly wage. Nonetheless, when Coco Chanel has lunch with him she tells him, "I adore you, but you dress women like armchairs."

Chanel was already world famous and had sold 20,000 dresses a year when Dior was still a schoolboy. She had exalted fake jewelry and that humble material, jersey, to the height of fashion; she had launched the famous Chanel No. 5 perfume. She reigned over Paris for twenty years, vanished for fifteen years, then reappeared because she was bored. And this winter everyone is imitating her designs.

Dior thinks above all about foreigners; Chanel thinks above all about Parisiennes. Dior shows 200 designs; Chanel shows forty. Dior fears being copied, and fashion buyers must deposit a "*caution*" of 100,000 francs if they are European, 350,000 if American, to see his collection. Chanel on the other hand likes to be copied and lets the press reproduce all her designs as early as she feels like it, because, she says, "discoveries are made to be lost." Dior loves lavishness, the million-dollar look; Chanel loves the impudent, the seemingly inexpensive. These two great couturiers, however, have one thing in common. Neither knows how to sew.

Contrariwise, Balenciaga—dark, gaunt, distinguished, and of indeterminate age—made

---

Reprinted from the January 27, 1957, issue of *The New York Times Magazine* by permission of *The New York Times*.

* Dior, deceased, is replaced now by Marc Bohan.

his first design with his own hands when he was 10. It was a jewelled collar for his cat. And in all his collections there is, according to superstition, one dress he has sewn entirely himself.

Balenciaga never shows himself, never goes out in society. His establishment is not a shop; it is a temple, in which 350 seamstresses and twenty saleswomen officiate. His dozen mannequins are not beautiful willowy girls, they are high priestesses of a sacred cult. His clients? They are a sect. When one of them requested an admission card for a friend a while ago, Balenciaga's assistant, the terrible Mademoiselle Renée, replied, "No, madame. Curious women do not interest us."

If Dior's ideal client is an elegant millionairess and Chanel's a witty, knowing Parisienne, Balenciaga's ideal is a tragic young widowed queen, always dressed in dramatic tones—black, white, red. Balenciaga is the couturier of night.

As for Marquis Hubert Taffin de Givenchy's ideal type, she embodies the notion of an American a Frenchwoman gleans from the American fashion magazines at her hairdresser's. Givenchy, the greatest of all dressmakers so far as height is concerned (he stands over 6 foot 6 and, since he is only 29 years old, may grow taller) uses clashing colors with an audacity that amounts to genius. That is why his spring collections are always bigger hits than his winter ones.

For all their dissimilarities, these four—and a few others, equally gifted—create twice a year a homogeneous commodity, one that is universally recognizable. They create Paris fashion.

The first hint of what this week's openings would be like came last November, when eighty cloth manufacturers displayed some 12,000 different fabrics here. Dior ordered 600 samples to experiment with; Castillo of Lanvin-Castillo, 400. Since then, these bundles of material have been stacked up in all the various designers' studios.

But it is in December and June that the creators create. And everybody with an ambition to become a couturier creates, too, in the hope of selling his ideas to an established house. Thirteen years ago, two young chaps were doing just that for Lucien Lelong; a third young man was an apprentice *chez* Jacques Fath. Their names were Dior, Balmain, and Givenchy.

This season's Dior collection began with 600 designs sketched by the master. These *croquis* Dior turned over to his two assistants, Madame Marguerite and Madame Raymonde, to be made up experimentally in muslin. Of the 600 "dry run" samples in muslin, Dior by now will have weeded out 400—after hot discussions with his staff. Two hundred remain. They have been modified, rectified, wrenched apart: the muslin model of a not particularly complicated tailored suit may require about 375 work-hours before it is considered finished.

Many different kinds of skill will have gone into the suit before that stage is reached. In the workroom, the *première main,* or "first hand," supervises the translation from sketch to muslin reality. She herself is a former seamstress who has climbed the ladder of the *haute couture's* rigid hierarchy, step by step, since her debut as an apprentice. (Apprentices currently start their careers at a salary of 550 francs a week, or $1.57.) By now, the *première main* is a woman whose back aches from kneeling at fittings, who has bad nerves from years of putting up with a couturier's creative anguish on the one hand and with clients' unreasonable ways on the other. "Dressmaking," says one such veteran, "would be a marvelous profession without the customers!"

To make up a muslin model, or *toile,* is infinitely more amusing than to endure the bad temper of some clients. First, the cloth is draped on a mannequin whose looks best correspond to the spirit of the design. Every couturier has a mannequin who represents the *jeune fille,* or "junior miss"; one who personifies the fair lady; one who is languidly distinguished; another, fresh-faced and piquant.

A spirit of collaboration develops spontaneously between the mannequin and the workroom *première;* commonly, they use the intimate *tu* instead of *vous* in speaking to each other. Summoned to the boss's studio, the one adorned in the muslin draped on her by the other, they are just as unnerved as pupils of Michelangelo might have been when called before the master. The *première* is entitled to utter an opinion if she is asked for it; the mannequin can only be silent and obey.

"Turn around . . . ." "Walk . . . ." "Come forward . . . ." "Raise your arm. . . ."

By the time the *toiles* have finally been perfected, the establishment will have been rocked to its foundations by a noteworthy number of "scenes," with resignations offered and withdrawn. And still the ideal fabric for each design must be chosen from among stored-up samples. The right button, ribbon, belt, and flower must be found.

At this point, the couturier is really living; he is a little boy again, playing at dressing his doll. All the great dressmakers of our day preferred dolls to electric trains when they were children. This is what makes them so different in their behavior and their creations from the great prewar leaders of Paris fashion. In those days, many designers were women (Jeanne Lanvin, Madeleine Vionnet, Chanel) who knew that women, first of all, strive to please. Or they were men (Poiret, Patou, Lelong, Rochas) who, in designing clothes, gave a talented expression to their taste for women.

As the new designs begin to shape up, the mannequins step forth to present them to their creator. He picks out the hat, the gloves; burrows into great cardboard boxes to find the appropriate earrings, a necklace. He tries one, another, a third, goes back to the first. Oh, what fun!

Then, all of a sudden, everything crumbles. On the evening of the pre-opening run-through, it all seems hideous, spoiled, unbalanced, boring. What has he done that's *new?*

Pretty dresses are not enough to keep the couture alive. Pretty dresses are everywhere—in every shop in America, Italy, Spain; maybe even in England. No. What the Paris designer must regularly provide, must indeed *impose,* is the stinging flick of the whip that keeps fashion in line, even though it cries with rage, each time it seems about to slip off into the soft, the seductive, the easy way. The lash that disciplines each time fashion, after having been first disturbing, then beautiful, becomes merely pretty.

Rare, indeed, is the couturier who doesn't panic at the eleventh hour. To be sure, he can still transform one dress, throw out another, whip up a third. But a collection always revolves around three or four basic themes: the set of the sleeves, the width of the shoulders, the location of the waist-line, the architecture of the skirt. Last-minute changes can be rung in; but it's impossible to create a whole new production overnight.

Meanwhile, other problems are rearing their heads. How to seat 500 people in a salon with a capacity of 100? How to make room for 100 in a front row that allows for fifty? Any executive who can't settle this problem had better get out of the business. But then, this is the reason so many retired diplomats' wives finish their careers attached to couturiers' establishments. Balenciaga and Givenchy, of course, have eased the problem in their own way, by banning the press from their premises for a month after the opening.

There is an eloquent contrast between the greetings and chatter "out front"—as each guest finds the chair that bears his name, and thus serves as an index to his importance—and the atmosphere backstage.

Trembling in every limb, the couturier takes refuge in *la cabine,* the mannequins' dressing room; he makes the sign of the cross, and in general behaves like a playwright at curtain time. The *cabine* has in fact the atmosphere, the lighting and the disorder of a theatrical dressing room. The mannequins, five at least, fifteen at most, have arrived early. Being harrowed with fear, they have eaten nothing. Each perfects her make-up before her mirror. Silence resigns, as before some great tragedy, while the guests in the salon read the printed manifesto in which the couturier sets forth his program, like a candidate for election.

A saleswoman announces the first number to the audience, in French and in English. The mannequins in the *cabine,* each wearing the first costume she is to show, rise and compose their features. Passing before the couturier, they gently incline their heads with a sort of grace that comes from the heart, and that seems to say, "Look, here I am just as you wished me, perhaps beautiful but perhaps ridiculous—and I go forth under fire, for you."

The spectacle begins. The mannequins walk the length of the salon, turning and whirling ceaselessly, a special skill which makes it virtually impossible to memorize the architecture of a dress and later copy it. Once they have swept offstage, they appear to disintegrate. The corners of their mouths fall, and if their bosoms do not also, it's because they are so firmly sewed into the dresses.

The couturier has begun to breathe again. And now, he tosses his bombshell—and listens. Where did it drop? Did it make a bang? Silence is not so good. Chatter is even worse.

There is a certain sound, recognizable among all others—the murmuring that accompanies satisfaction. Then, four times, five times (if this is an extremely successful collection), applause breaks out. And the manikin who has called it forth flounces backstage, prouder than Duse. Who remembers any more, either in the *cabine* or in the salon, that all this is only about dresses? The spectators and the actors are taking part in a kind of ceremony among initiates.

An hour passes; two hours. At last, the wedding dress appears that signals "The End." All 500 people present stampede to the *cabine*, gasping, "Marvelous! Divine! Where is he? I've got to kiss him!"

He (or she), on the verge of tears, is now scarred with a hundred lipsticks and bombarded with compliments, some of them sincere.

Slowly, the manikins take off their finery, shuck their jewels, and wearily find themselves with their own worries and their own little jersey dresses again. The seamstresses pour in through every door, asking, "So, was it O. K.?"

It is not always O. K.

Since World War II, three major houses have opened, but eleven have had to close. Each year there are fewer private customers, as the older ladies and the huge fortunes die out. The principle of *haute couture* itself is anachronistic: if a mattress manufacturer made his product today under the conditions of a century ago, he could not survive either. And that is possibly what gives this unique spectacle its truly emotional, dramatic character—it is like a fantastic circus act in which every year some acrobat will break his neck.

Beginning tomorrow, the acrobats of French high fashion will be leaping into space and displaying their new twists. Immediately, their designs will be flown out to foreign parts—some just as they were shown, others in muslin or as as paper patterns—for the buyers who have paid for the right to reproduce them commercially. In two months, copies of them will be in every shop window in America.

But they will not be seen in the shop windows or on the streets of Paris. Here, copying is forbidden; and there are not ten thousand Frenchwomen with the means to dress at a couturier's. That is why Paris has two kinds of fashion: the high fashion, set by the couturiers, and another, wholly spontaneous, which one sees all around on the streets. The couture inspires it, but every woman invents her own variations—and thereby makes it inimitable.

Style Piracy

by Kenneth Collins

As everybody knows, the latest Paris openings were marred by bitter charges of style piracy. No one claimed there was anything new about the situation except the speed with which the fashion thieves worked. That seems stepping up in tempo. And it appears that this practice of "lifting" styles is becoming more widespread than ever before.

On the above statements, I believe most people will agree. I offer no solution. Nor do I pretend to know the tricks of the trade. But the Paris bureau of *Women's Wear Daily*, certainly the most knowledgeable group in the fashion capital, knows the venal methods employed and has repeatedly commented on them. Still, the old game goes merrily and sordidly on.

Now let me turn to a different aspect of this subject. Every store in America which appeals to the masses knows that when European women of limited means come to this country, the one thing that flabbergasts them is the miracle of relatively high style garments at modest prices. Sure, they admire our gadgets, our cars, our major appliances—but these they

---

Reprinted by permission of *Women's Wear Daily* from "Today and Yesterday in Retailing," September 25, 1958. Copyright 1958, Fairchild Publications, Inc. After a long and successful career in retailing, Kenneth Collins became a columnist in *Women's Wear Daily*, commenting on the fashion scene.

can take or leave. But the clothes! These visitors simply cannot believe what they see. Nicely styled garments at $10, $15, $25. Accessories at prices which seem peanuts. These are the articles these women are bewitched by—and they are the ones they take home.

Why are such lovely things available at so little money? Well, much of the answer lies in mass production and in rapid distribution. But behind these factors is this custom of style piracy. And this piracy is a large element in the success of volume merchandising and of what foreigners call the "miracle" of good clothes at low prices.

Now with these remarks (including the unquestioned prevalence of stealing), let me turn to one final consideration. In 1947, Allen Raymond, a veteran newspaper reporter, worked abroad for the *Herald-Tribune*. I was then associated with the paper's European edition. Mr. Raymond made a study of the financial history of the haute couture; one fact astounded us. Before World War II, the complete industry, from buttons to whole collections, was, by American standards, trivial in the amount of money involved. But now the dress-making business in Paris has become big business.

I draw no conclusions. I make no apologies for robbery. "Thou Shalt Not Steal" remains in the Decalogue. Yet I wish someone would try explaining why this entire sequence, from creation, to pilfering, to wholesale copying, seems (at least to an outsider) a case where both the thief (a contemptible fellow) and his victim are ultimate gainers. Or is this all wrong?

Meet Manhattan

by Marilyn Hoffman

The real "Miracle on 34th Street" these days is Ohrbach's twice-a-year fashion "spectacular" of Paris originals, along with its own copies. One really has to see it to believe it.

More than 2000 women beat through the doors on March 16—some arrived when the doors opened at 9 A.M. to await the 1 P.M. showing.

The crowd included celebrities (we sat across from Eva Gabor, Ava Gardner, and Lauren Bacall), socialites, salesgirls, Bronx housewives, and ambassadors' wives, from thirty countries. Many arrived in chauffeur-driven limousines.

Some, of course, have shopped the couture houses in Paris. For others, these fabulous Ohrbach openings are as close as they'll ever get to a Paris fashion showing. That's pretty close —only the Atlantic Ocean is between. For Ohrbach's not only shows line-for-line copies of the originals they have purchased, down to the last seam, button, and pleat—and 92 per cent of the time in the same fabric—but also often the same hats, bags, gloves, jewelry, and shoes which were shown with the models in Paris are shown here.

This semi-annual fashion phenomenon has been going on at Ohrbach's since 1947, although only in recent years has it produced such excitement and near-hysteria. It has been likened to a Broadway first night and to a "Seventh Avenue convention." But Sydney Gittler, who is known as the coat and suit "king" of Ohrbach's, said the store worked a long time to get this kind of overjoyous response to its efforts.

Mr. Gittler is one of the most highly esteemed American buyers in Paris where he is much respected for his business acumen and intuition about which Paris styles will appeal most to American women. He is also known in France as an American professional buyer who is "one of the last of the big spenders." He and the store's vice-president, Rose Wells (who buys accessories in Paris), and Margaret Kennedy, dress buyer, descend on Paris each season with a very sizable budget.

The Ohrbach team is said to be the biggest

Reprinted from the March 24, 1964, issue of *The Christian Science Monitor*. Permission granted. One of the many ways in which Ohrbach's has made fashion history is its success in attracting wealthy and socially prominent women to the store for its line-for-line copies of Paris originals.

single purchaser in the Paris couture today. Once this trio has made its selections, the importing is arranged and the manufacturers are lined up here for the reproductions.

They use about thirty top Seventh Avenue houses to make the line-for-line copies, though which manufacturers are never announced. The copies must be completed on split-second timing. For instance, this time, the bulk of the models arrived from Paris by air on February 24 and February 27. They were put into the works, with Mr. Gittler and Miss Kennedy advising steadily with the manufacturers, checking first muslins, then patterns, then models.

Scarcely ever is the first finished copy accepted by the meticulous painstaking buyers. Last season Mr. Gittler had a Givenchy coat remade five times before he would accept the copy and allow it to go into production. Still, by March 12 the collection was complete, and by March 16, store stocks were ready to go.

Each seasonal show progresses with the original Paris model followed by the Ohrbach copy. It is difficult to tell one from the other. The price tag gives away the difference. An original violet and black printed silk dress was purchased from Balenciaga for $1250, while its counterpart made here is sold at $59.99 for the dress and $20 for the stole.

A St. Laurent two-piece navy blue dress was purchased in Paris for $1316, but reproduced for sale at Ohrbach's for $139.

How does a store do it? "Volume," said an official. "We'll probably sell more top-quality French copies this season than any other store in the country."

After the customer showing, the socialites and celebrities flocked to the Grey Room and the Oval Room to buy their favorite numbers. It's all cash-and-carry at Ohrbach's, but some leave the store with six and seven copies, which may range from a $59.99 linen copy of a Givenchy dress to a $350 copy of a Balenciaga double silk taffeta evening coat.

After the first day, there were but few left of the original stock of 150 Balenciaga khaki poplin rain suits, and 200 copies of one Chanel suit sold before the end of the day.

Mr. Gittler described the onslaught as the most sensational performance in the history of the store. Couture houses represented in this show included those mentioned plus Monsieur X, Castillo, De Barentzen, Simonetta-Fabiani, Patou, and Galitzine.

Linen was the top fabric shown. Wrapped or clutch coats represented the newest coat silhouette. The spring "gentlewoman" look from St. Laurent was apparent. There was nothing "far out" in the 51 selections; all reflected quietly elegant taste. And most were copied for very small women—size 4 to 12 was the most prominent range. Only a half-dozen models are made up to size 16, none above. Explanation: "We are catering these days to a younger and smaller audience."

Americans in Paris

by Eugenia Sheppard

American stores and manufacturers took off for Paris last month to get the semi-annual message that is fashion tradition. This time, after two weeks of made-to-order fashion collections in elegant Paris salons, the word came through direct and clear-cut: Back to the girly-type girl in navy blue and white, ruffles and pleats, and a rewardingly scooped out neckline.

If fewer Americans than usual went to Paris this time, it's not because the American fashion industry has declared its independence and decided to stand on its own feet. The reasons are more complex. In January the trip is harder than in July, when most of the fashion tycoons make a holiday of it and combine business with art gallery-going and the latest night clubs. What's more, the rising price of Paris originals is making Americans canny. On the up-and-up

---

 Eugenia Sheppard, Fashion Editor of the *Herald Tribune,* is considered by the industry to be a "top" fashion reporter.

for the past ten years, prices jumped $100 to $200 this season. Many stores and manufacturers are now in cahoots to share the cost—$1000 to $1500 for an average simple outfit that one will reproduce and the other sell. They take turns going to Paris. To save money, too, many manufacturers are making friendly deals with each other to swap their expensive Paris models when they get them home.

Tough competition between stores has made some of them give up and lose interest in the whole rigamarole of Paris fashion. Ohrbach's, now the biggest single American buyer of Paris models, has walked off with the socialite business—all the women who are willing to pay well for a real line for line, fabric for fabric, lining for lining Paris copy. Macy's has cashed in on the story of French fashion for everybody on a budget. Saks Fifth Avenue has specialized in the Chanel suit.

Instead of trying to tell the same old Paris story, many stores have found it more profitable to develop offbeat Paris names and to give their customers exclusive designs. Saks Fifth Avenue now has Louis Feraud, who rose to fame originally as designer for Brigitte Bardot, and Bergdorf Goodman carries the latest young Paris couturier to open, Jean Louis Scherrer. Even though Bergdorf is sometimes plagued by customers who cancel their orders in a huff when they find the same dress three times as cheap at Ohrbach's, the store still loyally buys a collection of originals and duplicates them to order, at prices as high as Paris. Other stores finesse the couture completely and buy European ready-to-wear.

For a long time after the war, this country was Paris' most potent customer. When the Americans arrived in Paris, it was like Santa Claus coming down the chimney. Over the past few years, though, the United States has been out-ranked completely in Paris by the common market countries. West Germany is the big, fair-haired buyer of fashions.

Nevertheless, the Paris fashion world, both its creative and business sides, still rolls out the red carpet for the crowd from the United States. Its press has the front seats for the opening shows. The American industry's whole cast of characters gets the first invitations to the luncheons, the cocktail parties, the little dinners at Maxim's.

Though sales to this country have fallen off, the French know the Americans have a great asset. After they have bought fashion, they know how to make it fashionable. The legend is that the French design, but the Americans make fashion. They know how to promote it so that thousands of wealthy, well-dressed women, more of them than in any other country, will accept the Paris look. They keep Paris in the headlines. They even understand how to move fashion along, to get women out of an old style and into something else. That something else really turned up in the recent Paris collections. There was a turn-about from the heavy, mannish shapes with easy shoulders and big sleeves, drawn with a black crayon, to such a delicate silhouette, that it looked sketched with a sharp pencil point. It's the kind of look women are going to want to buy, and men are going to be willing to pay for. The buyers hope.

Italy: The Tempestuous Decade

by Elisa V. Massai

Nothing is so bad that it cannot lead to something good. This is Italy's philosophy—and that was Italy's fortune after the war, when national pride reacted against frustration and misery in a flourishing of the arts.

Escaping from postwar ruin and chaos, Italy not only rebuilt the essentials, but burst forth in a tumult of creative design.

Movies and cars, architecture and fashions expressed a native desire for beauty combined with an innate ability to sell.

The renaissance of the Italian couture has been described all over the world with fairy tale accents. Her protagonists, however, are

---

"frontiersmen," who know the importance of every step they are to make.

A few words will explain why, when and how a phenomenon like Italy's boom in fashion sales could take place in a country where reconstruction of houses, bridges and roads had all the top priority privileges.

G. B. Giorgini. He was already in his 50's when, as a merchant of antiques and handicraft products, he organized an Italian furniture and home furnishings display at Watson & Boaler, Chicago, in 1948. The success of this exhibition and the signs of a growing interest of early United States buyers and visitors in some Italian apparel goods suggested to GBG the idea of another show including fashions.

First attempt to arrange a fashion display backed by New York and Chicago museums and B. Altman failed for lack of financial support. GBG decided, however, that 1950 was ripe for his own fashion export venture, cost what it might.

During 1947 and 1950, in fact, stores like Marshall Field, Lord & Taylor, and Hudson's had already contacted a handful of couture designers, from Simonetta to Fontana of Rome, Noberasco, Biki, Marucelli and Vanna of Milan. Emilio Pucci, on the other hand, was already the glossy magazines' pet for his new look in sportswear.

B. Altman, Bergdorf Goodman, I. Magnin, and H. Morgan, represented by GBG, could not resist the extremely kind, but hammering pressure of their Italian agent. They had to promise to send their buyers, after the Paris openings, to a private fashion show held at Giorgini's home.

While correspondence between Giorgini and his American accounts was going on, it was necessary for our enterprising Florentine to persuade the frightened or reluctant designers to make a score of models each for the event in preparation.

With a bit of necessary bluff, he finally got a first group of nine couturiers and two boutique designers officially ready with their first original line for the American market.

They were:

Carosa of Rome. Princess Giovanna Caracciolo and Barbara Dessalles who established this house in 1946 were among many Italian noblewomen eager to start a career in a field where refined taste and knowledge of their country's artistic patrimony can count as equivalent of stock capital.

Alberto Fabiani of Rome. As the second generation member of a long-established dressmaking house, he wanted to find his own way in the couture world.

Fontana of Rome. Zoe, Micol, and Giovanna Fontana, born in Parma among dresses, have shown their tenacity in training at Battilocchi of Rome and then in gradually expanding their business from Via Emilia to Via Liguria and then Piazza di Spagna.

Marucelli of Milan—is another couturiere who since elementary school days breathed the atmosphere of a couture house. United States residents and visitors to the Italian Riviera were her first clients in 1933 when she decided to open her Genoa atelier for reproduction of French models. War restrictions compelled this designer to carry out her own ideas. Having tasted the exciting flavor of individual creation, she forgot Paris and became an outstanding fashion personality in Milan.

Noberasco of Milan. Although as a couture house it disappeared in 1952, Vita Noberasco is still considered by fashion people to be a woman of great talent and technical capacity, achieved during many years spent in the prewar Paris couture. In 1950 Noberasco was both modelist and dressmaker.

Schuberth of Rome. The personal styling of this half-Italian, half-German designer procured him both success and limits in the frame of gorgeous "new look" fashions.

Simonetta of Rome. In 1950, still married to count Visconti, she was already a Vulcan in social and fashion life. In addition to native talents and fluency in foreign languages, she had listened carefully to the million-dollar-value-advices of personal friend Eleanor Lambert, making good contacts with New York's leading retailers and manufacturers.

Vanna of Milan. Another house which no longer exists—provided both original and French models. Experience, however, is never completely wasted: Anna Gandini, one of the three partners, is now sales director at Veneziani.

Veneziani of Milan. Couture models at this house were made as an additional line to furs in 1946, mostly on French toiles. Little by little couture overwhelmed furs and original designs Paris copies. Since February 1951 Veneziani has been a faithful member of the Giorgini couture group.

Emilio Pucci and the **Weaver of the Island,** another designer who does not appear any more at openings, completed the first Italian team. Mirsa for knitwear, Bertoli for handbags, and Bardelli for umbrellas were last-minute informal additions.

Foreign Ready-to-Wear

The three readings that follow highlight developments in the growing ready-to-wear operations of foreign countries. Notice that it is not only Paris to which this country turns for imported fashion merchandise, but also almost every country in Western Europe and some of those in Asia. Whatever a country's special talent, America's appetite for good fashion merchandise makes it a tempting market for that country's producers.

Menu Becoming Longer in Fashion Import Snacks

Ready-to-wear and accessories manufacturers all over Europe are cooking up the biggest batch of goodies in history to feed an America hungry for fashion imports. The menu is becoming longer, more varied. The fashion cuisine is being seasoned to American tastes, and even cooked to order. But for the present, and probably for many years to come, the output of the Continent's fashion chefs will be hors d'oeuvres in American stores, and not the meat and potatoes of a mass market.

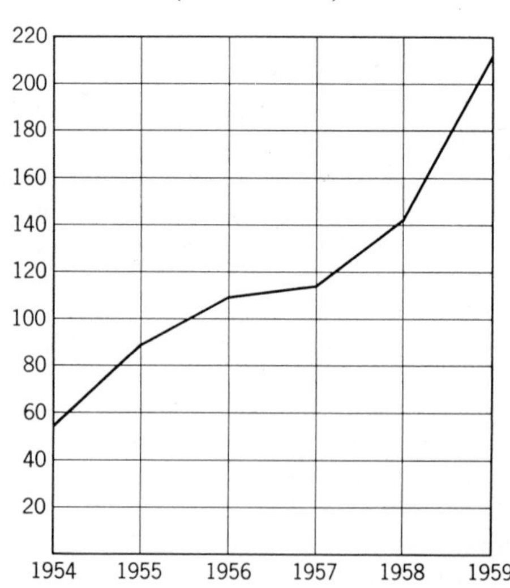

Source: Research Dept., Fairchild Publications, from U.S. Department of Commerce, Bureau of the Census Reports.

Few European manufacturers delude themselves that they can compete with low to middle bracket American-made ready-to-wear, except in certain specialty items like knitwear. Few, if any, European countries appear to have the productive capacity ever to become much more than a small thorn in the side of Seventh Avenue, or a minor blessing to retailers looking for a merchandise "sweetener."

Nevertheless, there seems little doubt that European imports have increased very sharply on the American scene in the past five years, and will accelerate in the foreseeable future.

Italian knitted sportswear and dresses are catching on like pizza. British outerwear, long an American import item as traditional as roast beef, is on an upbeat here. French pret a porter ready to wear, a mere soupcon now, is tantalizing the palates of American merchants. Swiss and West German apparel is commanding attention as is the costume jewelry and knitwear of Austria, and the sportswear of Spain.

The fact is, though, that when you add it all

up, European apparel exports to the United States amount to less than 1 per cent of American consumer expenditures on all clothing and accessories. And the combined shipments of Europe and Britain are almost matched by Japan alone.

The numbers game aside, in the American market European-made apparel has the glamour of a Follies showgirl or the neat respectability of a white-collar gal. Far Eastern apparel is more like a plain and inconspicuous, if highly productive, coolie. But trading up is developing in Japan and Hong Kong, and some segments of Europe have already felt Far Eastern competition.

What follows is an analysis of the major European apparel markets, based on reports by Fairchild News Service® correspondents on the scene.

Italy has rapidly developed as the biggest European exporter of wearing apparel to the United States. It probably has no more than 100 women's wear factories worthy of that designation, which employ 6000 or 7000 workers, and produce about 1.25 million units of coats, suits, dresses, and raincoats a year.

However, there are hundreds of small plants and thousands of cottage workers.

In 1959, Italy exported to the United States some $79.6 million in textiles, apparel and accessories, compared with $51.6 million in 1957.

Just over $30 million of the 1959 figure was textiles, compared with $22.3 million in 1957.

Very sharp increases were recorded in shipments of Italian-made merchandise to the United States in 1959—a peak year for United States intake of Italy's apparel. For example, women's knitwear—mostly cotton and wool one- and two-piece dresses—increased 50 per cent over 1958 to a total of over $2 million. Women's hats doubled to a figure of $400,000.

Italian man-made fiber textile shipments to the United States soared to $4.3 million in 1959 from $800,000 in 1958. Footwear rose 45 per cent to about $15 million.

On the other hand, traditional exports such as scarfs and squares have been declining because of Japanese competition. But this drop has been more than overcome by rises in United States-bound fashion accessories, ranging from buttons to couture millinery, and fur garments.

All told, the United States last year took some 19 per cent of Italy's total soft goods exports.

Ranking second to Italy in exports to the United States is Great Britain. No one really knows exactly how much British fashion goods goes to the United States because so much is sent by parcel post and isn't tabulated.

The Board of Trade reports Britain exported about $28 million in clothing and footwear to the United States in 1959, excluding parcel post shipments. The Apparel and Fashion Industries Association, mother hen to the industry, estimates that two-thirds of that total—more than $18 million—was women's wear. Hosiery, knitwear and rainwear added another $9 million, plus parcels.

The U. S. rates as Britain's best ready-to-wear customer. A steady climb in American patronage is in the cards between now and 1965.

The reason does not appear to be better British salesmanship or new products. Rather, it is the growing awareness of American merchants of the importance of the "Made in Britain" and "Made in Europe" labels.

"They are searching for novelty, and we can give it to them at a price," said a British industry spokesman. "The snob stores have always imported. Now the little fellows are following suit, and our exports have really jumped."

The British have had to tailor their production somewhat to cater to American tastes. The key is the American penchant for lighter weight fabrics. Woolens especially have to be ounces lighter than the British domestic market will bear, which poses a double production problem for the mills.

Also the British have learned to leave off the buttons, bows, belts, and bangles which the British customers love, and the Americans can't stand. Britons shrug off the sizing problem as not too serious despite real differences in the shapes of Britons and Americans, especially around the seat.

Moreover, in line with the English tradition that clothing must last, Britons insist that their apparel is superior in quality and workmanship to all but the highest price American ready to wear.

British prices are lower. Labor is plentiful. The average work week is about 44 hours; wages about $28. Materials, except for some specialty synthetics, cost less, too.

However, there are signs that prices are inflating. So much so that the Chanceller of the Exchequer warns that continuation of the upward price trend might cost Britain her export markets.

Meanwhile, British women's outerwear production hit about $900 million last year, exclusive of knitwear. British women, already noticeably better dressed, are buying more apparel. Austerity is a thing of the past.

French couture pret a porter (ready to wear) got off the ground last year. The French industry sees clear skies over the American market.

Twelve or 18 months ago, exports to America were negligible—probably more than $200,000 to the United States and Canada combined. In 1959, shipments to the United States probably exceeded $1 million. The figure could double in the next twelve or eighteen months.

The French industry produces about nine million coats and suits, four million skirts, four million blouses, six million dresses, and just over one million peignoirs. That adds up to $275–$300 million a year, of which about 5 per cent goes for export.

There are about 2000 manufacturers, mostly around Paris. Only 10 do over $1 million in yearly volume, and 25 over $500,000. About 1300 do under $50,000.

A great many of these producing units depend on labor working at home. This partly artisan approach may be the reason for the trade's creative strength. But it also underscores an inherent structural weakness to mass produce on the American scale at low prices.

All of which leads Jacques Casalino, head of the export division of the Association des Maisons de Couture en Gros, to the belief that it is only in the upper price and quality brackets that the French can compete with American makers. In the low to medium range, American manufacturers are unbeatable, says Mr. Casalino.

But, he adds, a stylish French suit in a quality fabric and of impeccable finish will retail in the United States for $150–$200, compared with $250–$300 for a comparable American-made suit.

Mr. Casalino also takes issue with contentions that French makers can't or won't work to American size and production standards. This is being overcome. But it remains true that the individualism of French makers makes it tough to attain scientific operations and rigid standards.

The impetus of the European Common Market is making French manufacturers more export-minded and more price conscious.

Swiss apparel exports to the United States have more than doubled since 1955. In 1958, the figure was $2 million. It was higher in 1959.

Main articles sold to the United States are knitwear, sportswear and cocktail and cotton dresses.

The Swiss needle trades are as modern as any in the world. Switzerland pays the highest wages in Europe. But the industry is limited when it comes to huge production. Its total output is about $100 million, exclusive of knitwear, which amounts to roughly $50 million for the inland market and $10 million for export.

Total garment production is increasing at about a 5 per cent annual rate. Shipments to the United States are rising. Associated Merchandising Corp., for one, increased its purchases last year 97 per cent over 1958.

Generally, the Swiss are alert to the potentialities of the American market. They are hep to United States sizing demands, flexible as to styling requirements.

"If American buyers come once," say the Swiss, "they come again."

Duesseldorf

Europe rtw Hub

Duesseldorf, Germany. Accident, a trick of fate, a dash of need stirred with a political swizzle stick is the recipe which created a heady cocktail—Duesseldorf, the rtw center of Europe.

In the exhibition grounds located on the

banks of the Rhine here, four times a year fashion buyers flock into the halls to see, to buy, and to check out what European rtw is doing.

And rtw sales in Duesseldorf are racking up a solid $1.5 million a year.

An American buyer could do worse than come here as an introduction to Europe; everybody comes here anyway, and it could save a lot of traveling, even if going round the halls is hard on the feet. At the last showing, there were 900 exhibitors from 14 countries running the whole gamut of the rtw field, and the event has reached such stature that showing dates carry authority, causing even Paris to amend its Salon de Pret a Porter dates.

However, it wasn't always that way, and Duesseldorf's place in the world of fashion is an anachronism. Duesseldorf exerts no fashion influence, it has no fashion industry of consequence, it is not even a fashionable city.

But the facts speak for themselves—last year, over four Fashion Weeks, 4500 exhibitors from 14 countries showed 12,000 collections in seven halls covering 700,000 square feet.

Last fall, the Americans staged a combined exhibition sponsored by the U. S. Department of Commerce, and in April the French will move in with a showing by 24 firms under the auspices of the Paris Salon de Pret a Porter. Now the international giants are vying for favors here.

The Fashion Week has come a long way from its birth in 1948 when 30 manufacturers banded together through necessity on a "united we stand, divided we fall" basis.

Berlin, the traditional home of German rtw, was in dire straits, the airlift had barely kept the city alive, and the fashion industry commanded no priorities, and buyers could not even get in or out. So 30 manufacturers, Berlin and West German, decided on a showing in West Germany, and by accident settled on Duesseldorf. Their exhibition, in one small exhibition hall, was known as the IGEDO (short for the jaw-cracking name of the association they formed, Interessengemeinschaft Damenoberbekleidung eV) and this name has stuck, even though the name of the event has been changed to International Sales and Fashion Week (International Verkaufs und Mode Woche) run by a limited company of the same name.

The accidental choice of site turned out to be a good bet. As the German economy rocketed upwards, Duesseldorf became an administrative center for the burgeoning industrial Ruhr district, the exhibition grounds grew and grew, communications improved, and the city became a bustling metropolis. The airfield is only 10 minutes away by automobile, the Trans Europe Express railroad network centers on Duesseldorf, as does the autobahn road net.

However, the hotel problem is acute, and there are only two hotels in Duesseldorf of international standard, which has proved frustrating and embarrassing. Influential buyers and important fashion personalities are arbitrarily dumped into a private family during Fashion Week, which poses certain basic problems.

Reportedly, there will be a new hotel soon in the intercontinental chain, if the financial snags can be overcome. Pan American is not talking, but it is common knowledge it has the site, the city fathers have given planning permission, but backers are scarce.

As the Fashion Week grew, and progressed, so the whole flavor of the event changed. Three years ago the halls were partitioned up into blocks, corridors were lanes between sealed off booths, and there was an air of secrecy behind closed doors. Anybody walking through had no idea what was in the booth, beyond the name of the manufacturer, whether it was coats, or suits, or dresses, or maternity wear, or even what price ranges were shown. To compound the puzzlement of a bewildered stranger, when business was slack, exhibitors had the habit of standing a model girl in the open doorway, giving the place an air reminiscent of a red light district "somewhere in Europe."

Today, the booths are all open, the halls are bathed in clear light, and attractive displays invite buyers in to look around, sample, talk, and even buy.

Across the road, right on the banks of the river, the Rheinterrasse restaurant has come into being as a rtw venue. Some manufacturers, either needing more space than available in the halls, or unable to rent space, have moved over into plushier surroundings. This has a double advantage: Bigger shows can be staged, and if the buyers are bored with the collection, they can always look out at the busting barge traffic on the Rhine running right under the windows.

As of now, American buyers are rare birds

here, apart from a few buying office scouts checking the market, but the rest of the world homes in twice a year for the main collections. (The supplementary collections are more of a domestic event.) Every European country this side of the Iron Curtain is represented, and even then, Polish buyers have registered. Scandinavia, Switzerland, France, Benelux and Italy probably account for the biggest percentage of non-Germans checking in, backed up by contingents from Iceland, Lebanon, Syria, South Africa, Northern Rhodesia, Southern Rhodesia, and Latin America.

Not only are foreign buyers on the increase, exhibitors from outside Germany are climbing. Last fall, there were 150 non-German manufacturers, not including the American contingent.

The cocktail has been mixed, and poured from the shaker. Duesseldorf is now the European rtw center.

Hong Kong Hits the Gong On Right Note in Fashions

by J. W. Cohn

Hong Kong. Hong Kong's growing fashion industry exported an estimated $7 million (FOB) worth of dresses, loungewear, and sleepwear to the United States last year and hopes to double this figure within two years.

Long-term potential is seen for a wide range of sportswear, brocade hostess gowns, silk slacks, quality coordinates, and the more exotic luxury items in addition to the traditional Hong Kong exports.

This British Crown Colony is becoming a crossroads for the world of fashion where French and Italian designs meet up with American production know-how and the traditional cottons and silks of the Orient.

Hong Kong's own contribution to this international fashion melange is the manual dexterity of its low-wage workers. Nucleus of this sizable pool of skilled garment workers is a group of ex-Shanghai tailors, claimed to be the best in the Far East.

Some months ago, Stanley Marcus, of Neiman-Marcus, Dallas, on a trip through the Orient, bought some unusual silk fabrics in Thailand, brought them here to be made up into dresses from designs he had purchased at couture houses in Paris. This is how fashion operates in Hong Kong today.

In this age of jet travel, some American buyers continue right on around the world from the European fashion openings to have their models made up in Hong Kong of Japanese or Thai silk.

Fashions—not to be confused with the Colony's low-priced textile-garment industry—are attracting American retail buyers in practically every price bracket. Spiegel's 1963 catalog devotes its top page to silk dresses priced at $19.97, manufactured here by Overseas International, Ltd.

Mandarin Textiles, Ltd., maker of the Dynasty line, produces dresses that retail in the United States as high as $300. Its customers sound like a Who's Who of top American retail fashion houses—Neiman-Marcus, B. Altman, I. Magnin, Bullock's, Lord & Taylor, Marshall Field, J. L. Hudson, Garfinckel's. Other stores active in Hong Kong include Saks Fifth Avenue, Bonwit Teller, Peck & Peck, Carson Pirie Scott, and the Broadway Department Store.

There are lots of labels—some of the larger manufacturers produce two distinct lines, aimed at different price brackets—but all roads lead back to Hong Kong.

There is a sharp demarcation here between the "fashion" industry and the "apparel" industry. What separates the sheep from the goats are all those wonderfully dexterous hands available here at low wages. These hands produce the hand-finished silk dresses that retail in the

---

United States at below $30. That is what permits Dynasty to use foot-treadle machines almost exclusively.

The greater the handwork required the greater the advantage of the Hong Kong manufacturer. That is why dresses can be produced on a fashion level while most blouses must fall into the apparel category. A May Co. buyer here this season bought dresses at a fashion manufacturer here but could not fit this producer's blouses into his retail price brackets.

As Hong Kong grows as an international fashion center, it is gradually discarding the strictly Oriental flavor that originally marked its products. Oriental motifs are still popular in lounge-wear and after-five wear but they have largely disappeared from daytime dresses. Here the emphasis is on Western design with fabrics playing up the vivid Oriental colors.

After its skilled workers, Hong Kong's chief asset in the fashion field is its supplies of fabrics—cotton prints and lightweight silks from Japan; heavier silks from Thailand; locally-produced rayon-silk brocades; silk-wool blends from Italy; linens from Ireland. There is small start being made to get away from the traditional silks and cottons. Double-knit jerseys are being made locally. Experiments are going on in wool and synthetics. However, at present the great majority of fashion goods are being produced in the traditional silks and cottons.

Black cloud over the fashion industry is the skyrocketing silk market. Silk fabrics have had five price increases since last August. This greatly adds to the retail price of the garment since the retail price in the United States is three to four times the FOB price here. Some manufacturers say their $39.95 silk dresses have been forced into the $49.95 bracket in the United States because of increased costs for silk fabrics.

Hong Kong's great lack is style creativity. Practically all styling here originates in the United States—either directly or modified from European originals. An executive of the Associated Merchandising Corporation recently expressed himself here as "fed up" with the shirtwaist dresses being shipped from Hong Kong.

"We're looking for something different this time," he said. "We want some diversification."

Most of the Chinese manufacturers here regard designers a waste of money when copying is so easy. Even the larger American-controlled firms depend largely upon designs from the United States, usually supplied by store buyers. Normal form is for patterns to be sent here, made up into samples, and sent back to the United States for final approval before being put into production. Fabrics are also submitted to the American headquarters for approval. A line may be in the planning stage six months before the first finished dress appears.

However, there is a growing awareness of the importance of design here. Dynasty has a head designer in New York, Doris Saunders, formerly with Lord & Taylor.

These Designers Made Fifty Years of Fashion History

As the pace of fashion quickened during the past 50 years, an increasing number of dressmakers all over the world emerged from anonymity. Leaders emerged in the wholesale ranks in America as well as in the traditional couture center, Paris. A few designers have stood head and shoulders above the rest. These have captured in their designs the spirit of the times, and their influence has set a trend for a period, not just a season. The ten creators discussed on these pages have helped establish the look of the past half-century.

Gabrielle Chanel's signature and look was as well known at the end of the 1950's as it was in the 1920's when she made the first short dresses in "humble" fabrics, like tweeds and jerseys.

Setting her stamp on a way of dressing, as

Reprinted by permission of *Women's Wear Daily*, July 13, 1960. Copyright 1960, Fairchild Publications, Inc.

Gabrielle Chanel

well as exerting a strong influence on other designers, Chanel is as responsible as any other individual for the look of the 1920's, and the movement away from corsets, ankle-length skirts, heavy hats, and long suit jackets. Her revolutionary simple short skirts, low waistlines, and loose jackets were easy to wear and to move in.

Chanel started her fashion career as a milliner, setting up shop shortly before World War I in the Rue Cambon, where she is still located. Her special look came in after the war, continuing until World War II, when she closed her house. The Chanel look was noticeably absent from the fashions of the 1940's, to return with strength in the mid-1950's. At 71, she reopened her couture house in 1954. By 1957, the open jacket suit and loose overblouse that she has consistantly endorsed was the big fashion everywhere.

The fake pearls, elaborate costume jewelry and sweaters that she put into fashion orbit had never died down, and the underplayed "poor look" that she catapulted into high fashion had become an accepted way of dressing.

While she has put her stamp on the loose-jacket suit and the jersey sports dress, Chanel has also always done evening fashions. Lace dresses are her perennial favorites.

Fashion is not always synonymous with change. It sometimes has a timeless quality that defies change.

Prominent exponent of this kind of fashion was **Captain Edward Henry Molyneux.** Born in London in 1894, he scored an immediate success when he opened his own salon in Paris in 1919, drawing an international clientele. His reputation was based on the fact that he "designs clothes for ladies." Fond of horses, dogs, and sports, he entertained extensively, knew the life a "lady" lived.

He explained that he designed by visualizing a particular woman in a special environment, engaged in a definite activity. He then selected the appropriate materials and color, making sure that "the modern note was present."

Disapproving of "costumy" clothes, he felt

Captain
Edward Henry Molyneux

that the woman should stand out, not the dress. Result was a classic style, simple and direct. Lots of pleats, supple jackets, slender dinner gowns were his forte.

He constantly gained prestige during the 1920's, and during the early 1930's was rivaled by Patou for the greatest volume in the French couture; by the end of that decade, he was ahead.

An art student, he learned the dressmaking business from Lady Duff Gordon who had an enormous vogue as Lucille just before World War I with her delicate chiffons, elaborated with ribbons, laces, and embroideries. Returning after the war, he found his emphasis on simplicity in conflict with hers, and decided to branch out on his own. His house closed in 1940; reopened in 1946, and closed again in 1951.

Elsa Schiaparelli

A modernist, not awed by tradition, **Elsa Schiaparelli** was delighted to try anything new, which ranged from original closures on suit jackets (dog-leash hooks, leather love-bird links) to knickers for ski wear (in 1937, anticipating a fashion which made an impression during the 1959 season, and promises to be increasingly important in 1960–1961).

One year younger than the century, Schiaparelli launched her fashion career with her hand-knit sweaters in modern designs in the 1920's. A big success among women with a flair for fashion, they inspired her to branch out to sports clothes in 1927. She added evening styles in 1930.

She would try her hand at designing anything, and in the 1950's made arrangements for wholesale production in America of lingerie, scarfs, stockings, and gloves bearing her name.

Her boutique in Paris carried accessories, perfume, beach and sportswear, lingerie—and table linen.

As a result of her daring, she left her mark in many areas of fashion: Jewelry (a bracelet carrying perfume was one of her ideas), fabrics (she was known for her exciting prints and use of tweeds), and sportswear. A jersey maillot for swimming in 1931, long stockings worn with pale corduroy shorts in 1937 (a precursor of tights and Bermuda shorts), and knee breeches for after-ski in 1952 were some of her off-beat ideas which clicked.

Gilbert Adrian boosted California as a fashion center, first with the glamour clothes of the film siren, and then with top-priced wholesale fashions.

He is associated with the silhouette that dominated the 1940's—broad, padded shoulders balancing a tapered hipline. In defense of this silhouette, he became involved in a tremendous controversy over the Dior-inspired New Look.

Sloping shoulders and padded hiplines brought forth his strongest attack, as he defended the "trim, square-shoulder suit."

His geometric handling and mitering of stripes, collarless jackets, slot seams, and waistline tie closings were other characteristics of his suit styling which were widely influential.

Born in Naugatuck, Conn. in 1903, Adrian served no long, tiresome fashion apprenticeship. A costume he designed for a fellow art

Gilbert Adrian

student to wear at the Grand Prix Ball in Paris won praise from Irving Berlin, and was followed by commissions to do costumes for Berlin's Music Box Revues. Soon afterward, he went to California, where he spent sixteen years with Metro-Goldwyn-Mayer.

Among the stars for whom he designed were Joan Crawford, whose clothes in "Letty Linton" in 1932 were widely copied, Greta Garbo, Katharine Hepburn, Rosalind Russell, and Norma Shearer.

He left films in 1939, and showed his first custom and wholesale collection in 1942. Cotton evening dresses, shirtwaist dinner dresses and one-sided drapery were some of his contributions.

Adrian retired in 1952, and died in September, 1959, at 56.

A spokesman for American designers, he was one of the first Americans to be copied by other native designers.

The first note of freedom for the feminine figure was struck by **Paul Poiret.** He emerged from the nineteenth century ateliers of Maison Doucet and Worth, to open his own shop in Paris in 1904. His daring approach to fashion made him a dominant influence during the years preceding and immediately following World War I. Some of the wild iconoclasm that was shaking the fine arts was translated into fashion terms, resulting in clothes with a new sense of drama, a fresh point of view.

The brash, clash colors of the Fauves (violent reds, greens, violets, oranges, and citrus yellows); exotic influences (primitive sculpture and painting, lavish Oriental motifs, the Russian ballet) and a new silhouette turned fashion to uncharted roads.

Trouser dresses and puffy harem skirts were

Paul Poiret

some of the Eastern themes that Poiret adapted for the Western world.

His major contribution to the silhouette was that he freed women from their corsets. Though he eased the silhouette in some areas, he shackled it in another, namely hobbling the skirt at the hemline.

His spectacular personal life, sometimes rivaling the luxury-living of the Oriental potentates who served as a source of fashion inspiration, presaged the press agentry that characterizes certain aspects of fashion today.

Especially identified with pre-World War I fashions is his high-waisted drapery that marked one of the many Empire revivals, his tiered lampshade-skirt sheer dresses and his dinner dresses with bat sleeve capelike wraps known internationally as dolmans.

Today, his name is invoked most frequently in relation to boldly colored, primary print motifs.

By 1924, his influence was definitely waning. When everything tended to simplicity, as Chanel led the way to the little boy look after World War I, he continued his Oriental lavishness.

Mme. Vionnet introduced not only a new silhouette, but a new technique to the fashion world. Her big contribution: The dress cut on the bias. This dressmaking technique continues prominent today in the work of such Vionnet pupils as Mme. Gres, Mad Carpentier, and Jacques Griffe. When it was introduced in the 1920's, it helped revolutionize and modernize the entire concept of dressing.

The effect was of overwhelming simplicity based on the bias principle.

On a wooden mannequin, two and a half feet high, which she later bequeathed to Jacques Griffe, she worked out her simple-looking cuts, which were translated by her associates into full-scale clothes.

When the fashion silhouette was flat, she worked in the round, so that her styles reflected the curves of a woman's body. Her bias construction permitted the elimination of foundation garments and fastenings, and freed the silhouette.

Among the styles with which she was associated: The chiffon handkerchief dress, halter and cowl necklines, the hemstitched blouse. She also liked long, fitted evening coats.

Mme Vionnet

Eighty-three years old today, Mme. Vionnet started her fashion career with Callot Soeurs in London, was "premiere" at Doucet, where she was known as Mme. Madeleine, and opened her own shop just before the war. Closing during World War I, she reopened in 1919, and proceeded to be a dominant fashion influence during the 1920's.

Among her nonfashion contributions was the provision of advanced social services for her workers, along with medical clinics and a gymnasium. She also organized the couturiers into an association against copying.

Toward the end of the 1930's, her influence dwindled, and she closed her house in 1939, at the beginning of World War II.

Informal in her manner and her approach to fashion, **Claire McCardell** brought fresh individuality and prestige to the characteristically American fashion field, sportswear.

Claire McCardell

Credited with starting the "casual American look," she concentrated on comfort and function, with the result that she established a special style.

She always claimed that she designed for herself, and always wore her own clothes. Her tastes and demands happened to coincide with those of many other American women who were as proud of their wholesale "McCardells" as other women were of their Paris couture styles. The fact that a "McCardell" endured for years was part of its appeal. And though widely copied, the original retained its individual stamp.

Her first big success was the monastic dress, a loose, flowing style which the wearer belted-in herself. This flooded the wholesale market in 1938. Characteristics of a McCardell dress were: surplice bodice, Empire waistline, hook and eye closing, halter neckline, little ties which could be varied, unpressed pleats. The dirndl for town-wear, the "Popover," an easy-to-get-into wrap dress evolved during the war as an aid to the hostess when she had to do without servants, and ballet shoes were some of her other inspirations. She liked wrapped waistlines, usable pockets, the kind of stitching associated with blue jeans. She made the shirtwaist dress her special province.

She gave a new lift to fabrics, especially cottons, which she used in distinctive colors and patterns.

Born in 1905 in Frederick, Md., McCardell joined the staff of Robert Tuck in 1929, and went with him to Townley two years later. Except for a stint at Hattie Carnegie, she continued there until her death in 1958.

The symmetry of **Christian Dior's** career as the head of the couture house that carried his name circled the decade from 1947 to 1957, during which period practically every collection was front page news.

His first collection, in February, 1947, put the term "New Look" into the general vocabulary. The designer, who had worked for Lelong since 1941, and with Piguet before that, was unknown to the general public. That first collection made his name a household word. It also made fashion a fighting word, as housewives organized clubs to defend the lingering short skirts, and men protested the descent of the hemline.

Nevertheless, the look took, and natural shoulder lines, flared full skirts, fitted waistlines, and suit jackets that were snug above stiff peplums became the prevailing fashion. This curving figure line, with echoes of the hourglass shape of the past, provided a dramatic change from the skimpy, short, broad-shouldered look that had endured with few changes since beginning of the decade. Wartime fabric economies were erased by lavish yardage—and Paris was again established as the world's fashion hub.

Subsequent collections continued to make news, and to help change the shape of the silhouette everywhere. Dark stockings were introduced in the August 1947, line. Scissors panels appeared the following year, and the "ligne verticale," pleated, straight dresses, were the newsmakers in February 1950, showing

Christian Dior

In that same year, Balenciaga's famous brown lace dress, a two-piece style that bypassed the waistline, broke with a shock on the fashion world, and was the direct ancestor of the numerous unwaisted styles that succeeded it.

Balenciaga started his couture house in Paris in 1937; previously, with houses in Madrid and San Sebastian, he had been a heavy purchaser of Paris models. His Spanish background still lingers in his rich embroideries, heavy passementeries, braids, fringes, and laces.

One sign of his mastery of dressmaking is that his line develops from season to season.

In the mid-1940's, Balenciaga was a proponent of the curvy, fitted suit that Dior popularized. In 1947, he introduced the barrel coat silhouette, which he worked over in ensuing years. In 1948, his contribution was the high-waisted coat; two years later, he introduced

that the master was experimenting with a straighter silhouette. The counter revolution in 1953, when Dior shortened skirts, also made news, as did his 1954 H line.

A major contribution of Dior to the fashion world was the use of elaborate inner constructions. His wide skirts inspired petticoats and his small waistlines, belts. He also influenced blouses.

A designer's designer, **Cristobal Balenciaga** de Eisequirre, while aggressively shunning the spotlight, has turned out to be a strong influence on some of the world's most smartly dressed women as well as on other designers. In 1951, his fitted front, loose back coats and suits set the ball rolling for an easier silhouette after the tautness of the New Look. This move, developed in subsequent collections, eventually changed the suit look all over the world.

Cristobal Balenciaga
de Eisequirre

back blousing. All-around bodice blousing was the news in 1952, and hipline belts appeared the following year. By 1954, the loose jacket suit had crystallized, and "demi-fit" was accepted internationally.

Spare, unwaisted tunics appeared in 1955, and bloused tunics the next year. The straight line, with no waistline demarcation, was the rule by 1957, the year of the chemise.

Recently, "the master" has shown some tendency to closer fit.

Acknowledged dean of American designers, **Norman Norell** generated the same kind of enthusiasm with his first collection bearing his own name in June of this year as he did with his first collection with Traina-Norell in 1941, when he was said to have exploded on the season "like an electrical storm."

The thunderbolt this time was his divided skirts for town wear, substituting a type of pants for skirts.

Some of his enthusiasms, which turn up repeatedly in his collections: Slinky, beaded long evening dresses, easy-waisted fashions (he had a middy dress as early as 1944), tunics, Empire waistlines (with no indentation at the normal waist), shirtwaist dresses, and fabrics that cling to the figure, like jerseys and crepes.

As a true style leader, Norell is often seasons ahead of his time, appealing to the woman with fashion daring. He also is watched closely by other designers.

Long known as one of the top-priced wholesale designers, Norell designs clothes that are "so simple only the initiated can see in them justification for their altitudinous prices."

While he has been established for two decades in the wholesale field, Norell has had diverse experience. Born in 1900, he came to New York from Noblesville, Indiana, in 1919 to attend art schools.

In the early 1920's, he designed costumes for Valentino and Gloria Swanson films, then worked with the Brooks Costume Company. After a few years with Charles Armour, he spent twelve years with Hattie Carnegie, where his name became known.

An articulate observer of the social scene, he considered the chemise a characteristic mid-twentieth century fashion, has had one in his collections for years. In his newest collections, he continues an exponent of the loosened line.

Norman Norell

Questions for Review and Discussion

1. How does a typical Paris Haute Couture house differ from a typical Seventh Avenue apparel firm?
2. Do you agree with Mr. Marcus, President of Neiman Marcus, who said that "We have some great creative fashion talent in the United States, but our industrial climate is not as favorable as Paris' to the growth and flowering of such talent."? Explain.
3. Why do couturiers show their new collections to trade buyers before they show them to their private clients, when the latter are so important to them?
4. Couture houses usually charge representatives of manufacturing firms a higher "caution fee" than they charge retail buyers. How would you explain this practice?
5. Does the practice of line-for-line Paris copies differ from that of style piracy? How?
6. From your personal observation of Paris line-for-line promotions by retail stores, which retailer do you think does the best job? Explain.
7. Has the Italian couture made much progress since the reading "Italy, the Tempestuous Decade" was written? Explain.
8. Do you believe that Paris-designed styles are as meaningful to American customers as they seem to be to the American fashion industry? Why?
9. How can you explain the interest by American stores in European ready-to-wear imports?
10. How does imported ready-to-wear compare with domestic items which retail at the same price? Consider styling, fit, value, workmanship, etc.

SECTION

V

The Retailers of Fashion

Retailing is the final step along the road that fashion merchandise travels on its way to the ultimate consumer. It is also the process that makes economically meaningful the work of the talented designers and efficient producers who have contributed to the creation of fashion products.

In the United States there are more than 1.8 million business establishments devoted to all types of retailing—stores, mail-order firms, and door-to-door sellers. Available information about these establishments does not permit an exact count of how many of these establishments, or how much of their total volume, should be considered as part of the fashion business. It can, however, be narrowed down to those who deal exclusively in apparel and accessories, and to those who deal in general merchandise (and do a substantial amount of their business in the fashion field). When this is done, one finds that those retail establishments that have at least a significant interest in fashion merchandise account for more than 10 per cent of the 1.8 million retail outlets; that they employ the services of more than one-quarter of the ten million men and women engaged in retailing; and that their combined sales of fashion and other merchandise constitute more than one-sixth of the $262 billion total annual retail sales in this country.[1]

This section is concerned with the development of fashion retailing in America, and with the different kinds of retail outlets that are engaged in the distribution of women's apparel. The readings which are included illustrate the fashion appeal and merchandising policies of different types of well-known retailers.

Fashion Retailing in the Past

Retailing is as old as recorded history, if not older. Forerunners of many of our modern types of stores existed in the days of the Greeks and Romans. There

[1] Audits and Surveys, Inc., New York, N. Y., 1964–1965 Eleventh Annual Sample Census of Distribution.

have always been traders and peddlers traveling by ship, in caravans, and on foot; there were shopkeepers in the earliest towns.[2]

Many of America's great fashion retailers of today came into being in such a manner—as peddlers, small shopkeepers, and custom-tailors. Brooks Brothers, for example, was founded in 1818 as a men's tailoring shop; the Gimbel organization, which owns Saks Fifth Avenue, had its beginnings with a store opened in 1942, in Vincennes, Indiana, by Adam Gimbel who had started his retail career as a traveling peddler; Lord and Taylor, New York, began as a general dry goods store in 1826. Arnold Constable, New York, was established in 1825 as a shop specializing in the sale of imported goods, mostly textiles.[3]

As towns and cities grew and factories began to produce goods in quantity, a country-wide network of retail merchants developed and assumed the role of getting goods from the producers to the ultimate customers. By the late nineteenth century, many of our modern forms of retailing and most of this country's large volume retailers were well on their way. There were specialty stores like Filene's of Boston, established in 1873; department stores like Macy's in New York, founded in 1858; and mail-order houses like Sears Roebuck and Company which began with a watch and jewelry mail-order catalogue in 1886 in Minneapolis.[4] There were also variety stores such as Woolworth's, whose first store in Utica, New York, in 1879, featuring small wares at 5¢ and 10¢, was a failure; and chain stores like the A & P food stores which started as a tea chain in 1859.[5] Supermarkets, discount stores and suburban branches of department and specialty stores did not make their appearance until well into the twentieth century, as did shopping centers.

Custom-Salons in the Nineteenth Century. The merchandise offerings of these early retailers could hardly be classified as "fashion goods," since they consisted mainly of staple and utilitarian products. The production of fashionable apparel was still largely in the hands of European couture houses and of American tailoring and dressmaking firms who bought the sketches or originals of Paris models along with the French fabrics from which they would make the reproductions for well-to-do customers.[6] Toward the end of the nineteenth century, a few exclusive big-city stores such as Marshall Field in Chicago and John Wanamaker and B. Altman in New York got into custom-dressmaking and began to send their own buyers abroad to purchase the latest French fashions.[7] Some of the stores whose names today are synonymous with fashion built the foundation of their fame in this manner—through their custom salons where people of means could order fashionable garments of good quality and workmanship. The retailing of ready-to-wear, however, awaited the developments of textile and apparel production and it was not until late in the nineteenth century that significant

---

[2] Dr. Paul H. Nystrom, writing in the *Encyclopedia of the Social Sciences,* Vol. 12, New York, The Macmillan Company, 1934, p. 346 *ff.*

[3] J. W. Ferry, *A History of the Department Stores,* New York, The Macmillan Company, 1960, pp. 35–74.

[4] Tom Mahoney, *The Great Merchants,* New York, Harper, 1955. Also see Ferry, *op. cit.*

[5] *Ibid.*

[6] "Fifty Years of Keeping Step With Fashion," Ethel Traphagen in the *Department Store Economist,* January 1961.

[7] John B. Swinney, *Merchandising of Fashions,* New York, The Ronald Press, 1942, p. 5.

amounts of manufactured apparel were even available for sale in stores. Department and specialty stores began to experiment with the new "store clothes" and as the wholesale fashion industry developed so did retail ready-to-wear departments.

Early Ready-To-Wear Retailing. The early years of ready-to-wear retailing were difficult ones for dry goods merchants who, up to that time, had had little or no experience with the vagaries of fashion. Apparel departments generally showed a financial loss which had to be made up by profits in other more staple lines. Apparel producers themselves were newcomers to the fashion business and could not offer much help. Together the retailers and manufacturers learned by trial and error. Custom-made clothing was still important but it was steadily giving way before the growing and constantly improving ready-to-wear clothing industry. By 1920, however, ready-made apparel departments were firmly established in all big-city department and specialty stores and in most general stores in smaller communities.

During the twenties, many department stores leased their apparel departments to ready-to-wear specialists who would install and manage an apparel operation in return for from 10 to 15 per cent of the sales. Some of these leasing concerns operated in as many as fifty stores, mainly in the Middle West.[8] During the 1929 depression, most of them went out of business and today, there are relatively few in the department stores.

Fashion Authority of Early Retailers. In the beginning of ready-to-wear retailing, the owners of great fashion stores would work with the manufacturers to produce their ready-to-wear designs to meet the styling needs of individual stores.[9] Many retailers helped manufacturers to get started by bringing them Paris models to copy and starting them off with substantial orders.[10] Although this is still a practice in the industry today, with production on so large a scale it is the exception rather than the rule. In those days, also, the retailer was the main source of fashion information for customers, as well as manufacturers; there were few movies, few telephones, no television, and only a few publications to keep people up-to-date on what should be produced or worn. Long before the fashion show, the bridal counselor, and the college shop advisors were commonplace, great department stores were publishing fashion magazines which they mailed to customers. John Wanamaker began publication of a magazine in 1909, Marshall Field and Company in 1914.[11] As fashion traveled its long, slow route from Paris to Podunk, customers looked to their favorite retail stores to bring it into their towns when the time was right for it.

Fashion Retailing Today

We have historically discussed fashion retailers in terms of a limited number of department and fine specialty stores. The years between 1950 and 1960, how-

[8] Swinney, *op. cit.*, p. 7.

[9] Lew Hahn, *Stores, Merchants and Customers: A Philosophy of Retailing*, New York, Fairchild Publications, 1952, pp. 177–182.

[10] Swinney, *op. cit.*, p. 5.

[11] J. Appel, *Business Biography of John Wanamaker*, New York, The Macmillan Company, 1930, pp. 114*ff*; and L. Wendt and H. Kogan, *Give the Lady What She Wants*, Chicago, Rand McNally Co., 1952, p. 293.

ever, witnessed what many refer to as a "revolution in retailing" and left many changes in its wake.[12] Today every conceivable type of retailer pours a steady stream of fashion goods into American homes.

In terms of their merchandise assortments, the retail stores that sell fashion merchandise today divide into two classes: specialty shops and general merchandise stores. In terms of the quality of goods they carry and the degree of service they render to the customer, the variety is infinite. There is everything from the bargain-basement type, in which the customers must scrabble through piles of merchandise to find what they want, to the salons where customers are seated and waited upon by expert salespeople. There are cash-and-carry stores, in which the relationship between customer and retailer begins and ends at the cash register; and stores that deliver, charge, and send on approval. There are also nonstore retailers, who do their selling by catalogue or door-to-door solicitation; and there are facilities in many stores for buying by mail or telephone.

There are little "mom-and-pop" stores that sell $50 or less a day and there are large-scale retailers who employ thousands of people and sell as much as $1 million worth of goods on some days. There are retail stores owned and operated by manufacturers, particularly in the men's wear field. In fact, there are almost as many different types of fashion retailers as there are different kinds of people.

Table 1 Retail Sales of Women's and Children's Clothing by Type of Retail Outlet (in Millions of Dollars)

Year	Total Sales	Department Stores	Women's Ready-to-Wear Stores	Family Clothing Stores	Other Retail Outlets
1958	13,659	4941	4462	1127	3129
1959	14,509	5379	4724	1185	3221
1960	14,754	5549	4677	1233	3295
1961	14,912	5793	4575	1268	3276
1963 [a]	16,500	6000	5600	1400	3500

Source: Trends and Prospects in the Women's Garment Industry 1959–1962, Research Department, International Ladies Garment Workers Union, New York, p. 2 for 1958 to 1961.
[a] Estimates.

The fashion industry's close watch upon the consumer is made easier as a direct result of the buying and selling activities of fashion's retailers. Large and small alike, while seeking goods that are acceptable to their particular customers, they act as a sounding board for producers—a series of listening posts on the consumer front. At the same time, in the course of their selling activities, they serve as a medium for educating and informing the public about fashion and, by the very nature of their business, do much to stimulate consumer demand for fashion products.

Department Stores. The department store is a descendant of the trading post

[12] For an analysis of changes see J. Wingate and A. Corbin, "Changing Patterns in Retailing," Homewood, Ill., Richard D. Irwin, 1956. Also see E. Gold, *The Dynamics of Retailing*, New York, Fairchild Publications, 1963.

and general stores of pioneer days. Many of the large and well-known department stores in the United States today came into being between 1840 and 1880 when the growth of cities and the increase in mass production created a need for this type of retailing.[13] One of its basic appeals to the consumer was that she could purchase under one roof merchandise for herself, her family, and her home.

By definition, a department store employs at least 25 people, and handles a wide variety of merchandise lines including home furnishings, apparel for the family, and household linens or dry goods.[14] Establishments which meet these criteria except as to number of employees, are classified as general merchandise stores. Department store executives add several points to this bare description: that the merchandise is offered for sale in separate departments, each of which is administered by a buyer or department manager; that sales service is provided; that credit, return, and delivery privileges are offered; that the customer may shop in person, by telephone, or by mail.

Department stores may be independently owned, or be parts of chains. If they regularly carry some home furnishings, but omit major categories of furniture and household appliances, the trade refers to them as junior department stores. If they do not offer the full complement of customer services, regardless of how complete their range of departments may be, the department store community refers to them as discount stores or mass merchandisers, or by any name except department stores. Manufacturers, too, tend to avoid attaching the department store label to stores that do not meet the criteria laid down above.

Having thus delineated the department store, we can proceed to its functions in the fashion business. From the customer's point of view, the department store is an important source of authentic information about fashion. Its advertising and its stocks permit her to browse and develop her own ideas; its refund policies permit her to buy with confidence. The offer of money back if the merchandise is unsatisfactory, or if it merely fails to please the family at home, has been a cornerstone of department store policy for at least a century.[15]

In the fashion industries, the department store represents a large volume of sales and accounts for more than one-third of the total retail business in women's and children's apparel.[16] It also offers producers an opportunity to expose their merchandise, often with considerable drama, to the public. It is not at all uncommon for department stores to have auditoriums or other facilities for staging fashion shows, or for them to stage shows outside the store for clubs and charities. They advertise, they display, they bring customer traffic into the store. Since they cover so many fields of merchandise, they can generate more traffic than a specialized clothing store; a woman who comes in to buy shoes for her child, or a lamp for her living room, may see and buy on impulse some fashion item that was not on her original shopping list. Department stores cater chiefly to women and typically do over 40 per cent of their business in feminine apparel

[13] See Ferry, *op. cit.*, for a history of American department stores.

[14] The retailing definitions in this section are those of the Bureau of the Census used in the 1963 Census of Retail Trade.

[15] Appel, *op. cit.*, p. 42.

[16] "Trends and Prospects in the Women's Garment Industry 1959–1962," Research Department, I.L.G.W.U. Also see Dr. R. Entenberg, *The Changing Competitive Position of Department Stores,* University of Pittsburgh Press, 1961.

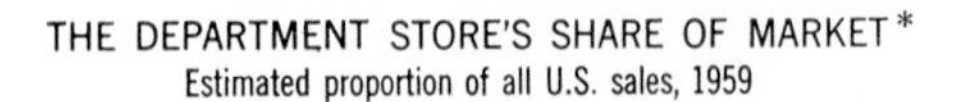

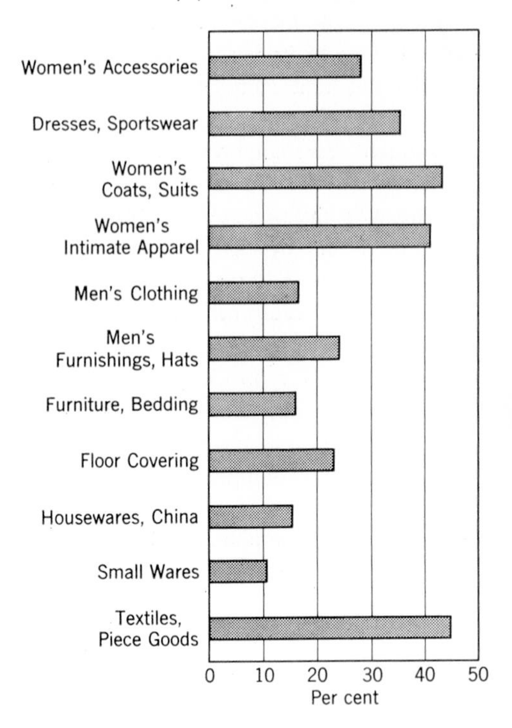

Source: University of Pittsburgh; after The National Industrial Conference Board, New York.

and accessories. Even in the departments which handle men's furnishings, women do a large part of the purchasing.

Preceding sections of this book have mentioned the trend to giantism in the textile and apparel industries. The same trend exists in the department store field, but it is not always apparent. We have a few individual retail stores whose tremendous size is obvious: Macy's in New York; Hudson's in Detroit; and Marshall Field & Company, Chicago. We also have the mail-order houses and chain stores, among whom the largest reckon their sales in billions, and the lesser lights, in hundreds of millions.

Less clearly recognizable to the layman is the trend to bigness among department stores through merger and affiliation. This is because a department store, when acquired by an ownership group or merged with a store in another city, usually retains its original name and personality. Thus, the largest of the department store groups, Federated Stores, has no store named Federated; it has Abraham & Straus in Brooklyn; the F. & R. Lazarus & Company store in Columbus, and so on. The Allied Stores, another large department store group, has no store named Allied; it has such stores as Jordan Marsh & Company in Boston and Stern Brothers in New York. The Macy and Gimbel groups have some units bearing the names of the parent stores, and others with such names as Davison-Paxon (the Macy affiliate in Atlanta), or Saks Fifth Avenue (under Gimbel ownership).

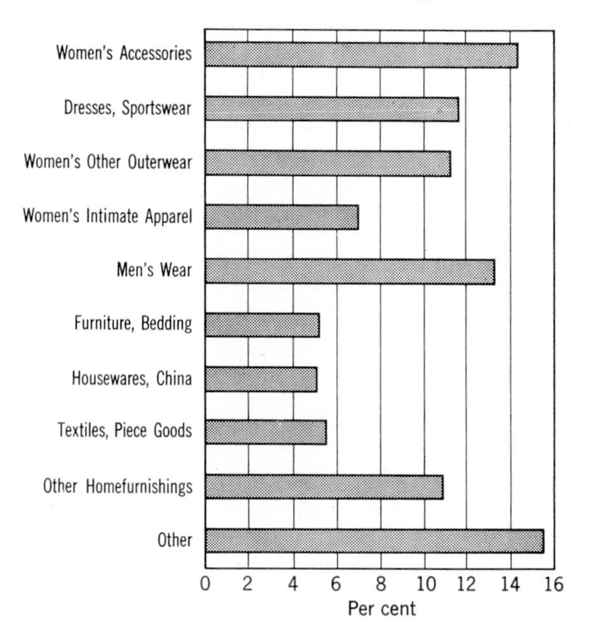

Source: Board of Governors, Federal Reserve System; after The National Industrial Conference Board, New York.

Although only one department store group, the Federated Stores, has crossed the billion-dollar mark in annual sales, the purchasing power of such groups in the fashion markets is enormous. They are thus in a position to develop brand names of their own, in fashion merchandise and other lines. So, too, are some of the remaining large, many-branched independent department stores. And so, also, are large and small independent stores when they team up with other non-competing retailers throughout the country. Just about every department store or departmentalized specialty store has a buying office to serve it in the fashion markets. By marshalling the buying power of its subscribing stores, the buying office can create a private brand that its client stores can use, each one in its own trading area.

Retail private brands for fashion merchandise are most common for hosiery, lingerie, sportswear, shoes, cosmetics, coats, and suits. Retailers cite as reasons for fostering private brands: control of price, better net profit, control of quality, and the development of distinctive merchandise, among other reasons. Against these advantages in having a brand of one's own, the retailer must weigh the time and cost of establishing acceptance for his brand instead of featuring a brand for which the manufacturer's national advertising is paving the way.[17]

[17] For a discussion of brand developments in department stores, see B. Judelle, "National Brands and Private Brands in the Fashion Departments," *Stores Magazine,* September 1962, National Retail Merchants Association, 100 West 31 Street, New York.

Chain Store Retailers. In the retail trade, the term "chain" is applied to a group of four or more specialized or general merchandise stores when they are centrally owned; when the units are very similar in physical appearance and in lines of merchandise carried; and when the individual stores are managed from the chain's central or regional headquarters where the buying, selling, and other operating policies are formulated. A department or specialty store which has several branches, or becomes part of a centrally owned group of other stores, is not usually described as a chain—it is called an ownership group, a parent store with branches, or a group of sister stores. In part, this bit of semantics harks back to the 1920's and 1930's when most department and specialty stores were individually owned and when most chains granted little or no autonomy to their local managers.[18] The situation has changed sharply since then. The chains have individualized their units more and more; department and specialty stores have sprouted branches and affiliated with units in other cities and even in other parts of the country. But the semantics remain. To retail professionals, chain store retailing continues to mean standardized stores and merchandise and remote central management.

From the point of view of the popular-priced fashion business, the years from 1920 to 1929 may well be called "the chain store era." During the preceding decade, the manufacturing and retailing of blouses, or waists as they were then called, was at a peak. Blouses were fashionable and blouses were also moderately priced in comparison with the ready-to-wear dresses which were then being retailed in department stores from $50 upwards. Induced by the demand of lower-income customers for lower-priced ready-made apparel, chains of "waist stores" made their appearance in the form of small specialized shops in the trading areas of large cities.[19] About 1919 blouses went out of fashion and the waist manufacturers turned to making dresses which could retail from $16.95 to $25.00 and which were lower in price than those being featured by the department and large specialty stores.[20] It seemed quite natural that the waist chains should add these popular-priced dresses to their merchandise assortments; with department stores catering to middle-income families, there was little competition for chains in the popular-priced apparel field. This period saw the start of many apparel chains that emphasized lower-priced ready-to-wear and catered to the class of new "working women" who had entered business during the manshortage of World War I. A notable example of an early waist chain is the Lerner Shops, which got its start during these years and which is one of today's largest apparel chains.[21] By 1929 there were reportedly 2240 chain units specializing in women's apparel [22] and featuring low-priced merchandise as a means of attracting customers.

These same years witnessed the peak growth of many other types of chain

[18] Godfrey M. Lebhar, *Chain Stores in America,* Chain Store Publishing Corp., New York, 1959, p. 287.

[19] Swinney, *op. cit.,* p. 25.

[20] *Ibid.* (Authors' note: Many of the most successful dress manufacturers of the 1920's and 1930's evolved from these early waist producers.)

[21] Lerner's 1964 sales were given as $235,987,000 in published financial statements of the McCrory Corporation, of which the chain is now a division.

[22] Phillips and Duncan, *op. cit.,* p. 206. (Authors' note: According to this same source there were 3062 millinery chain units in 1929.)

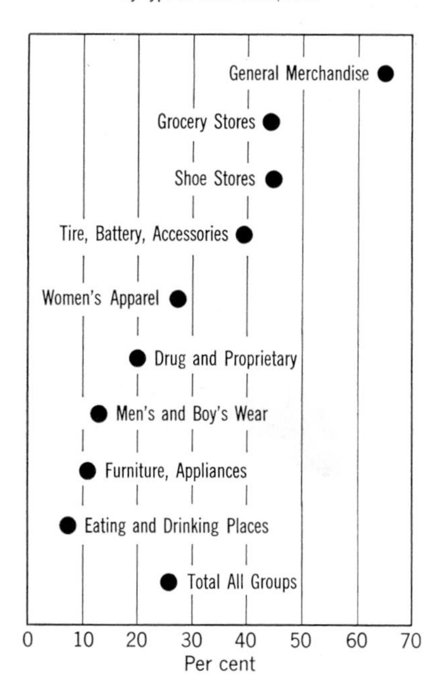

From: "1963 Graphic Guide to Consumer Markets," The National Industrial Conference Board, New York.

retailers that currently play an important role in the distribution of lower-priced apparel products.[23] Large mail-order houses like Sears Roebuck and Company established chain store divisions which since then have accounted for the largest percentage of their considerable sales volume; many of today's big shoe chains came into being during these years; and other previously established chains like the variety stores of Woolworth's experienced great sales increases during the twenties. Chains entered field after field of merchandise which, until then, had been considered quite unsuitable for their methods of operation, and by 1929 were doing almost 30 per cent of the total retail business in the United States.[24]

After World War II, many types of chain organization began to broaden their merchandise assortments and extend their price ranges upward. Variety stores, such as F. W. Woolworth and W. T. Grant, are today a mass outlet for many products of the fashion industry—undergarments, foundations, hosiery, sleepwear, gloves, handbags, costume jewelry, dresses, and sportswear among others.[25] The chain divisions of retail giants like Sears Roebuck and Company and Montgomery Ward and Company, are giving prime locations in their stores

[23] See Lebhar, *op. cit.*, for a detailed analysis of chain store developments.
[24] Phillips and Duncan, *op. cit.*, p. 205.
[25] *Variety Store Merchandiser*, December 1964, p. 50, estimates variety store sales of women's and misses' ready-to-wear as $383 million a year, or nearly 8 per cent of total variety store volume.

to women's apparel and accessory departments and trading up (selling higher quality) their fashion offerings. Even giant supermarket food chains, of which the A & P and Grand Union are but two examples, have been experimenting with staple clothing items. The quantities in which these larger chains can purchase are obviously enormous in comparison to the purchases of even good-sized individual stores of any type. They may not have the fashion authority of the department and specialized apparel stores, but they can and do move a great deal of merchandise.

Since the thirties, the development of specialized apparel chains has slowed down considerably from their almost meteoric rise in the 1920's.[26] Although chain stores in total still do 30 per cent of all retail business, this ratio varies widely by lines of merchandise. For example, although chains account for a large percentage of the retail sales of foods, variety merchandise, auto supplies, and other general merchandise, their relative share of men's and women's apparel, other than shoes, is very much smaller. Their function, as the fashion industry sees it, is that of moving large quantities of fairly standardized apparel intended for customers of relatively modest income.

Mail-Order Houses. The two major forms of nonstore retailers are house-to-house sellers and mail-order houses. Both have their roots far back in the past. House-to-house sellers, of which the Fuller Brush Company and Avon Cosmetics are two examples, usually deal in a single line of staple merchandise such as cosmetics or household wares. Their role in the distribution of fashion apparel is minor.

By census definition, a retail business that makes the bulk of its sales and deliveries by mail is classified as a mail-order firm.[27] Such establishments may be specialized as to the type of merchandise they sell, or may feature full lines of general merchandise. An example of the former is Spiegel's, Inc., a Chicago firm specializing in apparel, whose 1964 volume of sales was over $300 million.[28] The latter is best exemplified by Sears Roebuck and Company, the sales of whose catalogue division's sales alone are estimated to be one-quarter of their total volume of nearly $6 billion.[29] The oldest general merchandise mail-order retailer is Montgomery Ward and Company, founded in 1872.

The catalogues of both firms, along with those of their smaller brethren, were the standbys of rural customers for generations. Isolated farm life and inadequate country stores created the business climate in which the early mail-order sellers could develop and flourish. As rural families acquired mobility, thanks to the automobile, retail stores became more accessible to them, and their merchandise horizons broadened. Increasing awareness of fashion came also through improvements in transportation and developments in communication—publications, movies, and radio. Their shopping patterns changed—and so did the mail-

[26] Phelon-Sheldon's Resident Buyers Book (a directory) listed 120 specialized women's apparel chains in its 1964 edition. Published by Phelon-Sheldon Publications, 32 Union Square, New York City.

[27] Census of Retail Trade, *op. cit.* (Authors' note: Mail-order houses are not to be confused with the mail-order services offered by many large stores as a supplement to their over-the-counter selling.)

[28] Source: Published financial statements of company.

[29] Authors' note: Sears Roebuck is the largest general merchandise retailer in the world. The only retailer whose sales are larger is the A & P Company.

order house. In the 1920's they opened retail stores, and in the 1930's they initiated catalogue sales offices to which customers could come and have the help of skilled salespeople in filling out orders for merchandise listed in the catalogues.

During the fifties, they began to give considerable space to ready-to-wear and to upgrade all their fashion lines by "introducing and selling high-quality women's fashions through its catalogues (such departments being) the most rapid growing . . . in the book." [30] This upgrading has reached the point of commissioning noted European couturiers to create special collections "to offer *haute couture* to mass markets through its catalogues." [31]

To the customer, the mail-order catalogue offers the convenience of ordering her merchandise at home, by mail or telephone, whenever it suits her to do so. In addition to the catalogues of companies specializing in mail-order selling, the customer may also buy from catalogues published at intervals by retail stores and sent to their charge-account customers. Such catalogues are familiar at Christmas, back-to-school, and other peak shopping seasons. But whereas a store's catalogue may reach thousands or even tens of thousands of customers, a mail-order house's catalogue reaches millions of households. As far back as 1905, Sears was distributing more than 2,000,000 copies of a single issue of its spring catalogue.[32] In 1963, it is estimated that Sears distributed a total of 50,000,000 catalogues in the course of a year, and Montgomery Ward, 45,000,000.[33]

The mail-order houses represent a huge market for the fashion industry's products. When a style is purchased by their buyers, and placed in a catalogue that goes into millions of homes, the prospects of selling many, many garments of that one style are excellent. In their relationship with manufacturers, the mail-order companies exercise a great deal of leadership. Their testing laboratories check apparel for fit, workmanship, wearing qualities, fabric strength, stability, and color fastness. Their sales records provide them with a vast storehouse of information on the public's preferences. Their purchasing power and prestige make it possible for them to specify the thread count wanted in a fabric, or the number of stitches per inch in the seams of a garment, to make sure their customers get the wearing qualities they expect. More recently, their immense buying power has been used to bring smarter, more fashionable garments to their customers by the device of employing leading designers, both here and abroad, to design garments especially for them. As a result of their fashion and trading-up policies, current catalogues of leading mail-order houses list many well-known designer names and higher-priced apparel items.[34] However, the catalogues are not neglecting their more traditional popular-priced mass market merchandise which still accounts for the largest part of mail-order selling.

Discount Stores. Discount stores are not readily defined; some are department stores in every sense but those intangible ones described earlier in this chapter.

---

[30] Annual Report 1962, Montgomery Ward & Co., p. 7.

[31] *Ibid.*

[32] "Merchant to the Millions," Sears Roebuck & Co., Publication Service, Department 703, 925 S. Homan Ave., Chicago 7, Illinois.

[33] "Putting Out the Wish Book Is a Complex All-Year Production at Sears," *New York Times*, May 19, 1963, Section 3, p. 14.

[34] Authors' note: See current catalogues of Sears Roebuck and Montgomery Ward.

The editors of the magazine, *The Discount Merchandiser,* offer this definition: "A retail outlet offering one or more major merchandise lines—usually a broad selection of departments—on a self-service, semi-self-service, or self-selection basis. The policy of the store is to sell nationally advertised and branded goods below the prevailing price levels of other more conventional retailing outlets in its immediate trading area, on a continuing basis."[35] Some of these stores are open to the general public; others are of the "closed-door" variety, restricted to member customers. Those of the closed-door type usually solicit their memberships among people of nearly identical social and economic positions, whose merchandise needs will be similar.

Discount retailers, featuring nationally advertised brands of home appliances at less than "list" price, came into their own during the late 1940's. Their development and growth was sparked by the Fair Trade statutes enacted during the thirties that made it possible for wholesale suppliers to set resale "list" price minimums. At the beginning, these stores provided no customer services of any kind, relied largely on word of mouth advertising and confined their operations primarily to the sale of well-known brands of hard goods. During the latter part of the fifties, however, the situation changed rapidly. Discounters began to open additional stores in the burgeoning suburban communities and to broaden their merchandise assortments to include apparel. Many new discount stores came into being in cities and suburbs alike.

Although "underselling prices" remained their major appeal, alert discount merchants, aware of the higher profit margins and potential sales volume of ready-to-wear, began to trade up apparel offerings and stress fashion as well as price. As volume increased, discount stores increasingly carried larger quantities of clothing. At the same time, they began to up-grade their displays, advertising, and even their locations. E. J. Korvette's Fifth Avenue store in the heart of New York City's most fashionable shopping area is a notable example of changes such as these.[36]

Today, many of these pioneer discount operations call themselves "promotional" or "junior" department stores. Their appeal to the customer is still on the basis of bargains; their role in the fashion business is that of moving lower-priced merchandise rapidly and in large quantities. They can be enormous buyers in the wholesale markets because some of them are chains with many outlets. Others turn their ready-to-wear operations over to leased department operators who specialize in apparel concessions in retail stores. Their lessees, serving many stores or store groups, have great buying power also.

Many apparel manufacturers who wish to control the resale prices of their garments or who are fearful of antagonizing their older accounts will not sell to discount retailers who "undersell" their garments. There are other garment firms, however, who are glad to manufacture secondary brands for stores such as these or produce a line of lower-priced merchandise which is sold under the store's own label. There are also many who specialize in selling to discounters and there

[35] "Discount Retailing in the United States," by the Editors of *The Discount Merchandiser,* New York, Supermarket Publishing Co., Inc. 1963, p. 238.

[36] See "Discount Stores Put on Airs," *Business Week,* February 10, 1962, pp. 72–74. Also "Korvette Plans Prestige Centers," *Chain Store Age,* (Executives Edition), June 1963, p. 20.

are still others who sell them only their discontinued or marked-down garments. In an industry numbering thousands of apparel producers there is no shortage of merchandise or suppliers for discount buyers.

In one sense, the apparel discounting developments of the 1950's and 1960's are not new; stores such as Ohrbach's, whose underselling fashion operation and policies are described in a reading in this section, have been in existence since the 1920's. What is new, however, is the multiplicity of discount operators in the United States [37] and their increasing importance as distributors of popular-priced fashion apparel.

Specialty Stores—Large and Small. The term "specialty store" refers to a retail organization specializing in one narrow category of merchandise such as jewelry, shoes, lingerie, or blouses. It also applies to a store that specializes in several related categories of merchandise such as women's apparel and accessories, or men's clothing and furnishings. For census purposes, these are classified as apparel shops; in the fashion business they are referred to as specialty shops or stores. Among consumers, the larger versions are frequently miscalled department stores because they are departmentized, offer extensive customer services, and carry wide assortments of the merchandise in which they specialize. To qualify as department stores, however, they would have to carry home furnishings as well as apparel.

Specialty stores (or apparel shops) may be individually owned or units of chains. They may even be apparel discounters. They may range in size from a small neighborhood or rural shop to such large, universally known fashion retailers as Bergdorf Goodman in New York or Neiman-Marcus in Dallas, whose fashion operations are described in readings in this section. Great or small, apparel specialty stores usually cater to a restricted clientele—the woman of great wealth and discrimination, the suburban housewife, the outsize woman, the young woman on a small budget, the tall girl, the maternity customer. Atmosphere, displays, selling effort, and the actual merchandise are all pointed strongly toward the particular customer who is the store's target. Salesmanship, if only because it is specialized as to merchandise and clientele, is likely to be of a higher order than what the customer encounters in stores aimed at a broader market.

The small stores specializing in apparel for men or women play a very dominant role in the fashion business. Despite the competition of larger stores, their collective share of the total volume of fashion merchandise sales is substantial. Among women's apparel shops, for instance, those with annual sales of less than $500,000 each constitute 68 per cent of the total number of stores in the United States and represent over 62 per cent of the total volume of sales.[38] A large percentage of these small shops are independently owned and there is no small town or big city where they do not exist. Their attrition rate is high, of course, but so is the replacement rate. Figures released by the Credit Clearing House, a

---

[37] See "The True Look of the Discount Industry, 1964," *Discount Merchandiser*, May 1965. According to this source, there were an estimated 2951 discount stores in the United States in 1964 with a combined sales volume of $10.8 billion, of which approximately 18 per cent is in women's and children's wear.

[38] Based on figures contained in "Retail Trade, Sales Size," 1958 Census of Business, U.S. Department of Commerce.

division of Dun and Bradstreet, Inc., show 385 failures in 1964 among women's apparel retailers—and 1526 new retail apparel businesses in that year.[39] Their average capitalization was less than $10,000 per store. It is from modest beginnings such as these that most of today's great fashion retailers have evolved.

[39] From press releases issued by the Credit Clearing House, Dun and Bradstreet Inc., New York.

WOMEN'S APPAREL STORES AND SALES*

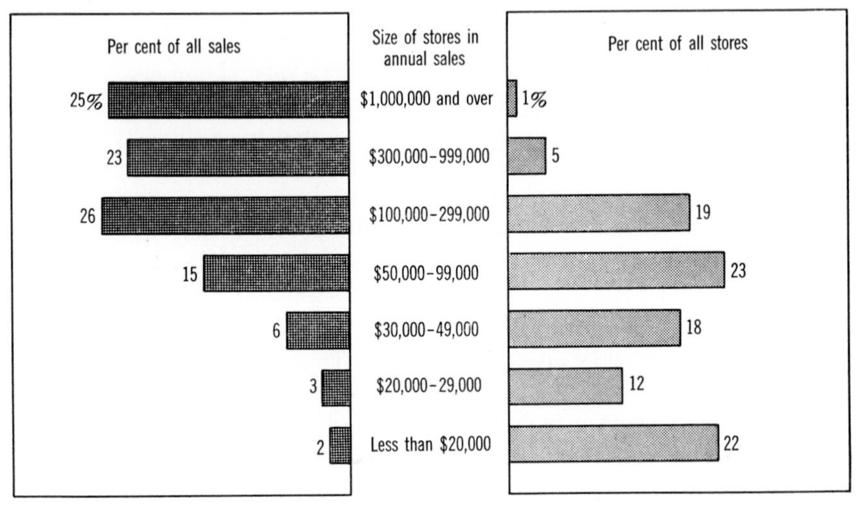

Each series, 1958 = 100%

MEN'S APPAREL STORES AND SALES*

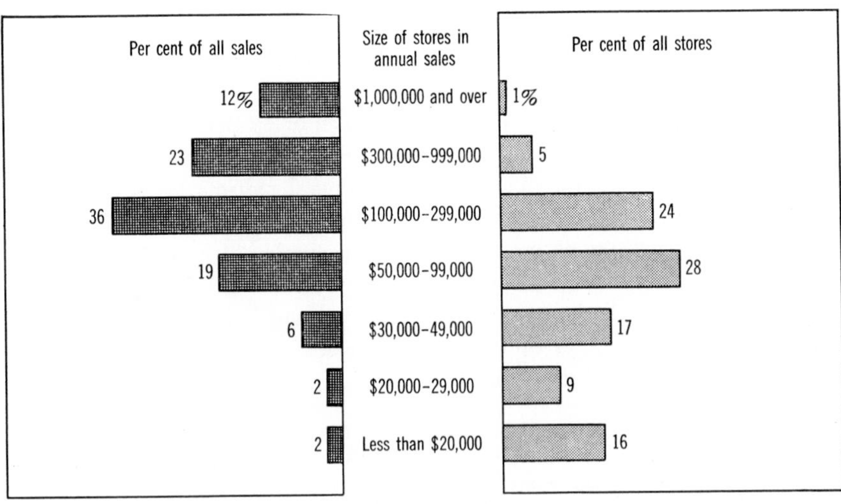

Each series, 1958 = 100%

* Retail outlets primarily engaged in the sale of apparel. Source: U.S. Department of Commerce.

From the consumer's point of view, much of the staying power of small fashion retailers can be attributed to the individuality of their operations, the convenience of their locations, and their intimate knowledge of their customers' needs and tastes. Their owners know the way of dressing in the communities in which they are located and many times will take the trouble to buy with individual customers in mind. Their importance to the fashion industry is best expressed in the words of an executive of the industry's largest volume producer of apparel who said:

> In our company we see the different role played by the various classes of retailers very clearly. Our nationally advertised brands have won their place in the sun, and maintain their leadership, primarily through the cooperation and good will of the independent retailers, most of whom are, relatively speaking, small retailers. . . . The independent retailer is highly important to our economy as well as providing valuable services to the customer. It is the existence of the smaller independent that really makes national distribution possible.[40]

Other Types of Fashion Retailers. Many stores of other types sell apparel items in addition to whatever merchandise constitutes their main line of business; supermarkets are a prime example. To the consumer they offer the convenience of being able to buy staple clothing items, such as hosiery, undergarments, and the like in the course of her routine household shopping. To fashion producers they are additional outlets for their merchandise, especially those articles that can be packaged or those which do not require the advice, help, or try-on facilities that an apparel or general merchandise store would provide. The dramatic presentation that has impact upon the consumer and stimulates demand for the industry's merchandise is not forthcoming, however, in this quarter.

Retailing Changes With Customers

The retailer's function in the fashion business requires him to change as his customer's needs and interests change. Each generation, even each decade, sees changes, not only in the fashion merchandise that women buy, but also in the manner in which significant numbers of them prefer to select and buy that merchandise. Customers, like fashion itself, are anything but static. Since the retailer's success depends on his ability to understand and serve the consumer, he changes as his customers do—or falls by the wayside.

Some changes within recent memory illustrate this point. Along with the postwar migration to the suburbs, for example, came the vast expansion of department stores into the suburbs via branch stores. With the increased income and sophistication of blue-collar families came trading-up efforts and greater individuality among units of the chain store field. The growing use of mail and telephone ordering, not only by families in rural areas, but also by quite sophisticated and well-to-do women in cities, led to the appearance of better styled,

[40] Norman A. Jackson, Financial Vice-President, Kayser-Roth Corporation in a presentation to the National Association of Credit and Financial Management, Los Angeles, California, May 19, 1964. (Excerpts reprinted in *The Apparel Outlook,* June–July 1964.)

and, finally, couture merchandise in mail-order catalogues. It has also led to improved telephone order equipment and techniques in many large city stores.

The introduction of self-selection fixtures and self-service devices into fashion departments all up and down the price scale reflects the willingness of busy shoppers to help themselves. The buy-now pay-later attitude that manifests itself in the purchase of housing, major appliances, and vacations on the installment plan has its retail echo in the revolving credit plans that almost every department and specialty store now offers, and in the credit plans that are offered by chain stores whose names were long synonymous with cash and carry. The eagerness of very young adults to run their own affairs is reflected in departments for teen-agers and preteens, and in the experimentation among stores with special credit plans for teen-agers.

The need of customers for evening shopping hours has led to night openings once or twice a week in most downtown stores, and several nights a week in suburban centers. In some parts of the country, customers show sufficient interest in shopping on Sunday so that merchants keep open seven days a week; in other parts of the country, Sunday shopping is restricted to convenience items. It is the public's attitude that decides the issue.

The eagerness of some customers for bargains, even if they must plunge into crowds to find them, has created an important place for the discount store. It has also led other types of stores, such as department stores, to curtail unwanted customer services in order to meet price competition, either on a storewide basis or in basement departments alone.

The list of changes goes on and on. And there will always be more. Just as fashion changes to reflect the consumer's changing way of life, so does the retailer have to change his way of doing business to conform to his customer's changing preferences in the way she wants to buy.

Readings

The readings that follow undertake to clarify the picture of fashion retailing from two viewpoints. One is through a series of articles describing the merchandising philosophy underlying the fashion operations of several great stores, each of which illustrate a particular type of retailing that has been discussed in the text. Bergdorf-Goodman, Henri Bendel, and Neiman-Marcus are leading fashion specialty stores; Ohrbach's is probably the best-known apparel discounter in the fashion business; Sears Roebuck and Company, the largest and most successful retailer of general merchandise in the world, is the prototype of mail-order and chain-store retailing; Federated Stores is the most profitable department store group in the United States; and Lane Bryant is a noted example of a highly specialized apparel chain. Other outstanding retailers are highlighted in "What Makes a Favorite Store" which concludes the series of store readings.

The second viewpoint is through the words of three great merchants, the presidents of stores renowned for their superlative merchandising of fashion; the late Mr. Escobosa of I. Magnin in California, Mr. Marcus of Neiman-Marcus in Texas, and Mr. Daniels of Burdine's in Florida. Note particularly the importance they each place on their customers' wishes, whatever they may be.

To conclude this section, the authors have compiled a list of prominent American retailers by location, ownership, and estimated dollar sales volume.

Retailers of Fashion

These readings offer the basic philosophies of each of several different stores: what the store stands for, and how it seeks to serve its customers. Each is quite different from the others in its aims and in the segment of the buying public to which it makes its strongest appeal. The selections have been chosen to show the broad range of types encompassed by the term "fashion retailer."

Posh Palace of Fashion

New York's Bergdorf Goodman—A Nine-Story Monument to Rich Women—Is Filled with Sables and Silks and Money, Money, Money

by Joan Younger Dickinson

Bergdorf Goodman is a lush, plus New York women's specialty store where all that glitters is probably gold, or at least a chic synthetic, acceptable this year from Palm Beach to Paris.

Nine stories high, this white marble citadel of fashion sits on the corner of Fifth Avenue and 58th Street, sharing the famous Plaza Square with such impeccable neighbors as the Plaza Hotel, the Sherry-Netherland, and the Savoy Hilton. Beyond lie the tree-shaded acres of Central Park. And here—in the privileged section of New York where Bergdorf Goodman is firmly entrenched—the city air is always crisply scented with the sharp green smell of money.

For nearly sixty years this extraordinary store, discreet, tasteful, and expensive, has catered to a customer list that runs the social and fashion alphabet from A to V (Astor to Vanderbilt). On most shopping days, Bergdorf's is as peopled with celebrities as Sardi's on opening night. One may glimpse Greta Garbo, conspicuously disguised in dark glasses and bucket hat, shopping the lingerie department for at-home robes. Mrs. William Paley, Mrs. Vincent Astor, and Mrs. Paul Mellon are frequent visitors to the custom-hat department. Mrs. Henry Kaiser became so enamored of a certain beach hat which matched her shocking-pink house in Honolulu that she ordered a dozen. And the late King Mohammed V of Morocco, on a state visit to the United States a few years ago, brought a male entourage to Bergdorf's to help him select gowns for his wives back home.

Some of Bergdorf's regular clientele buy as many as fifty dresses a season; others may order only a suit, a half-dozen dresses, and two or three ball gowns. But of a basic customer list of 1700 wealthy women who regularly buy custom clothes with the Bergdorf label, more than fifty spend from $80,000 to $90,000 per year. And when these gilded customers have a "fur year"—that inevitable time when a mink or sable goes tatty—they add as much as $30,000 to $50,000 to their individual fashion budgets for fur replacements. Tailored under the direction of designer Emeric Partos, a Bergdorf custom-made sable coat will cost about $55,000, and more for outsizes. There are less expensive furs, of course. A Somali leopard may be had for around $7000. Snug mink or sable babushkas, a combination specialty of the fur and millinery departments, are priced at $295 and $495—custom-fitted and lined with a fabric of one's choice.

For its merchandise quality, distinctive design and general solicitude for the tastes of the fashionable, Bergdorf Goodman is handsomely rewarded. Current sales receipts add up to more than $20,000,000 per year.

Yet there is nothing formidable about Bergdorf's. Careful planning in layout, personnel, and decor has kept it a comfortable, at-ease place to shop. Just as a well-run bank does not discourage small depositors or sully the atmosphere with vulgar displays of money, so Bergdorf's keeps much of its lavish merchandise carefully vaulted away. The first floor, separated from the street only by revolving doors, is baited with a supermarket array of umbrellas, handbags, costume and antique jewelry, toiletries, and less expensive millinery. To one side is the shoe salon and a small men's-wear shop. Merchandise is varied; prices range from possible to sky high.

In 1956 the store's owners, Andrew Good-

Condensed and reprinted from the April 14, 1962 issue of *Saturday Evening Post* by special permission; Copyright 1962.

man and his sister, the late Ann Goodman Farber, began making changes, with the aid of Leonard Hankin, Bergdorf's only vice president. One of the most successful innovations has been the introduction of the "Miss Bergdorf" department, featuring youthful, high-fashion clothes and accessories at moderate prices.

"To create this department we had to create clothes which had never existed before, clothes that had all the taste and quality of the other departments but were lower in price and younger in style," Mr. Hankin explains. "It was quite a task. Slews of companies came into business just to serve the Miss Bergdorf label, slews of new customers came in to buy—and slews of competitors began following our example. It's hard to believe that before Miss Bergdorf, good junior-size clothes were either terribly expensive or impossible to find. But it's true."

A woman vice president of a leading cosmetics firm said, "New York is a high-fashion city, and Bergdorf's was smart enough to know that the bloom years of a career girl's life mean big spending. Secretaries and receptionists are usually the best-dressed women in offices here. They may live four or six to an apartment, but they're on their way up and spend most of their money on clothes. They're dressing up to a dream of living and working in the big city."

Six stories up at Bergdorf's is another comparative newcomer, a children's department handsomely papered in a nursery plaid of yellows, browns, and pink. Here is stocked a complete line of young-children's clothing, including snowsuits and reinforced play clothes sturdy enough to indicate that the rich, as well as the poor, sometimes wear out their knees. The merchandise suggests that well-dressed children should be conservative, demure, and rather plain. Extremes are available. Bergdorf's once supplied a $750 vicuña coat for a six-year-old. Best-seller in children's furs, however, is a simple white rabbit coat priced at $200. And the silver-spoon-infant crowd can get a chic start in life in a hand-made christening gown: price —$250. Young John Kennedy's entire layette was purchased in this department. As a male customer, Baby John can be clothed and suited by Bergdorf's until he graduates beyond size 6XX.

On other floors—in the antiques and decorating departments, the salons devoted to custom garments, furs, and millinery—Bergdorf's becomes soberingly posh. Here the atmosphere and decoration are of controlled elegance, positive but never overpowering. Rugs, walls, and draperies are in a soothing gray-beige, crystal chandeliers give muted light, and flower arrangements are placed at random, as though by a graceful housewife. Saleswomen—there are 178 in all, with eleven men in furs and men's wear—are available but never pressing; they are quiet-voiced and genteel, as if by osmosis they had taken on some of the expensive quality of the merchandise. About one-third of the personnel has been with the store for more than twenty years; a handful more have had nearly a half-century of service.

High priestess of this inner sanctum of *couture* is gray-haired buyer-designer Miss Ethel Frankau, directress of the Custom Salon. So sure is her taste, so tigerish her insistence on quality in merchandise and design that last August—for the first time in history—the International Syndicate of Couture feted her with a dinner at Maxim's in Paris, solely to toast her influences in the fashion world. Miss Frankau dismisses her own talents lightly, saying she "only helps ladies to find ladylike clothes."

Such ladylike clothes, as conceived in the custom salons, come with husky price tags. Suit prices start at $750, dresses at $1000, and both can go up, up, up. Custom-clothing customers may select their designs directly from the collections of Bergdorf *couturier* Leslie Morris, or ask for adaptations of Paris originals. At customer whim, individual changes may be made —a variation in sleeve or jacket length, material, skirt fullness, or other details. Two staff sketchers create designs from customers' descriptions of their preferences. Many fashion-wise women are able to rough-sketch their own designs, which Bergdorf's then translates into workable patterns.

After the selection of design, fabric, and trims, a garment usually needs three or four fittings before it is ready for the final hand-sewing of the Bergdorf label. On the eighth floor of the store, in a room dubbed "ghost city," stand 2000 dressmaker's dummies, each labeled with the name tag of its human prototype. If a woman gains or loses more than ten pounds, she is expected to inform her fitter—who will then trim or pad out the dummy figure in appropriate places.

All patterns and fabrics are numbered, and

a careful listing of each garment on order is posted in every Bergdorf fitting room to avoid duplication among customers. Once—but only once—Bergdorf's sold the same dress to the mothers of both bride and groom at a society wedding. Now wedding notices and social pages are required reading at Bergdorf's, and perhaps gossip columns also. "They seem to know my income down to the penny," explained a Long Island customer, recently separated by divorce from one of the largest fortunes on the East Coast. "Since my divorce, the service and attitude at Bergdorf's are exactly the same. But they no longer offer me the most expensive suggestions as they did in the old days. They seem to know I don't get much alimony."

Two ladies who have availed themselves of Bergdorf's custom services are Mrs. Robert Kennedy—as the busy mother of seven, she often shops the children's department by mail—and Mrs. Henry Ford II, who wore a Bergdorf lace gown to her daughter's $250,000 Detroit debut last spring. Debutante Anne Ford was custom-supplied for the same party with a pearl-embroidered organza. Eunice Oakes Gardiner had her wedding dress made in the bridal salon; and, as an extra Bergdorf service, a rip in the heirloom lace once worn by First Lady Mrs. John Tyler was rewoven by hand for the bride.

While most of the names of Bergdorf's clientele are kept as secret as possible, sometimes a customer breaks into the limelight. Last year Jacqueline Kennedy, a Bergdorf customer since she was a little girl, was caught in the bright flashes of publicity when she ordered her Inaugural Ball gown from Bergdorf's.

Today this amazing store should properly be called Goodman's, but even the reigning Goodmans call it Bergdorf's. The enterprise was started at the turn of the century when a tailor named Herman Bergdorf designed a suit for his sister. Miss Bergdorf was a career girl employed as social secretary to the very social Mrs. Sidney Loeb. Mrs. Loeb's friends admired the suit and then asked for Bergdorf-made copies of it. Business grew in the little gaslit shop on New York's 19th Street until Bergdorf was forced to hire help—young Edwin Goodman from Rochester, New York.

In 1903 Bergdorf sold out completely to Goodman and went back to Alsace; but the name Bergdorf Goodman was already firmly established as New York's leading suitmakers to ladies. At that date Mrs. Cornelius Vanderbilt's mansion still stood at 5th Avenue and 58th Street. She and many of her stylish friends were Goodman customers, but they could not have dreamed that the young tailor would someday move up to the Vanderbilt end of Fifth Avenue.

From the very beginning, tall, handsome Edwin Goodman *was* Bergdorf Goodman. He went to Paris with buyers, dealt with wholesalers, trained the salesgirls, assisted in sales and fitting rooms, and sometimes lent a skilled hand at the tailoring. He added hats, perfumes, and even a limited line of ready-to-wear garments. In 1927, when the boom was on, Edwin Goodman had 15,000 loyal, fast-spending customers and a business of $3,000,000 a year. He decided then to buy the land on which the Vanderbilt mansion stood. The old landmark was torn down, and atop the new building Mr. Goodman built a large apartment for his family.

When Edwin Goodman died in 1953 at the age of seventy-six, his two children became co-owners of the store, with Andrew Goodman in charge of overall operations and Ann Goodman Farber concentrating her excellent talents on the antiques, gifts, and decorating departments. As youngsters the Goodmans had lived in the resplendent twenty-two-room apartment over Bergdorf's, immersed with their father in the business of running the store. Now Andrew Goodman lives with his family in Rye, using the apartment only on snow-blocked nights or when late Christmas shoppers keep the store open long after commuting hours.

Some changes at Bergdorf's were made by customer demand. The department of antiques, gifts, and *objets d'art,* for instance, was created because so many customers sought to buy the fine antique desks the store uses for its receptionists, as well as the excellent chairs and tables sometimes borrowed from the Goodman family apartment as general décor. Now fine pieces of every period except early American are on sale.

Back in the 1930's, when Edwin Goodman added furs and lingerie, shoes and hosiery to his stock, it was felt along Fifth Avenue that he was now a "tailor graduated," a complete "master of madame's ensemble." Andrew Goodman, as alert a merchandiser as his father, has since given madame one last touch of luxury—an ultralush, newly remodeled beauty salon. The foyer here is walled with antiqued mirrors and furnished with elegant sofas and coffee tables, topped with a housewifely collection of begonia plants potted in high-priced antique china. Customers are given a choice of pink or blue shampoo gowns, with a selection of leopard-cloth wrap-arounds for the young in heart and hip. Free stationery marked UNDER THE DRYER AT BERGDORF's is supplied for letter writing. Scotch is kept in supply for girls who consider it less plebeian than the usual beer or egg rinse. Many of the hairdressers and manicurists are bilingual, thus helping visiting Parisiennes or Madrilenians feel elegantly at home.

Bergdorf Goodman today, with an active charge-account list of 90,000 persons, has roughly three kinds of customers. First are the very rich, to whom custom attention and leisure shopping are part of a way of life. These customers want the best, and they don't care where the demical point falls in the price tag.

"As a middle group," says Mr. Goodman, "we have the shoppers—women who buy many things in Bloomingdale's or Ohrbach's, or do their everyday shopping in their home areas of Chicago, Detroit or Columbus, Ohio—who come to us for something special. We like that.

"We don't want to be the kind of store a woman dashes into, with the parking meter ticking outside. We want customers to feel we're worth taking a day off in town. In return we'll put forth every effort to make that shopping day pleasant and exciting. Eventually, we hope, they won't want to go anywhere else."

In the third customer category is the career-girl or young-matron group, a special breed of sophisticated New Yorker who has champagne tastes on a Martini income. For this group, the Miss Bergdorf department sharpens and satisfies the fashion senses. Today they may shop with shrewd lapidary eyes to find that perfect jewel of a dress, perhaps a black crepe with flaring skirt, or a slim, overbloused evening sheath—either for under $100. In later years, given adequate adjustments in their money belts, this group will probably search Bergdorf's higher-priced floors for a Givenchy or Balmain at nearly twenty times that $100 price.

And Bergdorf's, in its second half-century of service, will stand ready. Just as Tiffany's is not likely to switch to rhinestones, so Bergdorf Goodman is determined never to lessen the intrinsic quality of their fashion contribution. Exclusive and expensive, the white marble citadel stands firm.

"After all," explained Andrew Goodman, "we're not trying to sell the whole world, just those who like what we like."

High Style Cash-and-Carry

Ohrbach's Became a Big Success by Disregarding all the Rules

by Herbert Brean

Students of modern retailing have yet to produce a foolproof formula for successfully operating a store. They can, however, list a number of foolproof ways whereby a retail business can be hastened into bankruptcy. One is to locate the store in an area inconvenient to the customer. Another is to sell the merchandise at a low, profit-cutting markup but never to advertise these low prices, or better still, refrain from advertising the merchandise at all. Another device calculated to keep sales low is to hire a bare minimum of sales personnel and enjoin them to leave the customers alone unless they ask questions and never, never do any "persuasive" or high-pressure selling.

If these measures do not keep customers away by the thousands, there are more skillful

---

Reprinted from *Life*, January 26, 1953. Courtesy Life © 1953 Time, Inc. Although Ohrbach's is now in a different New York location and is under new ownership, their merchandising policies remain essentially the same as described in this article.

refinements for alienating the buying public. This is particularly true if the store caters chiefly to women, whose instinctual urge to shop has long been cultivated by certain little thoughtful acts provided by most stores and to which a woman by new feels entitled. So, to keep her out of your store, refuse to allow her a charge account. Sell her smart clothes, but refuse to alter them. Make her carry all her bundles home. Accept no mail orders, even if your location is inconvenient. If you feel obliged to provide a desk for wrapping packages to be mailed, supply no stamps; let the customer take the package to the post office herself. Of course the interior of the store should be kept as inexpensively plain as possible with a minimum of open space. Above all, never hold sales since they notoriously attract customers, especially women.

Any one of these hints to the would-be bankrupt can be depended on to discourage a portion of his trade. Put into operation *in toto* they should effect a business's early demise with predictable certainty. Nevertheless on New York's 14th Street, quite distant from the city's fashionable shopping center, there stands a retail clothing establishment which has so religiously followed this and all the other precepts that it is now exuberantly entering its thirtieth year of disobliging customers, and in recent years has even had to extend its program of studied disservice to Newark and to Los Angeles. Indeed, this week it announced a fourth store to be opened in fifteen months near Hempstead, N.Y., at a cost of $4 million and there is reason to believe that this is not necessarily the last expansion. During 1952 this enterprise sold at least $50 million worth of clothing, mostly feminine and mostly coats and suits but also 89¢ nylons, French handbags at $250, and American evening gowns at $295. It is not only one of the most successful operations in the whole field of U.S. merchandising, but some people believe it is the pattern of successful future retailing in the United States. Its name is Ohrbach's.

The proofs of Ohrbach's unorthodox success are many and varied. One is that while last month it experienced the usual Christmas rush, it did not, relatively speaking, feel rushed at all since its really heavy seasons come at the time of the major fashion change-overs in spring and fall. Another is the veneration in which its customers hold it for saving them money, whether on heavy woolen shirts for truck-driver husbands or velvet wraps in which to attend opera openings.

For while Ohrbach's originally stocked chiefly odd lots and job lots bought cheaply and sold quickly at a low markup, over the years it has found it practical and profitable to add more and more "quality" and fashion items, and even to originate them. All of this, high fashion or low, is sold at an average of 20 to 22 per cent below the prices of more stylish competitors. As a result Ohrbach's attracts a clientele which is extremely varied: bargain-conscious salesgirls from other stores, fashion-conscious models from top agencies, movie stars like Joan Crawford and Jeanne Crain when they are in town, cotton-clad housewives from the lower East Side and silk-rustling matrons from the upper East Side.

This unusually wide feminine cross section, incidentally, is regarded by some manufacturers as a sensitive barometer of what will and will not sell, and they often place two dozen dresses of a new style on sale in Ohrbach's second floor as a test. If eighteen have been bought by the end of the first day the manufacturer will order the materials for several thousand, confident that he has a best seller. This cross section occasionally produces some curious contretemps. There is a famous story of one genteel lady who was caught up in the crush milling around an Ohrbach's table of doeskin gloves and was pushed squarely into another woman. "Oh, I do beg your pardon," she fluted delicately. "I simply could not help myself." Her vis-à-vis regarded her with aversion. "If you are so goddam polite," she observed, "why aren't you shopping at Altman's?"

Ohrbach's offers other contrasts. A cut-price store in a cut-price neighborhood, the 14th Street establishment probably sells as many cashmere sweaters and top-quality woolens as any individual store in the United States. English Argyle men's socks are another best seller.

As much as 40 per cent of the approximately 150,000 garments which the store may stock at any one time is often "name" merchandise, the work of nationally named designers (whose labels have been ripped out, however, and Ohrbach's own substituted, because other stores supplied by the designers complain loudly at being undersold). It provides the clothes for a number of television shows, including Lucille Ball's in *I Love Lucy,* and many Broadway plays and movies. When the Los Angeles branch held a fashion show last year, guests included Princess Pignatelli, Lady Lawford, and Baroness d'Erlanger. Yet this store, like the other two, contains more than a trace of proletarian serve-yourself or supermarket element. Ohrbach's, a pioneer in the retailing trend toward self-service, believes that the reduction in labor costs more than offsets losses through shoplifting and damage from customers.

Ohrbach's buys as much as $45,000 worth of a single model of a suit at one time, in contrast to the $1500 worth that another store might purchase, and turns this stock over an incredible fifteen times a year in contrast to the average department store's six or seven. Ohrbach's accomplishes this by assuming that everything must sell within two weeks. If it doesn't there begins a series of scheduled price reductions calculated to move unsold merchandise within a month after it has come into the store. A dress which remains on the racks at $49.95 is reduced 20 per cent to $39.95. If it still does not move in a few days, it drops another 10 per cent to $35.95. If it still does not sell, additional cuts of 10 per cent are made until it does.

Such reductions are never announced by advertising or even by a "sale" sign in the store. The woman shopper who drops into Ohrbach's on any given day can never tell when she may find an original by a famous designer in the last stages of markdown and thus selling at half of what it costs elsewhere. This makes the 14th Street establishment a powerful lure to shoppers that benefits the whole business neighborhood, and as a result Ohrbach's receives weekly requests from real-estate developers and bankers in other cities to open branches. Similarly a steady stream of store owners from other cities and even foreign countries tour the store every year, studying how the Ohrbachs do it. Nathan ("N.M.") and Jerry Ohrbach, the father-and-son team which owns and operates the store, answer all questions fully and frankly, knowing well that their operation is a little more difficult to copy than might appear. Indeed, the chief argument against those who hold that Ohrbach's high-volume low-profit pattern is the shape of retailing to come is the list of stores which have tried to imitate it, sometimes within a stone's throw of Ohrbach's main location and even with former Ohrbach personnel—and failed.

To keep business flowing through the six 75-year-old buildings put together to form the 14th Street store, Ohrbach's employs a number of techniques. One is to hold operating expenses to 17 per cent of gross sales, which is about half the average department store's overhead. This is done in part by buying and selling for cash on the barrelhead always, even when, as in Los Angeles, the store sells in quantity to movie costume departments. Even MGM must pay cash. The elder Ohrbach argues, "The more billing, the less cooing."

The stock inventory department is equipped with a battery of I.B.M. machines that each night tabulate the stock tickets from every item sold during the day. When an Ohrbach buyer comes to work next morning he knows at once how his lines of merchandise have done and can reorder goods or reduce prices as seems indicated. Being able to react sensitively and quickly to public demand keeps the stock moving and enables Ohrbach's to limit its markup to 20 per cent. The businesswide average is 40 per cent.

The basic Ohrbach technique, however, is the store's aggressive dedication to the heartwarming proposition that the customer is a lot smarter than anyone suspects. In years past Nathan Ohrbach has proved this to his satisfaction by putting 100 handbags on sale at a very low price, 92 of them bags of high quality and eight of them shoddy ones. Ohrbach grinned from ear to ear at day's end when he found that that of the six bags left, four were "dogs."

This attitude is reflected also in Ohrbach's advertising which is entirely institutional. It simply advertises Ohrbach's as a place to buy fashion cheaply. Ohrbach ads were among the first to use cartoons. They have also employed old movie stills and modern art, and tend to be handsome, striking, and rather humorous, as the current series (which kids other advertising) illustrates. Though the average store spends 5 per cent of its gross on advertising, Ohrbach's spends less than 1 per cent and has even completely discontinued advertising for a year at a time.

Several years ago a well-known Hollywood actress, while visiting New York, dropped into Ohrbach's and bought some $1200 worth of dresses. When she got them back to her hotel she commented loudly and flatteringly on how much she had received for her money, and her vigilant press agent wrote Ohrbach's a letter saying she would be very happy to compose a free, publishable testimonial to the quality of their merchandise. Jerry Ohrbach wrote back thanking her kindly but declining the offer because Ohrbach's refuses to bother with testimonials.

"Promotion Is Like Taking Dope"

Ohrbach's in fact refuses to indulge in anything that smacks of promotion such as "birthday sales," January "white sales," and the like. "Promotion," says the elder Ohrbach (with whom this is a favorite subject), "is like taking dope. You use one dose of it and you have to have another, and another, and then another. These people who advertise enormous bargains such as $119 'values' for $39 simply insult their customers' intelligence. Everyone knows that you cannot sell a $119 item for $39 and stay in business." Dwelling on these matters, he is likely to brandish a newspaper containing a rival's advertisement, raise his voice until it is audible six offices away, and continue: "Or now you take the marked-down item. A store advertises a sale of shoes that originally retailed at $24.50 for only $14.95. Actually they are telling the customer: We thought we could get you to pay $24.50 for these things and you wouldn't. So now we'll try to get you to buy them for $14.95."

When Ohrbach's finds itself in this predicament it avoids the embarrassment of admitting it by never scratching the price on a price tag and writing in a lesser one. The entire tag, which includes a seal to prevent a garment being worn and returned, is removed and the new one inscribed with the lower price substituted. This practice can give an Ohrbach customer something of the pleasant thrill of a Wall Street operator watching A.T. and T. on the ticker tape. The housewife interested in a $19.95 coat knows that by holding out a day or two she may get it for $15.95—but she may also lose it to another, less patient speculator.

The fact is that both Nathan and Jerry Ohrbach are primarily agile merchandisers in an age when department store executives are more and more inclined to concern themselves with overall planning and long-range thinking. Both subscribe to the principle that intelligent buying automatically assures quick sales—"The goods just walk out of the store," in 14th Street's breezy argot. For that reason they give their buyers more authority than is customary. Far from maintaining losing departments, as do many stores for prestige reasons or to attract trade ("better" dresses are often losers), Ohrbach's has had no losing departments at all. Their space being at a premium, they do not launch a new department until they are sure it can make more money than the present one.

They have also helped extend the principles of self-service and self-selection to the field of women's wear. As a result, the amount of service which a customer receives in the 54 departments of the parent store varies enormously, being provided on a basis of what it takes to sell the merchandise involved. In the Oval Room, for example, where Ohrbach's sells its most expensive women's clothes, the customer gets individual attention from a saleswoman. In the better-shoe department, however, the customer is confronted by a display of 300 shoes from which she selects styles that appeal to her. Their numbers are jotted down for her by a clerk and handed to a salesman who brings out the shoes she likes in her size. In cheaper shoes, however, and inexpensive blouses, sweaters and house dresses the customer is likely never to be waited on at all but simply expected to choose what she wants from large tables, try them on herself and take her purchase directly to a cashier.

The Difference Plus 10 Per Cent

Nathan Ohrbach founded his store thirty years ago on low prices, and today if a customer can prove Ohrbach's is being undersold on a given item she is immediately rebated not merely the difference but 10 per cent of the rival store's price as well. However, in the past ten years Ohrbach's has become as conscious of fashion as it has always been of price. Now it sends buyers to Paris and Rome twice yearly to buy originals by Dior, Fath, and other top couturiers and fly them back here. These styles, some of which cost $900 apiece, are shown to manufacturers summoned from Seventh Avenue who are commissioned to make relatively inexpensive copies within 5 to 12 days. The result is that a week after she has read the fall or spring fashion news in *Vogue, Life,* or *Harper's Bazaar,* the less wealthy housewife can find competent reproductions of the new models in Ohrbach's for around $89.50. Meanwhile, knowing that their copies will be copied again by cheaper manufacturers, Ohrbach's tries to beat them to the draw by getting their own makers to do $49.50 versions, and even a $25 version, ahead of the competition. Since obtaining comparable materials on short notice has proved an obstacle in the past, the most recent Ohrbach refinement in this streamlined process of translating high fashion into low price has been to commission top French designers to do their originals in fabrics which are inexpensive and abundant in the United States. Additionally, the store regularly buys out virtually a whole year's output of certain European manufacturers of gloves, sweaters, and handbags to sell at cut prices here. These accessories are sold in the *boutiques,* or "little shops," which have been installed in the Ohrbach stores in a recent concession to elegance.

More typical, however, of an organization which still deals heavily in staples and "distress merchandise" is a schizophrenic department in the parent store which is called the "Cruise Shop" in early winter when it sells chic resort clothes, becomes the "Beach Shop" to sell bathing attire in late spring, changing into the "College Shop" to deal in campus fashions in early fall and, whenever it can catch its breath in between, straightforwardly sells sportswear.

Such luxuries as the *boutiques,* Cruise Shop, and even the modestly modern décor which is slowly replacing some of the 14th Street store's elderly fittings reflect, like the relatively new interest in high fashion, the influence of 45-year-old Jerry Ohrbach, now president of the firm. When the store opened in 1923 it faced the competition of such remorseless price cutters as Sam Klein, just across Union Square, who originated many of the fast-turnover, money-saving techniques now used to such advantage by Ohrbach's. In 1923 some of the 14th Street stores still employed shills and cappers to entice people from the sidewalk into the store where the proprietor charged whatever it seemed the traffic would bear. Such practices sickened Nathan Ohrbach, even though he had grown up in the trade.

Born in Vienna in 1885, Ohrbach came to this country as a child with his parents and took his first mercantile job when he was 14, sweeping out J. M. Tobias' wholesale coat and suit store. At 17 he became a traveling salesman and worked as salesman and buyer for a number of wholesale and retail firms. Later he opened the first of several small stores of his own. He and a partner, Max Wiesen, opened the original of the present one with a sale of dresses at $1 and coats at $5. On opening day crowds stormed the store and broke its windows; 20 were hurt and the cops had to be called. The opening was considered a success.

From the first the store stocked only staples, coats and suits, sold cut-rate. From the first the public affirmed Ohrbach's principle of one cash-and-carry price to everyone. However, the partners fell out in time on the subject of store policy, and Ohrbach tried to buy out his associate. Wiesen would not sell. In a demonstration of the hardheaded dollar sense that would propel him presently to much greater success, Ohrbach leased another store nearby and announced in the newspapers he was opening a business of his own. Wiesen caved in and agreed to accept half a million for his share of the business, which the partners had launched three years before with an investment of $62,500 each. Thereupon Ohrbach subleased the other store at a profit.

It was about this time that he advertised an unusual sale of bargains, and on the morning it began opened the doors himself, a practice in which he indulges to this day. A crowd had begun forming at dawn, and the instant Ohrbach twisted the bolt the mob burst in, carrying him to the very back wall of the store and smashing him against it, dazed and disheveled. His distaste for sales may date from this experience.

As the years passed, the store began to change its character, seeking more "quality" merchandise, toning down and presently abandoning flamboyant advertising and developing the friendship of quality manufacturers willing to sell to a price-cutter despite the objections of rival, nonprice-cutting stores. In fact, when the Los Angeles store opened on Wilshire Boulevard in 1948 it largely abandoned the Spartan plainness of 14th Street and revealed itself as a chi-chi emporium complete with murals. (Even so, on opening day the cops still had to be called.) Ohrbach's founder has been made a chevalier of the Legion of Honor, named Retailer of the Year, and lectures to college classes. Many of his establishment's uptown customers have taken to elegantly pronouncing it "Awebock's." But the proprietors themselves still pronounce their name "Oar-back" and their store has never lost its essential character as a place to buy "more for less or your money back." Said Nathan Ohrbach recently, "It makes no difference to us whether it's a wedding gown or a shroud—the markup is the same."

Considering the uncertainty of the fashion market, in which one rainy week during the height of the selling season can be a real disaster, Ohrbach's steadfast devotion to the low markup is as remarkable as it is seemingly masochistic. It evidences itself in many ways. One occurred several years ago when both the New York and Newark stores were selling umbrellas at an exceptionally low price. An executive of the Newark store telephoned "N.M." that it was raining in Newark and that the price could easily be raised and all the umbrellas be moved quickly. "We set that price to make our usual profit," Ohrbach roared apoplectically into the phone, "and that's all we want. Don't change it." For the same reason Ohrbach refuses to pay more than the legal maximum for a pair of theater tickets, although he could buy a couple of theaters without difficulty.

More significant, perhaps, is what both Ohrbachs regard as their most remarkable merchandising feat. They purchased the bankrupt Merry Hull line of costly and luxurious little boys' clothes and sold them out at a markdown of about 70 per cent, selling $6.95 boys' shirts at $1.95, for example. Mrs. Alfred Vanderbilt hurried to the Los Angeles store (after telephoning the younger Ohrbach that if he did not save her some of the clothes she would never speak to him) and bought $600 worth; Lauren Bacall bought $500 worth, went back later for $300 more. But what pleased both Ohrbach *père* and *fils* was not that they provided bargains for the families of an extremely well-to-do millionaire and an extremely well-to-do movie actor but that they enabled thousands of lesser scions to wear some very smart, long-wearing clothes they would otherwise never have owned. "That is the sort of thing on which our business is founded," Ohrbach senior likes to remind the help.

He has reminded them so well that when the Los Angeles store opened, the new manager there was able to include a curious, seemingly extraneous fact in an early report on how things were going. The employes' lounge in the store needed a cigarette machine, he said, and after shopping around he had been able to get one installed that would sell Ohrbach's clerks their cigarettes at 2¢ a pack less than they paid elsewhere. Jerry and "N.M." Ohrbach feel that their Los Angeles man is an able guy, with a real future in their business.

How Fashion Is Sold

Henri Bendel Has Staked Its Half-Century Reputation on a Brilliant Young Executive and Her Revolutionary Ideas. In Two Years She Has Given the Store a "New Look," Its Customers a "Bendel Look," Upped Sales 25 Per Cent

by Hannah Southern

Among the truly opulent purveyors of fashion, few can match—and none can exceed—the elegance of the Manhattan establishment known as Henri Bendel.

Here, in an atmosphere of hushed splendor, women to whom price is no object can indulge in the exquisite agony of choosing between a

Reprinted from the February 1960 issue of *Cosmopolitan* by special permission.

Dior and a Chanel, a sable coat (at $40,000) and a chinchilla (at a mere $30,000).

High prices, however, do not always mean high profits. Two years ago Bendel's, financially speaking, was falling flat on its elegant face. The Duke and Duchess of Windsor, it is true, were continuing to store her furs and his kilts there (Teddy Roosevelt had done the same with his African hunting gear and Franklin Roosevelt with his auto robes), but the store's proprietors were discovering, to their dismay, that they had more dignity than dollars. Bendel's remained the darling of the dowager set; debutantes were beginning to take their trade elsewhere.

General Shoe Corporation, which had operated the shoe department for a number of years, took over the entire store in 1957 and promptly launched a drive to restore Bendel's to its legendary place in the fashion firmament.

To spearhead the campaign, the firm nominated Geraldine Stutz, a young woman who had already made a name for herself as the *enfant terrible* of retailing, having attained a vice-presidency of the I. Miller Shoe Company at the age of thirty-one.

For the Woman of Taste

Now thirty-four, Miss Stutz, as president of Bendel's, inaugurated an overhauling operation for the entire store. Her aim: "a serene atmosphere, gracious personal service, the finest merchandise, for the woman of taste who is interested in beautiful things—regardless of cost."

As a starter, she converted the barn-like main floor into a "street" of small, specialized shops. ("It's hard to achieve a feeling of friendliness in wide-open spaces. It's easier and more pleasant to shop in small areas.") The "street," completed last September, contains eight shops in all, each with its own display windows and individual décor.

The Bijoutier, or jewelry-maker's shop, has a multi-arched roof supported by tapering columns of malachite. Display cases are suspended between the columns and all the stones shown in them are real. The Stocking Shop is a masterpiece of treillage, and The Perfumer boasts an authentic Louis XVI door from a Loire Valley chateau in its beige façade.

Strolling Bendel's "Street"

Across the "street," The Bag Shop has a gray and white décor with Corinthian columns. The Glove Shop, done in subtle shades of chamois and charcoal, is Directoire in feeling. The baroque façade of The Bagatelle, housing scarves, stoles, and handkerchiefs, is in light tones of aubergine; while The Gift Shop, in soft shades of gray and French blue, is done in circular Louis XVI style. The "street" ends with The Milliner, a two-story shop of Palladian influence carpeted and furnished in shades of beige and white. The total effect is reminiscent of such Old World luxury shopping thoroughfares as the Faubourg St. Honoré in Paris and Milan's Galleria Duomo.

When the main floor changes were well under way, Miss Stutz shifted her sights to the antiquated sixth floor. Here, under the direction of the Carita sisters of Paris, a posh beauty salon was established, complete with a podiatrist for foot care and an eye-catching wig department. Next came the second floor, which was redone in town-house style, with crystal chandeliers and rich draperies, as a setting for Bendel's most elegant Paris frocks and ball gowns. Ultimately, the entire store took on a new intimacy and charm.

The new décor, however, was only incidental in Geraldine Stutz' overall merchandising scheme. The key to her plan was creation of a "Bendel look." The woman dressed by Bendel's, she decided, must show it in every detail of her attire. She must become, in effect, a walking ad for the store.

What is the Bendel look? "It is an understated look," Geraldine Stutz says. "Elegant, chic, but not the last gasp. It is, rather, a contemporary, current look—one that plays up the woman herself rather than what she is wearing."

One of the designers most successful in capturing the Bendel quality of quiet tastefulness is Donald Brooks, who began by planning a line of sportswear for the store. This proved so successful that subsequently he was asked to concoct clothes of every kind, from fur coats to evening gowns. The full-skirted suits and billowing dresses with little jackets which he and other stylists have designed for the store are perhaps the truest expression to date of the Bendel look.

The Personal, Stutz Touch

To ensure attainment of this look for its customers, the store has adopted an unusual sales policy. "Each of our sales people," Miss Stutz says, "is trained to sell throughout the store. That way, the same clerk can assist in the selection of dress, shoes, bag—an entire ensemble."

In an era when most stores operate in an impersonal manner, this individualized service is rare. Even more rare is the store with a look, an identity, of its own.

As the originator of the look, and the philosophy behind it, Geraldine Stutz has become the personal symbol of Bendel's—one in which her employees take great pride.

"The Bendel look," they agree, "is the Stutz look."

Sears, Roebuck Has Discovered "A New Style-Consciousness among American Women." The Unprecedented Outcome: Paris-Designed Dresses for Its Famous Catalogue

Last fall thousands of women who, for several seasons, had resolutely rejected Oriental fashions as "not for me" suddenly blossomed out in Chinese brocade lounging pajamas.

What made them change their minds? Simply the appearance of the pajamas in the Sears, Roebuck Christmas catalogue. This, they knew, meant that Far Eastern styles were no longer a passing fad but an accepted fashion.

Through the years, Sears has made a practice of avoiding dubious items, concentrating instead on merchandise of proven sales appeal.

This policy has given the company unparalleled stature as a confirmer of fashion trends. It has also been—until recently—an almost foolproof way of doing business.

Changing with the Times

In the 1950's, however, this time-tested system began to run into trouble. Sales remained high ($250,000,000 worth of women's clothes were sold last year alone), but some of the supposedly surefire items failed to sell. "We came out with a denim wrap-around garment—a darn good item," recalls S. C. Hanson, supervisor of misses', juniors' and women's dresses. For some reason, the wrap-around failed to catch on. "Eventually," Hanson says, "it hit the overstock mail circulars, which, for us, is the equivalent of a store's marked-down rack."

What was wrong? Sears' marketing experts quickly discovered the answer. They were caught in a time-lag situation. Preparation of a Sears catalogue takes nine months—a period long enough for major style changes to occur. The wrap-around in question had "proven" its popularity, but now women were passing on to other things. For home wear, women were rapidly switching over to shorts, slacks, and blue jeans.

The time lag had never been a big problem before. Why was it suddenly becoming more important? Again, the answer was obvious. Communications media—television in particular—had speeded up the fashion cycle. Styles were catching on faster than ever before, and becoming dated more quickly. Sears would have to get in step, or lose customers.

They put their heads together and came up with a revolutionary plan. It was no longer feasible, they decided, merely *to follow* fashions; in the future, Sears would have to *foresee* them.

In 1956 a new fashion board was established. Its purpose: to judge the fashion pulse of the public and anticipate trends.

To head the board, the company tapped Mary Lewis, onetime style arbiter for Saks Fifth Avenue and Best and Company, who had joined Sears in 1940 because, "I'd rather sell 5000 of something for $10 than one thing for $500."

Her philosophy: "There are no hicks and no sticks any more. Today women everywhere know fashion and want to buy it. We've got to give it to them."

ues, she has been doing ex-
riental styles already men-
step in a long-range plan to
clothes to women through-
Sears' modest prices.
soon to follow. Last summer
ary Szur Barker, one of the
ers, went to Paris, visited the
and lined up some of their
favorite designers to concoct dresses especially for Sears.

These designs, adapted to mass-production techniques, are to be known as the Paris label line and will make their appearance in the company's spring catalogue. Will mail-order customers take to them? Mary Lewis feels certain that they will, and that they herald "a new era of fashion for Sears."

At Last, a Sears Bikini

Meanwhile, the company has by no means abandoned its old policy of waiting until a style is market-tested before stocking it. Sears has been holding up for years, for instance, on the bikini bathing suit, doubting that American women would ever buy it in volume. Now, however, Sears has reluctantly concluded that the bikini bathing suit is here to stay.

Sears officials are a bit embarrassed about this. "We don't like it," Vice President in Charge of Merchandise George Struthers says, "but we feel we have to go along with it." Accordingly, Sears will offer a bikini in next summer's catalogue.

"I hope," Struthers adds, "that is, I *like to think* that women who buy it from us will wear it only in the privacy of their own back yards."

The Man Who Sells Everything: Stanley Marcus

For the man with only $250,000 to spend on Christmas presents this year, there is a store dedicated to providing a wide selection of worldly goods tailored to his budget: Neiman-Marcus of Texas. There he may very well be waited on by the saturnine president of the company, Stanley Marcus, 55, who scours the world looking for unique, elegant, and offbeat items—and likes to sell them himself. This Christmas, for the well-heeled customer, he has a matched pair of Beechcraft airplanes neatly emblazoned "His" and "Hers" for $176,000, an espresso coffee-making machine at $250, or a roast beef serving cart for $2230 (which, Marcus points out, "includes 300 lbs. of steaks or 600 lbs. of beef on the hoof").

In the oil-welling land of the big spenders, Marcus has sought not only to create a store devoted to luxury but to provide standards that his often newly rich customers can rely on. Operating a store that is in many ways comparable to the best in Manhattan, he has effectively imposed Eastern and Continental taste on his customers. Though ready to indulge rich whims, he has been known to kill a good sale if he thinks a purchase is not suitable, *e.g.*, a mink coat for a college freshman. As a result, Neiman-Marcus is a respected name in stylish circles around the world. In the past decade Neiman-Marcus' sales have nearly doubled, will hit $41 million this year. The original store in downtown Dallas has branched into a suburban Dallas store and one in Houston. Last week Stanley Marcus announced plans for a new $2,000,000 store to be completed in 1962 in suburban Forth Worth.

The idea of a luxury store in a cattle-and-cotton city of 86,000 seemed slightly pretentious when Neiman-Marcus was founded in 1907 by Stanley's father, Herbert Marcus, and his aunt and uncle, Mr. and Mrs. A. L. Neiman. It was doing all right in 1926, with sales of $2,600,000, when Harvard-educated Stanley, then 21, went to work in the store's fur shop. Then the luxury goods really began to move. The year before the shop had sold only $74,000

---

worth of pelts. Using the casual low-pressure manner that he still assumes behind a counter, he sold $74,000 in furs in his first four months on the job. By the end of his first year, fur sales were $420,000.

His selling touch was matched by his talent for promotion and advertising. He instituted the annual Neiman-Marcus fashion design awards, which draw top designers from New York and Paris to the heart of Texas to show their originals. In his self-appointed role as the omninventoried merchant prince, Marcus window-shops Europe with his camera in search of ideas, on one trip spotted a French silk housecoat that he copied this year in chinchilla. Price: $7950. "We haven't sold any yet," he admits, "but we've had a couple of inquiries. I like it, and I like to keep my own appetite as a consumer whetted."

He pays his help well; a few Neiman clerks, working on commission as well as salary, can earn up to $25,000 a year. In return Marcus demands that they be unfailingly polite no matter how uncouth the customer may seem. He likes to remind them of the cotton-smocked girl who once came in straight off her father's farm. Papa had just struck oil, and Daughter spent $10,000 to outfit herself in style, including shoes for her bare feet.

Marcus married a Neiman salesgirl, Sportswear Buyer Mary Cantrell, in 1932. Today they live at No. 1 Nonesuch Road in a modern house jammed with paintings, books, and sculpture. A civic booster, he promotes Dallas with almost as much zeal as he does his store, works on everything from the Chamber of Commerce to the Symphony Society. But he likes nothing better than discovering things to sell. Once when a woman asked for a dress in a certain shade of buff yellow she had seen in a painting, Marcus had a fabric dyed to order in New York, made up a dress specially for her for only $42. The next season Neiman's "buff yellow" was a bestseller and a fashion hit.

Though it draws the biggest promotional splash, the carriage trade is only a small fraction of Neiman-Marcus' business. "We are geared to sell the oilman," says Marcus, "but even more, the oilman's secretary." Still, it is the very special sale that pleases him most. In one working day last week, Marcus came up with the gift for the "man who has everything, including a hangover," and sold a portable oxygen tank. Another customer who wanted "something new" got a watch specially made without numbers (it had only a single black dot). And then, of course, "the wife of the Vice President-elect came by and selected her inaugural gown along with a new suit."

We'd Like to Tell You about . . . Lane Bryant

"Maternity Dress, size 32, Amerika"—with only this address, a letter from a young woman in Poland was recently delivered to the Lane Bryant store—synonym for maternity wear—on Fifth Avenue, New York.

The founder of the nation-wide group of retail stores known as Lane Bryant, Inc., was an indomitable little woman who was born Lena Himmelstein in Lithuania, then part of Czarist Russia.

Orphaned as a baby, at 16 she was brought to the United States by relatives as a prospective bride for their son. When she met the young man, however, she would have none of him. Instead she joined a sister who was already in New York and went to work at $1 a week in a sweatshop making fine lingerie. Within four years she had learned English and machine sewing, and had advanced to the then high wage of $15 a week.

Marriage to David Bryant, a young Brooklyn jeweler, ended her job. But within a year after their son, Raphael, was born, in 1900, Bryant died, leaving his 20-year-old widow only a pair of diamond earrings. These she pawned to make a down payment on a sewing machine. In a tiny apartment shared with her sister, the young Mrs. Bryant returned to work.

Those were difficult days. She sometimes had to sew with the baby on her knee, and once the needle of the machine impaled one of his

---
Courtesy of Lane Bryant. Company booklet reprinted by permission.

fingers. She delivered the finished gowns and negligees herself. But her skill brought steady customers, finances improved, and she moved to larger quarters.

Into the shop one day came a young woman for whom Mrs. Bryant had done some sewing. "I am going to have a baby," she said. "Can you make me something practical in which I can entertain at home?"

Maternity dresses were unknown in New York in 1904. Mrs. Bryant met the challenge by creating a concealing tea gown with an elastic band attaching an accordian-pleated skirt to a bodice. The customer was delighted with it and told her friends. Other expectant mothers placed orders and Mrs. Bryant borrowed $300 from a brother-in-law for expansion of her small business.

This growth necessitated the opening of a bank account. Awed by the bank's marble lobby, the young widow's hand shook as she signed the deposit slip. The bank misread it and opened the account for "Lane" Bryant. She was too timid to rectify the mistake and later grew to like the name. It has been the company name ever since.

In 1909, Lena Bryant married Albert Malsin, a young engineer also born in Lithuania. They had three children within four years. With Mrs. Malsin wearing her own maternity clothes, her husband of necessity assumed an increasing role in her business enterprise. Where she had worked without patterns or measurements, he instituted engineering preciseness. It was his idea, too, that Lane Bryant should drop other items and specialize in maternity wear, layettes, and related merchandise.

Mrs. Malsin designed maternity dresses for street wear, a revolutionary move. Reluctant manufacturers had to be subsidized to make them in quantity. In those days, pregnancy was an unmentionable subject and the shop's side-street location was a great advantage. Some women left their carriages a block away and covered their faces as they entered the premises. Mail-order customers insisted on plain wrapping.

It was not until 1911 that the *New York Herald* was induced to accept a Lane Bryant advertisement for maternity dresses. It read:

> It is no longer the fashion nor the practice for expectant mothers to stay in seclusion. Doctors, nurses, and psychologists agree that at this time a woman should think and live as normally as possible. To do this she must go about among other people, she must look like other people.
>
> Lane Bryant has originated maternity apparel in which the expectant mother may feel as other women feel because she looks as other women look.

The advertisement brought such a crowd to the shop that all the street-wear maternity dresses in stock were sold by closing time. With the help of advertising and a World War boom in births, Lane Bryant sales passed one million dollars in 1917.

Malsin dreamed of additional specialties. A chance letter gave his thoughts direction. "Won't some ingenous man please take pity on us stout women?" a customer wrote. "Surely some way could be found for us to buy comfortable and stylish clothes as easily as our slimmer sisters do."

Malsin made a study of female figures, obtaining measurements of more than 200,000 women. He discovered that nearly 40 per cent of them were larger than the "perfect 36" idealized by artists and dressmakers. No ready-to-wear dresses were then available for these women.

Mrs. Malsin began to design clothes for this market. The new dresses were fashionable in appearance: vertical lines and slash pockets produced an illusion of slenderness. As a crowning psychological stroke, a size system was adopted by which a woman who requires a 42 elsewhere fits comfortably into a Lane Bryant 40.

After a slow start, Lane Bryant's outsize business boomed. By the time of Malsin's death in 1923, it accounted for more than half the $5,000,000-a-year sales.

Later, other groups were added for such special groups as tall women and chubby girls, half-sizes, Jr. Plenty and Minims for young matrons and short, plump women.

As business in hard-to-find sizes increased and the modern, wholesome attitude towards maternity developed, Lane Bryant stores were established in major cities across the country. In 1928 the Newman-Benton Midwest chain of clothing stores were absorbed. By 1941 the mail-order operations were shifted from New York to Indianapolis.

Although Mrs. Lane Bryant died in 1951, she lived to see her firm develop into a nationally known company. Her son, Raphael, is now president of the firm, guiding the organization in the same pioneering tradition formulated by his mother.

The First Family Of Retailing

In a Business where Tenths of a Cent Make the Difference, Federated Department Stores Easily Leads Its Competition. That It Does So Is Due in No Small Part to the Merchandising Genius of the Lazarus Family, Whose Watchwords Are "Dominance" and "Growth"

In Tokyo, the footloose shopper is likely to wind up at the Mitsukoshi Store (in business since 1673), which for a price will furnish not only complete weddings but the necessary boy-meets-girl introduction service as well. In Moscow, of course, the No. One store is state-run GUM, the cavernous gray emporium on Red Square which is not above staging capitalistic fashion shows. London has its Harrods, which will purvey a talking macaw, a funeral service, or an overcoat with the same unruffled efficiency.

The United States, too, has its share of great stores. In Columbus, Ohio, for example, "the" store is F. & R. Lazarus, the biggest and most estimable for many miles around. In New York's bedroom borough, Brooklyn, Abraham & Straus occupies a similar eminence. In Houston, the leader is Foley's; in Cincinnati, Shillito's; in Miami, Burdine's.

All of this latter group have one thing in common: they are members of the complex known as Federated Department Stores, the United States' biggest (1960 sales: about $785 million), most profitable (1960 net: an estimated $33.5 million) department store chain. With such other top stores as Bloomingdale's in Manhattan, Sanger's in Dallas, Boston's famous Filene's (home of the original bargain basement), and Rike's of Dayton, they make Federated the leading retailer almost everywhere it operates a store (and it operates, all told, 50 main stores and branches in 32 communities).

Reprinted from the March 15, 1961, issue of *Forbes Magazine* by special permission.

To achieve that $785 million in sales last year,* Federated's 15,000 selling employees (about 40 per cent of its total) averaged $50,000–$55,000 in sales apiece. They rang up more than 130 million transactions, or well over 700 each minute of each business day, with an average "ticket" of close to $6. They turned over their stocks of inventory, on average, five times during the year. Ninety-five per cent of their sales (including men's furnishings) were made to women. Understandably, Federated makes constant surveys to see what the *women* in its trading areas think of the local Federated store.

First Family. Federated has fought its way to the top of the bitterly competitive retailing heap through the efforts of a long line of predecessor merchant chiefs, including such famous names as Filene's Lincoln Filene, A&S's Walter Rothschild, and Frederick Rike of Dayton. But unquestionably the first name in retailing's first chain belongs today to Clan Lazarus, a tightly knit group of third- and fourth-generation retailers descended from one Simon Lazarus, a refugee from German religious persecution who opened a tiny men's clothing store in Columbus in 1851.

At Federated's helm today is "Mr. Fred" Lazarus, 76, one of Simon's four merchant grandsons. Second in command is Fred's son, "Mr. Ralph," 47, Federated's president. And scattered throughout Federated are no less

*Federated's 1964 sales were in excess of 1.2 billion dollars with pre-tax earnings of 9.6 per cent as against an industry average of 4.6 per cent.

than eight other members of the family which the retailing world respectfully calls "the Lazari." (Federated employees, to avoid confusion, invariably address them as "Mr.," followed by the first name.)

It would be wrong to assume that even so successful a group of merchants as the Lazari could (or would try to) dictate policy to the diverse group of highly profitable stores which constitutes Federated today. But in the largely advisory role which the chain's central management plays, theirs is certainly the most influential voice—just as the Lazarus store in Columbus most completely dominates its trading area and is, therefore, probably Federated's most profitable single unit.

About Face. Until 1945 even that advisory role was unknown. For the first sixteen years of its existence (the outgrowth of a meeting of Fred Lazarus, Walter Rothschild, and Louis Kirstein of Filene's on Rothschild's yacht in the summer of 1929), Federated was merely a paper holding company, designed to spread the risks among its four members (Lazarus, A&S, Filene's, and Bloomingdale's).

As the war neared an end, it became clear that Federated either had to grow or dissolve. It was making more money than could profitably be plowed back into existing stores, especially in the crowded metropolitan areas of the East. What's more, trade rumor had it, Clan Lazarus had some cause for dissatisfaction, since the F. & R. Lazarus store was contributing proportionately more and more of total profits.

Things reached the point at which serious talks were held in 1944–1945 to consider breaking up Federated. But some major interests were firmly opposed, and, in the end, it was decided to take the opposite tack. In June 1945, a central management office with Mr. Fred at its head, was established in Cincinnati. Since then, Federated's sales have nearly quadrupled, while profits have risen more than sixfold.

Growth-minded. In view of that remarkable record, management is understandably, strongly growth-minded. Last month, while Mr. Fred recuperated from a mild illness, Ralph Lazarus explained why growth is the key word in Federated's lexicon.

"We've often admitted that we are not good merchants in a 'control' situation," notes Mr. Ralph, "that is, a situation where you have to be concerned about the elements of expense rather than building greater customer acceptance. Grandfather Lazarus used to say 'You can't buy ham sandwiches with percentages,' and we believe it. The key to profits is not to cut *down* your overhead, but to build *up* your volume. And you do that by making your store the headquarters store for more people buying more different types of goods than any other store in your community."

What the Lazaruses mean by a headquarters store is well illustrated by Mr. Fred's story of a Brooklyn mother whose daughter was soon to leave for summer camp. Armed with a list of 38 necessary items, she shopped A&S—and emerged with 36 of them. "That lady," notes Mr. Fred with satisfaction, "will always think first of A&S, because she *knows* she can find there almost anything she wants."

Thinking Big. Federated's ambitions, however, are not confined merely to its chosen field of retailing. Says Mr. Ralph: "We want to be a company which will compare favorably in return on investment with the growth companies in *any* field" (see chart). Adds he: "Our objec-

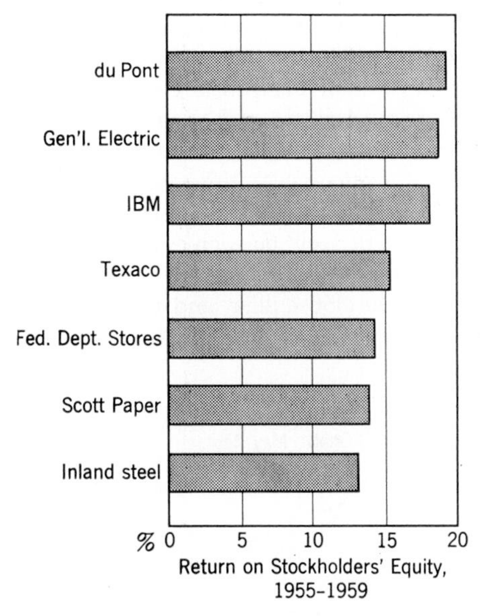

Blue-chip showing. Retailing has earned a reputation as a low profit business. Not so for Federated Department Stores, however. Its return on stockholders' capital has been roughly on a par with that of many of the most profitable giant corporations in other industries.

tive is a 20 per cent after-tax return, even though our average in recent years has been around 15 per cent."

Still, the 15 per cent return which Federated has been netting since the mid-fifties compares favorably, not only with leaders of other industries, but with the biggest names in two different types of merchandising, Sears and Penney. Thus, though Federated's 14.3 per cent average return since 1955 still trails Penney's kingsized 17.5 per cent, it is a trifle above Sears' 14.1 per cent showing, despite the lack of the nonmerchandising "kickers" (e.g., insurance) which have markedly boosted Sears' take in recent years. Within Federated's own department store group, it is simply no contest: the next best equity return is May Department Stores' 10.8 per cent.

Federated has achieved this impressive showing, what's more, with the benefit of very little leverage in its capital structure. As of January 31, 1960, long-term debt made up a trifling 8.1 per cent of its total capital, and that figure sank even lower last year. "We are not unaware of the advantages of leverage," says Ralph Lazarus with a grin. "But we don't think a high proportion of debt is consistent with the sort of quality company we want to be."

Vital Difference. It is axiomatic among retailers that they are all engaged in the same business. With few exceptions, they buy merchandise which any other retailer can buy and offer it for resale at a price which the competition usually can (and will) match. Yet Federated nets a snappy 4.3 per cent on each dollar of sales, well above the industry average of 3.1 per cent for stores in the $50 million and up range, which is where most of its major units fall. That 4.3 per cent is also more than twice the profit-poor 1.9 per cent which arch-rival Allied Stores, from whom Federated took the sales lead in 1957, netted in its latest 12 months (see chart).

Its above-average profit margin, in turn, is the key to Federated's top-drawer return on equity. For, like other retailers, Federated must carry the same substantial merchandise inventories, keep working capital tied up to provide liberal credit terms. Thus Federated's total assets work only a bit harder than its competitors': in 1959 it rang up $2.19 in sales for each dollar of assets, compared with $2.27 for Macy's, $2.02 for Associated Dry Goods, and a pace-setting $2.34 for Allied.

Yet since Federated hangs on to more of each sales dollar than the competition, its final profit showing is easily the best. If, for example, Federated had netted only the big-store average 3.1 per cent on its sales for 1955–1959, its return on equity would have shrunk from the actual 14.3 per cent to just 9.8 per cent, or just what Associated (which *did* have a 3.1 per cent profit margin) showed.

Profit Principle. Thus the question is: *how* does Federated manage to wring more profit out of each sales dollar than a group of competitors who are, presumably, equally devoted to the objective of making money?

"The answer is twofold," replies Ralph Lazarus. "First, we organize for maximum profit by pushing the responsibility for profit down to the lowest possible level—the department manager. Secondly, we try to be sure that the Federated store is always the dominant store in its trading area, the one which sets the pace for other retailers."

The role of the department manager within

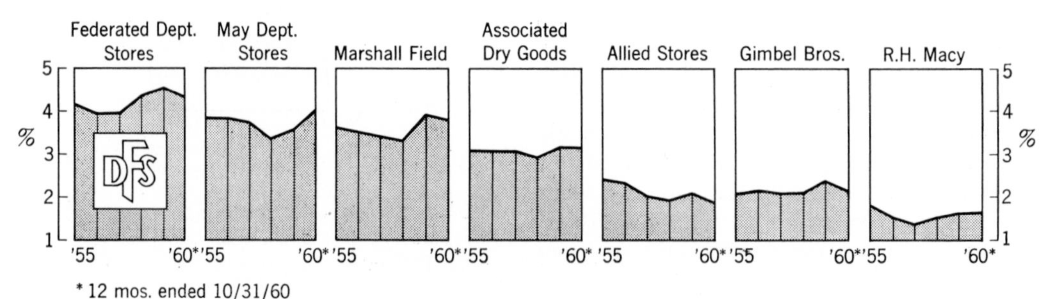

Well-run store. On two major scores, Federated's retailing skill has paid off in profits: (1) it has led all major retailing chains in net profit margins, and, (2) it has been one of the few able to increase those margins over the past five difficult years.

Federated is one of Fred Lazarus' many contributions to American retailing * (another: assortments grouped by sizes, an idea he picked up while on a busman's holiday at Paris' Galeries Lafayette). It has since been widely imitated by other United States retailers, but never with quite the same success.

The Entrepreneur. Dissatisfied with the old subdivision of a store into functional pyramids (*e.g.*, merchandising, services, accounting, and publicity—an organization pioneered at Filene's), Fred Lazarus first introduced the department manager set-up at Lazarus in the late twenties. Essentially, it puts one man in charge of both buying and selling all the merchandise in a single department. "Selling," however, includes floor displays, advertising, maintaining adequate stocks, scheduling special promotions, and training sales people.

The department manager is charged a proportionate amount of rent for the space he occupies, for its light and heat and for the supporting services (e.g., delivery) he uses. After all these charges, he is expected to show a satisfactory profit on his operations. Just what constitutes a satisfactory profit varies with the historical performance of his department and what the store management *thinks* it ought to earn. It is always expected to be above-average for the community.

"We're trying," explains Ralph Lazarus, "to make every department manager virtually an independent entrepreneur, to make his profit-and-loss statement as realistic as it would be if he were actually operating his own store. After all, many of our departments do a million or more dollars of sales a year, which is far bigger than many competing specialty stores."

To keep the department manager constantly reaching for profitable growth, each January and July he sits down with his store's top management to draw up two six-month plans. One projects the sales he expects to achieve during the next six months, and the profits he ought to realize on those sales. ("We encourage him to be conservative," notes Mr. Ralph.) The other is a "word plan," a verbal analysis of his department's strengths and weaknesses and what he proposes to do about each. ("We think that's even more important that the sales budget," says Ralph Lazarus.)

Building Dominance. Just the same, Federated"s management is keenly aware that even the most aggressive department manager is hard put to show a satisfactory profit (as Federated defines "satisfactory") unless his department is part of the community's leading store —what the Lazari call "the dominant store." How they go about building a store into a dominant position is best illustrated, perhaps, by the story of Shillito's.

When F. & R. Lazarus bought the John Shillito store for $2.5 million in 1928 (the year before Federated was founded), it was trading largely on its reputation as the oldest store west of the Alleghanies (founded 1830). It ranked no better than fourth among Cincinnati stores, with a 1927 volume of about $4 million. Many of its departments were leased, its merchandise was cheap to the point of shoddiness, and its building was 50 years old.

Fred Lazarus, assisted by his brother Jeffrey (who still runs Shillito's), set out to regain first spot among Cincinnati retailers. The old store was refurbished, the cheap merchandise quickly sold out. Then, department by department, Fred Lazarus set out to get the lion's share of the Cincinnati market. Shaving markups to the bone, profiting by the mistakes of rather feeble competition, the Lazari boosted sales more than 50 per cent, to $6.5 million, in 1929. By 1939 Shillito's was once again No. One, with sales of over $10.7 million. Last year it did an estimated $57 million, over one-third of all Federal Reserve department store volume in the Cincinnati area, and more than its two biggest competitors combined.

Once a Federated store reaches the top in its trading area, local management has two responsibilities: to stay on top and to keep growing. Federated's brass is unlikely to dictate *how* those jobs are to be done, but it will certainly want to know why if they are *not* done.

One important technique of staying ahead is a "lively" sales atmosphere. "Downtown stores," notes Mr. Ralph, "ought to generate at least $70–$75 of sales per square foot, and a branch that's been in business three years, at least $60." Of Federated's total sales, some 75 per cent still comes from its 11 downtown units.

---

* Although substantially the same idea has long been an article of faith for Canada's famed T. Eaton & Co., a pioneer of such other notable retailing innovations as the catalog order office, since adopted by Sears and Montgomery Ward.

The Beaut. Federated's management knows that each year's retained profits constitute, in effect, a new subscription of money by stockholders—who may withdraw their money if they are dissatisfied with the way it is reinvested. Says Ralph Lazarus: "We don't feel at liberty to use our undistributed earnings to subsidize marginal or substandard operations. They should be used as profitably as the proceeds from a new issue of stock."

Even so astute a management as Federated's, however, occasionally makes mistakes. And, as the late Fiorello LaGuardia used to say: "When I make a mistake, I make a beaut!" Federated's beaut of a mistake came ten years ago when, looking for new ways to reinvest its earnings at a profit, it decided to build a chain of small department stores (to be called Fedway, i.e., "the Federated way") in the faster-growing cities of the bustling Southwest and West.

Fred Lazarus was among the first to note the steady postwar drift of the United States population to the South and West. The first acquisition he made for Federated, in fact, was Foley's of Houston—a city in which he had already rounded up land to build a store when Foley's owners at last agreed to sell. (It was during this deal that Mr. Fred turned real-estate salesman to peddle a parcel of land which had cost $1,250,000 for $3,050,000, a price which gleeful Houstonites noted was the equivalent of $2000 a "front inch"—still a local record.)

Problem Child. But Fedway was another matter. The Lazari still believe that the concept was sound, and will ultimately prove profitable. But they freely acknowledge that Fedway has been a problem child for most of its ten-year existence.

"We made a lot of mistakes," admits Ralph Lazarus frankly. "We paid top prices for real estate in towns whose growth curve began to level off after we came in. We overbuilt our stores for volume growth that just didn't materialize. Those factors gave us a heavy burden of fixed charges to carry. Worst of all, though, we tried to superimpose our knowledge and experience from Cincinnati and New York on brand-new selling organizations thousands of miles away."

The results were predictable. Except for one or two, notably in Alburquerque, Fedway stores' results were (and are) far below expectations. They have also claimed a disproportionate amount of management time and effort. One Fedway unit, Halliburton's of Oklahoma City, suddenly went out of business last month. "It was a choice," explains Ralph Lazarus, "between chasing strong competitors to the suburbs or quitting. We had lost our downtown position and couldn't regain it without terrific added effort and investment."

All remaining Fedway units are now in the black. Most, however, are not yet returning what Federated brass considers a satisfactory profit. The result: plans for Fedway's future are being restudied. "We know now," says Ralph Lazarus, "that it is difficult to build profitable new stores in a community new to you except in unusually fast-growing towns which are drastically under-stored." Henceforth, Fedway may expand by acquisition, too. Last June the Lazari bought Levy's of Tucson and added it to Fedway.

Minding the Store. Fortunately for Federated stockholders, Fedway is not large enough (probably no more than 5 per cent of total volume) to drag down the group's overall results perceptibly. Moreover, in re-examining the idea of building new stores, the Lazari are returning to one of their own first principles. As Mr. Fred has often said: "We are retailers, not realtors. We have always believed that we could make more money selling merchandise than owning land. If not, we shouldn't be in retailing."

The Lazari have no quarrel with the several big retailers (among them: May, Allied, Gimbel's) who firmly believe in owning the land which underlies their stores—land which can be made to turn a profit through wholly owned, unconsolidated real-estate subsidiaries. But Federated prefers either to rent from a builder or to build itself for a sale-and-lease-back. True, it has sold no stores for several years; as a result, it now owns 40 per cent of the space it occupies, up from 25 per cent in 1957. Notes Mr. Ralph: "Recently the money market has been wrong, with rents high and attractive reinvestment opportunities scarce. When money rates ease, we might well sell off some stores."

The results Federated has achieved over the years certainly suggest that in retailing it pays to stay home and mind the store while letting others tie up dollars in real estate. In 1960, for example, Federated was one of the few retailers to raise sales in what Ralph Lazarus calls "the most unseasonable year in memory: bad winter, late spring, cool summer, warm autumn, then terrible weather during the peak Christmas selling season." The snows of December and January ("We got clobbered in New York and Boston, two mighty big towns for us," notes Mr. Ralph) trimmed Federated's nine-month sales increase, but it still wound up 1960 an estimated 3.3 per cent ahead of 1959.

But that modest gain, well below Federated's average 8.7 per cent increase in 1955–1959, was dearly won. To achieve it, Federated spent more promotion dollars, took bigger markdowns to keep its merchandise moving. Result: total net probably slipped modestly below 1959's $33.8 million, despite the sales pickup, and earnings per share fell an estimated 5 per cent to about $1.90. Even that somewhat discouraging showing, however, promised to outpace the as-yet-unreleased results of rival retailers, most of whose earnings were down far more sharply at the year's three-quarter mark.

Market Payoff. Federated's consistently above-average performance has by no means been lost on Wall Street, where its stock has more than quadrupled in the last decade. Equally noteworthy, perhaps, Federated is the only major department store chain whose stock commands a really substantial premium over its book value. Thus last month, each dollar of book was worth $2.78 in market value to Federated, versus Associated's next-best $1.63, May's $1.55, and a dismal 88¢ for Allied.

Federated is hardly strapped for cash. It is well able to afford its 50 per cent—plus payout of annual earnings to stockholders. But it knows that when and if it *does* need money, management's prestige in the marketplace will help get it on the cheapest possible terms. Which explains why both Lazaruses say, again and again, "We're not merely interested in growing. We're interested only in growing *profitably*."

What Makes a "Favorite" Store?

Overheard on the down escalator of a big, respected department store: "They didn't have a good selection. We should go to ————'s, but I wouldn't touch it with a 10-foot pole."

This chance comment serves a warning to retailers. Obviously, something in the minds of these customers overrode their conviction that they would find what they wanted at the store just down the street. It was the same something that sent the shopper in the picture into the store of her choice rather than the one next door. Part of the reason may be summed up in the words "store personality."

In the past year, there has been a flurry about the need of a sharp store "image" in the minds of consumers. Latest sign was the announcement two weeks ago of a study by Super Market Merchandising. The study reveals that housewives have highly personal feelings about the supermarkets in their neighborhood, and guide their shopping accordingly.

Reprinted from the June 14, 1958, issue of *Business Week* by special permission.

Danger Signals. Many retailers insist that maintaining a personality or image is no harder now than it has been. But some see dangers ahead.

For Stanley Marcus, president of Neiman-Marcus Co., the prime peril is mass production and conformity.

Big J. L. Hudson Company in Detroit is frankly worried. Rising costs threaten their whole concept of the utmost in service, Hudson executives feel. They are asking, Can we present in the 1960's the face we have shown in the past?

Yet the pressure to individualize is strong. It is one way a merchant can claim his market for his own, reinforce his bargaining power with his suppliers.

How—and Why? *Business Week* talked with some dozen retailers and found two main approaches:

There's the store that aims to be "all things to all people."

There's the store that holds, "You can't be all things to all people."

Certain outside factors play a part. For the

old store, heritage often dictates the kind of operation it runs. Location has an impact. And the physical size of a store may dictate the breadth of stock it carries.

I. "All Things to All"

Macy's-New York is one store that seeks universal appeal. Its market—the high-low to the low-high income—cuts a broad swathe. How do you cover the waterfront and still have a character of your own?

Macy's doesn't hesitate to use showmanship. "Macy's is theater," says Mrs. Frances Corey, senior vice-president. She proves it by citing events on a given day: on the first floor, a big promotion (such as a flower show); on the dress floor, a fashion show; in the arts and crafts department, a hobby show; on the home furnishings floor, a "Plan a Home" display.

Pianos to Underwear. Something for everyone means the widest assortment of goods. "I wouldn't know how many millions of items we carry," says Pres. Elliot V. Walter. They include such oddities as long underwear, pianola rollers, celluloid collars.

Macy's merchandise does exclude the low-low in price because, says Walter, there you get into shoddy goods. And the high-priced items serve mainly as frosting on the cake. In the vast middle range, it seeks individuality through private brands, "Macy's Own" label, covering 1500 to 2000 items.

Another Macyism: "We maintain." It cites its slogan, "It's smart to be thrifty," as a case in point. This was a Depression-born slogan but it hits the times just right, officials believe.

In all its 100 years, it has stuck by its 6 per cent less for cash policy. Customers who use a credit system pay for it, Walter explains. Cash customers still get their price advantage.

Family Store. John Wanamaker, in Philadelphia, says "Wanamaker has everything. It thinks of itself as a family store, with a friendly atmosphere. Like Macy's it has some very high-priced merchandise, but it also has national brands.

Emphasizing that it is more than a store, Wanamaker devotes 40 per cent of its space to institutional affairs. Its great organ puts on three concerts a day. Leading civic groups use its club rooms and auditoriums. Its religious window displays at Christmas and Easter are another way Wanamaker says, "We are more than a store."

Regional-Minded. No store puts more steam into the institutional approach than Rich's, Inc., of Atlanta. Its Christmas opening ceremony rings in the holiday for Atlantans. It entertains visiting notables. For visiting conventions it offers fashion shows, lunches.

Richard H. Rich, president, is deep in social and civic activities, and gives employees time off to do the same. One big display window is used regularly for community projects—the Boy Scouts, for example. It will put on "spend the day parties" for out-of-town groups.

Rich's throws an extra fillip into its institutionalism. It capitalizes on Southern loyalty. "Atlanta born, Atlanta owned, Atlanta managed," it proclaims.

The big store tries to individualize its "waterfront" policy of something for everyone by treating its departments as sharply differentiated specialty shops. At the same time, it makes a strong point that you'll find everything there. "If rice grew in Piedmont Park," an ad reads, "Rich's would carry the best chopsticks."

Community Power. J. L. Hudson is another big store that goes in for strong community activity. It seeks, in fact, a dual role: to be dominant store and dominant institution in its area. It was Hudson that decided that Detroit should have the most splendid shopping centers in the country. Hudson has been the mainspring, too, in Detroit's urban redevelopment program, and a big backer of such projects as Harper Hospital.

In the store, Hudson's slogan has been, "Tell us if we're wrong." This includes a policy of not being undersold—by discounter or anyone else; of liberal returns (they run around $25 million a year); of free delivery.

Carson Pirie Scott & Company in Chicago shoots squarely for the middle of the road: good merchandise, not too expensive, not too fashionable, not too dull. Its target: to achieve a friendly family feeling, to satisfy the broad market that might feel uncomfortable in a high fashion store.

II. For Special People

Says Dorothy Shaver of Lord & Taylor, "We try to have a well-bred store, run by well-bred people, for well-bred customers."

Breeding, to Miss Shaver, doesn't necessarily mean high prices. "There is no price tag on taste," she feels. So Lord & Taylor has a budget floor, along with merchandise for upper-middle income groups.

How do you project a well-bred personality?

One way, says Miss Shaver, is to treat every job with dignity. "No one has to punch a time clock," Mrs. Alieda van Wesep, vice-president, amplifies. "No one—not even the elevator operators—wears a uniform. We aren't open evenings, a fact that attracts the type of employee we want. There's no high-pressure selling."

Another Lord & Taylor tenet is to make shopping pleasant. "I felt you could apply a knowledge of art to retailing," Miss Shaver says. "People respond to beauty. This is a troubled world. We want to be gay. Why can't shopping be fun?"

Partly because its location is farther downtown than many Manhattan shops of its kind, L&T stresses exclusive merchandise—so people would have to come here, explains Mrs. van Wesep.

West Coast Tactics. Neiman-Marcus has a goal similar to Lord & Taylor: offering Texas the finest merchandise with the best taste. In fashion, Stanley Marcus sees his role as an educational one. "We introduced the chemise three years ago," he says. Such a policy means a willingness to gamble.

The Dallas specialty store is famous for its flair in putting over fashion ideas—such gala promotions as last fall's French Fortnight.

San Francisco's I. Magnin & Co. also is proud of its fashion education job. "Beautiful merchandise in pleasant surroundings," so President Hector Escabosa sums up his shop. Like Chicago's Marshall Field, Magnin goes in heavily for high fashion, French couture. And like Lord & Taylor, it belives that its prestige and attitude bring it the all-important personnel it wants.

No Frills. Robert Hall Clothes, Inc., is an example of a limited appeal chain that aims at quite a different group. President Harold Rosner describes this as "the average family, who wants their pound of meat without the fat." "Low overhead"—conveying to its customers that a shopper gets his full dollar's worth in merchandise value—is Robert Hall's advertising theme. And the chain backs up its promises with an extremely liberal returns policy.

Robert Hall stores are bare of frills. But Rosner doesn't consider service a frill. So he has fitting rooms, sales personnel, strives for a friendly store. That is one reason he keeps his stores relatively small; some people find a large store cold, he says.

III. Character Stores

A remarkable institution with its own flavor is Sattler's, Buffalo's No. 1 store in dollar volume. This is another one-stop store. Possibly because it is several miles from the heart of downtown, it set out to be the "three-ring circus," the "Hellzapoppin store." Be as crazy as you can—drag in the crowds, runs its theme song.

So Sattler's has had elephants in its dress department, weddings in its store windows. When Mrs. Stanton of Massachusetts sent 68¢ and asked Sattler's to send her "any bargain," the store organized a Mrs. Stanton's Day in no time. It brought her and her husband to the city, greeted them with a parade, showered them with $5,000 in gifts.

Much of its merchandise is distress merchandise. It operates on a principle of buying right, selling for less, creating a folksy atmosphere. Sales, sales, sales are its selling theme.

Offbeat. Another oddity, is Raymond's, the "Bargin Stoar," in Boston. It plays itself up as a country store, appealing to the shrewd Downeaster who knows a bargain when he sees it. Its misspelled ads are famous in its area.

Like Robert Hall, Raymond's makes a virtue of offering no frills. It sets up its wares in what it calls "horse-sense displays." Much of its merchandise is very cheap, but the whole set-up aims to flatter the customer into feeling he is a smart, knowledgeable shopper.

IV. Friendly Supers

Kroger Company is one food chain that works hard to overcome the coldness that self-service, vast displays create. Joseph Hall, president, concentrates on an air of friendliness.

The supermarket has two ways to achieve warmth, Hall feels: the decor, and the personnel. Time was when supers felt that shiny white was desirable. Kroger hired Howard Ketcham, color specialist, to give his stores warmth.

Extra-wide aisles, to give housewives room to chat, are another gesture to friendliness.

Personal Touch. The big food chain comes down hard on courtesy in its training program. At one time Kroger offered a free loaf of bread to every customer who didn't get a "thank you" from the checkout employee.

Up to his ears in charity himself, Kroger expects his managers to follow suit. His ads often have a personal tinge—introducing the manager as a man active in his community.

V. Problems

No store would say it is easy to make itself a sharply defined entity. Communications—putting management concepts into actuality at the counter level—is a major problem. Here is where the veteran employee plays a part.

Rising costs are another. "We've never thrown out a service on a profit basis," says an official of J. L. Hudson. "We weigh it against customer need. But we don't know how long we can keep it up." It has been chipping away at some of its time-honored policies. Customers can no longer return hats and bathing suits. Shopping bags, once free, now cost a nickel. Self-service has appeared in one department.

Projected Image. Branch stores present another problem. Most of the big stores project the downtown store image in their suburban shops. But Sattler's and Raymond's sometimes have to tone down their capers for suburban shops.

Time brings changes to some of the old concepts. Lord & Taylor was once the special stronghold of the conservative, mature customer. Now often it is the young that stretch their budgets to go there. Bloomingdale Bros. is in process of upgrading to match the growing affluence of its neighborhood on New York's East Side.

Hard or not, retailers agree with Macy's Elliott Walter: "You can't be a me-too store and survive."

Fashion Merchandising

The manner in which a store meets the challenges of fashion retailing is often decided by the man at the helm—the merchant whose understanding of people and of fashion is translated into sound management of the store and wise sponsorship of fashions particularly acceptable to that store's customers. Following are the philosophies of three great fashion merchants: the late Hector Escobosa, Alfred H. Daniels, and Stanley Marcus. Each has made a noteworthy contribution in this special field.

Fashion, The Heartbeat of Retailing

by Hector Escobosa

Fashion had always been I. Magnin's act and it is fashion we want to discuss today.

1. ***Fashion Is the Force behind All Discretionary Spending.*** . . . Fashion keeps the retailer in business, fashion keeps merchandise moving. Fashion is the most exciting, most creative, most dynamic force in one of the most competitive businesses in the world. Fashion produces obsolescence . . . an important factor in the American economy.

2. ***Fashion Is Our Most Effective Tool with Which to Meet Today's Competition.*** . . . Our competitor is no longer just the merchant across the street. Competition today goes beyond our

---

Mr. Escobosa, now deceased, was president of I. Magnin San Francisco, when he delivered this address at the Annual Convention of the National Retail Merchants Association, January 7, 1963 (Statler-Hilton Hotel, New York).

cities, our counties, our states and even our country. In our stores today we compete with the world at large.

We have discount houses selling dresses and other soft goods, supermarkets selling such items as hosiery, more customers buying clothes in Paris and Rome, more customers shopping in Hong Kong and Bangkok, more shopping centers, more branches of well-established stores, more mail-order specialists and unscrupulous and short-sighted manufacturers selling to customers directly.

Competition is keen between retailers. It is also fierce between different businesses and services, all striving for a larger slice of the consumers' total income. Should she buy a coat or a car, should it be a dress or dryer, go on a safari, or buy a sofa? To meet this competition we must work for the elimination of all waste.

We must achieve greater efficiency. We must use every tool at our command. We must learn to think of fashion not as an unpredictable and mysterious process but as a tangible force which can be charted and graphed . . . which can be understood, explained, and projected. The more we know about fashion, the better we can use it.

3. ***Fashion Know-How Is the Extra Ingredient Every Store Must Have.*** . . . Fashion is the quality which adds luster, life, character, personality, and interest to a store. It is the difference between death and survival, between dullness and sparkle.

Fashion is the retailer's most productive ally . . . our assets and attractions may include . . . beautiful assortments, attractive stores, convenient parking areas, brighter advertising, but fashion is the catalytic agent which keeps customers coming.

Fashion is the final spark that gets everything moving and parts the customer from her cherished dollar . . . provided we understand it and also provided we teach our salespeople what it is and how to use it. But more about our sales people later. Their importance is really my message today.

4. ***But What Is Fashion?*** . . . Fashion exists in all fields from dresses to diets, from furs to furniture, from cars to coats. It affects what we eat, the movies we see, the language we use, the way we think and vote and act. Fashion affects not only the way we dress, but almost every facet in our lives.

Fashion is a constantly evolving tide—seldom capricious—and generally orderly in its constant evolution. Fashion is a power stimulated by man's eternal desire to create something better or more beautiful—and praise the Lord for the designers, for the artists and for all the creative souls in this world.

Fashion feeds on new designs and new designs are created by a dynamic compulsion that keeps creators constantly experimenting . . . striving for something newer, more exciting, more beautiful.

5. ***And Where Does Fashion Come From?*** . . . Is it always and only from Paris? No, its sources today are many. To better understand it, fashion must be studied at all its sources.

Representatives from I. Magnin have been going to Europe regularly since 1906 and we try to keep up with what is going on in all the creative markets of the world.

Paris is no longer the only fashion fountainhead—but Paris still supplies the spirit, the mood, the essence, the overall direction that fashion follows. Paris is the best laboratory of fashion ideas, it is the place where many of the accepted styles are born. Perfect atmosphere for creation. Besides Paris we have: Italy—superb knits and exciting sportswear. Since World War II: exotic, far-away places such as Thailand—Siamese colors—textured silks. India—handwoven silks—exquisite saris. Japan—obi sashes—kimono sleeves—subtle, mysterious print designs. Hong Kong—Chinese brocades—tribute silks—frog fastenings. West Germany, Scotland, Spain all contributing to the eternal process of trial and error—of developing ideas with the hope that the customers will like them.

Many painters create purely for self-expression, but good fashion designers create to please the ultimate consumer as well as to express themselves.

6. ***In Discussing the World Influences on Fashion We Must Pay Tribute to America's Tremendous Contributions.*** . . . From the exclusive, expensive, and very fine designs of Norman Norell and Galanos down to the remarkable values of Jonathan Logan and Suzy Perette, the United States is very good at every price level. . . . The United States supplies the best values, most sizes (about 35 different sizes and proportions)—most scientifically cut—most quickly adapted—best mass-produced clothes in the world.

We have the greatest ability to interpret and adapt ideas from the world world—we can and do deliver the Dior A line, the St. Laurent tunic, or the Balenciaga shape three weeks after Paris presents it.

We influence other countries as much or more than they influence us—often an American idea goes to Paris and returns with a French accent and rave notices. But as great as the New York market is. . . .

7. *All Good American Fashion Does Not Come from Seventh Avenue.* . . . Good American clothes are designed in New York, but also in Chicago, Florida, and other cities. I must mention the influence and development of California as an important fashion source. Swim suit—sportswear—casual dresses—couture—began with Adrian in the 40's, now include such greats as Galanos, Kilpatrick, Jean Louis. California makes a distinguished contribution to today's one world of fashion—by working on a realistic delivery schedule continues to increase the share of the market that it takes.

8. *With Jets, Television, and Travel There Is Only One World of Fashion Today.* It is hard to tell the women from Madrid apart from the one from Montreal—more and more standards of what is good fashion have become international.

9. *Choice Today, from the Whole World, Is So Varied That Each Store Has to Edit and Present What Best Fits Its Audience.* . . . Its own interpretation of fashion or it ends by having assortments that confuse the customer. Fashion is not the same for every store—hot numbers in one store can fall flat in the competitor's.

Fashion is more democratic in the twentieth century than ever before in history—great similarity in appearance of people of all income levels—distinctions are subtle and often only apparent to the initiated. This democracy in fashion raises importance of status symbols—sable coats, square-cut diamonds, black alligator bags, understated simplicity and real quality.

Fashion acceptance in our materialistic society, travels down from the high to the lower income levels—startling exceptions such as denim play clothes or laminated fabrics sometimes begin at popular prices and by popular demand travel up to the better price lines. This reversal of the traditional process is strictly a twentieth century phenomenon.

10. *Besides the Acquiring of More Fashion Understanding by Its Personnel, How Can a Store Strengthen Its Fashion Reputation and Presentation?* . . . Each store must cultivate its own clientele. Must precisely interpret what its customers want—keep its eye on its own grandstand.

This is an important part of the philosophy of P.G. Winnett, Bullock's, Inc., Chairman of the Board—important cornerstone building the Bullock character and customer acceptance. Each Bullock store works on precisely reflecting its own individual clientele. The assortments in the new San Fernando Valley store are young, fresh, and keyed to the young families of the area—the Pasadena store reflects the wealthy conservatism of that community—Bullock's Wilshire is a fine sophisticated specialty shop. . . . They all follow the same quality and service standards, but each one develops its own flavor and personality.

Good fashion stores, like good sailors, choose their course and stay on it—I. Magnin's 86 years of devotion to the same objectives has resulted in a business producing enviable profits—a fine record of growth and development—an illustrious fashion name with worldwide recognition. This could not have been accomplished by a course interrupted by detours and changes of policy. . . .

11. *To Have Its Own Individual Appeal and to Succeed in Projecting a Clearly Defined Image.* . . . Each store must: (1) Develop its own buyers. (2) Train its buyers to lead—necessary to merchandise ahead not behind its consumers—to anticipate rather than to follow. (3) Guide its buyers first and its customers subsequently into investing in blue chip fashions—avoid fads. (4) Have a consistent fashion point of view (I. Magnin's is feminine, refined, ladylike, derived from Paris, rich). (5) Encourage good taste—a relative term . . . which needs interpretation. (6) Cherish, respect, and guard its fashion integrity—sell, promote and present what it believes in. (7) Protect its customers from making fashion mistakes by selling them only that which is becoming and suitable. And to live for the pleasure and the satisfaction of its customers—for profit can be the result of a job well done, rather than the first objective.

12. *We Must Never Underestimate Our Customer.* . . . She is more sophisticated, better educated, more traveled, better informed, more self-confident, and more independent in her choices than ever before in history. She is less loyal to one designer or to one store—more loyal to her convictions and to finding what she wants. She often knows more about competition than we know ourselves. Customers are revolting against uniformity—trying to express her individuality in a society that is pressing for monotony and conformity. We must understand who our customers are and how they live—their demands result from their way of life.

At I. Magnin & Company we believe all our customers are stylish, young, sophisticated, and able to buy what they want—we visualize them that way when we buy for them and when we sell to them. We respect their convictions. Admire their taste and ideas and live to bring to them what will please them. And this brings me back to our salespeople.

13. ***The Research, the Analysis, the Planning, the Hard Work, the Imagination, the Advertising, the Merchandise Can Succeed or Fail by the Actions of Our Salespeople.*** . . . Salespeople can make us or break us.

14. ***Management Must Pamper, Love, Cultivate, and Over-pay Salespeople.*** . . . We must encourage salespeople to work for the customer more than they work for the stores. Salespeople can teach customers to buy fewer but better clothes . . . to practice the economy of good quality . . . good fashion cannot exist with poor quality.

We must teach salespeople to sell their customers better clothes than the customers can afford—to sell merchandise which will make customers happy—to understand the customers' needs and desires.

In the final analysis the significant projection of fashion is ultimately made in the fitting room. To repeat let us pamper, love, and cultivate, and over-pay our salespeople—in their effectiveness, rest our fates. Too many retail executives in the daily pressure of a demanding business fail to find time to work with, help, and train and inspire their staffs.

15. ***The Broadway Play Succeeds in Business by Really Trying.*** . . . Today—the retailer succeeds by living, eating, dreaming, understanding, and loving fashion. Fashion is the heartbeat of retailing, providing and *only* if our salespeople have been taught all about it and use it as the effective selling tool it is.

Fashion Merchandising

by Alfred H. Daniels

Mechanics of Fashion Merchandising

To make for a better visualization, let us picture a ready-to-wear floor. We see on it not only a lot of pretty women but an inventory, and this inventory is comprised of these variables: (1) categories, e.g., coats, suits, dresses, skirts, etc.; (2) classifications, e.g., fur-trimmed coats, untrimmed coats, print dresses, plain dresses, etc.; (3) style numbers; (4) prices; (5) sizes; (6) colors.

These are variables in terms of what a customer wants, it should be noted, so it should be clear that one of the chief jobs a fashion merchant has is to control his variables so as to come out with the right composite of inventory. He has three basic problems: (1) How *much* of each variable to have—the quantitative factor; (2) what *kind* to have—the qualitative factor; and (3) *when* to have it—timing.

Quantitative Merchandising. Quantitative control of inventories, we know, is developed through dollar control and unit control. There is an overlap. Since the latter has even more to do with the qualitative factors, it will be discussed separately in a subsequent section.

A number of different procedures are useful in achieving dollar control. Under the Six Months Plan, each department plans its sales, stocks, and markdowns six months ahead in

---

Excerpted and reprinted with permission from *Harvard Business Review*, May 1951. Mr. Daniels is Board Chairman of Burdine's, Miami, Florida. He was formerly vice-president of Abraham & Straus, Inc., of Brooklyn, and later a vice-president of Federated Department Stores, Cincinnati. His article has become a classic on its subject.

dollars, and markups in per cent, by month or period. Planned purchases are a matter of simple arithmetic. Many factors are taken into consideration in the development of these plans, including economic trends, commodity trends, comparative performances, and so on. It is this plan that becomes the framework of reference for dollar control by departments. Incidentally, the store has an overall plan which is a composite of the individual department plans.

A second procedure is the Weekly Open-to-Buy Sheet. The control division releases weekly an open-to-buy sheet indicating by department current sales, stocks, markups, and markdowns as against plan and as against last year. Adjustments of the original plan are made periodically in view of the current trend. If customers show a preference for suits rather than dresses (as they have lately), the former departments will have a revision upward of their planned sales and/or stocks, giving them more spending power, and the latter will have revisions downward.

The Daily Sales Sheet is also useful in dollar control. Each morning in my company we receive such a "flash" sheet which summarizes, by departments, dollar sales yesterday and a year ago yesterday and sales month-to-date this year and last. This flash sheet is our ticker tape or box score. From it, sales trends are perceived that eventually are interpreted back into the open-to-buy market sheet. It is particularly helpful, even though the experience is not always merry, if you have a sister store with whom to compare daily departmental sales. By using another store as a measuring stick, you are in a better position to differentiate general trends from your own weaknesses. For example, your fur sales may begin to fall off. If this is likewise true of your sibling rival, a trend may be indicated—a switch into fur-trimmed coats, for example. If not, the trouble may lie in your sponsoring muskrats rather than persians, and capes rather than stoles.

Federal Reserve comparisons are a fourth method of dollar control. Monthly the Federal Reserve Banks collect and disseminate departmental sales figures for all stores in the various Reserve areas and in given cities. These statistics, like the store's own sales sheets, can be used to determine trends, weaknesses, and strengths. Much as baseball managers are judged by their standing in a pennant race, departmental managers are evaluated on the basis of their ranking in their district. "Going behind the district" is *lèse-majesté* in our business, while "going ahead" makes one a Casey Stengel.

Basically, the foregoing discussion is merely an application of the retail method of inventory. Fashion merchandising is no different from any other kind of merchandising, save for one very important factor. "Controller thinking" should never determine money amount to fashion buyers. A fashion inventory is worthless unless it is right; that is, unless the customers want it. Therefore, open-to-buy can never be completely mathematical. A department may have no money to spend according to its plan; but if the stock is comprised of fur-trimmed coats and customers want untrimmed coats, the buyer is what is known in our trade as "hooked," and he has to start all over, dollar mathematics notwithstanding.

One of our apparel departments recently had a sudden slump in sales, and its inventory was high. Rightfully concerned, several of us toured the department for an appraisal. The buyer reassuringly patted us on the back and said, "Don't worry at all. Prices in the market are going up. Further, this inventory is composed largely of 'classics' [a famous last word in the fashion business]. It's like money in the bank." The department's business fell off 40 per cent that day. Soon everyone in town broke with a sale on similar classics (sic!). The buyer had his money in the bank all right, but the bank had failed. This leads right into the problem of making qualitative decisions.

Qualitative Merchandising. Next to understanding the definition of fashion, qualitative merchandising is the most important aspect of this analysis. Once it is determined under dollar control that a department is going to spend a certain amount of money, the question is: Spend it on what? There are a myriad of possibilities. Should coats be trimmed or untrimmed, box or fitted? What kind of fur collars will sell best? What colors? What fabrics? Long coats or short coats? Ad infinitum.

The problem is not so complex as it appears, however, since there are two ways of determining what to buy qualitatively—or to put it another way, of determining what the customer is probably going to want. The first method is by talking to people; the second, by getting the facts together and talking to yourself, the soliloquy method you might call it.

One group of people worth talking to is the fashion advisory services—Tobé, Amos Parrish, and so on. These vary in type, quality, size, and fee. Let me use the Tobé office as an example because it happens to be one with which I am familiar (there are possibly others equally good). It is headed by Miss Tobé, a top fashion authority (and merchant). She has a relatively large staff of experts whose job it is to cover everything from what is being worn at the Opera and Dog Show to what is being shown on "Seventh Avenue" (i.e., the ready-to-wear markets). The office is jam-packed with information, some of which is published in a comprehensive weekly report. Tobé and her staff can tell you fashionwise what is considered *de rigueur* and *de trop* at Palm Beach or what is selling "like pancakes" on Fourteenth Street. They will offer opinions about skirt lengths next fall and why your sales were disappointing last Saturday.

Central buying offices—Associated Merchandising Corporation; Kirby, Block & Company; Mutual Buying Syndicate, Inc., etc.—comprise a second group worth talking to. As a member of Federated Department Stores, my own particular organization is a participant in AMC, a voluntary group of 24 department stores which maintains a large buying office and sees to it that member stores keep their books alike and exchange information on operations continually. The AMC stores have a sales volume in excess of one billion dollars and, therefore, obviously have a substantial soft goods business. The AMC office has a full and complete fashion organization, including market supervisors, buyers, assistants, and even a specialized fashion office. In most instances, these persons do no direct buying for us, unlike certain other offices, but act as advisers to our merchandise staff. Their advice is based on a wealth of information. Save for the matter of direct buying, most buying offices are like that of AMC and do not vary much in terms of function.

The fashion merchant also profits from comparing notes with other merchandise managers, buyers, and assistant buyers. Many a constructive tip has developed thus from a phone call or over a cup of coffee. And don't forget the customers! The simplest, and most direct, and *best* method of finding what a customer wants is to ask her (or him). Salesgirls can be helpful, too. If the salesgirl in question has gone home, you can "talk" to her by reading her entry on what we term a "want slip."

Last but not least, it is important to talk to your resources, who are necessarily in the position of having to anticipate what stores are going to buy and whose opinions about the future are, therefore, particularly valuable. It is well to believe their sincerity when they proffer advice; they have backed it with their bankroll! Months ahead they have committed themselves to bold prints rather than subdued ones, to clan plaids rather than flannel, to no fabrics at all if perchance their belief is in Bikini swim suits. Consider, too, that they have been more often right than wrong.

In other words, there is no paucity of fashion information, all intelligible, if you like talking to people. And there is consensus more frequently than you might think.

The Unit Control Card. A second method of determining what to buy qualitatively is essentially a process of getting the facts together and talking to yourself. Here I would like to introduce the subject of unit controls, which, as I have mentioned earlier, has to do with quantitative as well as qualitative merchandising.

The unit is the style number. A style *number* is a designation given by a resource to a particular garment and to all identical garments from that resource. The number has its own attributes in terms of design, classification, price, colors, and size range. Following its history intelligently is as important in the merchandising business as following a patient's chart in the medical profession.

The mechanics of unit control are relatively simple. An individual style card is devoted to each style number carried. Daily someone enters on the card yesterday's sales, receipts, customer returns, then sales-to-date, and finally, by deduction, number on hand. This forms a perpetual inventory control in units. The various cards are arranged by classification, price, and resource. The summary information about price and classification is developed daily and weekly in different forms by different stores.

The panel (that is, the receptacle holding the cards) gives the complete running history of a fashion department. It is alive with information and clues of all kinds. When you want to see how your wool dresses are "going," you look at your wool cards. If they are not going well, you might reason it was too warm out or you had the wrong ones. If you wanted to see how you were doing with wools at $16.95, you would look at that particular section. You might find none and remind yourself that several customers had asked for them at this price.

As far as the individual style number is concerned, obviously, you can learn exactly what to do by looking at the individual card and talking to yourself, even if you are unimaginative. If the number is not selling, you say to yourself, "I ought to reduce it." If it has sold pretty well, you say to yourself, "I ought to reorder a fair amount." If it has sold exceptionally well, you might muse that in fairness to all your other emulative customers, whom you do not wish to frustrate, you really should reorder a lot. After having done this with a hundred cards, you know how you want to spend your money qualitatively.

There will be a few question marks, of course. For instance, the classification summaries may have showed inadequate stocks of untrimmed coats. On the other hand, your cards show only slow sellers—what we call "pups." Therefore, you need to find, say, two new styles. You saw some new fur-trimmed coats at a favorite resource of yours, and he has told you to "check" (i.e., buy) a few. You do. He also whispered into your ear that they were selling at "better" prices (the fashion cycle!). So you earmark some money for this. Also, Tobé has indicated her complete disgust with you because you have no coats whose sleeve length shows the tip of the index finger. You have no confidence in the fashion, but feeling insecure about your job, you earmark a few dollars for it anyway.

It is difficult for me to overemphasize the importance of the unit control card. I know of a very successful department store buyer who used to boast that he never knew what a dress in his stock looked like (*not* that I recommend this, but it illustrates the point). He simply lived in, and made his living out of, his cards. Nine out of ten and he would reorder. None out of ten and he would try to return or "swap." Two out of ten and he would mark down; and so on. To refer again to my own experience, I used to pull the cards out of the panels and arrange them to see what common denominators I could detect. I might arrange them by resources, to see who was "hot" and who was "cold." Or I might take the ten best cards, get samples of the merchandise in the office, and see what they had in common. If it was dresses, it might be a kind of print, or a lot of fabric in back (what we call "back interest"), or a stripe, or what-not. The point is that I was able to find out what customers wanted even though I was neither a couturier nor a designer.

Let me give you an example, an instance where I supposedly showed fashion *flair*, fashion feeling, and heaven knows what else.

> About two years ago, our Blouse Department got "very sick." It was serious because we were going into our big Christmas season, during which a continued slump of the same degree would have been disastrous. Not being too close to the facts, I went at the problem administratively. I talked to the buyer and divisional merchandise manager, both of whom were rightfully dejected; called a few friends, who had no suggestions; had our competition shopped and found there was "no activity"; and had a complete survey made, finding that we were "covered." The sum total of my administrative efforts, therefore was nothing.
>
> As a last resort—it should have been the first—I requested the cards, together with samples, of the best sellers. Upon scrutiny, it was apparent that seven were wool jerseys. In desperation, we decided to run a wool jersey promotion. This decision, though, did not quite "hit home." Competitors had advertised wool jerseys, and our grapevine had indicated nothing startling. As our meeting was about to adjourn, I asked to see the *two* best sellers once more. Then the light came. Never did two necklines plunge so precipitously—and wickedly!
>
> No time for modeling. We hurriedly reordered the two blouses in large amounts, bought three new styles with the same common denominator (sic!), and scooped—both literally and figuratively, I guess—the country with "Deep Plunging Wool Jersey Blouses." Our blouse business became enormous. Some even said that a new fashion had been started, for the "deep plunging" look was soon advertised in dresses, slips, and bras all over the country.

Had I "started" a fashion? Of course not! There had been a general, and obvious, fashion trend toward bareness—"The Bare Look"—for some time. Subconsciously, that is probably why I had asked to see the two blouses again. Had I started a specific style? Of course not. We *all* had some blouses of this kind—and they had been selling. In other words, to revert to our definition, the fashion was "currently appropriate." One merely had to look at the record to see it.

It will be seen that much of what I have been discussing here is scientific, if by scientific one means a logical interpretation of *merchandise* facts. Undoubtedly, for this reason, many engineers have been successful fashion merchants. Several of America's top-flight fashion divisional men not only went to engineering schools but taught in them. Many successful dress, coat, and millinery buyers are men whose forte is operation.

Certain stores, from Ohrbach's to Jane Engel, have gone much further than what has been indicated above, literally mechanizing much of their fashion merchandising. IBM machines can be "souped up" in such a way as to tell you how many two-piece as compared with one-piece dresses were sold yesterday, how many dotted swisses as against voiles, and even, for all I know, whether you have got the right ratio between red-headed salesgirls and black-haired shoe clerks.

Timing. Granting that the questions of how much and what kind are settled, the next question is: When? This actually refers to two different issues—(1) the timing of a specific fashion and (2) seasonal changes and demands. To illustrate the former, a thousand dollars may be exactly the right appropriation, and a hundred red print dresses at $10 the right components, but if they come in two weeks late, you may be just as badly behind the times as if you had a batch of late-Victorian bathing suits on your hands. (Incidentally, this is one reason for being precise about delivery dates in the fashion business.)

As an example of the problem of seasonal timing, at a recent meeting of my company's stores, it was pointed out that for the past several years most of the stores had been doing more spring coat business per week in April than in March. Yet our stocks had been peaked for March 1. The results were big markdowns and lost business; for, when our customers wanted spring coats, the stocks were neither fresh nor right. The moral was like the delayed buck in football, in which the ball carrier does not plunge until he sees the right opening. By waiting until March 15 instead of bringing in coats at the end of February, we could see what was "currently appropriate."

Timing is a big and important subject in our business. Timing a fashion is a matter of alertness to what is going on. One gets to know seasonal timing by intelligently looking at the record. The heartening fact on this score is that there is so little change from year to year.

Arts of Fashion Merchandising

Some fellows in our business are big, others are medium size. They all seem to apply the same principles. What is the difference? It is a matter of degree of application. With a few exceptions, the arts of fashion merchandising boil down to the mechanics—only more so. There is very little about them that is mysterious or exotic. Let us take a look at three of the arts to see that this is so.

"Running Up and Down Stairs." A prominent retailer, at a Fashion Group luncheon, recently said:

> Basic utility cannot be the foundation of a prosperous apparel industry (because nothing wears out). We in the soft lines business have a responsibility to accelerate obsolescence. It is our job to make women unhappy with what they have in the way of apparel. We must do so by offering them something more desirable. We must make these women so unhappy that their husbands can find no happiness or peace in their excessive savings.

To my mind this statement is impressive because of its understanding as well as misunderstanding of our business. First, a few words of background.

The soft goods or fashion business has been a little ill in this past period for a number of reasons. The gentleman in question was attempting a pep talk to rally the fashion girls to do something about it. Two years ago, he pointed out, the fashion business was enormous because of a change in silhouette; skirt lengths dropped. Every woman had to buy a new wardrobe or else look like something out of *Gentle-*

men Prefer Blondes. He was recommending that it be done again.

Well, this is "nice work if you can get it." But if my earlier discussion has been convincing, it should be enough to point out that it cannot be done again—not on purpose. General fashion trends cannot be changed by masterminding on the part of any group. If they could be, the fashion business in total would always be enormous.

The retailer's remarks also had considerable insight. In effect, he said that our business is dependent on our being constantly able to seduce customers with something new—in other words, to get a lot of fashion cycles working within the general fashion trend. "New—different—fresh!" That is the vitality of our business. I think that the German poet, Heine, had something when he said that "When a woman begins to think, her first thought is of a new dress." The job of the fashion merchant is to keep her thinking.

When I was young in the business, I made it a point to make sure we brought in new things—anything new, just so long as they were in fair taste. In the trade this is called "running up and down stairs." I figured that, even though I did not know what I was doing, if the manufacturer could put half his savings into the production of a new idea, I could gamble Abraham & Straus money to the extent of 40 dresses. Naive? Perhaps yes, but my premise was a correct one.

Promotion. Every father has his favorite child, and promotion is mine. A psychiatrist might call the pleasure of promotion sadistic, for it involves torturing a competitor by selling quantities of something he usually has. Sadistic or not, it is fun. (Caution! Having the wanted fashions in stock at all times may be less fun, or more tedious, but it is more important. Thus, remembering the mechanics could well be labeled an art.)

To be a promoter requires certain technical knowledge. A promoter must know, first, how to make a plan—what the objective is and how to map out strategy. Just as important, he must know how and when to change a plan. Pity the poor persons in our business who compulsively stay with the blueprint. As football players change from cleats to sneakers when the field freezes, so must the fashion merchant change his strategy when the market changes.

He must also be able to differentiate between the values of different kinds of promotion: (1) sale promotion, which has to do with value events, typically in assortments; (2) item promotion, where the objective is to sell specific things (a butcher linen dress, for example); (3) idea promotion, where the goal is to sell quantities via an idea (e.g., pink shirts); (4) departmental promotion, where one attempts to establish the reputation of a department (e.g., the Junior Size Center); (5) brand promotion, where one plans a campaign to build a particular manufacturer's line (e.g., Carolyn Schnurer sportswear).

The promoter should have an understanding of media—how to reach his audience. Media problems are varied, ranging from which *kind* are appropriate (newspapers, direct mail, magazines, radio, TV) to which one (a certain paper, list, or station). Decisions are made, essentially, by knowing something about what persons are reached by a specific medium—where they live, how many there are, how they buy, what their age is, what they spend. As examples of how intricate this subject is, circulation *per se* can be meaningless, for some papers are read for their ads, in which case advertising receives high audience attention, and others are not; Sunday advertising in some communities receives more attention than comparable advertising midweek; morning papers may pull better than evening; and so on. This complexity does not deter store people. Everyone who ever entered our business felt he could be a self-labeled publicity expert after two weeks on the training squad. It is almost immoral not to feel that way. Incidentally, part of the fun of promotion is "kibitzing" the publicity director—which is sadistic, too.

Promotion problems are like so many others we have discussed. They should be kept as simple as possible, conclusions about them being reached through use of experience and direct judgment. For example, if you are planning a big mail- and phone-order response to a $7.95 fly-front gabardine dress, you use a paper with a geographically scattered circulation ("full-run") rather than a local one. If it is a floor promotion of high-price coats, you might consider a direct mail piece to your charge customers, who are your "best" customers; there is less dilution in this method than in using the typical newspaper. A "cutie pie" boxy sweater advertised in *Seventeen* should outpull the same item in *Charm* because of the different age composition of its readership, while a dress designed for the career girl might better be featured in *Charm*.

Aside from the technical aspects, the art of promotion requires several personal qualities which deserve comment here. The first is *alertness*. Now, it should be axiomatic that if his competitor does something successfully, the promoter should duplicate. Yet very few do. It should be obvious that if a sister store effects a coup, it is not unsporting to try to imitate. Again, however, not so many do. Finally, it should be clear that it pays off to be alert to the dictates of your own customers. For instance, the coat business was very poor last October. Like others, our store ran several coat sales in a row, all of which "flopped." Yet our buyer was alert enough to recognize that each time the lynx fox trimmed coats moved out. Therefore she contrived a promotion on *just* lynx coats—and really got results! As far as the first personal quality is concerned, in other words, it is not so much a matter of fashion as of glasses and a hearing aid.

A second vital quality is the *ability to reason inductively* (a phrase which appeals to me more than "imagination" because it puts it within the reach of ordinary businessmen). This has been mentioned earlier under the subject of qualitative merchandising, but let me present still another example. Several years ago, in going through the dress cards (here we are, back looking at the record, you see), it was found that virtually every black washable dress on our floor had been sold. Six out of eight, nine out of ten, and so on—all small quantities, but "sold out." We had our competitors shopped and found that they had no black dresses in stock either. According to our notes, there had been calls for such dresses a year ago at the identical time, namely, the end of May. On the basis of this and a few other facts, we bought 10,000 black summer dresses—the largest dress purchase in our history before or since.

I will never forget the weekend before the promotion; with no warning it had turned cold and wet. Before store opening on Monday morning, the stockroom was about as depressing a sight as possible: wave upon wave of dresses, each as black as the next. It looked like doomsday, and we braced for the worst. Then the store opened. Well, to cut the story short, the response was simply enormous—$150,000 of business in three days! Never underestimate the desire of a woman to be "appropriate."

The point is, this successful venture in fashion promotion came about as the result not of some great fashion imagination but of a little workaday logic. "Hunch" decisions are reminiscent of Mark Twain's comment that it had taken him three weeks to develop his extemporaneous remarks.

In the fashion business there are times when nothing succeeds like excess. This puts a premium on *courage*, which is another quality the promoter needs. He gets courage, not through a devil-may-care attitude or by tremendous internal security or fortitude, but by being reasonably sure of his premises and facts. In the case of the black dress mentioned above, facts pointed in the one direction. The promotion could be as sure, no more, no less, as if it had tried to corner the canned tuna fish market because of evidence of a switch in demand from canned salmon. After all, there is a certain amount of unpredictability in anything.

A final quality that needs mentioning is *speed*. This refers not only to the fact that fashion changes quickly, as per our definition, and that seasonal demand changes, but also to the fact that fashion is a highly competitive field. The promoter has to get his facts quickly and act upon them quickly. Had we been two weeks later with the black dresses, the party would have been over; we would still be counting them.

Resource Relations. Resources can help the fashion merchant in many, many ways—from giving him good deliveries to pushing him to big ideas and concentrating his stocks. In this third art it is important for him to know how to work with his resources and how to get them to work for him. The Nettie Rosensteins, Howard Hodges, Adele Simpsons, Sally Victors, Barbizons, Harris Classics, Shagmoors, Winfields, McKettricks, Brimbergs, Sayburys, Betty Hartfords, Jerry Gildens, Young Viewpoints, Monarchs, and others can, by themselves, build a huge business for the store. If there is a quick short cut to success, this is it. It does not require fawning or frolicking; the fashion business has become more mature than that. It does require an ability to listen, and to say "yes" many times and "no" sometimes. Also it requires loyalty.

This is one case where it is imaginative to be consistent.

The subject of resources has received more and more attention on the part of top-store management. An Associated Merchandising Corporation planning committee, comprised of several key store executives, spent a year developing a 150-page manual dedicated to "ideal resource relations." * It was presented to the AMC store principals at a meeting in White Sulphur Springs last fall and received a tremendous ovation. There was a recommendation that all merchandise persons in all the stores read it—and practically memorize it—as essential to their growth as merchants.

The great change which has occurred in the fashion field is in the development of strong brands and is, in my opinion, a stabilizing and salutary one. This development has been of such recent vintage that many persons are unaware of its existence, let alone its significance. The fact is, women are now developing as much preference for Red Cross shoes and Henry Rosenfeld dresses as for Uneeda Biscuits and Chevrolet cars. My company had for years an underdeveloped suit department. Analysis recently showed that we were missing perhaps the strongest brand, Handmacher, so we decided to concentrate on getting that line. I am sure our suit business will expand as a result. Needless to say, not only will we have the wanted merchandise (customers coming to us because of the reputation of the manufacturer), but we will also have at our command all of the know-how and genius of suit experts to help us build *our* department.

It is perhaps understandable why a store's relations with its key resources should be of such concern.

Feeling for Fashion

My final topic is that particularly mysterious piece of mumbo-jumbo called "fashion feeling."

Some bright fellow years ago, in order to get an increase, must have sold his boss on the idea that fashion feeling was like sex appeal—you either had it or you did not. Blarney! All the discussion in the preceding pages is fashion feeling, from the application of logic to resource loyalty. However, two points deserve a little amplification:

(1) We have discussed emulation as a prime drive in the purchase of fashion. How obvious, then, that it is important to keep in stock at all times merchandise that represents advance fashions, typically at higher prices than you ordinarily sell. The object is to be convincing to the people who buy a lot of your merchandise. We say that we carry "prophetic" fashions so that we can sell "accepted" fashions. Professor Copeland says "distinctive" fashions and "emulative" fashions. The customer says: "I am proud to wear that store's label."

How do you get advance fashions? You go to the name or couturier resources, and they do the work for you. A person who does this is known as a "fashion leader," which is the equivalent of a 33rd degree Mason.

(2) We have indicated that women buy clothes to look glamorous, young, attractive. I think it was Lin Yutang who said that "all women's dresses are merely variations on the eternal struggle between the admitted desire to dress and the unadmitted desire to undress." How elemental that fashion merchandise be displayed, stocked, advertised, and sold attractively? We call this a "soft" approach, and without it we would have no fashion business. Much as you judge a housewife by the way she keeps her home, you can evaluate an apparel man by the appearance of his fitting rooms. If the fashion merchandise manager need not be a couturier, he must scrub himself daily and insist that his salesgirls do the same. In this sense, fashion feeling can be defined as cleanliness. You cannot sell fashion in a fish market.

Summary. Let me summarize the main points about fashion merchandising that have been discussed above: There are three broad aspects of fashion merchandising. The first, the *mechanics* of fashion merchandising, concerns itself with how much to buy, what kind, and when. The merchant develops answers by looking at the facts and by talking to people, including himself.

The second aspect, the *arts* of fashion merchandising, has to do with the know-how involved in getting bigger and better than your competitors. This is done by bringing in new,

*Associated Merchandising Corporation, *Resource Relationship Manual* (New York, August 1950).

irresistible merchandise, by promotion, and by developing close working relations with prime resources and new sources who look as if they are going places.

The nerve center of fashion merchandising is the unit control card. The fashion merchant should always be close to these cards—pulling them out, analyzing them, summarizing them. It is helpful to have actual samples of merchandise available. This is the unmysterious road to what is enviously termed "fashion flair."

The third aspect, *fashion feeling*, is a matter of good grooming. This applies to yourself, your staff, and your floor.

Merchandising Fashion

by Stanley Marcus

The problems of merchandising fashions for a profit are multitudinous, and differ from one type of store to another. . . . Fundamentally, a *store* must know at what point it wants to get on this fashion cycle, and when it wants to get off. Since fashion is not static, this process may involve some leaps and some occasional skinned shins, but severe falls are most unusual. In our particular store we must be in at the beginning of a fashion trend, or as close to the beginning as possible. Our trick is to recognize the new trends quickly, represent them in our stock in small quantities at first and larger quantities as the demand accelerates, continue with them until we reach or just pass the crest, and then jump off and mount a new trend.

If we had only one fashion at a time to contend with we wouldn't have too difficult a problem, but at any particular time there may be a number of trends in varying stages of development. Some of them may be reaching the peak; others may be just beginning; and still others may be in an ascending or descending stage. All of this may sound extremely complicated, and it is; but it *is* possible to learn the criteria upon which fashion understanding can be developed. Fashion forecasting is more complex and requires certain innate sensitivities. To get the proper understanding of these fashion movements, there is no substitute for the experience gained from an internship in selling and buying. *The customer* is the buyer's best teacher, just as she is a designer's best inspiration. . . .

The fashion magaiznes, such as *Vogue* and *Harper's Bazaar, Glamour,* and *Mademoiselle,* are extremely helpful monthly guides and are essential reading to keep up with fashion development. *Women's Wear,* a daily trade publication, does one of the most remarkable fashion news reporting jobs in the world and tells of fashion changes occurring around the world. It is vitally important for anyone in the fashion business to keep up with the news of the day, because the news exercises a great influence in setting the economic and psychological atmosphere which affects the trends of fashion.

To sell fashion we have to use a number of promotional devices. First of all we try to educate our sales people so that they understand the new fashions and believe in them. This takes great organizational effort, but we believe it is the foundation for a successful fashion business. After we have educated the sales person we then start to educate the customer by advertising the new fashions in the newspapers and magazines, by showing them in our windows and in our interior displays and in our fashion shows. We have found that the fashion show is an extremely important device for education, because it combines visual presentation with a convincing verbal commentary. We have found that the personal appearance of the designers at fashion shows and on the selling floors is another important promotional device. Women are interested in the personalities cf designers just as ardent movie-goers are intrigued

---

Excerpted from a lecture delivered by Stanley Marcus, President of Neiman-Marcus, Dallas, Texas, at Harvard Graduate School of Business, March 10, 1959. Reprinted by author's permission.

by the personal appearance of one of their favorite stars. Most important of all techniques in the development of a new fashion is getting the new fashion on the right women to start with, for we must never forget that emulation works only if the example is inspiring.

In our stores we have found that new fashions properly timed and properly priced will attract more people than a value promotional event. We don't believe in planned obsolescence as a means of selling merchandise, for we think that theory is economically unsound. We do think there comes a time, though, in the evolution of the clothes when the designers and the customers alike get tired of the uniformity that results from a successful dominant fashion. The human desire for self-individualization is so great that customer demand begins to make itself felt, and the designer, having the sensitive perceptions of the artist, frequently anticipates his customer's requirements. Fashion merchandising has lots of hazards, for even small mistakes can prove to be tremendously expensive. As a business it is neither the easiest nor surest way of making a profit. There are few, if any, fashion merchants who will show the kind of net profit that merchants of more staple categories of goods, like Best & Company, or The May Company, will show. Profits they do make, as testified by the success of such as Bergdorf-Goodman, I. Magnin, and Neiman-Marcus. Not long ago I was having luncheon with an oil man who turned to me and asked, "What sort of profit do you fellows make in the retail business?" I told him that the Controllers' Congress figures showed the average store made anywhere from 1 to 2½ per cent on sales, after taxes, and that a few extremely well-operated stores might make as much as 3 to 3½ per cent. He thought about that for a couple of minutes and then turned to me and said, "Hell, you are in the wrong business. We spill that much!" What the fashion business lacks in profits, though, it makes up in the excitement of a fast paced business, the interesting people one meets both as customers and designers, and in the opportunities of exercising the qualities of judgment and prophecy and decision at home and abroad.

Some Major Retailers of Fashions in the United States — Location, Sales, and Ownership

To familiarize readers with the names of some prominent retailers of fashion merchandise, the following list has been compiled. Department and specialty stores are arranged alphabetically by cities, with approximate sales volume and ownership affiliation. Basis for selection has been dominance in terms of volume or fashion leadership or both. The choice has been arbitrary in some cases, as the authors were seeking to assemble a representative collection, rather than a complete one.

Sales figures are reported by some retailers, particularly those which are publicly owned. Others do not announce their volume, and, for such stores, industry estimates were used where they were believed to be reasonably accurate. Principal sources of data have been *Summary of Available Sales Figures, By Cities, for Leading Department Stores*, published by the Research Department, Fairchild Publications, New York, April 1964, and Fairchild's *Financial Manual of Retail Stores*, 1964.

Following the department and specialty store listing, some of the largest chain, mail-order, discount organizations, and store ownership groups are shown, with their corporate sales volumes. Figures are for 1964 where available, or 1963.

Department and Specialty Stores

City	Store	Approximate Sales (Millions of Dollars)	Ownership [a]
Akron, Ohio	O'Neil's	55	May Co.
Atlanta, Ga.	Rich's Inc.	116	Independent
	Davison, Paxon	56	Macy
Baltimore, Md.	Hecht	40	May Co.
	Hutzler	51	Independent
Birmingham, Ala.	Loveman, Joseph & Loeb	25	City Stores
Boston, Mass.	Filene's	135	Federated
	Gilchrist	28	Independent
	Jordan Marsh	155	Allied
Buffalo, N. Y.	Adam, Meldrum & Anderson	30	Independent
	Sattler's	30	Independent
Chattanooga, Tenn.	Loveman's	11	Independent
Chicago, Ill.	Carson, Pirie, Scott	176	Independent
	The Fair	60	Montgomery Ward
	Goldblatt Bros.	155	Independent
	Marshall Field	280	Independent
	Wieboldt Stores	98	Independent
Cincinnati, Ohio	H. & S. Pogue	30	Assoc. D.G.
	Shillito's	80	Federated
Cleveland, Ohio	Halle Bros.	59	Independent
	Higbee's	75	Independent
	May's	96	May Co.
Columbus, Ohio	F & R Lazarus	110	Federated
Dallas, Texas	Neiman-Marcus	50	Independent
	Sanger-Harris	45	Federated
Dayton, Ohio	Rike-Kumler	75	Federated
Denver, Colo.	Denver Dry Goods	36	Assoc. D.G.
	May's—D & F	35	May
Des Moines, Iowa	Younker's	65	Independent
Detroit, Mich.	Crowley, Milner	26	Independent
	J. L. Hudson's	280	Independent
	Winkelman Bros.	30	Independent
Fort Wayne, Ind.	Wolf & Dessauer	20	Independent
Hartford, Conn.	G. Fox	60	Independent
Houston, Texas	Foley's	65	Federated
Indianapolis, Ind.	L. S. Ayres	82	Independent
	Wm. H. Block	45	Independent
Kansas City, Mo.	The Jones Store	17	Mercantile
	Macy's	15	Macy
Knoxville, Tenn.	Miller's	25	Independent
Long Beach, Calif.	Buffum's	26	Independent
Los Angeles, Calif.	Broadway Department Stores	141	Broadway-Hale Stores, Inc.
	Bullock's	137	Federated
	May's	185	May
	J. W. Robinson	69	Assoc. D.G.
Louisville, Ky.	J. Bacon & Sons	15	Mercantile
Memphis, Tenn.	J. Goldsmith & Sons	30	Federated
Miami, Fla.	Burdine's	60	Federated
	Jordan Marsh—Florida	15	Allied
Milwaukee, Wis.	The Boston Store	45	Federated
	Gimbels-Schusters	60	Gimbel
Minneapolis, Minn.	Dayton Co.	130	Independent
Newark, N. J.	Bamberger's	175	Macy
	Hahne's	20	Associated
New Orleans, La.	D. H. Holmes Co.	36	Independent
	Maison Blanche Co.	35	City Stores

(*continued*)

Department and Specialty Stores, cont'd

City	Store	Approximate Sales (Millions Dollars)	Ownership [a]
New York, N. Y.	Abraham & Straus	210	Federated
	B. Altman	85	Independent
	Alexander's	156	Independent
	Arnold Constable and Co.	28	Independent
	Bergdorf Goodman	25	Independent
	Best (New York area)	33	Independent
	Bloomingdale's	134	Federated
	Bonwit Teller (New York)	34	Genesco
	B. Gertz	80	Allied
	Gimbels	119	Gimbel
	Lord & Taylor (New York)	75	Asso. D. G.
	Macy's New York	327	Macy
	Ohrbach's (New York)	55	Independent
	Saks Fifth Avenue (New York)	82	Gimbel
	Stern's	65	Allied
Oklahoma City	Kerr's	34	Independent
Omaha, Nebr.	Kilpatrick's	8	Younker's
Philadelphia, Pa.	Bonwit Teller	10	Genesco
	Gimbel Bros.	79	Gimbel
	Lit Bros.	88	City Stores
	Strawbridge & Clothier	105	Independent
	Wanamaker's	122	Independent
Pittsburgh, Pa.	Gimbel Bros.	66	Gimbel
	Joseph Horne	82	Independent
	Kaufmann's	83	May Co.
Portland, Ore.	Meier & Frank	71	May Co.
Providence, R. I.	Outlet Co.	29	Independent
Richmond, Va.	Miller & Rhoads	43	Independent
	Thalhimer Bros.	45	Independent
Rochester, N. Y.	E. W. Edwards & Son	25	Independent
	Sibley, Lindsey & Curr	30	Associated D. G.
St. Louis, Mo.	Famous-Barr	153	May Co.
	Scruggs-Vandervoort-Barney	25	Independent
	Stix, Baer & Fuller	80	Assoc. D. G.
St. Paul, Minn.	The Emporium	50	Independent
Salt Lake City, Utah	ZCMI	20	Independent
San Antonio, Tex.	Joske Bros.	25	Allied
San Diego, Calif.	Marston's	15	Broadway-Hale
	May's	15	May Co.
San Francisco, Calif.	Emporium-Capwell	152	Independent
	Macy's	25	Macy
	I. Magnin	30	Federated
	J. Magnin	28	Independent
	Ohrbach's	29	Ohrbach's
Seattle, Wash.	Frederick & Nelson	45	Marshall Field & Co.
Syracuse, N. Y.	E. W. Edwards & Son	30	Independent
Washington, D. C.	Garfinckel's	25	Julius Garfinckel
	Hecht's	84	May Co.
	Landsburgh	27	City Stores
	Woodward & Lothrop	94	Independent
Youngstown, Ohio	Strouss-Hirschberg	35	May Co.

[a] Full names of some of the groups mentioned in abbreviated form in this column are: Allied Stores Corporation, Associated Dry Goods Company, City Stores Company, Federated Stores, Gimbel Brothers Company, R. H. Macy & Company, Inc., The May Department Stores Company, Mercantile Store Company, Inc., and Younker Bros., Inc.

Sales of Selected Chain Organizations

	Type of Chain	Approximate Sales (Add 000)
Alden's	Mail-order chain	$ 193,900
Bond Stores	Apparel chain	90,300
Diana Stores Corp.	Apparel chain	94,500
Franklin Stores Corp.	Apparel chain	56,900
Grant (W.T.) and Co.	Variety chain	770,000
Holly Stores, Inc.	Apparel chain	39,200
Kresge (S.S.) Co.	Variety chain	683,000
Lane Bryant	Apparel chain	122,000
Lerner	Apparel chain	236,000
Miller-Wohl	Apparel chain	56,000
Montgomery Ward and Co.	Mail-order chain	1,697,000
Newberry (J.J.) Co.	Variety chain	334,000
J. C. Penney Co.	General merchandise chain	2,080,000
Sears Roebuck and Co.	Mail-order chain	5,740,000
Spiegels, Inc.	Mail-order chain	305,000
Woolworth (F.W.) and Co.	Variety chain	1,338,000

Sales of Selected Discount Retailers

	Approximate Sales (Add 000)
Arlan's Department Stores	$139,250
Interstate Department Stores	360,700
S. Klein's Department Stores	185,000
E. J. Korvette, Inc.	529,000
Mangel Stores Corp.	93,000
Vornado, Inc.	208,000
Zayre Corp.	176,000

Sales of Selected Store Ownership Groups (Combined Store Totals)

	Approximate Sales (Add 000)
Allied Stores Corp.	$ 829,800
Associated Dry Goods	460,000
Federated Department Stores	1,215,000
Gimbel Bros., Inc.	536,000
R. H. Macy and Co.	656,000
May Department Stores, Inc.	782,000

Questions for Review and Discussion

1. Is the retailer's primary function in the fashion business that of a distributing agent for producers or a purchasing agent for customers? Explain.
2. Discuss the statement that there are "Different types of stores for different types of people."
3. What, in your opinion, is the future of fashion operations by traditionally "non-fashion" types of retailers such as discount houses, variety stores, etc.
4. It has often been said that you can eliminate retail stores but you cannot eliminate the functions they perform. True or false? Why?
5. Why have most fashion retailers with very few exceptions discontinued the practice of making clothes to order? Why does a store like Bergdorf Goodman continue to operate a custom-made workroom even though they lose money in this particular department?
6. Do you believe that small independent fashion retailers will continue to play an important role in the fashion business? Why?
7. How can stores like Ohrbach's "undersell" other large retail stores on the same or similar merchandise.
8. How do present-day discount houses differ from early discounters?
9. Discuss the statement made by Mr. Escobosa in "*Fashion . . . the Heartbeat of Retailing*" that "fashion is not the same for every store."
10. Prove the following statement: "Continuing social and economic changes bring about new forms of retailing." Are there new forms of retailing emerging currently? What and why?
11. Cite examples of different types of promotional methods which are used by retailers to sell fashion apparel. Which methods do you feel are most effective and why?

SECTION

VI

Auxiliary Fashion Enterprises

There are many specialized services and advisory enterprises in the business of fashion whose roles are of major importance to its well-being. Among these are: fashion and trade publications, advertising and publicity agencies, fashion consulting firms, and resident buying offices. There are also many others whose highly specialized activities elude classification but whose function in the industry is a vital one. The activities of these auxiliary fashion enterprises, which supplement and complement those of the producers and retailers of fashion products, are the subject of this section. Many of the readings which are included are authored by different types of professionals in this area of the fashion business.

Fashion in Print

The amount of material which is printed about fashion and its workings staggers the imagination. Aside from the paid advertising messages sponsored by makers and sellers, there are editorial treatments in the daily papers, in news magazines, in the women's magazines, in specialized fashion publications, and in those segments of the trade press in any way concerned with the fashion business. Fashion is news, and news media cover it.

This printed material, along with what is done through broadcast media, serves as a vital means of communication between related parts of the industry and between the industry and the consumer.

Fashion Magazines. Fashion magazines, which have as their major activity the reporting and interpreting of fashion news to the consumer, as well as additional features for balanced reading fare, have been functioning in this country for more than a century. *Godey's Lady's Book,* which was started in 1830, carried pictures of the latest fashions, gave advice on fabrics, contained other helpful hints—and, of course, included advertising. Its distinguished editor, Sara Josepha Hale, gave early proof that a woman could have a successful career in the business world even in the days of hoopskirts and cinched waists. Its masculine counterpart, *Burton's Gentleman's Magazine,* also had an editor whose name acquired luster: Edgar Allan Poe. His editorial career there was brief, however, from 1839 to 1840. The present-day roster of fashion magazines consists of highly specialized publications, each appealing to its own carefully delineated market. *Mademoiselle* and *Glamour,* for instance, aim at the college girl and young adult market; *Seventeen* and *Ingenue* talk to the teen-agers; *Vogue* and *Harper's Bazaar,* the so-called high-fashion books, are addressed to older readers with more generous clothing budgets.[1]

The role of fashion magazines in the fashion industries is a dual one. In addition to serving as fashion reporters they often take an active part in the production and distribution of merchandise, working closely with manufacturers and retailers alike. On the one hand, their editors shop wholesale markets, both here and abroad, in order to select and feature styles that they consider newsworthy for their particular reading audience. On the other, the magazines keep readers informed about the retail stores in which their featured merchandise can be bought.

An important tool of their activities, and of other consumer magazines that cover fashions to a lesser extent, is the editorial *credit.* This is how it operates: The editors select garments that, to their minds, exemplify a trend important to their readers. They photograph and show them in their pages, identifying the names of the makers, the name of one or more retail stores in which the consumer can buy them, and usually the approximate price.[2] The magazine's sponsorship and the editorial mention encourage the makers to produce the garments in good supply, the retailers to stock them, and the customer to buy. Even in stores that do not have editorial credits for it, a fashion item featured in a strong magazine may be given special attention. If the magazine concerned has a good following among the store's customers, the editorial sponsorship becomes a selling point of the garment to the merchant as well as to his customers. The garment is then stocked, advertised, and displayed, and the magazine's name is usually featured in ads and displays. Hangtags on the garment and posters in the displays remind the customer that this is the style she saw in the publication. The magazine, of course, provides the tags and posters.

Like most publications, fashion magazines derive their principal revenue from the sale of advertising space. A single page of *Vogue,* for example, costs $4350; in *Seventeen,* it costs $4850; in *Mademoiselle,* $3450. By way of comparison, a page in *McCall's* costs $31,000; in *Life,* $33,860; in *Reader's Digest,* $49,800.[3] These are for black and white; color runs higher. Naturally, a high ratio of advertising to editorial pages means a prosperous magazine. In 1964, the 33 consumer magazines studied by the Lloyd H. Hall Company, a New York market research firm, were running about 47 per cent advertising to 53 per cent editorial. The fashion magazines were consistent with the general picture; *Vogue,* for example, had 53.1 per cent editorial for the first eleven months of that year.

---

[1] Authors' note: *Gentlemen's Quarterly* is a specialized fashion magazine which addresses itself to men.

[2] See "Fashion Magazines" in *Fashion Jobs,* a fact sheet from the Job Department, Glamour, 420 Lexington Avenue, New York 17, N.Y., p. 7.

[3] November 27, 1964, issue, Consumer Magazine and Farm Publication Section, Standard Rate and Data Service, Evanston, Ill., p. 11.

The money the advertiser spends for his page is, in simplest terms, spent to influence customers to buy his product. If a publication can show tangible evidence that it can move merchandise into the retail store and then out into the consumer's hands, its chances of selling advertising space improve.[4] One magazine editor has stated that, in order to attract advertisers, "Nothing is more important to fashion magazines than their relation to stores. This fact accounts for the increasingly large staffs of departments almost unknown to their readers—promotion and merchandising." [5]

The promotion and merchandising editors act as the liason between the fashion editors, the advertising staff, and the retail stores. Their job is to ensure that editorialized and advertised merchandise will be placed in retail stores where readers can buy it. They do this by telling the retailers what the magazine is featuring and why, and where to buy it. They then list these stores for their readers' information. The editor, quoted above, explains it this way: "Store listings of where merchandise can be found, ostensibly a service to the reader, are there to impress the advertisers, suggesting as they do a selling power that the magazine may or may not actually possess." [6]

There are mishaps, of course. Editors can make unwise selections; manufacturers can accept credits and fail to produce in sufficient quantity; retailers can accept credits and fail to stock, display, and advertise the style properly. One classic example, many years ago, involved a striking jacket featured on the cover of a fashion magazine. The editor was thoroughly justified in her confidence, and stores and consumers clamored for the garment. But the manufacturer did not share the editor's enthusiasm, and his production of the garment consisted of the one piece that was used for the photograph. Magazines try to circumvent such things by insisting upon firm promises of cooperation in return for credit.

The closer their relationship with both the producers and retailers, the easier it is for magazines to attract advertising. In order to cement these relationships, many free services are offered by fashion publications. They keep fabric and apparel producers informed on new trends, and advise them on ways and means of selling merchandise. The fashion editors encourage them to manufacture items for which they anticipate a demand and, secure in the knowledge that the item will be featured by the editors, the producer will plunge ahead. The merchandising and promotion departments provide advertisers with "as advertised" posters to distribute to their retail accounts. In addition, most magazines prepare, well in advance of each season, elaborate charts of their color predictions for the guidance of manufacturers and retailers alike. These charts show samples of the shades and colors that they believe will do well in fabrics and leathers. As described by one magazine: "The chart is a matter of inviting

[4] Authors' note: Several former fashion editors have charged that "editorial pages are being completely dominated by advertisers' dictates" and "that readers of fashion magazines today are getting only a digest of advertisers' offerings." (See Bettina Ballard, author of *In My Fashion* in "Eye on Advertising," *Women's Wear Daily*, June 6, 1961, p. 22. Also see "Decline and Fall of Fashion," *Harper's* magazine, October 1962, pp. 134–140.

[5] "Decline and Fall of Fashion" by Ann St. Code (pen name of a former fashion editor), *loc. cit.*, p. 137.

[6] *Ibid.*

everyone out on a limb—but at least on a limb that the magazine feels is strong." [7]

In developing a close relationship with retail stores, the fashion magazines make themselves a source of information for them. In order to make their editorialized and advertised merchandise desirable to retailers and ultimately to their customers, the merchandising departments prepare elaborate "retail store kits" that, along with the list of sources for featured garments, contain suggestions for advertising, fashion shows, and display. They also include selling aids such as hangtags, signs, and other promotional materials. If an important retailer requests one, the magazine will often send a representative to commentate a fashion show. Occasionally a magazine will set up a showroom in the garment district and invite retail buyers to preview the merchandise that will be featured in the forthcoming issues.[8] Many of them stage semi-annual fashion shows and clinics in which they preview their featured merchandise and analyze incoming style trends. Members of the magazine staff are also available in their offices to show samples of merchandise to retailers, and encourage them to visit the producers of the garments.

Most of the consumer magazines, including those primarily concerned with fashion, also maintain research departments. A function of these departments is to survey the readers of the magazine and compile information about their buying power, living patterns, and merchandise preferences. *Seventeen,* for example, annually surveys high-school girls and college freshmen and compiles reports which they send to retailers and manufacturers about what these girls buy, how much they spend, and similar information. The fashion magazines, then, not only interpret fashion for their readers but they also interpret their readers to the fashion industry. In the process, they serve as a clearing house for information in the fashion field.

As compared with the generalized consumer magazines such as *McCall's* with over eight million readers, or *Life* and *Look,* each with over seven million, the circulation of the fashion magazines is small.[9] *Vogue, Harper's Bazaar,* and *Mademoiselle* have circulations in the neighborhood of half a million; *Seventeen* and *Glamour* are the largest, each with approximately one and a half million. Their influence, in the business, individually and collectively, is great, and far out of proportion to their actual circulation. Fashion editors ignore styles and designers in whom they have little faith. They also give a great amount of free publicity to those that they favor. Ordinarily, however, what they do is, as one editor describes it, "Try to pick the most dramatic, the most exciting—not always the most wearable fashions—but the ones that will really stir things up." [10]

Newspapers and General Magazines. As mentioned earlier, almost all newspapers devote some space to fashion. Coverage varies, of course, both in

[7] "Are you Cut Out for Seventh Ave.?", *Mademoiselle,* March 1962, p. 119.

[8] Authors' note: Glamour's showroom is at 498 7th Avenue, N.Y.C. They open it seasonally and advertise their showings in *Women's Wear Daily.* See issue of April 14, 1964, for an example of their invitations to retailers.

[9] Standard Rate and Data Service, *loc. cit.*

[10] Helen Valentine, editor-in-chief of *Charm-Glamour* and former editor-in-chief of *Seventeen* magazine, speaking at a Fashion group lecture, reported in "The Making and Makers of Fashion," New York, Fashion Group, 1959.

amount and in depth. A *New York Herald-Tribune* may have its Eugenia Sheppard to report the Paris openings and express opinions which are read by consumers and trade professionals alike.[11] A small-town paper, on the other hand, may assign its society editor to fill out the woman's page with items about fashion, clipped from what the wire services send, what comes in by way of press releases, or what the local retailers supply.[12] The paper's resources and the lives of its readers determine how much original work its fashion editor is required to do.

The "credit" operation of the fashion magazines does not exist for papers. But it is within the scope of newspaper fashion reporting to mention sources and shops for items illustrated, and even to cover the opening of new departments in local stores or the arrival of the new season's merchandise in retail stocks.

Among the women's magazines not in the fashion magazine category, there is also coverage of fashion, and it varies with the nature of the publication. Their fashion editors, looking at the fashion scene through the eyes of their average reader, will select for illustration and comment only those items of interest to the young mother, the middle-class housewife, the ageless city sophisticate, or whatever the particular audience may be.[13]

Some of the women's magazines give credits. Some of the general magazines show merchandise; others, like the *New Yorker,* show no merchandise, but discuss what the shops are showing. The activities of their fashion editors, as in the case of newspapers, vary according to the importance that each publication and its readers attach to fashion information.

Trade Publications. There is a special field of journalism known as trade or business publishing. Some business newspapers and magazines in the fashion field concern themselves with a particular class of merchandise, from raw material to the sale of the finished product. These are addressed, not to the ultimate consumer, but to the fashion professionals concerned with the manufacture and distribution of that merchandise. Typical examples would be *Corset and Underwear Review, Boot and Shoe Recorder,* or *Infants' and Children's Review.* Other business publications devote themselves to only one aspect of production or retailing and have a horizontal readership. Examples of these publications are such monthlies as *Stores,* which goes to department store management, *Chain Store Age,* for chain-store management, and *Modern Textiles,* which is concerned with mill problems. Fairchild's *Women's Wear Daily,* which is published five times a week, covers the fashion waterfront in the women's fashion business—raw materials, manufacturing, retailing, and how the trend-setters among the consuming public dress. It is often called the in-

---

[11] Authors' note: Eugenia Sheppard, fashion editor of the *Herald Tribune,* won a Neiman-Marcus fashion award for her "stimulating writing in the field of fashion." She is the author of a reading in Section IV of this book, "Americans in Paris."

[12] Many newspapers send their fashion editors to New York to attend the National Press Week of the New York Couture Group, a semi-annual event subsidized by New York apparel manufacturers. *The New York Times* reported that 230 editors came to the January 1965 Press Week. (January 6, 1965 issue, p. 62.) A reading in this section describes Press Week.

[13] Fashion editors of general magazines also participate in the Press Week activities mentioned in footnote 12.

dustry's "bible". The Fairchild counterpart for the men's wear industry is the *Daily News Record.*

Business publications are not aimed at the general public and are inclined to discourage subscriptions from people not active in the fields they serve. They seldom are seen on newsstands, except for the Fairchild dailies in the garment district. Their circulations are quite small as compared with those of consumer magazines. *Women's Wear Daily,* for instance, is a giant in the field, with a circulation of nearly 54,000; *Daily News Record* has 23,000; *Boot & Shoe Recorder,* just over 20,000; *Stores,* nearly 12,000; *Corset and Underwear Review,* 4000. Advertising rates are correspondingly small. A one-time insertion of a black-and-white page in the magazine examples just mentioned ranges from $425 for *Stores* to $675 for *Boot & Shoe Recorder.* (The Fairchild papers, being newspapers, quote prices in terms of lines rather than pages.[14])

The capacity of trade papers, particularly the Fairchild Publications, for disseminating fashion information is out of all proportion to their size. Their readership, it should be kept in mind, is concentrated among people dealing in the merchandise they cover. They talk shop to such people. And, in terms of the amount of merchandise involved, when a manufacturer or merchant responds to information on fashion, that response moves a lot of merchandise.

Trade paper editors are usually in their markets every day of the business year, and cover every nook and cranny of their trades. They analyze fashion trends for their readers and show sketches or photos of actual merchandise, identified as to source and style number, to assist buyers and store owners in keeping abreast of the flow of new products. In addition, trade publications discuss business conditions and contain articles on how to manufacture, promote, or sell the trade's products. They analyze and report on foreign markets,[15] cover conventions and other meetings of interest to the trade, report on legislative developments of interest, and write up merchandising and promotion operations of retail stores.

Solid market research is also part of a trade publication's work. These magazines and papers make estimates of the size of their markets, survey subscribers on buying responsibilities and attitudes toward current problems; publish apparel directories,[16] help retailers and manufacturers find sources of supply, and sponsor clubs and associations for retail buyers.

Within their particular fields, trade paper editors and reporters are extremely well informed. Some of them are represented in the articles reprinted in this book and reading them is like listening to a group of experts indulging in shop talk.

Advertising and Publicity Agencies

Advertising Agencies. An advertising agency is a service organization whose original function was simply to prepare and place ads in magazines or news-

[14] November 24, 1964, issue of *Business Publication,* Section, Standard Rate and Data Service, Evanston, Ill., pp. 344, 363, 756, 770, 1293, and 1295.

[15] Examples of these foreign market reports were reprinted in Section III of this book ("Foreign Ready-to-Wear").

[16] Authors' note: For example, Fairchild Publications publish annual directories of apparel producers by name, address, and products.

papers for its clients. Today its job encompasses much more: research of the client's consumer markets, advice on promotional needs, planning of promotional campaigns, preparation of print and broadcast advertising, preparation of selling manuals, creation of selling aids such as labels and signs, packaging—anything that helps increase the sale of the client's product and makes the advertising itself more effective.

Advertising agencies in this country date back to the 1840's, but the pattern of operation that is common today did not begin to settle into its mold until the 1900's. The oldest of the agencies in existence today is N.W. Ayer & Son, which was founded in 1869 by Francis Ayer. Before this time, advertising agencies were more or less brokers of newspaper and occasionally magazine space. Ayer had the idea of acting as a buyer of space for his clients, the advertisers, and to give them every service that would make their advertising more effective, increase their sales, and thus make increasing funds available for future advertising.[17]

An advertising agency may consist of one talented, hard-working person with a few small clients, or it may be an organization with a staff of thousands and clients with hundreds of millions of dollars to spend each year. Revenue is derived primarily from commissions. These are paid, not by the client, but by the media from whom the agency purchases advertising space or time. Custom has fixed the rate at 15 per cent.[18] In recent years, there has been some effort to change the relationships, so that the client pays directly for the agency's services. Some agency services and a very few client-agency relationships are on that basis today, but this is not yet the prevailing pattern.

When an advertising agency makes a bid for a client's account, it studies the firm's operation thoughtfully and draws up a presentation that outlines the campaign the agency suggests and also the varied services that the agency performs. When awarded the account, the agency may delve into package design, market research, the creation of selling aids such as labels and signs, sales training material—plus its original function of preparing and placing advertising in publications, in broadcast media, and, in some cases, also in transit and outdoor media.

In the fashion industries, it is usually only the largest producers of nationally distributed merchandise who make use of advertising agencies. These include some makers of finished apparel plus the giant fiber and fabric sources. Retailers, whose audience is local or regional, usually maintain their own complete advertising departments which handle their day-to-day newspaper advertisements.[19]

The agencies which specialize in fashion accounts are not among the largest in the field; national advertising expenditures by fashion producers are small as compared to that of other major industries. This is largely due to the fact that the apparel industry is composed of many thousands of small producers who have very limited advertising budgets. The entire women's, misses', children's,

---

[17] December 7, 1964, issue, Section 2, *Advertising Age*, Chicago, Ill., pp. 2–4.

[18] "Advertising Agency Jobs," Job Fact Sheet from *Glamour* magazine, 420 Lexington Ave., New York.

[19] Ohrbach's Inc., whose institutional advertising pages have won several awards, employs Doyle, Dane and Bernbach to prepare and place its ads. Ohrbach's, however, is the exception rather than the rule in the retail field.

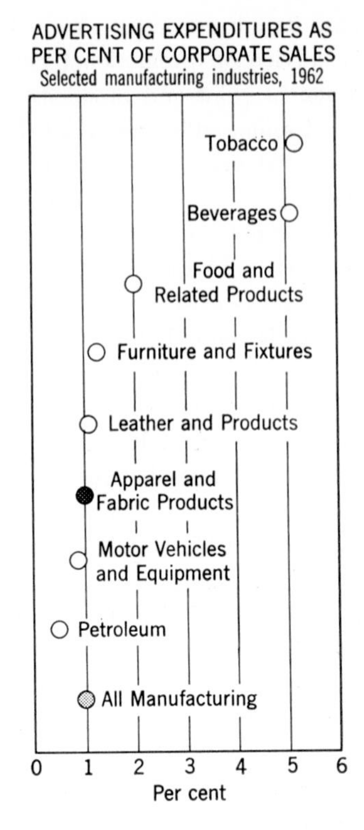

Source: U.S. Treasury Department; after the National Industrial Conference Board, New York.

and infants' outerwear and undergarment group spends an average of 0.96 per cent of its yearly sales on advertising—as compared, for instance, with 13.89 per cent of manufacturers' sales in perfumes and cosmetics, or 8.03 per cent for soaps and detergents, or 5.16 for tobacco.[20] The advertising expenditures of fiber and fabric firms, as mentioned in a previous section of this book, are relatively larger than those of the apparel group but are also minor in comparison with other major American industries.

The work of a fashion agency requires it to employ personnel who are expert in the language and background of the fashion business; account executives who work with clients and coordinate what is done; art directors who know how to visualize fashion; copywriters who are familiar with fashion appeals; and stylists or fashion coordinators who are responsible for the fashion slant of the ads.[21]

People with similar talents are also to be found in the larger, more general agencies, of course. The work of the fashion expert in the agency is not neces-

---

[20] July 6, 1964, issue, *Advertising Age,* Chicago, Ill., p. 59.

[21] Authors' note: Two of the leading fashion agencies are Hockaday Associates Inc., 575 Madison Ave., N.Y., and Trahey-Cadwell, 667 Madison Ave., N.Y.

sarily limited to fashion accounts, however. If a woman's figure appears in an ad for cigarettes, or automobiles, or soft drinks, it is a fairly sure thing that a fashion advisor in the agency that placed the advertisement has checked the model's outfit to make sure that it is in tune with the current fashion picture, and that the styles worn are in keeping with the occasion and the level of society that is being represented.

Thus the advertising agency, whether or not it has a fashion account on its roster of clients, contributes both indirectly as well as directly to the business of fashion.

Publicity and Public Relations Firms. Publicity, like advertising, has as its purpose enhancing the client's sales appeal to his potential customers. The space or time supplied by the media, in this case, is free, but the public relations firm's services are not. Working on a fee basis, with provision for expenses, the publicity agency develops news stories around the client's product or activities and makes these available to editors and broadcasters.

The key word in effective publicity is "news." The publicity expert's first job is to find or "create" news value in the product or activity he wishes to publicize. Next, he considers the media that might conceivably find this news of interest to their readers, and writes his story (called a press release) in a form appropriate to the media that constitute his target. If they are likely to use illustrations, he may attach a suitable photograph to his release.

Typical publicity activities include getting editorial mentions in consumer and trade publication, "plugs" on television and radio, school and college tie-ins, representation in fashion shows, feature articles in newspapers and magazines, and anything else that makes the products or the client's name better known and more readily accepted by the consumer—or by an industry, if the industry is the client's customer. An example of a simple publicity device might be to try to place a photograph of maternity wear on women's pages of newspapers. The news angle might be the fabric, the occasion for which the garment is worn, the "un-maternity" appearance, or whatever seemed most likely to win acceptance. Then photographs, captions, and story would be mailed to newspaper women's pages. Alternatively, they would be made available to retail stores selling the line, so that the publicity directors of the stores could "place" the publicity locally. That is to say, the store's advertising and publicity department would offer the item to the local papers in the store's name.

The publicity firm does not simply use contacts to place material for its client. It also prepares press releases, distributes photographs,[22] writes radio and TV scripts, sometimes works out an elaborate fashion show and hires and coaches professional actors to sing, dance, and model for the audience. If a medium, whether print or broadcast, is working on a special feature touching the client's field, the public relations people swing into action to provide the writer of the feature with facts, photos, and other help.

A broader term than publicity is *public relations.* A public relations firm does not limit its efforts to getting the client or his product mentioned in the press via press releases and similar efforts. It may supply expert advice on how to improve the client's public image, and may develop some of the less obvious

[22] Authors' note: Many out-of-town fashion editors depend upon press releases and photographs for the content of their fashion pages.

ways of getting publicity for the client: suggesting him as a speaker at conventions of appropriate groups, having him give scholarships, establish awards, and foundations, and so on.[23]

There are many independent publicists and public relations agencies who specialize in Seventh Avenue publicity, but the three leading ones are generally considered to be the firms of Eleanor Lambert Inc., Rosemary Sheehan, and Ruth Hammer Associates.[24] All three have their headquarters in New York City. As is the case with advertising agencies, their clients are generally fabric or apparel producers rather than the retailers, who usually maintain their own internal publicity staffs. Rosemary Sheehan has been described "as the closest thing Seventh Avenue has to Perle Mesta . . . She is renowned for the parties she throws and the (fashion) shows she stages for fabric clients like Galey and Lord Cottons, Hartford Fibres and the like. Miss Hammer, on the other hand, sees publicity as 'an adjunct to selling', wastes little time on frills that won't pay off . . . or on projecting any images of herself." [25] The many activities and clients of Eleanor Lambert, who is considered to be the kingpin of them all, are described in a reading in this section, "Jaunt with Fashion."

So far as the fashion industry is concerned, the public relations and publicity fraternity performs the very useful function of feeding information about it to the news media and thus stimulates business by keeping it in the limelight.

Fashion Consultants

A fashion consultant is an independent individual or firm hired by fashion producers or retailers to help them in their fashion operation. Although all manufacturers and retailers of any size have experts of their own within their firms, many use outside consultants for their more objective viewpoints, against which to check their own analyses and conclusions.

One of the oldest and most widely respected consulting agencies is Tobé Associates, whose founder, Mrs. Tobé Coller Davis, died in 1962.[26] Tobé, who had a background of experience in the retail field, established a retail fashion and consulting service in 1927. She hired a staff of reporters to survey the women's apparel and accessory markets, and report on the trends, successes, and reorder numbers, as they came in from stores across the nation. The staff also covered important social events, such as opera openings, charity balls run by celebrities, or college football games, and commented on the new fashions or the preponderance of a particular color or fabric or headgear.

The firm sends to their clients a weekly mimeographed brochure with fashion

[23] Authors' note: Two noted examples of concerns who receive a great deal of publicity for their award activities in the fashion industries are the annual Coty Fashion Awards to outstanding fashion designers, and the Neiman-Marcus annual award for "contributions to the fashion field." An example of an educational award is the Chair of Fashion, given by Bergdorf Goodman to the Fashion Institute of Technology.

[24] "Eye on Plugola," *Women's Wear Daily*, December 19, 1960, p. 1.

[25] *Ibid.*

[26] Authors' note: Tobé and Associates, Inc., is located at 11 West 42nd St., N.Y.C.

illustrations, compared by one retailer to a "fashion dopesheet complete with names and numbers of all the horses, jockeys, weights, and handicaps." [27] From these reports, retailers can get a confirmation of their own interpretations of fashion or they can be stimulated into a different appraisal. Further services rendered by consultant agencies such as Tobé Associates include annual or semi-annual fashion clinics, special analyses of weak departments, and other individualized reports for which clients may be charged extra, in addition to a yearly fee.[28] Consultants do not necessarily always come up with all the right answers, but in the case of Tobé's firm, there is testimony to the worth of their services in the fact that several hundred successful and well-known retailers in this country and abroad have been willing to pay annual fees of up to $10,000 for them, year after year, for a period of almost forty years.[29]

Although there are other fashion consulting firms in the industry today, no one person or firm has yet attained the stature of Tobé herself,[30] or even of the organization that she founded which is still considered to be the "cream of the crop."

How fashion consultants function is best described by the "master of them all" in her own words. In addition to the following description which was given by Tobé herself in a presentation that she delivered at the Harvard Graduate School of Business Administration,[31] reprints of some of her other fashion talks are included in Sections I and VII of this book.

> If you walked into my office on Fifth Avenue and 42nd Street in New York, your first impression might be that you'd made a mistake and gotten off at the wrong floor. There are no pretty models parading around, no luxurious displays, and not a single crystal ball to foretell the trends of the future.
>
> Instead, there is a kind of madhouse confusion which would remind you more of a newspaper or magazine office than the popular conception of a fashion business. In fact, this is precisely what our business is—*Journalism.* We are the reporters and interpreters of the fashion world, speaking to the fashion-makers and the fashion-sellers—"Opinion Molders"—that's the extent of our influence. We act as liaison between our retail clients, the department stores and the specialty stores, and their sources, the manufacturers. Our job is to tell the makers what the sellers are doing, and vice versa. Most of all, we interpret and evaluate for each what is happening to fashion itself.
>
> *How do we know what is happening to fashion?* First, we make it our business to stay abreast of just those economic, social, and art trends which I maintain are the great formative currents of fashion. Even music inspires fashion. Today, for example, because Harry Belafonte has made Calypso

[27] Stanley Marcus, President of Neiman-Marcus, in a presentation at the Harvard Graduate School of Business Administration, Cambridge, Mass., March 10, 1959.
[28] Authors' note: According to trade sources, Tobé received $1000 a day for personal consultations. (Source: *Women's Wear Daily,* December 26, 1962, p. 16.)
[29] "Eye on Tobé," *Women's Wear Daily,* March 13, 1961, p. 4.
[30] Authors' note: Tobé won many awards, among them a Neiman-Marcus fashion award in 1941 and the Chevalier of the Legion of Honor award in 1953. Prominent retailers have endowed Harvard's Graduate Business School with the Tobé Lectures in Retail Distribution, an annual lecture series.
[31] April 25, 1957. Reprinted by permission of Tobé Coller Davis.

the music of the moment, we have lots of Calypso fashions. Blouses, skirts, scarves, dresses. But you will also find we spend a good deal of time poring over such seemingly nonfashion journals as the London *Economist,* the Manchester *Guardian,* the *Wall Street Journal, Fortune* magazine, the *Harvard Business Review,* yes, and *Variety,* the weekly journal of the entertainment world.

From all of these we try to pick the significant trends that will change our lives, and hence our fashions. The series that *Fortune* ran some years ago on suburbia was a prize example of this: it gave us the facts and figures to back up a hunch we'd had for a long time.

Shifts in the international news are another clue we watch. To give a hypothetical example: when the Near East finds a solution to its terrible dilemmas, all creators will become "Near-East minded." While that does not mean that the American woman will be eager to go into Purdah, it very likely does mean that she will look with a newly-awakened curiosity and interest at Persian- or Egyptian-inspired designs.

The fashion business also presupposes lots of travel to forecast these straws in the wind. I made two trips within this year to lands that seem likely to inspire future fashions: one to Russia; the other to Japan, Hong Kong, and Bangkok. If the awful tragedy of Hungary had not taken place, I think that quite likely there would have been a genuine interest in Russian fashions. Though their current fashions are far below our standards, their museums are full of beautiful clothes in traditional style based on the old Russian culture. The influence began to appear in Paris last August, led by Lanvin Castillo, one of our top creators. It showed up in our hats this past winter, for many of us wore hats of Russian inspiration.

Meanwhile, the fashion influence of Japan and other Oriental countries is growing in every way. In Tokyo and Kyoto, for example, I saw geisha girls who wore Dior and Balenciaga necklines. No, of course they were not designed by Dior and Balenciaga. On the contrary, I think these traditional gowns, hundreds of years old, gave inspiration to, and influenced, Dior and Balenciaga. So you can see I needed a first-hand impression of Oriental life, old and new, in all its facets, to see what we could use, or translate, or adapt, to our American taste.

Our business does not only watch for fashion's ground swells, but it keeps track of the little ripples as well. For example, we recently made a survey in four cities among women of three different age groups, and on an average income of $7500—beaming to the great middle-class fashion market I've been talking about. We sought to find their preference in fashions, and how much they really know about it. We learned some facts that were astounding.

Plus all this, we keep an eye on what those in the fashion vanguard are wearing and doing and seeing. This not only means reporting on what smart people wear in such key places as the theatre and the opera, important social gatherings, and the smart restaurants. It also means keeping abreast of what plays, films, and TV presentations they are seeing, which are successful, where they travel, and what books they read.

All of this information flows into our offices, where it is digested, sorted out, evaluated, and then disseminated through a weekly 50-page report. That's our contribution to Journalism. Our clients—many department stores in America, a specialty shop in Australia, department stores in Europe, a wool manufacturer in Finland—they can all shop the Fifth Avenue stores and the Paris showings without budging from their desks. They can keep track of resort life without going to Monaco or Florida or the Caribbean. They can read about the fads, as well as the foundations of fashion, without spending much time or effort in research.

So it is our business as a whole to interpret the current scene to the makers and sellers of fashion wares.

Resident Buying Offices

In strategic market centers, notably New York, there are hundreds of resident buying firms which act as market representatives for, and render other related services to different groups of member stores.[32] Their major function is to scout the wholesale markets daily and keep their client stores informed of fashion, price, and supply conditions in the wholesale markets. Their work supplements, but does not replace that of the store buyers.

Half a century ago the resident office was likely to consist of one employee of a single store at a distance from the city, stationed in the market to service his store alone. Most of the retailers in those days bought from traveling salesmen, or drummers, who called on them perhaps twice a year. The New York buyer "in residence" was in the market, however, to follow up on orders and see that they were shipped on time, to take care of special requests and additional needs, and to be alert for bargains. Today, the typical resident office serves many stores—anywhere from a handful to several hundred—of similar type and customer appeals, but each store in a different trading area and thus not in direct competition with one another.

Types of Resident Offices. The majority of the resident buying firms are independently owned enterprises to which client stores pay a yearly fee. A few others are cooperative enterprises, owned and supported by the stores that they service. A third type is owned and financed by a parent corporation that also owns the stores for which they are run. There are also some, called merchandise brokers, who represent stores but collect a commission from the manufacturers with whom they place orders. Among the largest of the independent type are firms like Kirby, Block and Co., Arkwright Inc., and Atlas Buying Office, each of which represents some 150 stores. An example of a cooperative office is the Associated Merchandising Corporation which is supported by and serves 28 major department stores located throughout the United States; an example of the corporate type is Macy Corporate Buying Office, serving the stores that are owned by the parent R.H. Macy Corporation. Typical of the fourth kind of office, the merchandise broker, is Apparel Alliance, Inc., which services several hundred small independent stores in all parts of the country.[33]

Many of the larger buying offices maintain branches in other market centers like Los Angeles or Chicago. A few of the biggest also have offices in foreign countries to assist their stores in foreign buying; some also have client stores abroad and export American goods to them. One example is the Associated Merchandising Corporation which has branch offices in Chicago, Los Angeles, Paris, Florence, and represents eight stores located in foreign countries. Some buying offices serve only apparel specialty shops and report on fashion markets

[32] For a listing of resident offices and their member stores, see 1964 Phelon's Resident Buyers, 53rd Edition, Phelon-Sheldon Publications, Inc., 32 Union Square, N.Y.C. The 1964 edition contains the names of 202 resident offices and 132 merchandise brokers.

[33] *Ibid.*

only;[34] others, like the Macy office and the A.M.C., cover the whole range of department store merchandise. Some are even more highly specialized and deal only in children's wear or millinery. All, however, perform similar services and serve the same function as representatives of their member stores in the wholesale markets.

Fashion Services of Buying Offices. At the start of each season, the resident buyers in the offices cover the market and send analyses of fashion and market conditions to their client stores. During the season, bulletins go out with regularity—weekly, as a rule, in addition to whatever flash bulletins are needed to report on new items and special developments such as manufacturers' fast selling styles, price changes, new supply conditions, and so on. A typical bul-

[34] An example of this type of office is Specialty Stores, Inc. Mrs. Elgart, the executive director, describes this office in a reading in this section.

ATT: MERCHANDISE MANAGER, BUYER
HANDBAGS

STRAW VOTE!

Imported Plastic Vinyl Coated Straw handbags are heading the winning ticket insales all over the country!

Get on the bandwagon -- and poll the votes in your territory!

STATE		INITIAL	REORDERS
TEXAS	$35.65 group	78 dozen	150 dz
	$57.00 group	36 dz	60 dz
ALABAMA	$35.65 group	4 dz	12 dz
FLORIDA	$35.65 group	28 dz	52 dz
	$57.00 group	18 dz	33 dz
NEW YORK	$35.65 group	44 dz	86 dz
	$57.00 group	34 dz	69 dz

$35.65 group includes:

#539 PVC East West Vanity
#596 PVC Attache Case
#518 Novelty Basket
#538 Novelty Basket
#500R Baskets (assorted styles)
COLORS: Natural, white, black, colors
#599 PVC Football
#530R Baskets (6 styles)
COLORS: Natural, white, black
#4720R Gold-mesh baskets

$57.00 dz group includes:

#756 PVC Attache Case
#5722R Plasticized Raffia
#744 PVC Basket
#791 PVC Basket
#754 PVC Basket
#760R PVC Baskets with metal handle
COLORS: Natural, white, colors
#700R Assorted wicker baskets
COLORS: Natural, white, black, colors

FOB: New York City
DELIVERY: 2-3 weeks
TERMS: 3/10 EOM
RESOURCE: Simon Straw Bags Co.

FELIX LILIENTHAL & CO., INC.

HAROLD PARIS, MERCHANDISE MANAGER
GRETA SCHEUER, BUYER

FELIX LILIENTHAL & CO., INC., NEW YORK

Typical buying office bulletin.

letin may include such facts as, for example, a tightening supply of a wanted fabric or an early demand for a certain type of swim suit or a new style trend in the wholesale markets. When the buyers of the client stores are in the market themselves, the resident buyers act as advisors and time savers; when the store buyers return home, the office buyers follow up on the shipments of orders that the store buyers have placed.

Most of the actual purchasing by the resident offices is done at the specific request of the individual store buyers and is ordered in their name. Some offices, however, have set up a wholesale jobbing division which buys large quantities of reasonably staple products that are resold to member stores at a close markup. Private brands are also developed by many buying offices, and the merchandise bought under the office label is available to client stores. An example of such a private brand operation is the A.M.C. brand which can be found in many large department stores throughout the United States.

Some offices do centralized buying of lower and moderately priced ready-to-wear and accessories. This means that a resident buyer in the office makes the selection of styles for the store's stock, within the framework of a budget set by the store. The office orders the merchandise and, guided by sales and stock reports from the store, reorders some styles and discontinues or replaces others. With the experience of many stores to draw upon, the office has a national picture of fashion trends to guide its selections.

In addition to the buying and fashion advisory services, buying offices maintain departments which prepare catalogues and other mailing pieces for use by the stores; supply advertising mats and copy; offer assistance in finding merchandising personnel. Offices also hold special merchandise clinics for client stores during certain months of the year when the out-of-town store buyer influx in New York is at its peak.

The degree and extent of services may vary from one office to another but essentially they all serve the same function in the fashion business: they keep the producers informed of what retail stores want and they keep the retailers informed of what is happening in the wholesale fashion markets.

Other Fashion Enterprises

There are many other types of enterprises which play an important behind-the-scenes role in the business of fashion. Their activities, however, are too varied and too highly specialized to be described in detail. A few examples and some well-known names in the business can be briefly mentioned.

Display specialists design and construct fashion display materials for manufacturers, retailers, fashion magazines and so on. Some well-known names are the firms of Tom Lee, Ltd., and Lester Gaba Enterprises, whose visual merchandising activities also include the staging of fashion shows.

Specialized consultants in the fields of sales promotion or marketing are retained on a fee basis by manufacturers, retailers, and even magazines. The firm of Estelle Hamburger is an example of a sales promotion consultant; Estelle Ellis, president of Business Image, Inc., numbers *Glamour* magazine among her many other fashion clients.

Market research agencies do consumer surveys for retail stores and manufacturers, or retail surveys for producers. Among those who do work in the fashion field are the Eugene Gilbert organization, noted for their studies of the youth market, and Audits and Surveys, which has made some interesting studies of the buying patterns of retail store customers.

Trade associations serve businesses and business executives with interests in common and are set up for joint action or study of a common problem; some examples are the National Retail Merchants Associations, to which most retailers of department-store merchandise belong, the National Board of the Coat and Suit Industry, the National Association of Women's Clothing Salesmen, the New York Women Buyers Club, and so on.

There are also associations of publicity and advertising specialists, associations of children's wear buyers, accessory buyers, and fashion designers. A well-known association that encompasses many different types of fashion specialists is the Fashion Group, whose activities are described in a reading in this section.

In short, there is a whole army of creative people who contribute to making the fashion business what it is today and who will undoubtedly contribute to its growth in the future.

Readings

The best way to find out about a highly specialized fashion enterprise is to get a specialist to talk about his work. That is exactly what the readings that follow undertake to do. In each case, a professional in one of the service enterprises discussed in this section tells us what it is like to labor in that particular vineyard. Some, like Press-Week director, Kittie Campbell, ad-man Mr. Winters, and resident-office director Mrs. Elgart, speak to us directly. Others, like fashion editor Nancy White and publicist Eleanor Lambert, are brought to life through the medium of a skilled magazine writer.

The article by Inez Robb, a reporter herself, does not discuss her own job but is a provocative commentary on the editorial selections of fashion reporters. The reading on the Fashion Group describes a trade association of professionals in the fashion business.

The Fabulous Life of a Fashion Editor

In a Diamond-Studded Paris-Rome-New York World where Trench Coats Are Mink-Lined, Obsolescence Is Dreaded; Nancy White of Harper's Bazaar *Sits at the Crossroad of the Most Glamorous Business on Earth*

by Elizabeth Honor

"There's more *bazazz* in the *Bazaar!*" Amid the fierce, step-on-your-hand competition, the tearful rages, the feminine jealousies, the beauty, money, and brains—*Harper's Bazaar,* top magazine in the fashion world, pounds home its high-fashion pitch to the American woman. Behind the frenetic activity (editors darting off to India, Egypt, or merely out to New York's Aqueduct racetrack to photograph models Suzy Parker, Sunny Harnett, China Machado cavorting with jockeys in silks)—behind all this: the magazine's shrewd concern for the hard-core fact that each year American women spend, on clothes and accessories, twelve billion dollars.

From "A Diary of Fashion," *Cosmopolitan Magazine,* February, 1960. Reprinted by permission of Nancy White and Cosmopolitan.

The Scent of Fashion

At the helm of this jet-propelled world is forty-three-year-old, brown-haired (undyed), tennis-tanned Nancy White. Dedicated to loosening women's purse-strings only in the direction of exciting good taste—whether the price is five dollars for a pair of straw sandals discovered in Italy, fifty dollars for a bathing suit from California, or ten thousand dollars for a Paris original—editor-in-chief Nancy sends her editors zipping around the world. Chief cohorts are a handful of key photographers, an art director, and fashion editor Diana ("*Dee*-ann") Vreeland, of whom a rival editor complains, "She can smell out a coming fashion so far ahead that she makes a bloodhound look like something with asthma."

Bazazz-leader Nancy White was born with a silver lavaliere around her neck ("This year it's the emerald choker"), grew up in a big, rambling house in Smithtown, Long Island, got her first fashion job at fourteen—delivering packages at fifteen dollars a week. At seventeen, under the aegis of her famed aunt, Carmel Snow, long-time editor of the *Bazaar,* she made her first trip to the Paris collections (salary then twenty-five dollars a week) and found herself hopelessly hooked. There followed her twenty-six-year-long initiation into the field where the tooth-and-nail competition for fashion leadership is said to resemble the torture rites of a boy's coming-of-age in the South Sea islands.

Along with her passion for showing the American woman how to shake off conventional shackles, Nancy White believes women in this country are sophisticated concerning fashion. One afternoon, assembling clothes for a feature in the magazine, a neophyte fashion editor complained that the copy did not describe the model's panties. Miss White turned on the whiner a flashing eye: "We do not presuppose that our readers are starting out naked with a checkbook."

On the theory that "the lady from Dubuque knows as much as Noel Coward," Nancy, claims an associate, "fills the lady in on what's new—as one might catch up a friend on gossip she has missed."

A less kindly view of the *Bazaar*'s pioneering drive to put American women into Capri pants and elegantly tousled hair-dos holds that it is possible because "fashion editors are snobs, and therefore anti-conservative. Nothing is too modern for them. The readers are the same way." Denying the snobbishness, one *Bazaar* editor claims a white-hot flame of dedication: "At *Commonweal* they're a bunch of heretics compared to the *Bazaar*—the way people here *believe,* so deeply, so seriously."

The way Nancy White herself sees it, the reader of *Bazaar* "wants to know not only the new silhouette—she wants to know what goes on in art, architecture, music. She is as interested in a summit conference as in what is happening at the hemline." Claiming that "the woman of taste is a woman of adventure," Nancy lets her readers have culture right between the eyes. Literature and the arts are called on to imbue the American woman with what she may lack in the way of a Rhodes scholar's background. In one issue, Cocteau discusses Picasso. ("He is very small, with charming hands and feet and terrible gimlet eyes that pierce through skin and bone. Intelligence pours from him like a jet of cold water.") The next issue displays an emaciated-looking Suzy Parker in a green bikini. In this, reads the copy, a woman may "retire to the club solarium or her own patio to catch the sun *au naturel.*"

This photograph brought screams of outrage from husbands and old ladies. Says the *Bazaar,* "A lot of people thought the picture was ugly—but a lot thought it was beautiful." Whatever they thought, points out the *Bazaar,* "stores were flooded with orders for the exact bikini Suzy was wearing in the photograph."

Theme: Diversification

This past year *Bazaar* screamed the prophesy, "Blondes Preferred," letting readers in on the fact that tans, ivories, "bone," and off-white would be the coming fashion for spring. It also launched China ("Cheena") Machado, the delicately boned, Shanghai-born, half-Portuguese, half-Siamese model whose lesser abilities include speaking seven languages. Along with the American collections, the Paris collections, the Young Perfectionist (fashion at a price issue), appear such stunners as the full-page cat-face of Brigitte Bardot. Reads the typical *Bazaar* copy: "The bardot is the first international divinity since Isis." The culture-conscious woman could find everything from Maurice Chevalier high-stepping it out on the Champs Elysées, to "Dieting at the Great Restaurants," to Simone de Beauvoir's "Memoirs of a Dutiful Daughter." Though such choice literary efforts as Dylan Thomas's "The Beach of Falesa" and Vladimir Nabokov's new book, *Invitation to a Beheading,* appeared in its pages, the guts of fashion is the guts of *Harper's Bazaar.* Along with these doses of esoterica that are supposed to make a woman unerringly tasteful in dress, is dress itself. Though not necessarily expensive, each item pictured in *Bazaar* is staged to be thunderbolt effective: a model rides a donkey on the beach at Puerto Marques in Mexico to show off a simple black bathing suit. Even a $2.98 T-shirt, classic of its kind, has hit the fashion pages of the *Bazaar.* Yet another page may mingle society and celebrities—Baroness

Thyssen-Bornemisza in furs, facing Sophia Loren in more furs.

With her belief that the American woman is a fashion pro, Nancy White aims her shells at three groups: Those whose income is in the millions and who will spend any amount on the *dernier cri;* those who are rich and have good taste and will spend a *good* amount, but think it is immoral to spend five thousand dollars on one dress; those who have only very little money but plenty of taste, and want to know the right place to put their cash—three dollars and up—to reap the most style.

"Even if a woman can't buy a mink-lined trenchcoat," says Nancy White, "or a Van Cleef and Arpels jewel, she has a right to know what's available. With such knowledge, she becomes more free-wheeling in her choices."

Elegance Plus Excitement

Some shockers come from the impact of the photographs themselves. Explaining last year's spectacular success, art director Henry Wolf (who does such things as persuade Mrs. Andrew Mellon to let him photograph her priceless jewels in a dishpan of water) says, "It is easy to be both in good taste, and boring. And it is easy to be elegant and boring. But elegance plus excitement is the great thing—and that is *Harper's Bazaar.*"

Tantrums on a fashion magazine are not news. This is the world of the blow-up, the head-on collisions of personalities—fighting for their ideas. Explains one photographer who *tries* to keep his emotions on ice, "The amount of unrelated noise that comes out of these women could really sink you, if you let it. You'd never get anything done." The art director, known for his tantrums, also claims to be unemotional. "Then why do I lose my temper and yell? I learned that if I say to a fashion editor, 'I don't like this picture,' it means nothing. She doesn't believe me. I must throw my fists in the air, and scream, 'It's terrible! I think it's terrible! Terrible!' Then she begins to think that maybe I don't like it."

The Hub of the Hubbub

All this frantic and dedicated activity emanates from the tenth, eleventh, and twelfth floors of the *Bazaar's* Madison Avenue office, once described by a visiting socialite as an "elegant rabbit warren." The hub of the hubbub, Nancy White's tenth-floor office, has a midnight-black rug topped by an oval, hot-pink rug, generally covered with photographs. One of the two geranium couches with black cushions that cling to the wall by way of antiqued-gold plaques spills swatches of striped material onto the floor. Brilliant sunny light pours through translucent, yellow, four-inch-wide strips of vertical Venetian blind. A distracted fashion editor dangles a diamond necklace: "It's wrong, wrong, *wrong.*" A liquor advertiser arrives; can Miss White give him a "fashion approach" to liquor? Du Pont has created a sparkling, gold-dust stocking—but what to do with it? "It must be promoted as an 'after-five' stocking," remarks Nancy. A copy-girl appears with a layout; Nancy stares at it, inquires, "Where is Edith Sitwell? Oh—not big enough." Probably only in the *Bazaar* would Edith Sitwell be quoted as saying, "I never think about clothes; I've got so few. It's only when I suddenly realize I'm all in rags that I consider them at all."

But undoubtedly the sting is taken out of this statement when, later in her article, Dame Sitwell remarks, "Tchelitchev designed my red velvet gown. He's painted six or seven portraits of me, and he designed me a black dress out of very soft woolen stuff when I lived in Paris."

From this jewelry-photographs-clothes-strewn room, Nancy White jet-flies the *Bazaar's* fashion editors, models, photographers to Hawaii, the Caribbean, or on an around-the-world trip ("You'll have to make it in three weeks"). Some of her jobs: traveling to California each year to cover the West Coast collections; keeping in touch with the Rome editor, the Paris editor, the anything-in-the-world editor; discovering a fabric and suggesting to a manufacturer that he use it. "If the *Bazaar* says it will be a coming style, we know they'll promote what they believe in," says one Seventh Avenue manufacturer. Meanwhile, ten thousand buyers a year arrive at the *Bazaar* office for the "word." Nancy is on constant call to give awards, work on the fashion committee of the "Lighthouse," speak to the Jewelry Council, appear on radio and television. With kangaroo-agility she hops around the country, but must be back at home base for the big "Fashion Group" September show. As producer-director to the cream of the fashion world, who last September crammed into the Grand Ballroom of the Waldorf, Nancy and her staff spent weeks gathering the clothes, jewelry, shoes, gloves, hats, models. The fashion show could not be rehearsed because Khrushchev was being feted in the ballroom. Security police mingled with models, who spent valuable time peeking at the then-jolly Russian big-wig; security police peeked at models. The night before the show, Nancy worked at the Waldorf until 5 A.M., by eight o'clock was checking the models, got them on the runway for the 9:30 breakfast, commentated the show until 10:30, and, breakfastless, greeted the breakfast-filled fashion leaders as they departed to give way to the lunchtime batch of fashion greats. Lunchless, Nancy saw *them* out, by 2:30 in the afternoon said the last goodbyes, and, while the newspaper women rushed to make press deadlines on the Paris fashion story, hurried back to work.

"Vacations don't exist," marvels a manufacturer who, in his angrier moments, has referred to fashion editors as "brittle, soul-less, jealous creatures." What Nancy does get, instead of a vacation, is a twice-yearly—July and January—trip to Europe to see the collections.

Fashion: An Olympian Job

Typical itinerary for last fall, for Nancy, smacked hard of a relay race. She got to Rome on Thursday noon, July 15, checked in at the Excelsior on the Via Veneto, rushed away to a formal collection, then boutique shows, shoe shows, right through Friday, Saturday, Sunday. "In Rome you always work weekends." After a midnight sandwich, Nancy was so excited she could not get to sleep till two—she rose at seven and rushed to see as many collections as she could.

By Sunday night, Nancy was on her way to Florence; she spent the first day covering fifteen boutique collections, selecting clothes, having sketches made, and side-stepping the Rome-Florence feud about which city has the right to be the Paris of Italy. "It would be easier to settle the steel strike than the Rome-Florence fight."

Converging on Paris, Nancy, the photographer, art director, models (who in 1959 were Audrey Hepburn, Mel Ferrer), and assorted assistants totaling a round dozen, moved into the St. Regis Hotel, base for the *Bazaar* twice a year.

In and out was seventy-ish Marie-Louise Bousquet, famous *Bazaar* fashion editor, known in Paris for her Thursday afternoon *salons*, and of whom Truman Capote has observed: "Signed photographs of her victims, what she calls 'my lovairs,' are thick as Persian flies on the gewgaw-laden tables of her Place Palais Bourbon apartment . . . her lasting allure goes unquestioned." Mme. Bousquet is better known in the United States for her May 1959 visit to this country, during which the *Bazaar* sent her to fifteen cities ("They shipped me around like a package," she complained), the French Embassy in Washington honored her with a dinner, and she shocked some sensibilities by admonishing the American woman to "wear perfume on the thigh."

In the cloak-and-dagger secrecy of the Paris collections, where editors (who get first look at the clothes) must show passports, and sometimes must even leave them at a suspicious couturier's door, Nancy again covered collections from dawn to midnight. How sure of herself must fashion editor White be? It is the fashion editor of a top magazine like the *Bazaar* who stands under a Damoclean sword—she must unerringly choose the *crème* of fashion from thousands of clothes; she must then interpret these clothes to fit the purses and needs of women in the United States.

"Will Explain Later"

Secret, too, was the Paris photographing. Recruited to populate the scene was Zsa Zsa Gabor. From New York, *Bazaar* photographer Dick Avedon had, weeks earlier, prepared another recruit, Paris columnist Art Buchwald, cabling him in Paris: "What is your hat size will explain later dick avedon." Came the Buchwald answer: "Size seven will explain later." Complicating things further, other photographers followed the group to take pictures of *Bazaar* in action, for publication in *Life*.

Weighing several pounds less at the end of a week, Nancy wrote descriptions and salient news features on the backs of the photographs and sent them by jet to Idlewild, where they were picked up by a staff member and rushed to Madison Avenue, where the staff worked for two days until 3 A.M. completing layouts and writing copy. Nancy arrived in New York, picked up the layouts and a corps of assistants, and hurried to Philadelphia, where the presses had been kept open a week late.

Got to Have a Gimmick

To the uninitiated, this is the world of incomprehensibility, the world where fashion editors covering the best of the seventeen thousand fashion shows in New York every year get a door prize of an egg-cup topped by a mink cozy; where Luis Estevez sets up a pink-and-white safari tent in the Sheraton East ballroom to put editors in the right mood; where swans of ice swim in champagne at a bathing-suit fashion show; where a model falls shrieking into a set-up-that-morning swimming pool—all in the interest of arousing editorial attention. The fabric editor visits some of her two hundred fabric houses, and arrives back at the office to find fifty-five messages. Two editors war over which one is getting a page more than the other. A manufacturer betrays the magazine by not making the dress photographed. Another feels a rival's clothes are getting a better break, and begins a feud. The Paris couturiers say they are not getting enough of a hearing—so do the Americans.

"This Dress Will Be a Ford"

The jargon, as well as the habits of the fashion world, sometimes defies analysis. Among those in the know, the word "new" has nothing to do with the first time. Translation: "not like last year." There is "new" Victorian, "new" 1930's, "new" white. A "Ford" is a fashion that becomes popular. Pencils start scribbling when Nancy White, announcing a fashion show, says, "We predict this dress will be a Ford." A famous fashion story concerns the neophyte editor who asks a fashion editor for a raise, and gets the sweet reply, "My dear child, I can't give you more *money*—but I'm going to do even better." She pauses portentously, then, "From now on, *you may wear your hat in the office!*" The neophyte faints dead away at the great honor.

Yet, underneath the glitter, the feuds, the jet-speed, under the sometimes-zany hats, are minds that apparently work not only with electronic-calculator precision, but with that mysterious "X" quality—that extra sense of style. To keep buyers aware, the *Bazaar* provides a twice-yearly color-fabrics forecast that is studied by ten thousand buyers, reporters, and manufacturers from coast to coast.

Accusations that *Harper's Bazaar* often makes last year's clothes obsolete, forcing women to buy outrageous but new styles, shower the magazine. Pooh-poohing this, Lord & Taylor's Europe-roving buyer, Jack Vane, says, "The American woman is born with a built-in dread of obsolescence—if she doesn't have something new, she's unhappy."

The *Bazaar's* philosophy bears a startling resemblance to that of the late Dorothy Shaver, who was president of Lord & Taylor. One day, on a periodic checkup through the store's departments, Miss Shaver was shown how successful each department was; everything was perfect. Said Miss Shaver finally, twitching her shoulders, "But where are your *mistakes?*" Playing it safe, to Miss Shaver, was being dead. "Unless there is 15 per cent of a risk," she once stated, "we are not in business."

Risks are even greater at the *Bazaar*. But, points out Diana Vreeland, "There are the sheep and the goats—the followers and the leaders. The leaders must take chances." Working in her green-walled office with its leopard-covered couch, Mrs. Vreeland pushes back the sleeves of a Balenciaga dress; a model walks past in a Ben Zuckerman suit; another girl models a Scaasi coat. Insists Mrs. Vreeland, "We do not force—we force *nothing*. Fashion is like the space age—it is here, though you can't see it. We get it out of the air." And, going further, "We make no such things as decisions —you contemplate, then finally you know— and then you go, go, GO. And things hit right along the line."

Some of the hits: the Italian hair-do in 1952; the planter's hat discovered in Jamaica in 1954, and that, says the *Bazaar*, was effective in getting rid of "the bitsy hat"; the seamless stocking that the *Bazaar* fought for fiercely, showed exclusively for two years. Today the seamless stocking is turned out by practically every major hosiery mill. In 1952, the *Bazaar* tore apart a Dior dress, took out the skeleton, a built-in waist cincher, blazoned it through the magazine. The waist cincher promptly was taken over by Warner's corsets, became the best-selling "Merry Widow." Sticking its neck out again, the magazine went all out for hair-coloring, drove out the taboo against it, turned a million-dollar business into a billion-dollar business.

Bazaar Beatniks

For some of its "firsts" the *Bazaar* gets castigated—the thong sandal in 1938; more recently—the pale Italian mouth. Says Mrs. Vreeland, secure in the distinction of having "come out" socially on *both* sides of the Atlantic, "I prefer even a Beatnik look to the nothing look."

Manufacturers and buyers long ago gave up driving themselves to distraction trying to discover *why* women readers buy what is in the pages of the *Bazaar*. Many have been known to flinch and cry out when they opened the magazine and saw the photographs of their clothes. Yet women buy. Explains one photographer, "A blurred, hazy, Avedon-type of photograph doesn't sell a woman one dress—it sells her an aura, a dream."

A case in point is the story of how, three years ago, Mrs. Vreeland was suddenly struck with the horrifying thought: "There is not a single white silk shirt in the United States—the *right* shirt a woman wants!" What to do? A ransacking of continents turned up such a shirt in Milan. Price would be $39.50, with a small markup. Knowing the *Bazaar* was determined to give the American woman her white shirt, one Fifth Avenue department store agreed to stock the shirt, rubbed its hands in anticipation—until it saw the photograph of the shirt in the magazine. "They had made the shirt look out-of-focus," said the buyer. "You couldn't tell what it was. Besides, they had rolled up the sleeves. They had pulled the shirttails up and knotted them over the model's stomach. My God!" The result: orders flooded the department store from as far away as South America.

Fantasy Will Out

Readers opening the magazine sometimes react as though they have come face to face with a rattlesnake. This is, in part, calculated by the *Bazaar*. "They want a woman to think, 'What are they doing now?' " says a manufacturer. "They are after shock and surprise. They want something that is liked, in every issue, but they also aim to have something that someone doesn't like."

Invariably there are both. Pointing to a mistily photographed pink-lipped model wearing a necklace inspired by a maharani's jewels, Nancy White broods, "Some readers may say the model's face is dirty." Of another page, showing a model breakfasting in a four-poster bed under a willow tree in a glade: "Someone will ask, 'Why is a woman wearing a nightgown in the *woods?*' " Occasionally a reader runs across an earlier issue of the *Bazaar,* writes sarcastically to inquire whether "Gloria Vanderbilt, swinging on a child's swing, is an accurate portrait of that young lady's life."

Putting it on the line, Diana Vreeland says, "If it's bread and butter you want, you don't want us. This is the world of adventure. Fashion has a universal flavor. We like exultation—go to the moon!"

The woman who wants cakes and champagne will get what she wants in the *Bazaar*. "We put this magazine out for the reader—she pays sixty cents," says Mrs. Vreeland. "There are no pretty, pretty pictures in it. What we show, you can *buy.*"

Out of the tornado that is Nancy White's office or Diana Vreeland's office, the *dégagé* look for a single issue takes shape in one afternoon—after months of work. The talk becomes deceptively quick, seemingly casual. Mrs. Vreeland may approve a model with "that scarf—it makes the difference between Genghis Khan and nothing." To an accessories editor, "That gold won't do—it's not bright enough, no *bazazz.*" And to a blouse editor, "Please, get that shirt out of here before we all *die!*" An editor gets a fresh assignment, is advised, "Better get cracking with Daché." A fashion editor who has been trying to wring the needed hat from a temperamental hat designer is told, "My dear, don't *talk* to that woman on the telephone—*seduce* her, make your voice sort of idiotic." A model is given an accolade. "Terriffic! But blouse it all back, get the geisha look—full of air at the back of the neck. Keep it away from the body." Later, when Henry Wolf, Nancy White, and Diana Vreeland are in accord, the selections go to the photographer's studio.

Money in the bank for the *Bazaar* is the unconcealed desire of society, models, writers, photographers, to be in the magazine. "Models want the prestige—the *cachet*—of being in the

Bazaar," points out Nancy White. The cachet—signet, stamp, seal—will let them command big prices for modeling for advertisements. With an eye to the success of earlier *Bazaar* models Lauren Bacall, Dorian Leigh, and, later, Suzy Parker (modeling fees: $210 an hour, $420 after five o'clock), most would be willing to model for the *Bazaar* for less money. Why not, when it may mean movie contracts, theatre contracts, a rich marriage? Photographers will shoot and reshoot pictures until it costs them more than they earn—just to be represented in the magazine.

Paging Mrs. Paley

"Asking socialites to appear in the *Bazaar,"* says one society columnist, "is like asking them to do what they are dying to do anyway." From Mrs. William Paley to Britain's Henrietta Tiarks, to the Duke and Duchess of Windsor, to Mr. and Mrs. Henry Ford II, the pages glitter with society. It has even been said that international society, rich and poor, is rated by the *Bazaar* as being worth a full-page, a half-page, or a quarter-page photograph in the magazine. Making a full-page of the *Bazaar* can be equivalent to having really "made it" in society.

Despite the fireworks, the razzle-dazzle, *Harper's* strikes blows which knock the old chrysalis off the American woman. Reads a gift ashtray on the coffee-table in Nancy White's town house: "You're mad—all of you Whites—stark raving mad!" In the view of rival fashion editors, the White variety of madness is similar to being crazy like a fox—with *bazazz.*

American Designers Urged to Cast Off Their Paris Chains

by Inez Robb

It is one woman's opinion that the untimely death of Claire McCardell, American fashion designer's designer, has pinpointed the worm in America's fashion rose.

As was pointed out at the time of her death last week, Miss McCardell was to her own self and to America true. She won international fame as an American designer of American fashions for American women. Neither French, Italian, nor Hottentot couture influenced her. She had not attended a Paris showing in more than 25 years.

In short, she had faith in herself and her gifts, and it paid off in fame and fortune. She did not attempt to cage women in 18-inch waists one season and in barrels the next. She knew anatomy and she neither insulted nor flouted it. Museums collected and exhibited her timeless creations.

She stood on her own feet on her native soil, and she was good. No tricks, no fads, no stunts. When Paris sneezed Miss McCardell did not slap a mustard plaster on her customers!

So now, let us focus on that worm in the national fashion posy. It is also one woman's opinion that most American fashion designers, with few exceptions, lack the courage of their own great talents. So they grasp at a crutch they do not need, a crutch variously marked "Made in Paris" or "Made in Italy." Even when the mode is ugly and degenerate, as at the moment, they do not have the intestinal fortitude to say "No!"

And it is also my opinion that the chief reason that gifted American designers lack the character to stand alone can be directly traced to a small, powerful and snob section of the American fashion press that is more fascinated by its own navel than ever Buddha was by his.

In its book, the French designers can do no wrong, and anything an American designer can do a Parisian couturier can do a thousand times better. This group of the fashion press has ab-

---

Reprinted with permission from the March 28, 1958, issue of the *New York World-Telegram and Sun,* Copyright 1958. This article appeared, in Inez Robb's feature column, shortly after the death of the noted American designer Claire McCardell.

dicated its responsibility as reporters, much less as critics, and simply become unpaid drum beaters for French fashion. Recently they greeted the appearance of Yves St. Laurent, successor to the late Christian Dior, with panegyrics that would ordinarily be reserved for a combination of Ghandi, Churchill, Joe Di Maggio, and Venus rising from the sea.

And while I am handing out my licks, let me include a clutch of newspaper editors. They will publish any picture or story about French fashions, but they are affronted at the very though of publishing pictures or stories about American designs or designers.

A few American designers, such as Miss McCardell, the great Mainbocher, Sophie of Saks Fifth Avenue, and Pauline Trigere, have had the courage to be themselves and design American. Not a sack in a carload of their beautiful clothes.

Their example, for all are extremely successful, should encourage other American designers to get up on their own hind legs and be themselves. They have only their chains to lose.

How American Fashion Got There

The New York Couture Group Press Week Was the Ladder

by Kittie Campbell

Few of the 300-some editors in attendance for the presentations during this recent Press Week remember the war-torn days which shrouded its birth. From that original gigantic effort of assembling the country's important press came the continuity of semi-annual events which, more than any other single factor, has helped catapult American fashion to equal footing with Paris, projecting the American look around the world for women of other countries to admire and envy.

Fifty-three fashion editors accepted that hastily worded, telegraphed invitation to attend the first Press Week in July 1943. In awed wonder, the New York Dress Institute reckoned at the week's conclusion that it had received more than 696,000 lines of publicity, estimated at about $200,000.00.

At the recent 41st Press Week, which attracted the largest July press attendance in its history, these figures were probably passed during the first day, as daily newspaper reports were cabled, live TV went on the air, and radio shows were taped, all through the Couture Group's well-organized press set-up. Western Union revealed with astonishment that cabled word at mid-week during July's Press session were running 10 per cent higher than any other in its history.

Three attractive and powerful women in the fashion world helped spank Press Week into existence, but it took a man with a keen business sense to conceive the idea and wrap it up in capsule form for fellow-manufacturers to follow and understand.

Ben Reig, whose collection ranks every season with the top newsmakers, sparked the Press Week idea which has been fanned into semi-annual flames by the busy pens of the nation's press since July 1943.

In spite of living in the shadow of the great French couture until World War II blacked out all news from Paris, New York's clothing industry had grown to an awkward, sprawling, unorganized giant by 1941. Largely through efforts of the union to promote the "made in New York" label, manufacturers at last found a common meeting ground under the general title of The New York Dress Institute, organizing with admirable timing to take full advantage of the wartime blackout of fashion news from abroad.

In spite of the extremely diverse activities of its 1500 members, who sold dresses from $5 to $500, the New York Dress Institute prospered. After Reig conceived the idea for National Press Week, a publicist by the name of Eleanor Lambert, a former journalist who had won distinction for her coverage of the sensational

Excerpted and reprinted by permission of Kittie Campbell, Press Director of the New York Couture Group, 141 West 41 St., N.Y.C., 1963.

Hall-Mills murder case, helped guide it, as Press Director, through all its semi-annual explosions for nearly twenty years.

In 1952, a crisis developed for the New York Dress Institute. Manufacturers of lower-priced merchandise re-examined the advantages of participating in Press Week, and came up with the feeling that the top cut of designers was getting the lion's share of the news coverage. At about the same time the original union fund reached the bottom of the barrel. The result was a reorganization on a "club basis" with a nucleus of high-quality houses forming the New York Couture Group and assuming the obligation of carrying on Press Week.

With Press Week the established success it is today, it frequently finds itself with new sets of problems. Although completely supported financially by the members of The New York Couture Group, Press Week also plays hostess to affiliated businesses which are invited to be auxiliaries. Such auxiliaries as the Millinery Institute of America; International Silk Association, USA; National Shoe Institute; du Pont; Clairol, etc., pay a fee to be placed on the Press Week schedule so that the members of the press can be presented with a well-organized plan of events to attend and see without conflict and with a minimum of confusion.

Enterprising fashion houses sometimes "jump the gun" on official Press Week, run counter to the schedule, or hop on the bandwagon afterwards without paying for the privilege. This practice became so heavy that in 1960 Miss Lambert complained at a Couture Group's Board of Directors' meeting that some such interlopers even had the effrontery to phone bona fide auxiliaries to say there was a time infringement! The Press Director had already written to fashion editors about such offenders. While reporting that the press stood loyally behind the efforts of the Couture Group, Miss Lambert discussed the possibilities that a protest be launched to the "free loaders" by letter or telephone. Despite such efforts, the attractive opportunity provided by the Couture Group, which arranges to have the valuable fashion press of the nation in one spot at one time, proves too much of a lure for many firms who often prefer the morally questionable satellite approach.

The Fashion Role of An Ad Agency

by Arthur A. Winters

Calling an advertising agency by any other name may not be just as sweet—but it could be more accurate. The ad agency is now involved in so many marketing functions that the mere preparation and placement of ads in print media would severely limit its usefulness to most clients. This is especially true in the fashion industry where the agency helps primary and secondary level firms develop the right product in the right package at the right price and gets it the right distribution in the right markets. Merchandising becomes an agency function which helps a mill or a manufacturer stimulate his sales force, design sales presentations, train salesmen, plan sales conventions and exhibits, and organize sales drives. The agency can research markets or customer motivations and preferences. Dealer aids, cooperative advertising, tie-in promotions, and point-of-purchase materials are planned and produced. These functions are offered by agencies as a full service or a supplement to the firm's own staff. The agency role today is to assist a client in *marketing his product.* In the full sense of the meaning of marketing this includes merchandising and any of the direct sales promotion activities—advertising, display, publicity.

Most agencies who work for fashion producers are extremely retail-oriented. They realize the vitality of selling activities which get their inspiration from consumer wants and needs. Those efforts which best supplement personal

---

Mr. Winters, President of Arthur Winters Advertising Agency which specializes in fashion advertising, wrote this article especially for this book. He is professor of advertising at the Fashion Institute of Technology, New York, N.Y.

selling and coordinate sales promotion are the basis of ad agency service. The extent to which the agency gets involved is largely up to the client and his requirements. Many primary, and some secondary firms, have substantial staffs of their own which perform the aforementioned functions.

Ad agencies have generally found that regardless of how limited their original arrangement is—if they can really help a client—they are gradually asked to do more and more. A good agency is considered a staff element in the organizational structure of many firms in the fashion industry.

We haven't mentioned the retail level yet—and purposely. Here the story is quite different. It is difficult for the average ad agency to provide service for retailers. Agencies which have been most successful serving retail accounts found it necessary to institute "local" advertising departments that specialize in retail store advertising. These departments are specifically designed to handle daily newspaper advertising with its problems of quick deadlines and last-minute changes.

The advertising agency which equips itself for this service is prepared to plan and produce *all* of a store's advertising. This, however, is not as common as the case of agencies which undertake to prepare *special* advertising material and research, and offer counsel on planning and copy concepts. By limiting their service, they are not involved with the constant pressure caused by the day-in, day-out advertising and sales promotion in which retail stores must engage.

Several large stores, who have their own advertising departments, use outside agencies to prepare institutional advertising while they themselves prepare product advertising. Other stores may engage an agency to handle their radio advertising while handling all their newspaper advertising themselves.

The most successful example of a large store-advertising agency collaboration is the long-standing effort of Ohrbach's in New York City and their agency, Doyle, Dane and Bernbach. The institutional advertising produced by this combination has not only advanced the progress of the store, but is universally regarded as a classic in retail institutional advertising, and the series has been widely imitated and developed into an established and recognized style.

Agencies with clients such as fabric mills and garment manufacturers are now engaged in a full range of activities which serve to help originate, develop, package, distribute, and promote products. They also provide public relations programs which include research and publicity. The range of services which agencies render to retailers is much more limited. The number of agencies seeking business on the primary and secondary levels of the fashion industry grows daily. The problems of handling the promotion of retailers inhibit the agency's full-scale entry.

Promoting Fashion through Effective Fashion Advertising

What is fashion advertising and what does it take to create it effectively? In order to answer this question it is necessary to discuss what fashion is. But first, I would classify fashion advertising into two distinct categories: (a) exclusive fashion advertising, as exemplified in fashion magazines and in advertisements for exclusive stores, and (b) volume fashion advertising, as exemplified in volume selling in department and promotional-price stores.

The definition of what is and what is not fashion has confounded the so-called fashion practitioners for years. It has been analyzed and defined by poets, scholars, researchers, and advertising men, and no two explanations have been exactly in agreement. It seems that fashion is as elusive as it is illusive . . . and by nature a most capricious commodity. Therefore, rather than add to the long list of controversial definitions, I would choose to explain fashion in terms of the human motivation and desire which help shape it, applying these to a discussion of how they affect fashion advertising.

I am sure you have heard of the socioeconomic theory that wars, depressions, social and business environments determine the nature of fashion. I've never accepted this theory beyond the point or premise that all things affect fashion, which is *what people want.* Fashion is a personal affair, an individual's reaction to his own needs and desires. In women, the approach is so personal that it often takes a woman to sell a woman. A man might understand how important it is to a woman to wear a skirt that is shorter and tighter this season. But he is at a loss to explain how she actually feels in it. A woman can sell fashion because she knows the intimate feel of the sheath dress . . . she sells the feel of fashion, the tight skirt or flared skirt, the high waist or low waist, almost before she sells the particular garment. The basic difference in the salesmanship of fashion advertising is emotion. The appeals are emotional, the approach more imaginative. Effective fashion advertising will use a knowledge of the particular set of emotions concerned with the desire and need for individuality, romance, recognition, acceptance, compensation, career, etc. The partnership of illustration and copy must create in the customer the feel of fashion, and generate a specific satisfaction or emotion which can be attained with this fashion. Fashion advertising is extremely effective when it lets the woman know exactly how she will feel, and what will happen when she wears this black satin sheath on her next date.

Creating exciting fashion advertising must rely upon constant exposure to what makes people want and feel as they do. It requires comprehensive orientation on what is happening and what has happened in our world. And most important, it necessitates an understanding *of your customer* and *your store* and the particular appeals which it has for them.

We are now ready to discuss fashion advertising in terms of our original classifications, "the exclusive fashion customer," and the "volume fashion customer."

Exclusive fashion advertising can be formal or informal, but it must be authoritative and signify leadership. Fundamentally, this advertising is directed to women who want to *lead* in wearing a fashion and is designed to sell a concept rather than a specific garment in stock. Lord & Taylor's advertising is a good example of this most important characteristic. The approach is usually one of breathless excitement about what the fashion will do for you. The message is directed towards people who want to set the pace; the appeals are prestige and individuality. The atmosphere created is illusionary and full of mood. There is more concern with mood than details, and this type of advertising should try to convince the reader that she is influencing the fashion, rather than being influenced by it. Copy is usually brief, but dramatic and descriptive. Art work should be dynamic, fresh, dramatic.

The techniques in volume fashion advertising are designed to sell the woman who must keep up with fashion rather than be a leader. Here a knowledge of customer, product, and salesmanship are perhaps more exacting . . . for the advertising must be effective enough to influence much larger groups. Here, in a certain sense, an awareness of buying patterns merchandising, and customer preferences are more important than writing ability. The style of volume fashion advertising must be forceful and emphatic and geared to attract attention, maintain interest, arouse desire, and prompt to action.

This customer wants to dress smartly, but she is also concerned with budget, keeping her family healthy, her home attractive, leisure activities, etc. Many other considerations and products are vying with fashion for this customer's attention, and a dozen other stores are competing to sell her the same garments. If the advertising is to work, it must say it better and be more compelling. The appeals here are somewhat different from the specialized appeals in exclusive fashion advertising. Here we try to convince the customer that she is buying and wearing what is new and smart, and infer that she has the good judgment to recognize smart fashion. We emphasize why it will be becoming to her and try to leave no doubt that she is well dressed due to the merchandising skill of our store—*her store*. The fashion is related to her activities, her way of life. The copy gives details, wearability, washability, width of seams fabrics, colors, sizes—and gives more importance to price as the type of store goes more promotional.

Selling fashion today relies upon a very accurate knowledge of what your customer wants and what you have to offer in the way of product and conditions of sale. It is the blend of this, plus the emotional excitement of buying "something strictly for one's self."

A Jaunt with Fashion

by Jean Cameron

A fashion publicist bases her work on the premise that a woman must be ill if she doesn't want to know the latest about clothes. We are, apparently, a remarkably healthy nation.

Eleanor Lambert of New York, fashion publicist of great skill, is a prime generator at this wild side of a $15 billion industry. In its more drab end, that of production, it gives fruitful, if sometimes shaky, employment to one million U.S. citizens.

Among Miss Lambert's clients who participate vicariously and fruitfully in the excitement she generates in the press, are a distinctive group of fashion designers, here and abroad. Manufacturers who pay her court and costs admire the high plateau to which she raises the newsworthy in their fashion.

With a quick mind for timing, she analyzes fashion in New York, then Paris, to determine what will, and what will not, make fashion news. At two yearly meetings with the press, and in a myriad of releases during the year, she feeds out news; she bolsters opinion—and she sways it.

A blonde dynamo, Eleanor Lambert travels regularly between New York and Paris, loved by many, envied by many. An associate says, "Anyone who has become a success has critics. Eleanor Lambert has hers certainly."

Her world is fashion, and fashion has been good to her. She is at home in these worlds—divergent as Paris and New York—and thanks to her energies, all her worlds are luxurious worlds.

Her energy is expended on behalf of—in America—names such as Lilly Daché, Anne Fogarty, Ceil Chapman, Adele Simpson, Ben Zuckerman, Coty, Jean Louis, Rudi Gernreich, Arnold Scaasi (spell Scaasi backwards and see what happens). In Europe, Simonetta et Fabiani, Roger Vivier, Sybil Connolly, Castillo, Ferraras.

Although she has a staff of 17 people (she hires more at busy times), she does all the writing for each of her accounts herself. "She works all the time," says one associate in New York. Her experienced hand and mind guide, influence, and direct much creative talent in fashion. Producer of large and lavish fashion shows, she has produced the gala March of Dimes show, originated the Cotton Fashion Awards shows. And the fashion extravaganza, the Cherry Blossom Festival Fashion Show, has been staged for two years with a Lambert touch.

For 20 years Miss Lambert directed the New York Couture Group's semi-annual Press Week showings of new fashion. This year she gathered her group of outstanding designers into an aggregation known as the American Designers Group, and held a press week showing. Fashion editors from all over the country were treated to nearly two weeks of new designs.

The most interesting fashion show she ever produced? In 1959 she selected American fashions shown in Moscow by the U.S. government. They caused a sensation among Soviet women and brought frowns of displeasure from the Soviet government. There was no acceptance by the Soviet that it was at all suitable for their women to think, look or dress as Eleanor Lambert thinks women should. (It was at this show that sample Coty lipsticks were snatched with glee by Kremlin belles.)

Scores of designers attribute their success to Eleanor. She "put Arnold Scaasi on the map," is now promoting Pepe Fernandez, the Cuban refugee designer. He arrived in the United States from Cuba with only the clothes on his back, and unlimited talent and ability.

Eleanor is always attracted to new, young, striving talent. In the beginning, her publicity for the struggling designer costs him practically nothing. She has a list of distinguished clients, true, but many of them are distinguished as a result of the Lambert flair.

She has great know-how, a keen sense of

Realm, October 1963. Abridged and reprinted by permission of Medalist Publications, Inc., Chicago, Illinois. Miss Lambert is one of the best known and most effective public relations experts in the fashion field.

fashion. A friend says, "She has a fantastic memory. If she goes to the art gallery or the theater, she is able to mentally pigeonhole what she has seen, and sooner or later she will relate it to fashion. She relates *everything* to fashion." Another friend terms her a very "current" person, says she has a great sense of the past in relation to the present.

The pro's and con's of the *Ten Best Dressed* list, which Eleanor transplanted here from Paris in 1933, are debated hotly. Eleanor thinks it is important, mails 2500 ballots each year to qualified judges of these matters, such as society editors, columnists, and the like. She also thinks it important that the not-so-wealthy are dressed best. She worked out the uniforms for the women of the military as special consultant on publicity to WAC and U.S. Army Nurse Corps. She saw to it that Mainbocher, her client when he returned to America from Paris in 1940, designed a smart, feminine uniform for the WAVES.

"No matter what they're up to, women should look like women," maintains Eleanor.

"In America," she continues, "women have a tendency to either over-dress, or to be too conservative. That's why I try to spark the dull clothes, and eliminate all the fuss and nonsense from fussy clothes. If clothes are presented to the press as dramatically as possible, and properly, it's certain to get through to readers of women's pages. Because of all this vital fashion publicity, American women have become well dressed. It's a matter of fashion education."

The Resident Buying Industry

by Adele C. Elgart

Here in the United States there are thousands of retail stores, large and small, scattered throughout every village, town, and city in every state in the Union. On their shelves and selling racks one can find merchandise from all over the world. This merchandise is bought by buyers who are responsible for procuring the merchandise os that it will be in the store at the time customers will buy it and at a price which will make a profit for the store.

Market Coverage

New York City is the largest single market in the entire world for feminine wearing apparel. There are thousands of dress manufacturers among thousands of other ready-to-wear and accessories manufacturers in this market.

When the dress buyer from out-of-town comes to New York City to do some buying, with the thousands of manufacturers to choose from she doesn't have time to see them all. How will she know whom to see, and whom to leave out? Each trip is a big job and this job continues to get tougher because the dress market is not a static thing. Manufacturers come and go. Someone may be very good one season and just as bad the next. The buyer must see all and know all, before she can make her selections and write her orders, if she is to come out with a profit.

The dress buyer from out-of-town is in the market for two or three days to two or three weeks. Within the buyer's limited time and the enormous size of the market, the task of efficient buying becomes impossible for one person without help.

The Operating Procedure

At precisely this point the resident buying office comes into the retail picture. Here is the way it works in our office, and in similar fashion in other offices:

Again, the dress buyer, when she plans a trip to the market, will notify her New York Office

---

Mrs. Elgart is the executive director of the Specialty Stores Association, a resident buying office owned by a group of independent apparel specialty stores. She was the president of the Association of Buying Offices when this talk was presented to a group of college advisors in November, 1958. Reprinted with permission.

two or three days in advance of her arrival, and indicate what she needs to buy—the kind of dresses, the price lines, whether for regular selling or special promotion—and any other information pertinent to her contemplated purchases. The resident dress buyer will then proceed to check her records and re-examine the relevant portion of the market to this buyer's needs.

When the store buyer arrives in the New York buying office, she will find, ready for her, a list of the resources where she can buy the merchandise most suitable to fill her needs on that particular trip.

The resident buyer is in the market every working day of the year and it is his or her job to know the market thoroughly—stylewise, pricewise, valuewise, deliverywise, and every other factor which might have bearing on the merchandise recommended to the store buyers.

Departmental Organization

Now, what I said for the dress buyer in the store and her counterpart in the resident buying office is more or less true for every other buyer for all manner of merchandise the store buys.

Time and space does not permit enumerating every item of merchandise, or every category of buyer employed by stores or by resident buying offices. It will suffice to indicate that where the store has a furniture buyer, a rug or carpet buyer, its resident buying office will also have corresponding buyers. Likewise in ready-to-wear, the coat and suit buyer, the sportswear buyer and various dress buyers—such as the women's, misses, juniors, teen-age and children's wear buyers—each has his counterpart in the resident buying office.

Of course in stores as in resident offices, the number of categories given to any one buyer will depend on the extent of the market to be covered, and the volume done in any given category.

Kinds of Offices

Resident buying offices are owned by individuals or corporations, as private business ventures, or they are owned mutually by a number of stores banded together to share the cost and to gain from each other merchandise experience in the market and in the operating of their own stores.

Resident buying offices differ as to the kinds of merchandise they cover, and the variety of services they render to their clients or members. But in one respect they are all alike—in that the store buyers and merchandisers have a base of operation when in the market, and have available carefully screened market information to save useless expenditure of their time and energy examining lines which are not for their needs.

In addition to the buying service, they provide a place to meet with other buyers from noncompeting stores and to discuss their business plans for promotion, experiences with certain manufacturers, and success or failure with certain styles.

Research Activities of Office

Some of the mutual buying offices also gather statistics from their member stores covering all manner of costs of doing business: cost of selling, buying, advertising, alterations, delivery, maintenance costs, how much business done per cubic foot of space on the main floor, on the second floor, etc., and also all manner of statistics in regard to such merchandising data as stock inventory, at the beginning of the month, at the end of the month, the sales, turnover, and markdowns.

When all this information is gathered from the various member stores, it is correlated and worked out into averages and made available to each member store for its own personal benefit, and I hope for their enjoyment. If you have any students who like to have their imagination run riot in a mass of figures, this controller's department in a resident buying office would be a heaven on earth for them.

Personally, an abstract number of more than five loses all significance for me. But let me walk into a stockroom packed with wearing apparel, and I can tell you at a glance about what percentage of the stock is headed for markdowns, and what is missing in order to do a good business.

There is room for all sorts of abilities in our industry.

The Association of Buying Offices

The 38 members of the Association of Buying Offices alone in New York City represent an annual volume of over $15 billion and there are quite a few additional resident buying offices representing only one or two large stores, or small groups whose annual volume runs into the millions.* Whether the total is $15 billion or $25 billion doesn't much matter for our discussion because these astronomical figures have no meaning unless we can intelligently compare them with a quantity our minds can grasp.

Any way you look at it, you will agree the resident buying industry in New York City is big—in fact, very big.

Buying Office Centers

It would be well to tell your students who enroll in college for retailing to also study French, Italian, Spanish, or some other foreign language because there are resident buying offices in London, Paris, Zurich, Florence, and many other cities throughout the world.

In the United States there are buying offices on the West Coast, in Chicago, and other cities —in fact wherever in the world there is a market for merchandise which can be sold in a retail store, you most likely will find a resident buying office. The basic services in a buying office, no matter where it is located, are the same.

*The ABO is a trade association of major New York buying offices with headquarters at the NRMA, 100 West 31st St., N.Y.C. Its membership numbered 39 offices in 1965.

Importance of the Business

It seems to me that this is a rather fascinating and glamourous side to the resident buying business. It would be quite normal for you to think that since I am in the resident buying business, I therefore am painting a rosy picture for you and may be laying it on a little as to our importance.

Then just listen to what the manufacturers of merchandise have to say about our industry. A few weeks ago the Association of Buying Offices celebrated its 25th Anniversary and one of the speakers was Mr. Robert A. Seidel, Executive Vice President of the Radio Corporation of America. I quote from what he said:

> We at RCA have come to realize that the quickest way to get our message to the stores is to work closely with the buying offices. We know that their advice and guidance is highly regarded by stores and buyers as well. Recognizing this fact, our company has established a specialized selling group to work directly with the buying offices. As a result, our department store business has increased steadily and we are looking towards continuing increases in department store sales.

RCA, a very large corporation with its own highly trained selling staff, found it paid off to create a special department to contact the resident buying offices.

Polka Dots Are Poison in Georgia

The Work and Life of a Resident Office Buyer

by Sonia Arcone

 An excellent description of a buying office girl's duties.

Bounded on the north by Forty-first Street, on the south by Thirty-fifth, on the east by Broadway and on the west by Eighth Avenue, there is an island of industry known as the Garment

Center and, to people in the business, more familiarly as Seventh Avenue or the Market. Here a group of people gets paid to know that there are towns in Georgia where polka dots are poison, that southern Alabama hates red, that the heat in San Diego comes in September, and that sleeveless, low-cut dresses are taboo in Mormon country. These people are called resident buyers.

A resident or buyers' buyer can spot a Midwest accent and often the exact state in which the accent was acquired. She can sometimes tell a home town from a dress or its color. And she knows, oddly enough, by the number of dresses she's to purchase for a town in Pennsylvania whether the coal miners are working, on strike, or have a three-day week. She also knows when the law has clamped down on a wide-open gambling town (requests for formals drop to nothing).

Sometimes she knows from the type of dress a store may request, or by the urgency of cancellations, or demands for off-priced goods to stimulate business. Sometimes her strange conglomeration of knowledge comes from a word, phrase, or paragraph in hastily written letters—the tip-off to news that will break into headlines a week later. Her job, buying (and planning) fashions for perhaps a hundred stores in a hundred cities, is part of a billion-dollar business—one that has played a large part in influencing the growth of stores and the tastes of women all over the country. And her work and life have special interest for college women excited by the touch-it, try-it, own-it-temporarily glitter of a department store buyer's job. For the resident buyer, unlike her store counterpart, is not responsible for daily sales volume—the strain of making each day's profit figures equal or surpass those of a year ago. And she does not work on Saturdays. She may, however, have to travel more miles (breaking home ties) than the would-be store buyer to get her start and keep her power; resident buying is not any-city kind of work. There are a few resident buying firms in Chicago, some in Los Angeles. But most, well over two hundred, are in New York.

If it's hard for a regular department store buyer, say in Minneapolis, to anticipate the multifaceted needs and wants of her store's clientele, you can imagine what octopuslike vision is required of the resident buyer whose job it is to satisfy the needs and desires of customers shopping at stores all across the country, not to mention customers in Africa or Japan. Indeed, the resident buyer's business has such scope that if she longs to identify herself with something big she may gravitate to international dress-buying. Thus one buyer we know took her pattern-cutting knowledge to England to show an English coat and suit manufacturer how to style his garments for good United States sales; she advised Italian silk houses that Americans wanted to buy their silks but not in lingerie tints.

Supposing it were possible for you to pay a visit to one of these progress-and-prosperity-minded buyers. Her office is in a tall, tall building on Broadway among some shorter buildings where ribbons, hats, and leggings are sold wholesale. On the seventh floor of the building, after you've passed rows and rows of glassed-in, semiwalled offices teeming with busy women, you come to a separate semiwalled office of frosted glass and guarded by two secretaries. Inside you find a very, very busy woman who sits in quiet authority under a black hat of dignity and breadth reading a big book of reports. She nods for you to read a magazine until she's through. The secretaries whish in and out, the high heels echo briskly up and down outside the door, the buzzer buzzes. Finally: "And what is it I can tell you about resident office buying?"

She pauses. Then, "To begin with, our stores own us. We don't own the stores."

Actually, she might go on to explain, only a few (about six) of the New York buying offices are literally store property—they are owned cooperatively and operated by groups of major big-city stores. Other offices—about a hundred—are maintained by nation-wide or territorial chains. A hundred more are independent organizations commissioned by the stores and paid annual fees based on the volume of their services (another way of being owned). Our big-time buyer would point out, however, that all buyers in resident offices, even offices that live by commissions, are salaried and work on a year-round basis. Maybe this sounds secure. It isn't.

In the Market

For the resident buyer of dresses the New York market is a vast jungle of manufacturers, factories, and showrooms where merchandise is born, bought, and shipped out. From the catacombs of ancient buildings on Thirty-fifth Street (called Chinatown by the trade) where the cheaper dresses are manufactured by the thousands to the more modern edifices on Broadway and Seventh Avenue where more expensive clothes are made, the resident buyer knows her way around. Because there are over two thousand New York dress manufacturers plus many, many offices of out-of-town firms to be shopped, each dress buyer has to specialize in a particular size and price range. The budget dress buyer of misses sizes, for instance, knows of over two hundred makers of dresses that retail from $8.95 to $17.95. She shops as many as are humanly possible, can recognize top value for the money, and may do business with thirty-five to fifty manufacturers within a season.

The manufacturers are the resident buyer's friends and often her problem children. They seek her advice and opinion on styles fresh from the designing room. She, in turn, tries to see and hear everything that goes on in factories and showrooms. To a bit of information about a color or a sample cut of fabric she gives serious consideration, storing it away against some future project. And each week she writes a long report (plus many shorter ones) telling her store buyers what's happening. Usually, she'll give advice on what to buy—from then on it's up to the store buyer.

The buyer's long, full day—like Maureen Nilan's—regularly starts at nine sharp with at least three long-distance calls from stores, a heavy pile of mail as well as a line of people impatiently waiting, requesting merchandise or information. (Maureen gets up at six to make it by bus and subway from Long Island, rarely gets home before seven.) And a buyer's morning usually starts off, too, with a series of headache calls from salesmen—salesmen on the phone or arriving with bulging sample cases. Either way, they must be put off until the special hours set aside for "looking"—usually in the late afternoon. It's important that a buyer get out into the market early if she's to make all the stops, often at least ten, necessary to fill that day's requests and to collect information from salesmen on what's "hot" at stores she doesn't buy for: How many stores bought item X? How fast was it reordered in three big stores? What colors were reordered in what quantity?

"I Get More Nervous Sitting Still"

Twenty-one-year-old Maureen has the title of assistant buyer at Specialty Stores—a store-owned resident office for expensive specialty shops all over the country. Her chief job, one that, like maternity clothes, is often turned over to bright assistants, is buying and following up orders for bridal gowns. (Maureen has no special plans, isn't anxious to get married but already has a wedding gown picked out for herself, costing $165 wholesale.) Maureen also shops formals in "missy" sizes eight to twenty, retailing up to $69. (Her boss handles all the street wear, cocktail dresses, and expensive clothes.)

Hurrying from manufacturer to manufacturer each day (poor, tired feet), Maureen hugs to her blond sheared raccoon coat a nine-by-twelve-inch Manila envelope and a black loose-leaf notebook, the insignia of the resident buyer. The brown envelope contains sheaves of yellow memos (teletypes from stores), of white papers (manufacturers' original orders), and a flurry of torn scraps of notes to herself. The black notebook is even more precious. In addition to telephone numbers, it has her only listing of manufacturers' lines. This is the bible of information on which she bases her daily advice to store clients. Every dress has a number—e.g., 281—which she has written down and alongside it a buyer's shorthand description of the dress. If it's a Bianchi bridal number maybe her description reads "silk mist with glotz [fancy stuff like pearls and sequins] . . . has panels extending into things [refers to side panniers] . . . and a Maypole skirt." "Maypole" is an adjective Maureen made up to describe this number so it will come vividly back to mind when she sends off teletypes and bulletins to her stores—the skirt was wound with ribbons like a child's Maypole. Little tricks like this are important, Maureen says, because many of the bridal dresses look very much alike. In fact, one of the earmarks of a successful buyer is a good memory—the visual kind that can note, from week to week, the exact, subtle differences between similar numbers and styles: the kind that, in the market, can keep in mind what particular stores want: "California stores like sexy dresses—like colors—and black with floating panels." ("I can remember a style from three years ago and who made it," says one buyer. "I can walk into a dance with my husband and tell him whose number it is over there and what price.")

Taking a look at her own qualtities, Maureen Nilan might see a girl with a good memory, a girl with a mania for clothes, and also a girl who is happy only when she is chasing around. The fast pace of resident buying suits her: "I take my work very seriously and get nervous about it but I get more nervous sitting still. Sitting at a typewriter makes me disagreeable. I get twitchy."

Actually there is plenty in Maureen's job that would keep anybody twitchy, no matter how fast she could run. (Maureen herself gets lots of headaches, cures them with aspirin, doesn't like to go out weekday evenings for the sake of her health.) "Aggravation" is the word she uses to describe the climate of her job. Bridal clothes, first of all, are generally spoken of as irritating because delivery dates are so important and orders often involve exact measurements. But there are other sources of frustration. Example: A store buyer cancels after merchandise has already been shipped, then forgets to return it, then orders merchandise in another—e.g., ballerina length. Example: A difficult "personal" (individual order for store owner's wife)—e.g., to find a black lace size eighteen for a woman six foot tall. Worst of all are late shipments from manufacturers.

For in this field well-meaning promises are made every day—and broken by manufacturers who have fallen behind in production. A broken promise can mean that a store would come dangerously close to having a big promotion fall on its face. It can mean the loss of thousands of dollars. It's the resident buyer's responsibility to see that this doesn't happen by keeping after the manufacturer.

This kind of thing happens: Mr. A., a successful Seventh Avenue manufacturer, had promised one of the Pittsburgh stores a large shipment of dresses to cover a newspaper ad. The dresses were not ready.

When the resident buyer called frantically that afternoon Mr. A. wasn't available and one of his young salesmen took the call. The salesman, who knew nothing of the promise, told the buyer the dresses hadn't been shipped.

"Why did you tell the truth?" Mr. A. raged. "Why didn't you say they were shipped? A little white lie is important in this business. Until you learn to lie you'll never be successful."

What do *you* do, we asked Maureen, if you are worried about a manufacturer's promise? "Well," Maureen said, "I don't think they lie to *me* . . . I make them laugh. I look them straight in the eye—if they're lying they just have to laugh or else they blush."

What else?

"You go," Maureen said, "into the shipping rooms and ask the shipping clerks about shipments you ordered. Sometimes they say, 'They're all coming in and they're all going out.' Then you can check the invoices (supposed to represent the merchandise that has been shipped). But invoices don't prove a thing. I look up the order cards in their files. The order cards should have date shipped and name of shipper—e.g., Air Express. I try to find a trucker's or shipping company's receipt. In most cases I call the trucker to find out when he delivered the merchandise and ask him to get me the packing company's receipt number so I can call and find out what flight the parcel went out on."

Key Seasons

The resident buyer is both Midas and menace to the manufacturer since she is the guide for the store buyer, who, unless she's with a major Eastern department store, averages only two to four trips to the New York market a year. It is often the word of the resident buyer that influences a large purchase or none at all.

January and June are the months of the heavy buying weeks when the bulk of spring and fall purchasing is done—hectic weeks when every day is devoted to working along with one or a group of store buyers, guiding their steps, suggesting "resources" (manufacturers) in order of importance, demanding where possible that valuable time be saved by showing only preselected samples.

Sometimes the resident buyer is greeted by wariness and even a certain amount of hostility on the part of the store buyer who feels that he or she has been coming to New York's market long enough to know the score. Mostly, however, the store buyer is grateful—or learns to be —for the additional services of a buyer who scouts the market regularly and who, after all, is supplied by her own employers at a substantial cost. It's to the advantage of the resident buyer if she has the liking and confidence of a store buyer: it can mean the privilege of "open money" and the right to buy on her own, in small quantities, any new item that looks right for the store. This added power, sought after by resident buyers, turns every month into a rush month. More details mean more errors and more promises mean more broken. Even a good idea may backfire.

A recent purchase was made in New York for a California store. When the dresses arrived the store buyer turned pale. There were twelve dresses in the package, six blue and six brown. Brown is difficult enough to put over in California and this was the most monstrous shade she had ever seen. Furious, she sent the dresses back direct to the manufacturer without troubling to writer a letter of explanation.

The package was refused and returned to the store because no explanation arrived. In great disgust and not wanting to be bothered any more, the buyer put the dresses in stock and muttered with heavy sarcasm to her assistant: "Lovely new color."

The dresses sold out in one day. Resident buying is full of these mysteries: the good guess gone wrong, the unspectacular style that suddenly becomes "hot."

Small wonder a myth has grown up that the successful buyer has a sixth sense. No one has devised an aptitude test for this, however. Key questions for beginners are rather "Can you write?" and "How's your health?" For many who make otherwise excellent buyers become bogged down with the constant and heavy writing of reports. And since every buyer runs a little business of her own, employers figure she'll manage it better if she knows the details of planning stock, markups, gross margin, and bookkeeping to start with—learned perhaps in a department store selling or stock room job or from merchandising courses, or sometimes in the market itself.

The lowliest of lowly jobs (fate of the inexperienced) is that of a "follow-up." The follow-up girl does nothing but check on shipments of merchandise. She's slave to the assistant buyer she works for and at the mercy of the shipping clerks. Even an assistant buyer must go through months of following up orders, observing, note-taking, placing small orders. Then one day, she'll say to herself, I shouldn't be placing that reorder for wools now—by the time they reach San Francisco it will be late spring. Then maybe she's on her way—a girl who will one day sense the trend in colors, fabrics, styles, can advise her stores whether Dacron blends are more important than rayons or tell them what is the coming thing in shoe shapes. Most important is the ability to forecast a major market break—the frantic time when the sudden arrival of, say, the sheath demands fast reporting, buying, and promoting, when if a buyer misses she makes a million-dollar mistake.

Some say the excitement of the buyer's job lies right here: the power to make big decisions affecting big money. For the buyer who helps to earn dollars for other people doesn't always carry away a purseful for herself. A beginner's meager live-with-your-family wage can grow gradually until it reaches, in three to five years, an average of five thousand dollars—that's the pay that goes with the job of full buyer. A chosen few reach ten thousand. A handful even higher.

They say a buyer's work either becomes a passion with her—or that she can't stand it. All those faces. All those people—some she can trust, some she can't. Everything a crisis. Concessions. Cancellations. Lost packages. Sometimes the glamour of being a very special person. Sometimes the feeling she's just a letter carrier—"neither rain nor snow . . ."—with aching feet. And eventually, perhaps, a buyer meets with flattering reminders of her influence. Traveling across the country, she is startled to see it: in the skirt a Lancaster schoolgirl wears or the Saturday night date dress on a farm girl in Iowa. These were samples she took a flier on—all in a day's work.

Fashion Is Their Business

The 2,841 Women Members of the Fashion Group Influence the Way You Look and Live

by Eleanor Pollock

When you hear "women's club" or "women's organization," you're apt to think of a group of Helen Hokinson characters with large fronts and "little more than 'arf of that behind" holding forth on the beauty of Browning or the song of the birds. Not so the Fashion Group, which represents the largest industry in New York City. The influence of the 1400 resident members is far-reaching. It goes way beyond the clothes on your back; reaches into your refrigerator, to your bathroom—even gets into bed with you. For fashion is not a funny hat. Fashion is a business that affects not only the way we look but the way we live and think.

New York is undeniably the fashion center of the United States. The huge ready-to-wear industry (which is young—about 35 years old), is located in a concentrated area, six blocks long and three blocks wide. Responsible for more than a billion-and-a-half dollars' worth of business, it gives employment to 179,545 women and a like number of men. It is the fashion trades that have given women who work an opportunity to create jobs where their special skills and aptitudes can be used and developed without stint.

The first faint sign of women's place in fashion appeared in the 1920's when department stores suddenly became aware of the very evident fact that the majority of their customers were women. At the same time, they awakened to the fact that most of their master-minding was being done by men. Something seemed to be wrong. So the stores created an anomalous job for someone called a "stylist." They hired women of good social background (but with no business knowledge) to advise their buyers and merchandise men. Any woman who had a finishing school education and who knew how to enter a room and use an oyster fork had the red carpet put out for her. This resulted in a flock of women with some taste and not too much business sense getting good posts at hefty salaries.

The reaction was not long in coming. The store moguls discovered that while good taste was important, a knowledge of what the public would buy was even more important. But from these beginnings came a whole new job field for women who could learn fast and who could translate their style sense into merchandising.

It was just about this time (1928) that some "stylists," who found themselves alternately jeered and cheered in their jobs, decided that there should be an organization of women engaged in fashion work that would give the job of stylist some dignity and standing. Such a club would also act as a clearinghouse for information and would enable members to get together to explore problems affecting their jobs.

Initiators in this move were Harriett Ainsworth of Filene's in Boston and Lois Hunter who was with the NRDGA (National Retail Dry Goods Association). So one hideously stormy night a group of determined pioneers met at Mary Elizabeth's tearoom at Fifth Avenue and 37th Street. Everyone agreed that the idea of a club or organization was a fine one. And it was decided that the group would become an adjunct of the NRDGA with Miss Hunter as chairman. But at a luncheon at the Hotel Pennsylvania in 1929 it was decided, for reasons now lost in history, that the NRDGA was not quite the right aegis for the group.

Things then stood still, or at least they did so as far as the rank and file were concerned. But behind the scenes women who were important in the fashion business then (many of them still

Reprinted by permission of the Fashion Group. The Fashion Group is an organization of women active in any of the many branches of the fashion business.

are)—such as Mary Brooks Picken, Julia Coburn of the Tobé-Coburn School, Marcia Connor, and Mary Lewis (who put cotton on the map as a fashion fabric)—were meeting and discussing ways and means of getting a group together.

At a luncheon at the Women's City Club in 1930 some 45 women gathered to hear Marcia Connor, then an associate editor of *Vogue,* expound on the idea of a Fashion Guild.

In her book, *Always in Vogue,* Edna Woolman Chase gives Marcia Connor credit for seeing the idea through. Miss Connor enlisted the interest of Marion Taylor, a dynamic woman who even a quarter of a century ago succeeded in carrying fashion and the women's point of view into industries which, although they "viewed with alarm," had sufficient prescience to recognize a good idea when they met up with it.

Then in 1931 another general call went out, and 75 women attended a luncheon at the Hotel Pennsylvania. There without further ado Miss Taylor was elected first president of the Fashion Group.

Even the founding mothers didn't know what they had started. No one could foresee then, in the depths of the depression, that fashion would extend its tentacles to every phase of our lives. At that time fashion meant mostly ready-to-wear, hats, accessories. It had just started to mean decoration and home furnishings—given a push no doubt by exhibits of "modernistic" furniture and décor from Europe. But it would have taken more than a swami to foretell the day when fashion was to mean the upholstery of your new car, the color of your typewriter, the shape of your vacuum cleaner, the design of your kitchen stove, the packaging of your breakfast food, as well as the length of your skirt and the shape of your eyeglasses.

But in 1931 some 75 women had enough faith in their own place in the sun to join forces. That they were right was proved by the very first luncheon meeting in March, 1931. About 100 people were expected; some 200 turned up to hear Kenneth Collins, then advertising director of Macy's. Success was assured.

Today, nearly twenty-five years later, the Group has 2841 members. Of these, 1452 belong to the New York Group. But there are also twenty regional groups with 1389 members in major cities throughout the country. Requirements for membership are rigid. Three years' actual experience in some phase of the fashion field is requisite. This may include newspaper work, advertising copywriting, personnel work—anything that touches on the fashion periphery. A prospective member must have a member sponsor and be vouched for by five others. There must be a record of actual achievement in some phase or other of the fashion field.

The roll call of Fashion Group members is a Who's Who in fashion. Among the presidents have been Mary Brooks Picken; Kathleen Howard, former opera singer and onetime fashion editor of *Harper's Bazaar;* the late Winifred Ovitte, moving fashion force of *Women's Wear Daily* for nearly a generation, and Dorothy Wallis, "D.L.W." of the same publication; Helen Valentine, editor of *Charm;* Julia Coburn; and others of similar stature.

When it became clear that the Group was growing so rapidly that a president alone could not cope with its problems, the office of chairman of the board of directors was introduced in 1933. The first chairman was Dorothy Shaver, now president of Lord and Taylor.

The roster of membership includes Edna Woolman Chase, a true pioneer in fashion and editor of *Vogue* for fifty years; Carmel Snow, editor of *Harper's Bazaar;* Beatrice Auerbach, president of G. Fox in Hartford; Tobé, whose style service has influenced stores for a quarter-century; Mrs. Ogden Reid, board member and former chairman of the board of the New York *Herald Tribune;* and many women who head their own firms, are vice-presidents of advertising agencies and manufacturing companies, or hold high posts in department stores. In addition, there are designers, writers, publicists, promotion experts, fashion editors, decorators, and women from almost any other field you can mention in which fashion plays a part directly or indirectly.

A measure of the growth of the Fashion Group's prestige is pinpointed by the fact that it is not unusual for a prospective employer to ask a job applicant if she is a member of the Group.

What does the Group do? Its original purpose was to promote good taste and to act as a clearinghouse for ideas and problems. It has not deviated much from these twin purposes in its twenty-five years. But gradually it is becoming clear that the focus of interest of its members is narrowing down to what is valuable to their jobs, so that while at one time the monthly luncheons featured speakers only remotely related to the fashion world, almost every luncheon program now deals with some phase of fashion.

Recently the programs have turned into what might be called "spectaculars." Twice a year there is a showing of French clothes staged alternately by *Vogue* and *Harper's Bazaar* with members of the ready-to-wear committee working extracurricular hours to assemble the merchandise and stage the show.

So great is the demand for tickets for these events that they are now run twice, one showing at breakfast and one at lunch. The first time this was done, last March, some 800 members and their guests came to the breakfast showing, 1400 to the luncheon.

Also twice a year is a showing from the American market, given the same spectacular runway sendoff as the foreign clothes. Prominent retailers give the commentary: last January Andrew Goodman, president of Bergdorf Goodman, spoke, and at this June's showing, on the 23rd, Stanley Marcus of Neiman-Marcus will be the guest speaker.

There is an enormous fabric exhibit twice a year; and other divisions have their day in the sun, too—millinery, cosmetics, accessories, home furnishings, and now the newly created children's-wear committee.

Members look to the Fashion Group to keep them informed on what is going on in the various related fields. Many of them do not get into the markets themselves, although their work is closely tied in with them. So they depend on these showings to keep them up to date. It is a feather in the Group's cap that more and more male bosses and important clients of the members ask to be guests at the luncheon showings.

One development in the Group's progress has been the erasing of the lines of demarcation of the various divisions. Nowadays the full membership is invited to all the luncheons, because it is impossible for anyone working in the fashion business to segregate her interests. The cosmetic people are naturally interested in what is happening in millinery. Women in the hosiery field care passionately about what the shoe people are doing. The fabric people have more than a passing interest in the silhouette. In the old days, difficult as it may be to believe, hosiery stylists chose their colors without checking with the fabric manufacturers. The Fashion Group was certainly instrumental in convincing manufacturers in every field that a correlation and interchange of fashion information would benefit the industry as a whole.

Nursing the Group until it came of age was the job of Ethel M. Kremer who, as executive secretary, lived and breathed for the Group and its members. Many of the standards rigorously adhered to today were set up by her. When Mrs. Kremer retired two years ago her place was taken by the current executive director, Dorothy Waddington, who enthusiastically maintains the standards of her predecessor.

There is a governing board of nineteen women, all of whom have top reputations. The current president is Florence Goldin, vice-president of Grey Advertising Agency. Chairman of the board is quondam president Mary Brooks Picken. An advisory council is made up of former presidents, board chairmen, and prominent women in the field. They are called in on questions of major policy.

Each regional group has its own director and officers. These groups head up to the parent group in New York, however, and any major project undertaken by any one of them must have the approval of the board of governors.

The Fashion Group has managed to keep aloof from any tinge of promotion or commercialism. Because the board reviews each program idea it has been impossible for any exuberant press agent to use the Group as a springboard. In fact some excellent program ideas have been vetoed because there was just a chance that some of the membership might consider it special pleading.

The regional groups have done some extraordinarily interesting things. The Fashion Wing at the Philadelphia Museum of Art, for one, was a Philadelphia Fashion Group project. And in Cleveland, Fashion Group officers were invited to make suggestions for designs and color schemes for the city's transit system. In Chicago, the Group has embarked upon a scholarship project for costume design at the Art Institute. Funds were raised for this purpose by the same Group. In 1948 the Los Angeles Group presented the Los Angeles County Museum with a check for $1000 to be used for a costume storage vault. Other groups have put on shows which benefited local hospitals, symphony orchestras, museums. St. Louis in 1948 gave three performances of "Symphony of Fashion" and turned more than $13,000 to the St. Louis Symphony Society. In Pittsburgh, the Group adopted a Carnegie Library project enabling the Art Division to build an important collection of magazines, plates, and books on costume design. Last year the Boston Group gave $1000 to the Art Institute there. In Cleveland, the Society for Crippled Children received $3000. The Cleveland Group has made this a continuing project. Los Angeles, St. Louis, and Portland contributed to their local museums and historical societies; Dallas helped a children's nursery.

These are but a few of the projects undertaken by the regional groups. In each of the twenty cities the Fashion Group is a continuing force in fashion and in the community.

Chief among the New York projects is the annual Fashion Training Course, a series of weekly lectures given by prominent members who are tops in their fields. The 1954 course drew 200 girls who had jobs in the fashion and allied fields who wished to learn more about their own and other phases of the business. At the end of the course prizes are offered for the best essays on what the students got out of the lectures.

Also there are scholarships for night courses available to girls who attend the entire training course series. The Elly Honig Scholarship makes it possible for a limited number of applicants to study at any night school or college offering fashion or advertising courses. This last year four girls were accepted for these scholarships. An additional scholarship was recently made available by an anonymous donor in memory of Michele Murphy, the fashion director of the Brooklyn Museum, a member of the board who died last autumn.

Proceeds of the Fashion Training Course go to augment the library of the Fashion Institute of Technology.

The Group is about to celebrate its twenty-fifth anniversary, plans for which are still in the making. As Kenneth Collins pointed out in a speech during the tenth anniversary year when he played a return engagement: "The Fashion Group has, in some sense, a part in the scheme in this whole business of the emancipation of women. . . . This organization, it seems to me, is one of the first organizations of women who are actually in the stream of events, and are having a tremendous influence on the business of this country." Mr. Collins also emphasized that the Group was born "when the economy of the country shifted from an era of production to an era of selling, and," said Mr. Collins, "that's where the Fashion Group came in."

That Mr. Collins was right fifteen years ago is incontrovertible, for it is no longer enough that an automobile should be mechanically perfect, that a refrigerator be noiseless, that a fabric be durable. Fashion has become the plus which makes the merchandise sell. All anyone has to do is to look at the revolution in automobile designing to realize that how a car looks, what color it is, how the interior is upholstered affects how it sells.

Recently one of the large automobile companies took stock of itself, realized that its very excellent cars were not selling in competition with other makes. What did they add? Not another cylinder, not something underneath the hood—they added style in new color combinations, new fabrics. They improved the appearance which after all sums up, in elementary fashion, the meaning of style. The results were instantly noticeable, the cars began to sell, the company went back into full production.

But even though fashion has penetrated every corner of the house and garage, it is still the apparel and textile industries which offer the greatest opportunities for women in New York. For the rest of the country, though recognizing the native talents of California, Texas, and St. Louis designers, still looks to the big names located along what is known in the trade as the "Rue de la Seventh." Seventh Avenue is still the mecca of embryo designers, the fountainhead of fashion trends.

The Fashion Group in its twenty-five years has become an interwoven part of this enormous industry. By maintaining its rigid membership requirements and by gearing its programs to the needs and demands of its members, the Fashion Group has maintained its equilibrium through the years of growth.

That it has come of age is pointed up by the fact that men speakers no longer feel impelled to start their speeches with some quip about the hats in the audience. For years, members winced visibly when some overgallant male guest speaker would try to make things cozy and bring them down to what you could only think of as his level by pulling the hat trick. Now perhaps the men are inured. But we prefer to think that the Fashion Group has so grown in prestige that men feel free to address us as equals.

Questions for Review and Discussion

1. Explain the difference between "editorialized" merchandise and "advertised" merchandise in fashion magazines.
2. Do you believe that fashion editors can divorce themselves from "pressure" by advertisers to feature their merchandise on their editorial pages?
3. Analyze the fashion columns or pages in your local newspapers. What types of information do they contain?
4. How great is the influence of fashion magazines and fashion pages in newspapers upon their reader's actual purchases of apparel? Why?
5. Many large producers use both fashion magazines and trade papers for advertising purposes. Would they be likely to run the same type of advertisements in these two media? How might they differ and why?
6. Many large producers and retailers who employ fashion specialists in their own organization, also retain outside consultants. Why?
7. Why do retail stores who have their own specialized buyers utilize resident-buying offices? Why would a New York store use a resident-buying office which is located in their own city?
8. Consider the factors that might influence fashion editors in their selection of merchandise to be featured editorially. Compare them with the factors that might influence a retail buyer in her selection of merchandise to be purchased. Are they the same? Why?
9. How can you explain the "free" advice and helped offered by fashion magazines to manufacturers and retailers as contrasted to the "paid" advice and help given by fashion consultants?
10. As compared to producers, very few retailers use "outside" advertising agencies. They generally maintain complete advertising departments of their own. How can you explain this?
11. What is the difference between an advertising agency and a publicity agency?
12. Why should business people pay for advertisements when they can hire publicists to get them free publicity?

SECTION

VII

The Consumers of Fashion

What lies ahead in the fashion business? To answer that question, we must look to the ultimate consumers of the industry's products, for as they change, so will the industry and its operations change. The business of fashion is a dynamic process requiring an understanding of consumers—and constant adjustment to their changing needs and desires. This is a responsibility of makers, buyers, and sellers alike. One noted economist has even gone so far as to say that "the central function of the entrepreneur in a fashion industry is far less the efficient organization of the production of a given commodity and much more the shrewd anticipation of the changing preferences of his numerically restricted clientele—his own small niche in 'the great neighborhood of women'." [1]

This concluding section discusses buying motivations and spending patterns of consumers. It also explores the social and economic changes, past and projected, that have significance for the business of fashion.

Understanding the Consumer

The goal of everyone in the fashion business is to have the ultimate consumer buy his merchandise. There is much that can be done to stimulate consumer buying, but in order to do this effectively, one must first understand people, their buying motivation, and purchasing patterns. This need to understand why and how customers buy is not uniquely a fashion industry problem. Every business that serves the public has to guide its operations in the light of consumer demand. The fashion industry, however, moves at a fast tempo. The rewards of success are great and the cost of failure correspondingly high. As Dr. Nystrom put it:

> Consumer demand is the guide to intelligent production and merchandising . . . a knowledge of the fundamental facts of what consumers want and why, is clearly of the first importance . . . to those who plan the policies, design the product, determine the price lines, prepare the adver-

[1] Dwight E. Robinson in "Economics of Fashion Demand," *Quarterly Journal of Economics,* Vol. LXXV, August 1961, pp. 395–396.

tising and sales promotion, sell the goods and make the collections, in fact all who deal with the problems of the consumer.[2]

The Power of the Consumer. The role of the ultimate consumer in the fashion business is an important one and, in the final analysis, controlling. This is a fact recognized by successful fashion professionals and repeatedly stated in their own words throughout the readings in this book.

Ordinarily the part that consumers play is a passive one. People do not actually demand new products and designs of which they have little or no knowledge; neither do they demand change. Their individual and collective power is exercised in the selections they make on one hand and in their refusals to buy, on the other. It is by their acceptance or rejection that they influence the goods which will be presented for their favor and even the methods of presentation.

The history of the fashion business is dotted with examples of unsuccessful efforts to make the consumer buy what she did not want. One classic example was the promotional campaign by producers of millinery trimmings to arrest a buying trend towards simpler millinery. They received the cooperation of Paul Poiret in their efforts to bring back hats "smothered with leaves, fruit, flowers, feathers, and ribbons" but even the sponsorship of the great Poiret could not make customers buy the decorated hats of earlier years.[3]

A second classic case was the failure of textile manufacturers to persuade women to purchase fuller skirts requiring more yardage than the tight hobble skirts which they were buying in 1912. In the course of their promotional activities they secured the endorsement of Paris couturiers, fashion editors, and retail distributors. The whole campaign was a failure. Consumers continued to buy hobble skirts almost as though the different business groups were backing this style instead of fighting it.[4]

There is no question that the promotional activities of the industry can influence what people buy. There is a big question, however, as to whether such activities could succeed in creating sales for products which consumers do not want. The high ratio of markdowns in the apparel business [5] is evidence enough that consumers are not "pawns in the hands of advertisers" [6] but rather the voters in the marketplace of fashion.

Why People Buy Fashion. In an effort to achieve an understanding of the consumer in relation to her buying response to fashion, we find ourselves joining the social scientists and the marketing experts in a continuing search for answers to a few basic questions: Why do people buy apparel? What factors influence their choice?

---

[2] Paul H. Nystrom, *Economics of Consumption,* New York, Ronald Press, 1929, p. 111.

[3] Quentin Bell, *On Human Finery,* New York, A.A. Wyn, 1949, pp. 48–49.

[4] Paul H. Nystrom, *Economics of Fashion,* New York, Ronald Press, 1928, pp. 11–12.

[5] The median markdown rate of women's apparel departments in department stores is 14 per cent of net sales as compared to an overall store average of 6 per cent. Source: "1964 Departmental Merchandising and Operating Results," Controllers Congress, NRMA, 100 West 31 St., New York, N.Y.

[6] Dr. Eva Mueller, reporting on the results of a consumer buying study conducted by the University of Michigan, in "Buying Habits of Women Found to be Inconsistent," *New York Times,* May 1, 1964.

There are some commentators on buying behavior who view us as puppets whose purchasing activities can be manipulated almost completely by the power of advertising. Vance Packard, for instance, gives this impression in *The Hidden Persuaders* [7] and some of his other books. Others would have us believe that almost every fashion purchase we make is in search of status. Edward Sapir, the social scientist, saw people's fondness for new clothes as "an outward emblem of personal display" and a desire to impress others with their spending power.[8] Veblen's "conspicuous consumption" value was, in his eyes, the major buying motive.[9]

Not all students of buying motivation, however, see the picture in such simple terms. A consumer study sponsored by the University of Michigan concluded that many elements condition what and why a purchase is made, among them "habits, background, individual caprice, quality and price." [10] Steuart Henderson Britt, long an authority on marketing, pointed out in *The Spenders* that every purchase involves a balancing of three factors: what one likes, what one needs, and what one can afford.[11] Decisions on any points are bound to be colored by emotional reactions—even the question of what is needed, unless one lives at the bare subsistence level. Thoreau tried that at Walden Pond more than a century ago, and found that he needed very little—so little, in fact, that he came to think it childish and savage for people to want new clothes or to follow the fashions of their day. He found it difficult, when he lived so austerely, to understand why other people wanted and worked for variety in their wardrobes, or why they cast aside garments that were not utterly worn out.[12]

The wellsprings of these wants that he did not share lie deep in human nature. Men and women are complex creatures whose actions are seldom governed by reason alone. Some people are always interested in change—as a relief from boredom with what they own, or as a means of differentiating themselves from others. They see in new styles a chance for distinction or self-assertion. The attention attracted by wearing a new style may be attention the individual wants but is unable to obtain readily in any other socially acceptable manner. Youth, particularly, tends to express its rebellion against existing social conventions by adopting different styles of dress. For the large majority of people, however, fashion buying is strongly motivated by the natural desire to imitate others or to identify with a group.

Fashion buying motives, then, are seldom either rational or simple, nor do they spring purely from physical needs. Emotional needs and the natural human wants and desires must also be taken into account.

---

[7] Philadelphia, David McKay, 1957.

[8] Edward Sapir, "Fashion," in *Encyclopedia of the Social Sciences,* Vol. VI, New York, Macmillan, 1931, pp. 139–144. Also see J.C. Flugel, "The Psychology of Clothes," London, International Psychoanalytic Library, 1950, p. 15.

[9] See Thorstein Veblen, *Theory of the Leisure Class,* New York, Mentor edition, New American Library of World Literature, Inc., 1963, for a discussion of conspicuous consumption.

[10] Dr. Eva Mueller, *op. cit.*

[11] Mc Graw-Hill Co., New York, 1960.

[12] *Walden and other writings of Henry David Thoreau,* Modern Library, New York, Random House, 1950, pp. 21–22.

Patterns of Spending.[13] Apparel expenditures represent a substantial amount of total consumer expenditures but the proportion of total spending varies from year to year. Consumer expenditures for women's and children's wear and accessories—excluding footwear—have grown from some $10 billion in 1947 to nearly $18 billion in 1964.[14] For some years, however, the fashion industry has been faced with the fact that, despite a period of great prosperity, expanding population, and rising incomes, the share of total consumption expenditures absorbed by clothing has been steadily shrinking. Many explanations have been advanced to explain this development: a greater percentage going to housing, recreational pursuits, automobiles, personal services; the trend towards sportswear separates which encourages the purchase of less expensive clothing units; the decline in the prestige status of clothing; and other factors. The statistics of this declining trend are illustrated in Table 1; the reasons are analyzed in depth in one of the readings in this section and therefore do not require an extended discussion at this point.

The long-term trend, however is unmistakable; in 1947 the proportion of the consumer's disposable income spent on womens and childrens clothing and accessories (excluding footwear) was 5.9 per cent but only 4.1 per cent in 1964. Apparel dollar sales did go up, of course, as personal incomes rose, but to a smaller degree. However the dollar spending in 1964 was nearly 80 per cent above the 1947 level.

Table 1 Consumer Expenditures for Apparel and Accessories (Rounded in Thousands of Dollars—Add 000)

Year	Women's and Children's Wear	Per cent to Total Disposable Income
1947	9,900	5.9
1948	10,900	5.8
1949	10,200	5.4
1950	10,000	4.8
1951	10,800	4.8
1952	11,600	4.9
1953	11,900	4.7
1954	12,000	4.7
1955	12,500	4.5
1956	12,900	4.4
1957	13,700	4.4
1958	13,900	4.4
1959	14,800	4.4
1960	15,100	4.3
1961	15,300	4.2
1962	15,900	4.1
1963	16,500	4.1
1964	17,800	4.1

Source: U.S. Department of Commerce annual reports of personal income and consumption expenditures.

[13] See statistical section of readings for all sources of data.

[14] See U.S. Department of Commerce annual estimates of personal consumption expenditures.

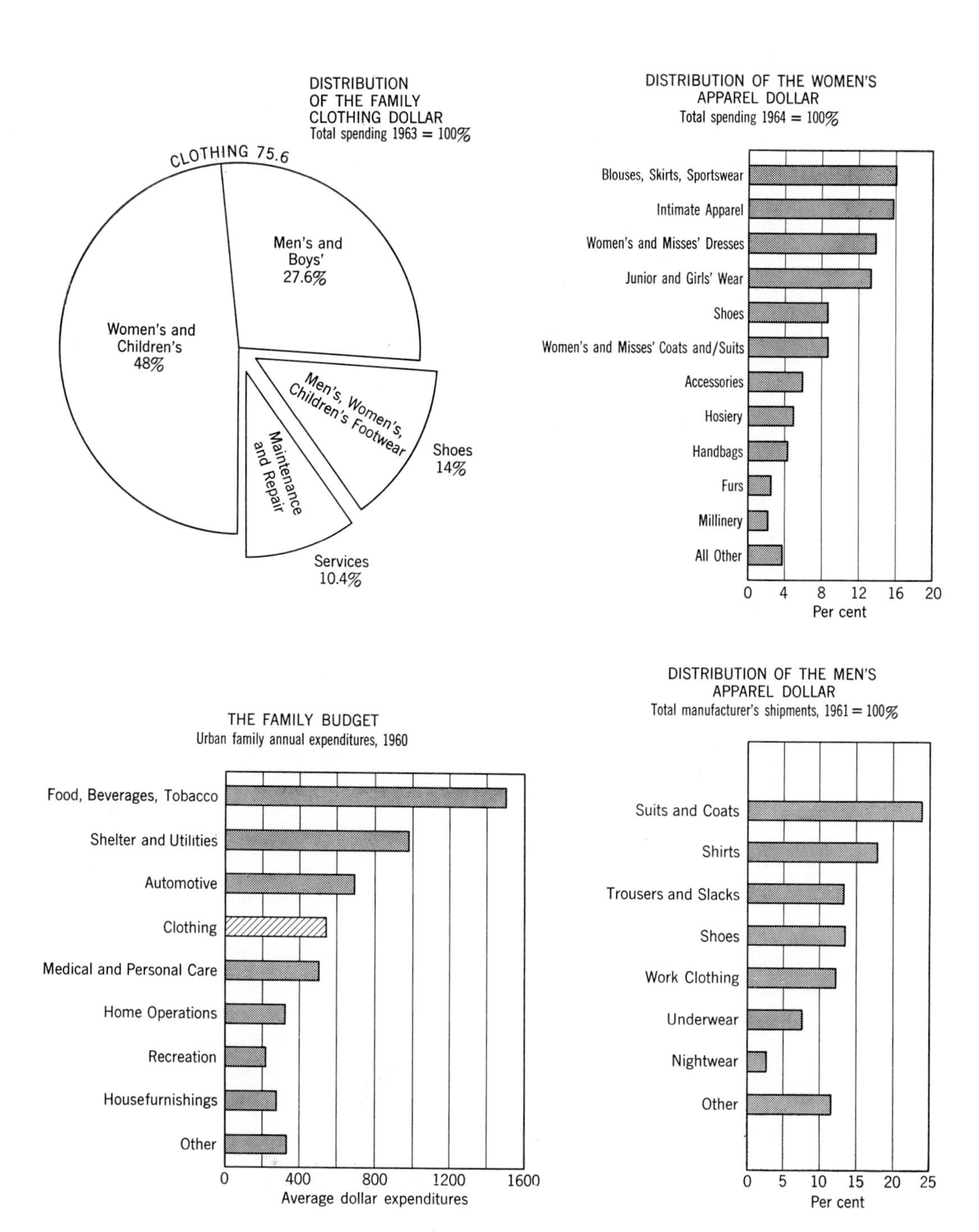

How much is spent on apparel? (Sources: U.S. Department of Commerce, after The National Industrial Conference Board, New York, N.Y.; U.S. Department of Labor, after the National Industrial Conference Board, New York, N.Y.; Board of Governors of the Federal Reserve System; and U.S. Department of Commerce.)

It is not enough simply to know how much is spent on apparel. It is also important to know how consumers spend their money on the other kinds of goods and services available to them. Of further significance to the industry is when the money is spent, and how it is distributed among the different categories of apparel. These and other related factors influence not only what the industry produces but also how much of its output it can hope to sell at a given time. Spending patterns are charted in this section; other related retail selling patterns were shown in Section V.

Table 2 Seasonality in Spending for Women's Apparel (Women's and Girls' Wear)

Month	Women's and Children's Wear—Total	Women's Coats and Suits	Women's Dresses	Women's Sportswear	Girls' Wear
January	6.0%	10.1%	6.0%	5.2%	3.7%
February	5.5	6.9	5.9	4.9	4.3
March	8.3	11.0	9.0	6.8	8.3
April	9.0	9.3	10.3	7.8	9.3
May	8.4	4.3	11.6	9.1	6.2
June	7.0	2.7	8.6	8.7	5.7
July	6.0	3.6	6.3	7.5	5.7
August	7.5	6.9	7.3	7.9	11.5
September	8.6	9.4	9.2	8.7	8.9
October	9.1	12.0	8.8	8.6	8.8
November	10.1	12.4	7.8	9.4	11.4
December	14.6	11.4	9.2	15.4	16.2

Source: Board of Governors, Federal Reserve Board Reports. The figures above, which are based on department store experience, reflect general spending patterns.

Studying the Customer

The makers and sellers of fashion merchandise have methods of their own for studying consumers. They examine their past experience for clues as to what will succeed today, and they watch today's activity for indications of what may happen tomorrow.

Analyzing Purchases. There is in the fashion industry a constant flow, back and forth, of information about what the customer is buying. In most retail stores, some recrod is kept as to the styles, colors, fabrics, and so on, that have been purchased for resale. On this record are also entered the day-to-day sales. Every garment bought by a consumer thus becomes a ballot cast by the customer for the size she wears, the color she selects, the fabric, and so on.

From the records of an individual store, the retailer can discern sudden or gradual changes in the preferences of his own customers. These changes become apparent whether the same customers are turning to different fashions, or whether there is a change in the kind of people who make up the store's clientèle. In either case, the proprietor or buyer sees that there is less demand for this, and more for that.

These variations in what consumers are buying at that store are reflected in what the store buys from the manufacturers of fashion merchandise. Multiply that store's experience by the hundreds or even thousands of stores that buy from one manufacturer, and you see that the producer has a pretty broad spectrum of consumer response represented in the rate at which his various styles are sold. If he has country-wide distribution, he may see that certain areas are buying certain colors, styles, or fabrics faster or more slowly than others. If he has no reason to believe that this is due to special effort (or lack of effort) on the part of his retail outlets in those areas, he can assume that a regional difference is influencing his sales. Typical of such differences are the West Coast's quickness to accept what is new, and especially what is casual and relaxed, or the Middle West's fondness for shades of blue, to go with the blue eyes that predominate among the German and Scandinavian groups who have settled there.

From the manufacturer of the finished garment, information about customer preferences, as expressed in customer purchases, flows in several directions. One flow is back to the retail stores, via the manufacturer's salesmen, to alert them to trends they may not have noticed for themselves. Another flow is to the fabric producers, in the form of the garment-maker's reorders for the best liked materials and shades.

Information about the customer and the balloting she does from day to day at the retail cash register is also collected by others in the fashion field. Editors of consumer magazines, for instance, check regularly on trends with manufacturers of raw materials and finished products. They do this to see if their own previous editorial judgments of fashion trends have been right, and to establish a basis on which to select styles to be featured in future issues. What the customer does or does not buy is watched as closely in the fashion industry as stock brokers watch the ticker.

Often the customer is a guinea pig on whom the experts test their judgment. Sometimes she is a member of a committee formed by retailers or editors to represent a particular section of the public, and to be available for consultation on reaction to new ideas, or just to sound off on subjects that interest her. Typical are the teen-age committees and teen-age clubs that many retail stores have sponsored.

More often, the customer serves unknowingly as a test subject. When a new style, color, fabric, or silhouette is introduced, makers and retailers usually proceed on a "sample, test, reorder" system. This means that only small quantities are made up and placed on sale in retail stores. At the first inkling of customer reaction, the retailer reorders the acceptable numbers, and discontinues those for which his customers have shown little eagerness. The garment manufacturer, meantime, is watching the retail reorders to see which numbers he should cut in quantity, and which ones he should drop.

No one, least of all the customer, may fully understand why she buys or selects one style in preference to another, but everyone in the fashion industry is looking over her shoulder while she makes her selection, and she thus decides the fate of the individual styles among the infinite number created each season.

Predicting Fashions. Predicting which styles will become the fashions at a given time is an occupational guessing game for the fashion industry, with millions of dollars at stake. People in the fashion business seem to develop almost a sixth sense for weighing various factors, and judging the probable ups and downs of trends. They learn to study signs that may escape the untrained observer, and to predict which styles are most likely to succeed, just as a weather man becomes adept at forecasting the weather.

Forecasting errors can be costly, however, and guiding rules and principles are used to keep these to a minimum, in fashion as in weather. The meteorologist arms himself with data about wind velocity and air pressure and the known results of certain combinations when they occur; the fashion professional arms himself with information about customers, trends, and modifying factors.

Whether one is designing, producing, or selling, the first step is to have a clear picture of the customer group that constitutes one's target. Just as there can be no universal weather forecast, but only one that is pinned down, as to time and area, so it is with fashion prediction. There is no universal group of customers: there is city, suburban, or rural; there is young or not-so-young; there is the blue-collar or white-collar background; there is the middle-income or well-to-do; there is the conservative or the *avant garde*. And so on. What one forecasts for, say, the young juniors in a wealthy suburb of the West may be all wrong for the same age group in a poor neighborhood of an Eastern city.

With a specific customer group in mind, the next principle is to collect all the facts one can get. How numerous are these customers? What are they buying from day to day this season? What are the activities and occasions for which they dress? What people, periodicals, or other influences will affect their choice? The more answers one has to such questions, the clearer the picture becomes, and the easier to forecast.

Simultaneously, as in weather forecasting, the fact gathering procedure of the fashion forecaster embraces looking for beginning trends in related areas. Measured by reports of what the customer is wearing or buying, and judged in the light of what the customer's ideally dressed women (motion picture stars, campus leaders, society women, whatever the case may be) are wearing, it becomes possible to evaluate trends in terms of their growth potential. In the meantime, popular fashions are watched for signs of a possible downturn.

Thus a forecaster—whose official title may be dress designer, fashion coordinator, magazine editor, or department store buyer, but whose work requires an awareness of fashion currents—may decide that ruffles have run their course for the time being, or that sleek hair-dos are coming in and will give millinery new opportunities, or that brighter and gayer colors will be better received than they were last year, and so on.

This fact gathering process, to pursue the analogy to weather forecasting, is like preparing a meteorological map, with isobars, temperature readings, wind indicators, and everything else that is needed to evaluate the current situation. A fashion forecast, once made, whether in one's own mind or in print, is seldom final and immutable. In fashion, as in weather, the study of conditions and influences is never finished. The unexpected often happens when some new final and immutable. In fashion, as in weather, the study of conditions and influencing forces, are essential at all times if one is to succeed or even to survive, in the fashion business.

Fashions' Customers—Past and Present

The development of the fashion business in the United States reflects the vast changes that have taken place in women's lives during the period of its growth.

In the early years of the industry, spending power was concentrated in the hands of the very few.[15] A majority of the population lived in rural areas. City dwellers included many immigrants who came to this country with little or no funds, skills, or knowledge of the language. Women constituted less than one-fifth of the labor force in 1900, and nearly half of the women then at work were domestic servants or farm workers, who were paid little more than their board.[16] Woman had no vote, and had few political, social, or economic rights. To dress fashionably was the privilege of the wives and daughters of the relatively few well-to-do.

Today, the majority of American families are comfortably in the middle class. Two-thirds of the population lives in urban areas and even the rural population is thoroughly abreast of fashion, thanks to newspapers, magazines, motion pictures, and television—to say nothing of the immensely improved private and public transportation facilities and the great amount of pleasure travel that persons of even moderate means enjoy. Women constitute one-third of the labor force, and of these working women, fewer than one in seven is a domestic or a farm employee. A majority of women over the age of 14 have money income of their own, usually at least partly from their own earnings. The normal activities of the typical woman today expose her to fashion influences, and if she responds by wanting to buy fashionable apparel, she has the means to do so. The readings in this section provide some of the statistics of change. They show the gains in women's education, employment, and income, against the background of changes affecting the population as a whole, and discuss some of their many implications for the fashion business.

These changing social and economic factors created new wants, new needs, and different mores. New wants, in turn, caused changes which required the industry to revise its products, methods of production, and distribution. In the yesterday of the industry, expectant mothers went into seclusion; today they buy maternity apparel. The emancipation of women when, in the years between 1910–1920, they won the right to vote and to attend some of the same colleges as men, pointed the way for less unwieldy dresses, giving them greater freedom of movement. The First World War gave many women their first view of an occupation outside the confines of the home and accelerated the need for ready-made clothing. Rising incomes opened markets for goods previously considered to be luxuries for the "idle rich." Shorter working hours and a wider choice of recreational activities increased the need for special purpose garments for a variety of occasions. The tremendous growth of the suburbs, or what one industry professional has called "the backyard way of life," brought about a "revolution in dress" for suburbanites and city dwellers alike. An example of how this last-mentioned change has affected the industry's production is illustrated in Table 3 which shows the large increases in "sportswear separates" compared to the smaller increases in dresses, and an actual decline in suits and coats.

These influences, among many others, have permeated the fashion com-

---

[15] See reading in this section "Statistics of Change" for detailed figures and sources of data.

[16] "Occupational Trends in the United States, 1900 to 1950," Bureau of the Census Working Paper No. 5, U.S. Department of Commerce, Washington, D.C.

Table 3 Variation in Growth, 1948–1963 [17]

Product	Unit of Measure	Production, 1948	Production, 1963	Percentage of Change
Women's skirts	Millions	35	119	+240
Women's blouses	Millions	94	196	+108
Women's dresses	Millions	227	263	+ 15.9
Women's coats	Thousands	25,574	24,558	– 4.1
Women's suits	Thousands	14,963	9,941	– 33.6

munity with an altering influence. It would be impossible to pinpoint which style changes have been initiated by the industry and which have been paced by consumers, with the industry following in their ever-changing footsteps. In any event, these shifts have created a mass market for fashionable apparel and a broadening of the fashion field, such as was impossible to conceive in the days when the well-to-do had their garments custom-made, when women of moderate income did what they could on the home sewing machine, and when poorer women had so pitifully little to spend that a woolen shawl was likely to serve as hat, coat, scarf, and gloves for all occasions. The same influences have made themselves felt in other parts of the world, but it is in the United States that the trend has been most marked. It is here that the development of mass markets, mass production methods, and mass distribution of fashion merchandise has been most rapid. In the process, American design talent has been developed; fashion schools have been established to teach design; schools and colleges have been established to teach the many other attributes required to produce, publicize, and distribute fashion merchandise in quantity. It is to this country that manufacturers and retailers of other countries turn for the know-how of making and selling fashionable ready-to-wear merchandise.[18]

The Future

If past progress is any indication, the fashion industries have an even bigger and brighter future ahead. The country is growing and women are growing in numbers, in spending power, in multiplicity of interests, in responsiveness to fashion. But if this book has put across its message, you, the fashion professional of the future, will not supinely take anyone's word for what lies ahead. Like everyone else in the fashion business, you will look, listen, think—and keep your eye on the consumer.

[17] *Survey of Current Business,* September, 1964, pp. 24–27. (Authors' note: The men's wear industry has reflected the same trend. See "Sportswear Races to a Sales-Lead," *Business Week,* December 5, 1964, pp. 54 ff. which shows that the yearly output of 20 million suits is unchanged since before World War I, and that production of topcoats has shrunk, while all leisure apparel categories have more than doubled in the same period.)

[18] Madge Garland, in *Fashion* (Penguin Books, Ltd., Harmondsworth, Middlesex, England, 1962, page 67 *ff.*) tells how a delegation of French businessmen came to the United States to study ready-to-wear manufacturing methods in 1947. In that same year, M.L. Disher published an elaborate study of American methods in *American Factory Production of Women's Clothing,* (Devereux Publications, Ltd., London) for British readers.

Readings

The consumer, on whom all successful fashion professionals keep a watchful eye, reveals herself to the industry in many ways. The readings that follow illustrate how she is observed and analyzed by producers, marketing experts, fashion directors, consultants, and store presidents. Each reflects the intense preoccupation of the fashion community with interpreting and adjusting to customers' changing wants and tastes. Note particularly the analysis offered by Tobé Coller Davis in 1953. With one eye on statistics and the other on fashions, she was able to analyze the changing American way of life as she saw it, and explain its effect upon the fashions American women would accept. Far from being dated, her evaluation is every bit as sound today as when she first offered it.

The concluding charts and tables give the statistics of past and projected changes that have significance for the business of fashion. When a study of the figures is combined with an understanding of fashion itself, and with careful observation of the consumer, one has a sound basis for drawing conclusions about present and coming trends.

Fashion's Declining Share of the Consumer Dollar

Are the Reasons Economic?

by Alfred V. Sloan, Jr.

To those engaged in the manufacturer and distribution of American fashions, it is hardly news that the percentage of consumer income spent for clothing has shrunk materially over the past generation. The refrain is familiar and dreary: in an otherwise expansive age the portion of his dollar that the consumer now utilizes to clothe himself and his family is—by any relative measurement—on a downward slope.

To add to the gloom, no upturn appears to be in sight. A decline of 3½ percentage points in the three decades since 1929 (11.9 per cent to 8.4 per cent) represents, in relative terms, a "popularity loss" of close to 30 per cent—a chilling statistic from any viewpoint.

This knowledge has caused both pessimism and soul-searching in the fashion industry. But is the dismay completely justifiable? Should the industry hold itself responsible?

Perhaps not. Or at least not to the extent that might be suspected at first glance.

To a certain degree, gains in industry efficiency, coupled with the market conditions surrounding free enterprise, may largely be to blame for the decreasing share of the consumer dollar which has plagued the apparel trades for the past few decades.

An analogy may be found in the precarious

Reprinted from April, 1962, issue of *Stores*, official publication of the National Retail Merchants Association. Dr. Sloan is Associate Professor of Marketing at Fashion Institute of Technology. Professor Jarnow is the co-author of this book.

situation of the domestic airlines today. Here the dramatic increase in "productive facilities" (i.e., large numbers of jet aircraft with more seat capacity) is perhaps more to blame for the diminished load factor than any failure in marketing techniques or management skill, or any decline of public enthusiasm for flying. Mechanical progress, coupled with severe competition, may well show negative results on the profit and loss sheet.

Uncontrollable Factors. In any "downtrend situation" there are frequently outside elements —let us call them the "uncontrollable factors" —which influence the decline.[1] Political developments, economic trends, and changes in social patterns can hardly be disregarded in seeking the cause of downward industrial movements.

A number of such "uncontrollables" suggest themselves when we examine the cause of the relative decline in apparel expenditures. Let's examine the four chief "uncontrollables" in this situation, with the full knowledge that they are not answers in themselves, but only contributing factors to the percentage decline in clothing's share of the consumer dollar.

Uneven Population Growth. For about two decades there has been a continual but uneven spurt in the size of the United States population. A well-documented "bulge" has developed at either end of the age scale, thus causing the lion's share of the population increase to be concentrated in the sub-18 and post-65 age groups.

What effect has this imbalance had on apparel expenditures? Essentially, it has been unsalutary—at least in a relative sense. It can hardly be denied that the clothing needs of the very young and the very old are far less, comparatively speaking, than those of the population who are in the midst of the career-shaping, family-forming, and traveling years. Although this imbalance promises to right itself in the relatively near future, as the current generation of children grows into adulthood, the unevenness of population growth in the past generation has been a relative hindrance to increased fashion expenditures.

Casual Styles and Synthetics. For over a quarter of a century—and particularly since World War II—the trend toward casual dress has been a fashion influence of major significance. While this has, in many cases, caused a near-revolution in styling and design, it has tended, generally, to have a negative effect on apparel expenditures. The reason is simple: casual clothing, in the majority of cases, is less costly than more dressy attire.

The car coat or surcoat beloved of suburbia is generally less expensive than the "street" coat. Scarves and hoods cost less than hats. A man's shirt-and-slacks outfit—now so favored by urban as well as country dwellers for off-hours wear—hardly compares to the cost of a suit, shirt, and tie. Indeed, the trend toward more leisurely living and the resultant decrease in demand for "proper" clothing has been most unproductive, dollarwise, for those in the fashion trades.

To parallel this development, man-made fibers have spawned a whole new family of fabrics which in turn have set fashion on an entirely new tack in the past generation. One of the heralded features of these "miracle" fabrics is their ability to take wear, in contrast to the more conventional textiles. This very gift of long life has made replacement less necessary than in the past. Nylon hosiery tends to outlast silk; an Acrilan blouse is likely to outwear a cotton one—as well as to be more flexible, climatewise. Decreased apparel expenditure is the inevitable result.

Structure of Apparel Industry. It has been a proud and oft-repeated boast that the apparel trades stand forth as one of the last strongholds of completely free enterprise—in its classic sense—in this country. Cartels, oligopolies, price leadership, "gentlemen's agreements," and administered pricing are all but unknown in this field. Unlike a great many of America's "better organized" industries, apparel manufacturers have been faithful exponents—by force of circumstance if not by design—of the principle of price competition. The relative ease of entry into (and departure from) the field assures this.

Furthermore, despite a spat of recent mergers, consolidations, and public stock offerings, no single firm has ever controlled more than the barest fraction of total industry output. Laudable as this achievement may be from the viewpoint of the consumer or society in general, it is most assuredly not productive of great or

[1] The outside factors causing the sharp falloff, for example, in the anthracite coal or railroad industries—to cite just two well known cases—are too familiar to bear repetition here.

frequent price increases, regardless of the justification for them. One need only compare the relative price rises in the past generation of the great bulk of American goods and services [2] with those of a man's shirt or a woman's dress to see the effect of unregulated competition upon the price structure. Free enterprise, like a large standing army, may be a splendid thing for the security of the country as a whole; for those most immediately involved, however, the burden is often irksome if not downright dangerous.

Maturing American Society. Economists and social statisticians have been in general accord —ever since the promulgation of "Engel's Laws of Consumption" a century ago—that as any society matures economically it begins to spend a decreasing share of its income on the basic needs of human existence. At the same time it diverts a growing proportion of its spending to the "discretionary" areas of consumption, such as travel, education, and recreation, to name but a few.

Since the closing of the frontier about three generations ago and the shortening of the work week in more recent years, American life has swung around from concentration upon merely "staying afloat" to an intensive cultivation of newly discovered inner resources. A simple manifestation of this has been the desire of the average American family to utilize more fully its recently found leisure. The apparel field has not been the only one to feel the effect of this "social maturation." In the past five years, for example, the percentage of the consumer dollar spent for food has decreased from 23.1 per cent to 21.2 per cent.[3] Yet who would label the food industry's approach to its problems unprogressive!

The fact seems clear that the clothing industry, as a relative "basic" of existence, has felt the force of this irrevocable change in American living patterns. It may well be that in the future it will have to adjust itself to riding with the punch since the elimination of the causal factors would hardly appear to be a reasonable expectation.[4] The metamorphosis of society, in the final analysis, would seem to be a factor beyond the control of any single industry or interest group.

Thus, the "uncontrollables." Like Mount Everest, they "are there" and no amount of wishful thinking can put them aside. To deny their existence would be unrealistic—and the fashion industry, to its everlasting credit, has never been known for living in a world other than that of harsh reality.

[2] It is estimated that in New York City since 1942 the following percentage price changes have taken place:

Evening newspaper	up 233%
Milk	up 100%
Subway ride	up 200%
Haircut	up 125%
Women's apparel	up less than 20%

[3] *U. S. News & World Report,* December 18, 1961, p. 65.

[4] An interesting question here—and one which is beyond the scope of this discussion—is whether clothing must be considered a "basic" only, or whether the stimulation of fashion is able to remove it from this catgory and place it into that of discretionary spending.

Fashion's Declining Share of the Consumer Dollar

Is It Merchandising Myopia?

by Jeannette Abelow Jarnow

I find several fallacies in the traditional argument that economic factors can explain away the declining percentage of consumer apparel expenditures.

First, it fails to consider that this continuing decline may be due to weaknesses in fashion offerings or in fashion merchandising.

Second, it is seriously to be questioned whether fashion is a "basic necessity" to which Engel's Laws of Consumption can be applied.

And, third, the argument that prices have remained relatively stable in the apparel industry does not take into account that these "stable" price lines have been maintained at the expense of quality.

I believe that current practices in the fashion business are creating customer buying resistance. There is an increasingly esoteric approach to fashion, combined with hackneyed thinking on price lines, seasons, styling, and methods of presentation. And the marketing approach has become much too product-oriented when it should be customer-oriented.

Consumer Sophistication. Our country is in the midst of a remarkable customer revolution which is making profound changes in people's fashion tastes and needs. These changes, immensely significant as they are for the fashion business, have yet to be recognized by fashion retailers and fashion manufacturers, with a few notable exceptions.

The belief that sales and profits are assured by an expanding and richer population is a dangerous one in itself. Certainly it is true that when customers are multiplying the future is brighter than if the market were shrinking—but marketing studies show that an expanding market has also kept many industries from thinking very hard or imaginatively about how to keep it growing.

What Is Fashion? The majority of retailers today seem to confuse fashion with an outdated concept of something called "high fashion." But times and conditions are not what they were when fashion was the prerogative of the four hundred. The diffusion of wealth, education, culture, and sophistication in America today has made fashion the property of the 40 million. The fashion business is the business of making and distributing the goods best suited to our times and to the lives of our customers—our 40 million customers. There is no reason why the fashion business should be dominated by the pronouncements of a group of self-appointed "fashion intellectuals" who are motivated only by their own vested interests and a desire for personal publicity. Today's customers are fashion intellectuals in their own right, and it is to them that the fashion merchants should be paying attention.

The idea that fashion is a thing apart from the bulk of apparel and accessories merchandising persists in the retailers' promotional approach to their customers. There's a scramble to establish "fashion leadership," to promote "designer names." Fashion "directors" (rather than coordinators) are appointed; there are even separate "fashion" budgets. And in all this drive to create a "fashion image," what attention is being paid to the customers' proven preferences about how and when they want to spend their money?

Artificial Seasons. The most obvious example is the timing of seasonal merchandise offerings. The retailers' current seasonal procedures are in direct opposition to the changing trends in consumer buying patterns. Fashion retailers continue to offer merchandise out of season, long before the wearing time, and are too often out of it when customers need it and are ready to buy it. I seriously question whether merchants are even aware of how much buying resistance they have created by this practice. Customers today may have the money to buy ahead of the season, but most of them are far too busy and sophisticated to shop for apparel to be hung in a closet for months before it can be worn.

Furthermore, it is a known fact that consumers' fashion wants and buying habits are no longer ruled by the seasons as they once were. Many changes are occurring in the public attitude towards the purchase of seasonal merchandise. Seasonal demand has been lengthening for an increasing variety of items, changes have occurred in the seasonal peaks for many classifications, and many other industries have already capitalized on second and third seasons and even "no-seasons" for a growing number of merchandise categories.

People want and expect to buy the kind of clothes they need *when* they need them. Why does the fashion industry keep itself shackled in artificial seasonal habits that leave so much consumer demand unsatisfied?

Three Lost Months. Here's a typical example of obsolete timing—the three-part fashion story with which, since the beginning of this year, merchants have been trying to persuade customers into giving them a bigger share of their dollars. In January the customer was offered clearance merchandise, made up either of styles which customers had refused to buy in the fall or of merchandise which, while suitable for January needs, was broken in size and color assortments.

Overlapping the clearance story and lasting into February was the stubbornly traditional promotion of "resort season" fashions. By resort fashions this industry means clothes for southern wear. But travel destinations and winter vacation spots now mean, equally, north, east, and west. The pattern of southern travel itself has changed completely (see Table 1).

Table 1 Influx of Visitors into Southern Vacation Areas[a] *for 1960*

January	8.6%	
February	8.3	
March	9.3	25.6%: First quarter
April	6.0	
May	5.3	
June	10.6	21.9%: Second quarter
July	12.7	
August	12.8	
September	6.0	31.5%: Third quarter
October	5.9	
November	6.5	
December	8.6	21.0%: Fourth quarter

[a] Excludes Cuba. (Source: Southern Travel Association.)

Then came the third and major part of the fashion story: new "spring" merchandise which was completely unwearable at the time it was shown. In the first place, spring doesn't arrive, either by date or by temperature, until late March. Besides that, the so-called "spring" merchandise was made up largely of summery colors, fabrics, and styles that could hardly be worn before May or June.

Some readers may believe this last statement is exaggerated. I urge them to take an objective look at the advertising of their own stores and their own competitors for the period in question, keeping the customers' viewpoint uppermost in their minds. The fact that many of these ads for denims, Dacron-cottons, linens, pastel jerseys, and other summer fabrics and styles were being heavily subsidized by manufacturers and textile producers was no excuse for retailers to run them.

Certainly a moderate amount of pre-season testing is a basic merchandising principle. But fashion merchants should take a fresh look at this game of fashion timing played only by rules which make life easier for producers and their publicists. Customers will not change their needs and wants to accommodate the industry. If the fashion industry wants more of the consumers' dollars, it will have to key clothes closer to the wearing season. It is high time for retailers to start re-educating themselves, their buyers and their resources on this question of timing—and to stop trying to re-educate the customers.

Price Lines and Quality. Another situation that requires more action and less conversation involves prices and quality. For the past few years there has been a great opportunity to trade up, with the rise in income levels and taste levels. However, to judge by the relatively unchanging price structure of apparel offerings (see Table 2), it appears that the fashion industry has not been quick to respond to this demand for quality and this willingness to move into higher price lines.

A keen student of retail advertising has said that there's been no real trading up evident in the prices of women's apparel advertised in leading United States cities by department stores in the past few years. This seems almost unbelievable in view of all the retail talk one has heard on the subject, but the proof that it's so can be found in the apparel industry's production figures for the past five years. Two facts stand out: one is the relatively small increase in the production of higher-priced garments (in some cases there's even been a decrease) and the other is the continuing predominance of very low-priced merchandise.

Surely no merchant can fail to realize the implications of these "stable" price lines. Other industries have realized that prices are ceasing to be the only consideration for larger and larger segments of the buying public. But the relatively static distribution of apparel price lines seems to indicate that fashion merchants are confusing the familiar with the necessary.

Price is important, of course. But insistence on quality and taste is growing. With the remarkable upgrading of the whole quality of American life, surely more money can be made by operating on the assumption that today's customers are eager for "something better," both functionally and esthetically.

Imitative Styling. In the face of the customer's increasing sophistication, styling grows more imitative and uniform. Like poor timing and the failure to trade up to better price lines, this sameness discourages the most eager customer.

Despite the attractions of Paris (and its tax-deductible aspects), it's hard to fathom why different manufacturers and retailers, with supposedly different personalities and operations, are all paying fabulous sums for exactly the same (and increasingly commercialized) Paris

Table 2 Changes in the Production of Selected Women's Garments

	1955 (%)	1960 (%)	Change (%)
Coats, untrimmed			
Under $16.00 per unit	42.7	51.0	+8.8
$16.00–$38.99	40.2	36.9	−3.3
$39.00 and over	17.1	12.1	−5.0
Suits			
Under $16.00 per unit	60.6	59.2	−1.4
$16.00–$38.99	24.3	30.0	+5.7
$39.00 and over	15.1	10.8	−4.3
Dresses, unit-priced			
Under $6.00 per unit	47.3	40.4	−6.9
$6.00–$9.99	27.2	33.0	+5.8
$10.00–$15.99	16.8	16.9	+0.1
$16.00 and over	8.7	9.7	+1.0
Skirts			
Under $39.00 per dozen	47.1	55.1	+8.0
$39.00–$75.99	40.0	31.8	−8.2
$76.00 and over	12.9	13.1	+0.2
Blouses			
Under $23.00 per dozen	60.4	57.6	−2.8
$23.00–38.99	25.2	28.1	+2.9
$39.00 and over	14.4	14.3	+0.1

Source: ILGWU from the U.S. Bureau of the Census.

originals to copy and adapt. Why this continuing industry dependence upon Paris designers to interpret the wants of our American customers? After the January Paris openings, *Women's Wear* reported that St. Laurent had sold 125 models for copying, *sight unseen.* American fashion merchants, lured by a questionable "exclusive," collectively invested over $100,000 in models without seeing them, without making any judgment of their own as to whether they were suitable to be copied and offered for sale to American customers!

Signs of growing customer dissatisfaction with imitative styling and fashion sameness are prevalent. From a recent report on a consumer survey conducted by FIT students come these comments:

> The woman of today is beginning to realize that the great American institution of Paris copies and adaptations is turning her into her neighbor's look-alike. . . . One of the great weaknesses we find in junior size merchandise is the similarity of styles. Practically every dress in every store is the same except for the color and some slight variations. . . .
>
> Women are more discerning in the type and quality of clothing they want. They are well on the way to becoming completely disgusted with the pallid, unimaginative and similar styles which confront them, rack upon rack.

Competition by imitation seems to have become the buyword of fashion retailers and their vendors. I would venture a guess that more merchandise is being ordered by buyers today because competitors have it than because they haven't. The situation has reached the point where a progressive and successful manufacturer is moved to make this public statement:

> Stores are finding the same merchandise in nearly every showroom. . . . Manufacturers for the most part are running with the mob, copying each other.

It is a marketing fact that today's knowledgeable shoppers are tiring of mass-produced and mass-consumed products. Witness the growing number and increasing success of the little, individualized, off-beat shops springing up all over the country, and the incipient "off-Seventh Avenue" movement.

It is true that best sellers have an important place in every well-run store and showroom. But the *same* best sellers for all stores and all vendors cannot supply the color and excitement that will get the fashion business a bigger share of the consumers' dollars. There are too many fashion products and too many advertising and merchandising programs that are imitative. Uninspired conformity will not produce growth.

Confusion About Sizes. Another situation that makes fashion shopping discouraging for the customer is the multiplication of size ranges. They're created and promoted at the drop of an off-beat measurement. They confuse the customers; they're fast creating an occupational guessing game for even the retailers and manufacturers. As if retailers had not already created enough shopping problems for customers by scattering similar merchandise in different departments all over the store, they are now confusing customers even more with the addition of "junior petites," "misses petites," "young juniors," "junior juniors," "juniorettes," and the like. There is even a movement afoot to give a new designation to half-sizes, the reason being that customers associate antiquated styling with these sizes.

To fashion professionals, the distinction between these many size-type designations may be apparent, though often they are nonexistent in styling, pricing, *or* sizing. But if retailers will look at it from the customer's point of view they will see they're only making it more difficult for women to figure out what size they're supposed to wear and to which department on what floor they're supposed to go. This in itself discourages the buying urge, and even creates positive buying resistance.

Outdated Physical Presentation. In this era of intense competition for the discretionary dollar, people cannot be forced to fit their buying into the way that merchants find it most feasible to buy and stock merchandise. The extra dollars that could go into fashion wardrobes will be spent for something else if fashion shopping is difficult or dull. Customers couldn't care less about retail problems of stock-taking and control, buying specializations and separations, or how and when retailers must buy merchandise.

No discussion of current fashion merchandising would be complete without pointing out that many retail stock arrangements, fixtures, and general methods of merchandise presentation are outdated. Departments and classifications are arranged to facilitate stock-counts and inventory control rather than for customers' convenience. Many floor fixtures still in use simply store merchandise instead of dramatizing its appeal. Many fixtures are so jammed with merchandise that looking and shopping have become a chore and a bore.

Be Willing to Change! I do not underestimate the great accomplishments and potentials of the fashion business. But it must change as its customers change. Traditional ways of doing things cannot be continued just because they are traditional.

A bigger share of consumer spending can be obtained for apparel. It requires a coordinated effort on the part of all segments of the fashion business. I believe this effort must begin with the fashion merchant. He must re-educate himself, his buyers, and his fashion directors to work *with* manufacturers, *for* customers, to bring out new and better fashion products at the right time and in the proper price lines, and to present them in the way that best suits the *customer's* convenience and preferences.

Analyzing Fashion Trends

by Rita A. Perna

Let's dispel some of the fiction associated with fashion straight-away. Fiction about forecasting, prophesying, having a "fashion feeling" being an *expert,* a seer, or omnipotent in a fashion decree. All of us have been in the position of looking with awe to someone who is reputed to have these special occult qualities. If I can but shorten the learning period of others

---

Rita Perna, Fashion Director of Montgomery Ward and Co., Inc., wrote this article especially for this book.

by stripping away the mystery—by reducing the steps to their simplest terms—I will at least have made the growing pains a little easier to bear.

Research

Although fashion is not considered a science many scientific steps are applied. The number one step being that of *good hard research*—which means *leg work* and consultation with the primary sources of information. The *mills* and *tanners* working months and years ahead of the market are in the best position to guide you on basic facts. Their information will include the approaching season's *promotional plans* plus ideas in the incubator stage that you can look forward to in the future seasons. Remember that they have *had to take a position* on raw goods and machinery well in advance. Their research should be of benefit to you. Next, the *magazines* whose fashion editors have also tread the same steps of basic research. Consult with them, tossing ideas back and forth searching out their convictions.

Let us not forget the *trade magazines* and newspapers, again, whose expert staff mulled over the very same problems—check *again!* If you are lucky enough to be a member of or have access to any special fashion services, such as Color Card Association, Tobé Reports, etc., once again you have *another pipeline* of information on basic research at your command.

Analysis

If you have the fortitude, stamina, strong legs, and unbending spirit to have completed a thorough job of research then you are in a perfect position to analyze this knowledge. In scrutinizing the facts it is important that you first put the information in *order of importance;* for example, let's talk about color. You may have learned that beige, pink, and yellow are slated for promotion. How will you determine their *degree* of *importance?*

Timing

It is not possible for all three colors to be equally strong at the same time. One color is probably right as a cruise color in January; a second color might be right as an early spring color; the third one might be perfectly timed for the summer. After seasonal timing, another question to ask yourself—what is the timing for *your* particular store or company? Are you a high-fashion specialty shop, a volume department store, an exclusive boutique, a window chain or mail-order catalog? Is your store located in New York, Kansas, California, or Texas? Are *you* the *best store* in town or the price promoter in town? The reply to these questions will determine *how timely you* should or must be, Being early or first is just as destructive as being late.

Classifications

Determining the *one, two, three colors* is step number one. Determining the *correct timing* for the image of your store is step number two. Determining the *kinds of goods* that are right in the selected color for a particular time of year in a *particular climatic* and *geographic* location is step number three. For example, the color beige as an early spring color would be adaptable for *all classifications* of goods, but, obviously the depth and breadth of stock behind yellow would be much shallower than the classic beige. The *degree* of *newness* would also be a factor in determining the *risk element* for your store. Purple is far riskier than pink; therefore, you would put it into short-lived fashion garments that would move in and out of your stock quickly rather than investing the color in merchandise of a relatively long life and basic character.

Newness

Newness is the life blood of the fashion business. It is absolutely necessary to take calculated risks in new ideas whether it be color, silhouette, length, or fabric. Investing wisely in newness will pay dividends. By exposing any new idea to the consumer you are *bound to learn* the *degree of acceptance* or the problems caused by the change. This enables you to take action based on your *own* findings. Allowing someone else to experiment for you may seem wise, but since you cannot always apply someone else's experience to your company you will still have to go through the experimental pains. This makes you *late* because you are a *follower* and *not* a *leader*. This mars your fashion image because *customers* will *not look to you* for newness. This lateness *destroys the momentum* that you would have gained had you been in at the inception of the trend and *ready* when it reached its crest.

Sensitivity

Basically we are pleading for the development of a *sensitivity* to the changing currents of fashion. This sensitivity comes through an awareness of what is going on at the mill level, manufacturer level, retail level, and consumer level. With this sensitivity and knowledge of what is eminent on the fashion horizon, you should be able to jump on the bandwagon at the proper time.

Day-to-Day

So far we have dealt with some methods used in fashion analysis in its early or beginning stages. What happens on a *day-to-day basis?* Once you have set your plans for the promotion of certain colors, silhouettes, categories of merchandise, you must then watch with a keen eye and ear for those ideas that have met with customer acceptance. This is obtained very simply in *reading sales records.* Did it *sell; how well* did it sell; *how fast* did it sell; *when* did it sell? Based on the responses you are able to add *strength to your convictions* or delete the ideas that have not won customer sales. Remember, it is the customer who sets the trend by parting with her disposable fashion dollars. No matter how you personally love a fashion feature you must abandon it *in depth* until you see evidence of a customer's change of heart. You will keep it alive through repeated investments in newness where they have refined the original idea. How long has it taken the majority to accept loose-fitting clothes since the advent of the chemise? How long did it take the majority to accept short skirts? How long did it take the majority of the women to accept the understated look? These ideas were *not abandoned* along the way, but were tried repeatedly with a new disguise—with better fit, better construction, better understanding on the part of the customer and manufacturer. Some trends take hold like a whirlwind, others maintain a slow and steady growth. Let us look ahead—how long will it take for the return of fitted clothes and the longer skirts? It will be interesting to watch!

Personal Attitudes

The personal qualities that I am about to speak of are applicable to everyone from the president to a lonely stock boy. I speak of:

1. A Sense of Urgency. Demanding *immediate* delivery, lugging merchandise from the receiving room now, sending the report out *immediately.* In other words, *action!*
2. *Dedication.* A sense of perfection that is not fanatic, but simply a matter of personal pride of *doing* something *now* and *well.* In other words, *thoughtfully!*
3. *Self-Evaluation.* You will always hear the blame and hardly ever the praise, that is the nature of our business. You should be able to determine if the job was A plus, good, or only fair. Get into the habit of *rating yourself* after every job assignment. Compare yourself with the *best people,* not the mediocre characters around you. In this way you will be pulling yourself up to a higher standard. In other words, be self-*critical!*

Living Down to the Joneses

by Tobé Coller Davis

It's a funny thing, but in all the years I have lived in New York, I have met very few people named Jones. But I'll tell you a secret. In Milwaukee I lived next door to a family of good Western Joneses all my school day life so I think I know a lot about the Joneses. The few I have met in New York were very nice but not particularly remarkable. Yet it seems to me that not only I, myself, but most of my friends, have spent those years desperately trying to live by the standard which *somebody* by the name of Jones has set. And during most of those years, living by the Joneses' standard meant scrambling for a place on an elevator which ended up in some smart penthouse.

Today America is still living by the Joneses' standard. But the elevator on which we ride seems to be headed in a different direction. It's going down to the bargain basement. For the Chauncey Montague Joneses who once ruled the social roost are now in permanent retirement on their old estate in Southampton where they can't afford the three caretakers they used to have. Their place has been taken by the Charles M. Joneses whose estate in Suburbia, U.S.A., has only one caretaker whose name, curiously enough, is also *Charles M. Jones.*

Today there is a new pace-setter—not only in the world of fashion, but in the fashion of living, as well. We are all of us going through a tremendous change in the accepted standards of what we call The Good Life. And the nature of this change is that we are no longer living *up* to the Joneses, but living *down* to them.

Why has this change come about? First, because there is an entirely new pattern of incomes in the United States.

To begin with, the mass market has shifted. It is no longer at the bottom of the scale, but in the middle. Fortune calls it the booming middle class—18 million families which spend 42 per cent of the income of America. In 1929 only 20 per cent of all American families got more than $4000 a year—in today's dollar values. In 1953, 50 per cent of American families have crossed the $4000 line. Indeed, six families out of ten get incomes of between $3000 and $10,000.

And not only has the mass market shifted upward, but something remarkable has happened to the creme de la creme market at the very top. In 1929 the top 1 per cent of American families received nearly 20 per cent of the nation's income after taxes. Today their share is down to less than 8 per cent. The heavy creme is a good deal lighter.

As a result of these economic changes, the Chauncey Montague Joneses no longer command a *vital* section of the American market. That privilege has fallen to the Charles M. Joneses.

But there is another important reason why our standards of living have changed. Something has happened to that mythical person who is described in the United States *Statistical Abstract* as Average Female. "Average Female" has a new look. For one thing she is much more likely to be married: only 19 per cent of American girls over 14 are *not* married—as against 28 per cent in 1940. She marries younger—20 is the average age today—she is having her first baby earlier, too. If she does not have a child—or if her child is old enough to go to school—she is working: *working wives outnumber working single women two to one*—a spectacular reversal of only a few years back. Working or not, she has a larger family than her parents did; witness the fact that the birth rate both for first and second children is significantly higher. And she intends and does bring up her children herself.

Let's speculate on what brought these changes to pass. Partly, of course, it is the great rise in American productivity; partly it is the impact of higher taxes. Some of this change is

---

Address delivered by Tobé Coller Davis, fashion consultant, before the 25th Annual Boston Conference on Distribution, October 19, 1953. Although the statistics in this article are based on 1953 figures, the fashion implications of these trends are still valid.

certainly due to new ideas and to a different attitude on the part of most of young America toward work and wealth.

But whatever the causes, these groundswell changes have brought with them a new standard of *good* living—and a new standard of *good* fashion.

The new *Good Life* is a great deal more casual. The day of the elegant soiree has gone, along with the chauffeur-driven car and the lorgnette. Today the big social event is the cocktail party or buffet supper. The limousine is a station-wagon—sometimes with mushrooms growing from its moldy old canvas. Instead of the imitation Spanish castle there is the *bona-fide ranch-type home.* In place of the Social Register there is the local P.T.A. This casual life has changed our needs for clothes; one evening dress is all that most of the Joneses own. They're out shopping for easy good-looking clothes that belong to a cocktail or supper party and yet do not look too conspicuous while they're waiting at the station for their husbands. Even our smartest young mothers wear sweaters and skirts to smart country weddings. They dress down even to the bride.

After the opening of the play, "The Little Foxes," Tallulah Bankhead stayed up to read her notices. They were all raves—"Thank God everybody knows I'm a hit," Tallulah said. "It means that now I don't have to worry about being seen wearing old clothes."

Secondly, the *new* Good Life is built more and more on the *do-it-yourself* attitude. This is partly a response to the times—young people can't afford domestic help, and the number of domestic servants has fallen by nearly 25 per cent since 1940. Partly deep down it is the expression of a new joy in the do-it-yourself hobby. A lot of young married couples I know who could afford a full-time servant or a nurse choose to do without them, *because their friends can't afford them.* The new trend in the fashion of living is to do *like* the Joneses *do*—not to get "embarrassingly" ahead of them.

Thirdly, this new Good Life is a good deal more independent of the past than the Good Life of our own generation. Many past restrictions have been discarded, but the new freedom has *not been used* as an *excuse* for license. Indeed, while most new young marrieds think and talk far more freely about such things as sex and morals, they often act more conservatively than older generations who paid more lip-service to rigid notions of conduct. What I think this means is that young America is determined to think for itself. That has a deep bearing on fashion, too. The *Charles M. Joneses* are not so ready to accept the verdict of any Four Hundred. Of course the movies, the stage, cafe society still influence fashions strongly—although note that this is an elite of accomplishment rather than wealth alone. Of course the young homemaker looks at the fashion magazines and is curious and interested about what Paris has to say this year. You recall in August that "Dior short skirt was biggest news since Stalin died," said a press service. But while she is ready to look, she is not ready to follow slavishly. Few will wear these 17-inch skirts even though Dior showed them, though his influence is undoubtedly felt.

And finally, the new generation has a different scale of values about what makes the Good Life good. Charles M. Jones has a good deal more money than he used to have. But he spends his new-found affluence in very different ways than Chauncey Montague Jones chose. As I have said, he has decided not to have full-time servants. He has not bought a *fancy* car—the middle cars like the small Buick are styled and priced right for Jones' tastes and pocketbook. He has built a modest house in which the kitchen and not the living room is the center of attraction. He spends more money for his children's *schools.* He has purchased more exciting leisure time for himself and his wife. Takes more vacations with travel—usually in his car—another informal attitude. He has a television set. If he lives in a big city, he eats out more. He has bought himself a raft of home appliances and his children have bigger and better toys. But although his family is larger he spends even less for clothes! The increase in clothes industry is a population increase, but a decrease for family—right up to the top, too. Out of his new, bigger income he spends less than 8 per cent for everybody's clothing needs. Two percentage points less than he spent before the war.

I think this is a pretty fair picture of the *new style leaders in the United States*—the Mr. and Mrs. Joneses who are not at the top, but in the big booming middle-income heap. There is a moral here, both for distribution and for fashion. The moral for distribution is clear and I need hardly emphasize it: it lies in recognizing that the old market—*big and poor at the bottom,* and *small and rich on top*—simply doesn't live here any more.

But the fashion moral is more subtle—more difficult to bolster with facts and figures. Today more than ever it expresses the taste and needs of the booming middle class of this huge American market.

Is that taste good? Yes! Every visiting fireman in his first trip to America, even members of the Paris couture exclaim about the style of our young girls as they pour out of their jobs at noon-day. Unlike the European family, the American working girl spends 25 per cent of her income for clothes. The new big middle class of America is style conscious. They have the same chic that French midinettes used to have before the war and better figures.

They believe in culture too. The sales of inexpensive prints of modern art masters like Dufy run to the millions of dollars. Women's magazines report great interest in modern architecture and interior decorating. A pocketbook of Old Masters' drawings, put out as an experiment, sold out its edition of several hundred thousand in a matter of weeks.

But it is a taste which, while excellent, cannot indulge in expensive originals—*in clothes* or *in art.* Those who have been accustomed to designing their models for the select few must learn to think in terms of more general types and sizes, and these must be accurate reflections of Mrs. Jones as she really is. The designer may sigh for Mrs. Chauncey Jones who had three cars and fifteen servants and bought ten dresses at a clip, but she will sell to more of the Mrs. Charles Joneses who has three kids and fifteen household jobs to do herself and who buys one dress for a special occasion at one time—and carefully, too.

One aspect of such fashion designing requires more attention to the matter of sizing. Technology and research will make big contributions to the fashion industry of tomorrow. Precision sizing long looked for is still in its infancy but will grow by leaps and bounds in the next ten years —just as frozen orange juice has grown since the war. There are many fine points in sizing— long waists—short waists and so on—all need a lot of study and engineering. All this will have the same effect for growth in the fashion industry.

There are, for example, over three million tall girls in the American market—girls over 5′ 8″. Tall girls alone provide a whole mass market by themselves. So do tiny girls, fat girls, and so on. Catering to these special demands is merchandising to the Joneses at its best. For the pacemaking Jones family comes in all sizes, and each of them offers a chance for some enterprising designer, maker, and distributor to cater to an entire submarket within this huge general market.

Even more important than sizing is style itself. And by styling, I mean not just designing clothes that are too utterly utter but designing clothes that belong to the way of life priced at the levels Mrs. Jones can afford. Style experts —who are as rare as good violinists—must remember that the final arbiter is Mrs. *Charles*— not Mrs. Chauncey—Jones. Remember Mrs. Jones doesn't want to look like Mrs. Chauncey Jones—she wouldn't if she could afford to: she wants to look like herself and her neighbors and her friends but still express individuality within the gamut. She leads a more casual life—a more comfortable life—but with plenty of glamour whether she lives in the big city or in Suburbia, U.S.A.

The young wives who play with their children, who give progressive dinner parties, and throw bring-your-own-bottle parties (at which Mrs. Chauncey Jones would turn up her nose), won't move into middle-age anonymity so easily. The whole accent, the emphasis, of these new communities is on youth—on the vitality and energy of young womanhood. That mood is reflected in the clothes they choose whether it's gay and unrestrained for television, glamour for a party, or functional for taking the baby out.

Just one more thought occurs to me. Fashions that follow Mrs. Charles Jones are apt to be more stable. By this I most certainly do not mean that fashion will come to a grinding halt; if there is one thing we *do* know about American women, it is that they like new fashions and they buy them quickly. But I think its extreme swings may narrow down a bit, none the less. In the days when fashion was set by the very uppercrust and imitated by the masses below, fashion often indulged the whims of its pace-makers. But as fashion gears itself to the middle-class Joneses, it is swapping a very temperamental client for a very steady one. The new Joneses, in addition, cannot afford to junk their wardrobes every year. They buy with an eye for the future—and may well veer away from styles which threaten to be *too* extreme to last more than a season. Suburbia wants to be different but not *too* different, but she wants quality in what she buys and is willing to pay for it. Hence, while fashions will most certainly change and change ceaselessly, we may avoid sudden *violent* changes to a greater degree than in the past.

When anyone asks me what fashion will be good next year—I answer if I knew I wouldn't be sitting here. I'd make my millions and retire to my hobbies. But one thing I'm sure of, is that the new fashion queen—that Mrs. Charles Jones I've been talking about—is *quite a person in her own right.* She is far poorer than the other Mrs. Jones, but as a personality she may be a great deal richer. She is more independent, more resourceful, more considerate, more intelligent. She's a real vital, exciting person and often has more culture, or strives for it. Her feet are firmly planted on the ground and her head is well below the clouds. She knows pretty much what she wants for herself, her children, her husband.

She offers a new challenge to the American multibillion dollar fashion industry. Mrs. Charles M. Jones is not one rare bird, but a flock numbering over 30 million women; she doesn't command one income of, say, $4000, but a Niagara of incomes of nearly one hundred billion dollars. If ever there was a market, this is it. If ever there was challenge to distribution, here it is.

The New Era of the Sophisticated Shopper

by E. B. Weiss

Culturally, as well as economically, the American shopper has gone through vast changes over the last decade.

The world of marketing has been keenly aware of the marketing impact of the shopper's *economic* improvement. Indeed, the world of marketing is almost constantly submerged in a sea of economic statistics.

But marketing men seem to be only dimly aware of the *cultural* progress of the American shopper—and even more dimly aware of what cultural progress must mean in terms of marketing policies and methods.

Over the next few years, our *cultural* progress may outstrip our *economic* progress. Yet much marketing is still directed at audiences that presumably have not changed intellectually since the Indian medicine fakir strummed his guitar.

This is not to say that Barnum's famous dictum no longer has any application whatsoever. We are by no means a nation of sophisticates. We still have millions who are "suckers" as Barnum defined a sucker. But a sucker is no longer born every minute. And a sucker no longer comes into shopping adulthood every minute.

Maybe the rate is now a sucker every *two* minutes—or better still, every three minutes. Even the lower rate, statistically, in a nation of 175 millions, represents a gigantic change in shopper sophistication.

But the important point for marketing men is that shopper sophistication is, today, not merely marching ahead—it is *leaping* ahead. It is leaping ahead both qualitatively and quantitatively. It is in a stage of *explosive* growth.

Marketing men will be hard pressed to match shopper sophistication with *sophisticated marketing programs*—even if they are fully aware of this remarkable change in our society. Where this awareness does not exist, *marketing* sophistication will fall farther and farther behind *shopper* sophistication—and that has been, is currently, and will in future be damaging to volume and profit.

Barnum would have been the first to spot the

Introductory chapter of "The New Era of the Sophisticated Shopper," a study-in-depth by E. B. Weiss, Marketing Director of Doyle Dane Bernbach, Inc., advertising agency.

change—and to base his calculations on a sucker born every *two* minutes. But marketing is loaded down with programs specifically aimed at a nation that presumably will continue to buy snake oil for every ailment.

Detroit continued to accept Barnum's precept. Its belated and frantic rush to climb aboard the compact car trend is one result.

The ethical drug industry has ample reason to understand that larger and larger segments of the American public are becoming more sophisticated. It is under strong attack from this very cause.

Ditto for the druggist—who never ranked so low in public appraisal as at this very moment. The reason? He rates public intelligence too low.

Even the medical profession is becoming aware of a tendency, among mounting millions, to look at the doctor somewhat more questioningly, somewhat less with a "God and doctors can do no wrong" attitude. (Remember the series of articles in *Life* in October, 1959, reporting on this very phenomenon?)

Economic and social progress ultimately go hand in hand. Our fantastic economic progress has provided multiplying millions with a remarkably elastic "discretionary" dollar. Perhaps 70 per cent of our total bill for national advertising aims at moving merchandise whose purchase is deferrable.

Well—a sophisticated shopulation is showing a remarkable discretion (and will show vastly more) in expending its discretionary dollar!

Even in our present-day remarkable era of high income for masses of people, by far the *lion's* share of discretionary dollars are in the hands of the *smaller* number of our families. These families are the *very ones* whose members are rapidly becoming increasingly sophisticated shoppers. The planning of too many marketing men shows an unawareness of this fundamental.

We have larger and larger numbers of our shopulation with higher education. We have larger and larger numbers who continue to improve their minds. (A large book publisher recently decided he might appeal to this self-improvement trend by reprinting a self-help series of volumes that achieved enormous popularity in the 1920's. After reviewing them, he decided that today's market would consider these tomes childish!)

Millions of our people followed the elections in England last October almost as closely as they follow our own. This would not have happened a few years ago.

An annual volume of over $2 billion in paperback books is proof of a literate public. Paperbacks are not exclusively fodder for low-level readers; check the titles. Nonfiction books never sold in such numbers.

The phonograph record industry reports a simply fantastic upturn in demand for the so-called "classics." And stereo, despite its technological state of utter confusion, is hard-pressed to keep up with demand.

A most interesting demonstration of increasing sophistication among even low-end shoppers is found in the experiences of the credit clothing chains in the South. These low-end shoppers now have an inkling of the high credit charges of the traditional credit clothing stores and therefore they are turning to Sears and other outlets where terms and prices are more reasonable.

The egghead is assuming a new position in our society. His very numbers make this inevitable. Once he was a queer—because he was so unrepresentative. Today, the *various degrees* of eggheadedness are common enough in our total population to begin to assume somewhat the proportions of a norm.

Talk to magazine editors—they are doing a vastly better job of reflecting changing social mores more than can be said for the TV networks. The magazine editors know that their audiences are more sophisticated (in the broader sense of that term) than their audiences of even ten years ago. And they look ahead to still more rapid advances up the ladder of culture by still more of our people in the near-term future.

Do not miss the significance of the editorial changes in *Life*. The reception it has won for its magnificent presentations of art and for its serious discussions of vital subjects—both total departures from its original editorial policy of pictures almost exclusively (sex, blood, and news)—reflects the smart awareness of its editors of vast changes in the degree of sophistication among its millions of readers. (Some of *Life's* recent editorial features would have been considered highbrow by *Harper's* years ago!)

The fundamental point is that the magazine editors, the book publishers, and some others in the world of communication (*not* including

TV) have moved faster, and more purposely, to conform with a newly sophisticated shopulation than have many marketing men. So have some politicians who realize that our huge and rapidly growing independent vote reflects intelligent thinking.

We hope to show in this study *why* marketing must more accurately reflect the new era of the sophisticated shopper—and *how* marketing may program toward this great cultural change in our shopulation.

The essence of sophistication is a greater willingness to accept—and demand—*change*. The world of marketing must therefore gear itself for a new tempo in the obsolescence of established marketing concepts and in the creation of new marketing concepts.

The New York Times in a November 8, 1959, editorial commenting on the TV quiz scandals stated:

> A wise editor once said, "You may easily underestimate the ignorance of great masses of the people, *but you had better not underestimate their intelligence.*" The degree of information possessed by most persons has improved since that day with better schools and with better means of communication. The intelligence is doubtless about what it always was. It is high enough to detect in the end the excesses of hypocrisy, condescension, and falsehood.
>
> This is something for purveyors of goods and ideas to think about now and for a long time to come.

We agree.

Looking Forward

by Andrew Goodman

Our fashion ready-to-wear business which reflects our nation's sociology in clothes can be expected to continue to change dramatically as the sense of taste and quality evolve.

All of us remember clearly the days when only a privileged wealthy few had good taste in clothing, in furnishing homes, and indeed in all phases of their lives. When my father first established BG in 1901, he was aiming at meeting and satisfying the needs of the smallest possible segment of the American population; those people who wanted and appreciated the high standards of custom tailoring and dressmaking that he knew so well. And, less than a decade before father's death several years ago, we still had a customer who had all the uniforms for her maids, nurses, and governesses made in the custom-made department at BG. She just did not know that there was any other way of buying apparel, and our own people did not work too hard trying to educate her.

Time was too when the big city stores would buy styles and price lines in dresses, coats and suits that would never sell in smaller cities and especially smaller towns and vice versa. There are still, as you know far better than I, New York and Chicago styles on the one hand and the jazzed-up numbers for out of town on the other. It's still true, for example, that the recent line-for-line RTW copies of French and Italian couture dresses have been much more successful in big city stores than in small stores belonging to the same buying groups and chains. But the difference between big city and small town taste is gradually disappearing. Gone are the days when the housewife in East Cupcake, Illinois, or the farmwife in Iowa did not know, and could not care less, about what silhouette was new or what skirt length was smart.

Today, through the mass media of TV, radio, newspapers, magazines, and the movies she knows what's new and she has a pretty good idea of what she wants. Just think of the impact of Mary Martin's and Dinah Shore's clothes when they appear on TV. They have affected the taste and standards of all of our people. Just look at the Sears Roebuck catalogue today and compare its stylish contents with those of the Chic Sale outhouse era. No longer is good taste, in any area of our lives, the exclusive property

---

Excerpted from an address delivered by Andrew Goodman, President of Bergdorf Goodman, Inc., at the Garment Salesmen's Guild Dinner, January 14, 1960 (Hotel Plaza, New York). Reprinted with permission of author.

of the few or of the rich. And this fact is becoming manifest in our homes and in the way we spend our time and in our purchases. People who five years ago did not know the difference between a Picasso and a piccolo now own excellent reproductions of well-known sculptures and paintings and are beginning to buy fine originals. Another part of the great cultural wave that is inundating our country is a renewed interest in fine music, with local opera and philharmonic orchestras spring up in many cities. Symphonic and classical records, which as recently as ten years ago were dying, now are selling in the millions and more people are in fact attending symphony concerts than baseball games!

You will notice in this approach that I have avoided any statistical references. I don't find them particularly revealing as a general rule, but in this area I find them even less so. During the next decade you can bet Americans will learn to live even better. More leisure time will be available. Thousands more college graduates will have upgraded tastes. This will have its effect on our business, yours and mine, because a richer, more tastefully decorated home creates a desire for more beautiful and appropriate clothes to go with it. So does the taste for travel and the opportunity to gratify it and jet travel will shrink the globe and create greatly increased demands for apparel. So many people are traveling these days that it is no longer a luxury and the need for more fashionable clothes in greater variety is being created all the time. My own feeling is, that within the next 10 years, price will cease to be the major criterion for larger and larger sections of our buying population. I think that the trend towards more luxurious and sumptuous homes, hotels, office buildings, and restaurants will continue. Interior decorators, custom cabinet makers, and custom carpet designers are all so rushed that you must wait months before they will take your money. Have you noticed, for example, what has happened to the bathroom faucet? Time was when the height of elegance was chrome. Then along came the special bathroom interior decorators and suddenly there are 24-karat gold faucets shaped like swans and flowers and done in Renaissance shapes reminiscent of Cellini.

My own thought is that in people's homes [illegible] toward the stark modern will give way during the next decade to a craving for many of the soft, decorative features of previous eras, adapted to modern functional living. I think that new efficient ways are going to be found to make decorative moldings which were once important and decorative chandeliers that people will be delighted to enjoy once again. going to work very hard to create their own personality and individuality in their physical appearances as well as in their merchandising and customer policies. I think that store management people are going to become tired of having branch stores all look alike and are going to work very hard to create their own personalities and store images again because customers will appreciate it and spend accordingly. There are signs that American women, to speak of an area with which I am somewhat more familiar than others, are coming of age in fashion.

Regarding furs, for example: think back. Ten years ago the purchase of a mink coat was itself a symbol of everything which we held dear in the United States. Now, the mink coat as an end in itself is already old hat to a growing section of our population. They now are interested in a mink coat that has distinction, that is more than just a mink coat, and they don't hesitate to try to express their own personalities in its design. Remember the mass-produced mink stole of which millions were sold in the United States? I have often thought that it was an outstanding example of the insecurity and uncertainty of American women in the field of fur fashion. Every woman wanted to look exactly like every other woman because she did not trust her own judgment and would not risk making an error. Just think how far we have come today. If you look around at the furs in this very hotel tonight, the outstanding characteristic is not the sameness but the difference in shapes, colors, and treatment of skins. People no longer feel it necessary to look alike. They want to look like individuals and stress their differences.

Consider automobiles, for example. More and more it is becoming obvious that to American car buyers the car is simply a device to get you from place to place and no longer is a status symbol. Some of the richest people in the United States drive around in cars that cost $2000 and feel no necessity to make any apology. And this will continue. The owning of a

Cadillac, as such, will become less and less important as proof of someone's position in society. It will simply mean in the future that he chooses and elects to move around in a large comfortable car and that someone else chooses to get from place to place in a small, economical, easily parked car.

During the 59 years we have been in business at BG, we have probably created more made-to-order clothes and millinery and furs than any other specialty store in America, but, as recently as this past year, of the $20 some odd million volume we did in the store, over $4 million was spent for made-to-order fashions. This is an astonishing figure during times when many famous houses have found it necessary to drop the custom business entirely. I am not suggesting that made-to-order customers are the pattern for the future. I don't think so for a moment. But, there will always be a small section of the buying public which has developed connoisseur's taste and which has so much money that it can afford to indulge its whims. But, in a year such as 1959, you might be interested to know that we sold hundreds of ready-to-wear dresses which retailed over $500 and a remarkable quantity over $1000. This in the RTW department! No matter what you are selling, no matter what the price line or which end of our fascinating, stimulating, and frustrating fashion business you are in, you should note these trends.

We recently opened a new floor—the B & G (for Boys and Girls) (and Bergdorf Goodman) Shop—after planning it for several years. To a degree, we were influenced in this decision by the statistics on the increased number of children in our future: the "population explosion," and by a desire to attract a new group of customers. Beyond that, we decided to go into this business now, because so many of our discriminating customers expressed a desire for fine, tasteful clothes for their children. That this was not a pipe dream is attested to by the fact that from November, when we opened this new section, through today (about 2 months) we have sold $200,000 of high-priced quality children's wear!

Fashion—A Very Hot Tin Roof

Fashion Creators Woo American Womanhood with a Few Guesses and Lots of Aspirin

by Harry Serwer

'Twas said yon Cassius was a cloak-and-suiter because he had a lean and hungry look; and that's the first thing you note about his modern counterpart—the harassed countenance so symbolic of his trade.

You can never tell when your number is up in the ready-to-wear business. Today store buyers break down your doors to get at your fashions. Tomorrow you're on the cafeteria-line scrounging for a cup of Java.

Who is responsible for this scary situation? The Union? No! The Union provides seasoned workmen who will make good merchandise if you tell them how you want it made.

Are the suppliers responsible? No! They confine themselves to providing the fabrics and findings out of which your fashions are made.

Are the store buyers responsible? In all fairness, No! They are only human too.

Well, who *is* responsible? With the utmost directness we must blame the American Woman, the lady known as the arbiter of fashions. Why is she responsible? Because she has no loyalty to particular versions of smartness since Fashion begets no loyalty. Thus, the American Woman contracts a thousand love affairs with Fashion, but never a marriage; and because she flaunts her waywardness in the market place she is responsible for the turbulence and volatility of the ready-to-wear industry.

Reprinted from a "Picture of a Union," May 17, 1959, by special permission. Harry Serwer was a well-known fashion merchandising consultant.

That is the reason for the constant gripe: "Howya gonna figure a woman out? Offer her red and she hollers for green. Give her lace trimming and she wants buttons. Make her a high waistline, like it says in fashion pages and suddenly she wants it around her knees. Everything she asked for two months ago, when nobody had it, she don't want it now when everybody's got it."

Now you understand why the lean and hungry look and the nitroglycerine tablets. And if you are in the explosive business you must agree with the Seventh Avenue philosopher who said, "Verily, Fashion is like ice cream melting on a hot tin roof."

The apparel manufacturer loves the American Woman but he has no delusions about her. He has her pegged as the real Czar of the industry from whose dictum there is no appeal.

But he is constantly confronted with the inevitable realities and deadlines of his business, and so he constantly reminds buyers that "Making women's apparel takes time; it ain't no Mickey Mouse climbing on a ceiling with the flick of an artist's brush.

Creating a new fashion collection for the coming season has all the frightening aspects of a nightmare. Shall he buy wools, silks, cottons, synthetics? And what percentage of each? Shall he buy solid colors, checks, stripes, plaids? Shall he mix fibers? All this is important because his styling is influenced—and often limited—by the fabrics he adopts. So he goes into the fabric markets with his designers and piece goods buyers. He buys a thousand sample cuts—half of which will never see the cutting table, and thus are destined for the rag bins. He listens to a thousand conflicting prophecies most of which are not only valueless but dangerous. He sends his designers to foreign markets, his copyists to the new plays, the Opera, the smart restaurants, to see the new ideas the women are wearing.

The very great fashions are usually the divinations of the gifted. The rest are rehashes. The number of "new styles" created every year are legion to the few that really succeed. The cost of all this "creation" is like a millstone around the neck of the industry. Ironically, in Fashion as in Politics and Social Structures, the good is not always new, and the new is not always good.

It doesn't have to make sense. There is only one yard measure; if your styles walk out of the stores at a profit you're okay; if they have to be marked down you're dead—and it makes no difference how hot you were last year, that was last year!

So the race against the crazy clock runs something like this. The designing staff works at white heat for about six weeks living on benzedrine, coffee, and quarrels. The collection is finally finished: some of it is original creation; some is downright plagiarism; some models are ingenious copies so trickily conceived that no one can tell exactly whose swipe it was and where the swipe started. Then the whole sales staff is brought in, including the resident salesmen from far-flung cities. The collection is paraded by the appetizing models like a first night dress rehearsal. The salesmen sit around, looking very wise; and instead of confessing they couldn't pick the winners in a hundred years, they handicap the collection like professional touts at a race track.

So what happens when the season opens?

Some of the styles become sensational sellers—to the stores, that is. And in the stores many of these die. Why? American Womanhood gave them the Bronx Razoo. Don't ask her why.

Many of these pre-season "flops" have become sensations. One, in particular, had an eight-year run, and more than a million and a half dresses were sold in a single color! But as a rule, nobody knows what's going to sell—except the liars, and they don't know either.

Isn't Fashion ever influenced by events? Of course it is! Look how terrifically the migration from the city to the suburbs has influenced Fashion. Suburban living has sparked gigantic markets in play, sports, and classic clothes. The garden needs special clothes. So does the school pool. So do the beach and the woods. And what about the automobile journey called shopping?

But what about the manufacturer's nightmare and his seeming inability to divine the Fashion needs of the distaff public? Is this shrinking the overall volume? It is not! This nervous and perpetual need to keep on one's toes has spiralled the volume to fantastic figures. More women are wearing more clothes in America than in any country in the world. Our stenographers are better dressed than the upper crust in Europe or elsewhere. A great compliment can be paid to the apparel manufacturer of this country: he is always on his toes, but never on those of the Fashion Consumers.

The Business of Fashion Is Change

by Estelle Hamburger

Since any business, most of all our own sensitive, mercurial, responsive business, must be part of its moment and the movement of its times, let us first take a quick look at some pertinent changes around us.

✓First, surely, is the phenomenon of accelerating distribution. The miracle that made the supermarkets of food is now pushing forward the super-distribution of clothes. Discounters are proliferating, enlarging, trading up. More and bigger shopping centers are springing up all over the land. Department stores battle the discounters or join them, adding their own discount branches, or multiplying their suburban stores. Mail order, telephone order, self-servicing, vending machines, all speed up clothing distribution, pressing its frontiers onward, forward, outward, not only in America, but all over the world.

What is the force that has caused this multiplication to be so fast, on so vast a scale? It is desire, world-wide, to have and have now. This must-have, have-now drive, powered by mass communication, is not only propelling the world into the industrial age of science and technology, but transforming great areas of the world into "Western dress." Apparently, there is an association of ideas between Western technological know-how and the special breed of Western clothes with simplicity, youthfulness, verve, freedom, easy care, easy fit, and moderate prices, that promise faster fulfillment of the desire to have, and have now. With a "Western look," women feel a sense of participation in hitherto unattainable freedom, a sense of emancipation from a restricted past into a liberating present.

Fashion makes a vital contribution to the elan of life. Knowing what is new, becoming, attractive, exciting about clothes, and knowing how to wear them with taste, authority, and flair is a pleasure that each can make her own, at whatever price she can afford to pay. That is the marvel of American fashion.

✓Second, we must note the dissemination of fashion information, its speed, intensity, degree of penetration, based upon the recognition of fashion news as big news. Fashion magazines, edited for many "publics" are being more widely read all the time. Fashion reportage is a consistent feature of local newspapers, not only in large cities, but in moderate-sized communities, in ever more prominent position in the paper, in ever larger space. Moreover, there is now fashion reportage also in almost every other publication that has a chance of being read by women, from company house organs of insurance companies to handbooks for nurses.

There is fashion on the stage, in the movies, on TV, and there is fashion in the ads in all media, from the woman swathed in sables gliding into her custom-body car, to the woman in her shirts and pants, effortlessly waxing her floor with an electric polisher.

✓Third, let us bring into focus a few more stimulants that will have increasing impact on our business and its future opportunities. Begin with America on the move—whole families in the family car, over the unending miles of superhighways that spin across the continent. Pants, shorts, tops, shirts, of no-iron, drip-dry fabrics, sneakers on the feet, a kerchief over the chair, sun glasses to shade the eyes, and a swimsuit in the luggage compartment. They're off, seeing the sights, sleeping in motels, feeding the gang at drive-ins with franks, burgers, and popsicles. More and more with less and less formality.

Whole families on skis. Whole families in boats. Bowling. Outdoor cooking. Leisure pursuits of activities newly glimpsed by the five-hour, five-day week. The impact on clothing has just begun to be understood, still to be explored and developed.

✓Finally, although nothing is final in a business so sensitive to its environment—credit

---

Estelle Hamburger, fashion and sales promotion consultant, delivered this address to a Retail Workshop in Fashion Merchandising, January 24, 1962, at FIT, New York. Abridged and reprinted with author's permission.

cards. Have, and have now. Desire, and fulfillment now. Do it now. See it now. Go now. Pay for it later. The credit card has become a badge of belonging. It began as a zephyr. It is a strong wind now. It may be the hurricane that blows up our economy.

Let us consider one more factor unique to our trade, the raw materials of which its products are made. Fashion does not start with raw materials, but with ideas. There are no fixed raw materials like the oil in petroleum or the tobacco in cigarettes. The materials of fashion are as scattered as the earth's geography. . . . Any or all of these raw materials could stay where they are, and never become part of the substance of fashion, if some idea were not generated, beyond mere utility, that demands use of a specific material to give a special look, character, appeal, desirability, excitement, to something taking form in a designers' mind . . . making something that preceded it seem old, drab, uninteresting, undesirable, and unexciting, regardless of the price that was paid for it, or how recently it was purchased, or how desirable it was when it was new.

This has nothing to do with obsolescence due to advancing technology, like the passing of gaslight after the invention of electric light. It is the outcome of a vitalizing idea! Whole industries and the skills on which they depend can prosper or perish with the birth or demise of a fashion idea.

If the business of fashion is change, it is always unfinished business. You, with the thrust of an idea, may be the one who changes it. Good luck to you!

Statistics of Change

Unless otherwise noted, all charts are adapted from *Graphic Guide to Consumer Markets,* published annually by the National Industrial Conference Board. Reprint permission granted.

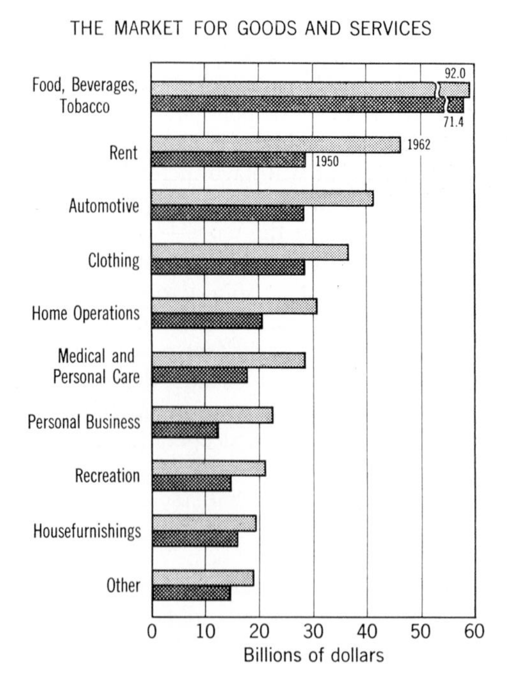

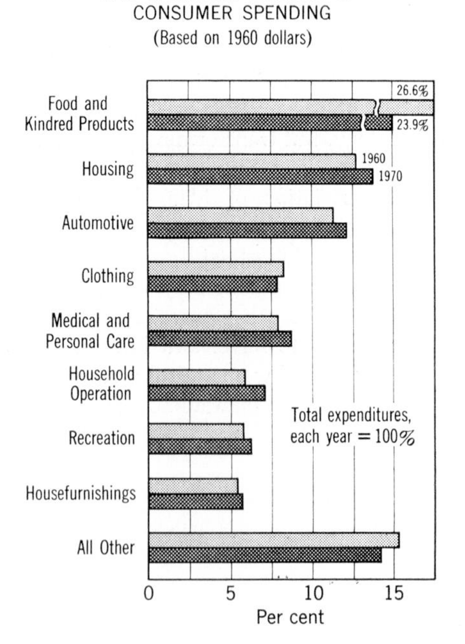

The changing pattern of consumer spending in dollars and as percentages of total spending. (Source: U.S. Departments of Commerce and Labor, after The National Industrial Conference Board, New York, N.Y.)

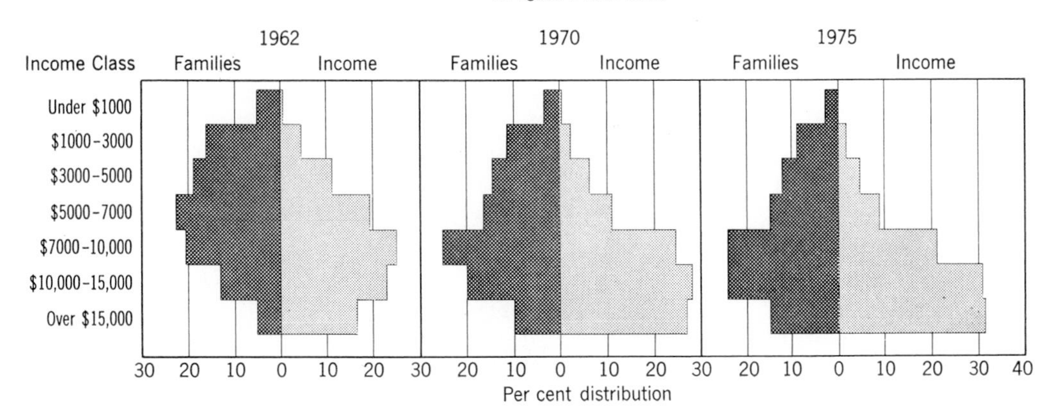

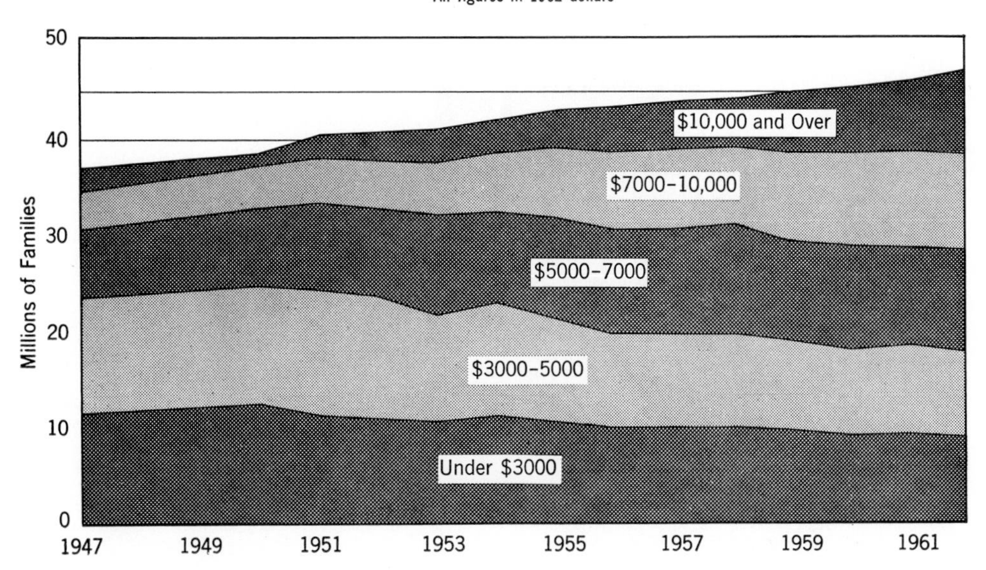

The changing pattern of family income. (Source: U.S. Department of Commerce, after The National Industrial Conference Board, New York, N.Y.)

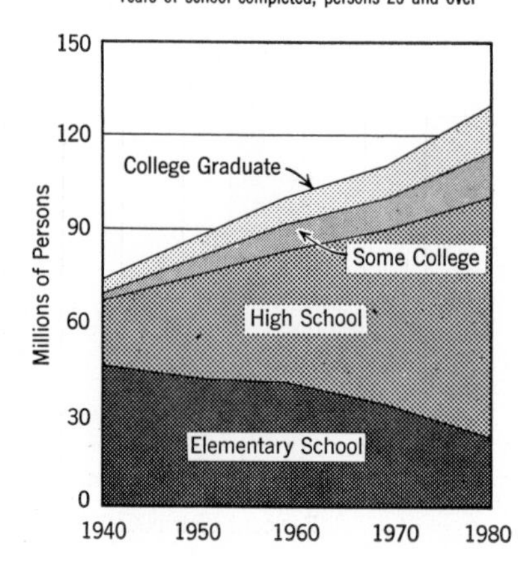

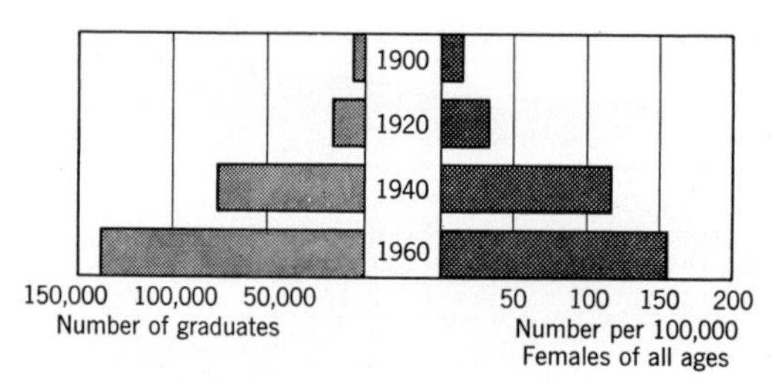

Education: more widespread. (Sources: The National Industrial Conference Board, New York, N.Y.; U.S. Department of Health, Education and Welfare for number of graduates; U.S. Bureau of Census for number of females; figure per 100,000 is derived, Statistical Abstract, 1962, pp. 24, 131.)

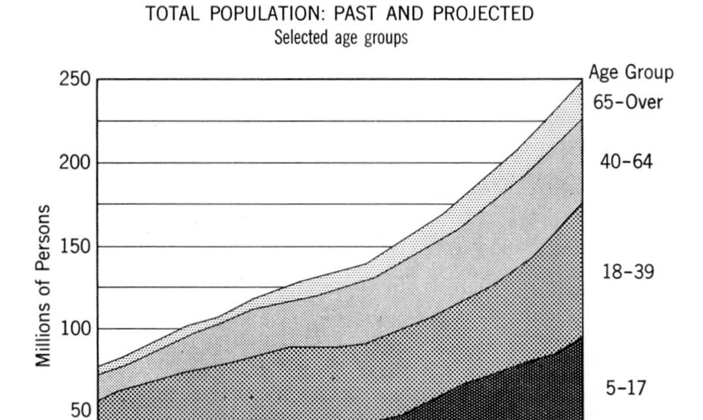

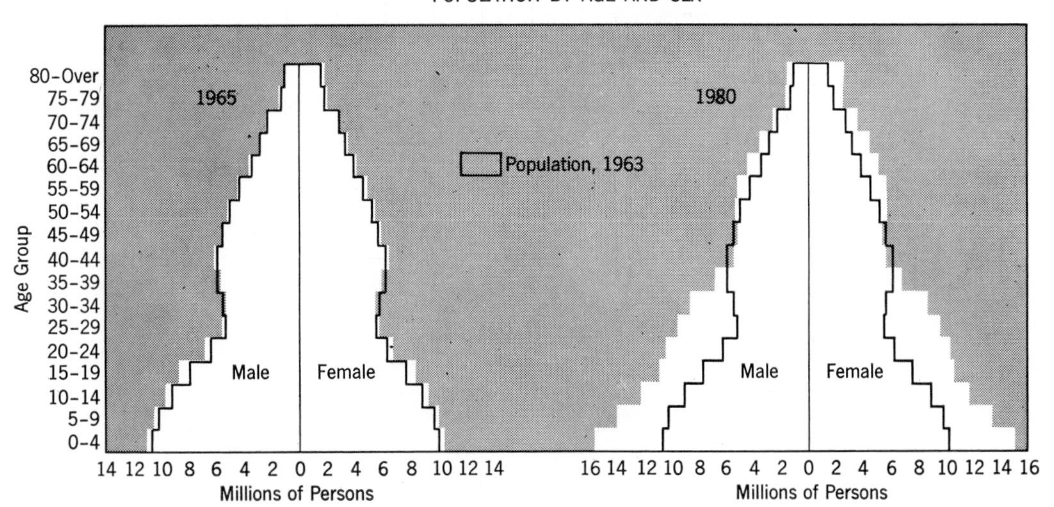

Population growth by age and sex. (Source: U.S. Department of Commerce after The National Industrial Conference Board, New York, N.Y.)

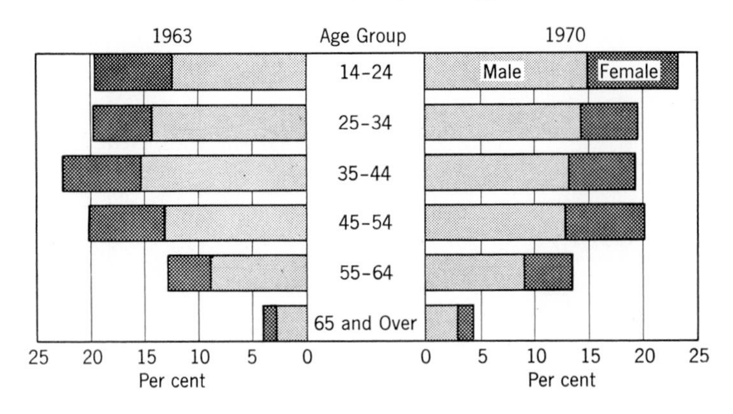

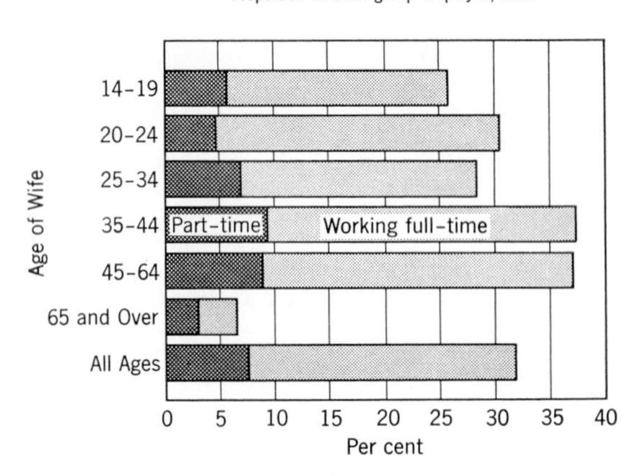

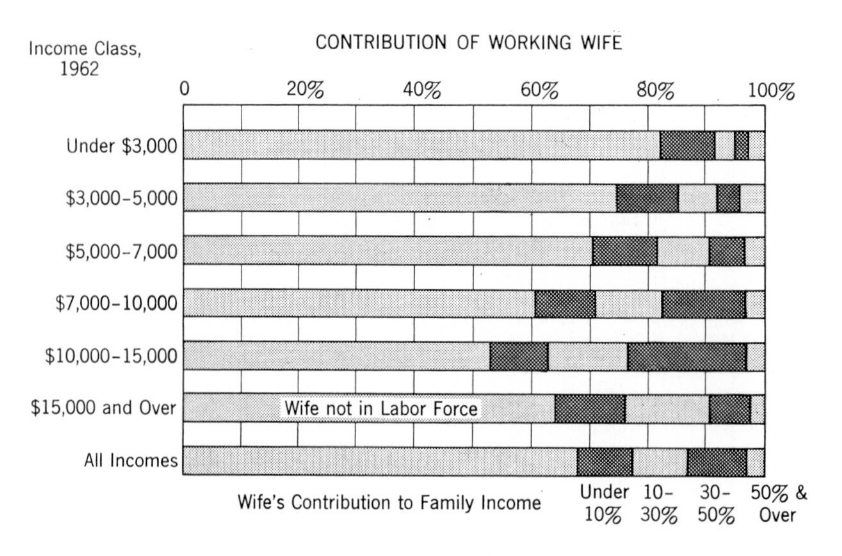

Women at work. (Source: The National Industrial Conference Board, New York, N.Y.)

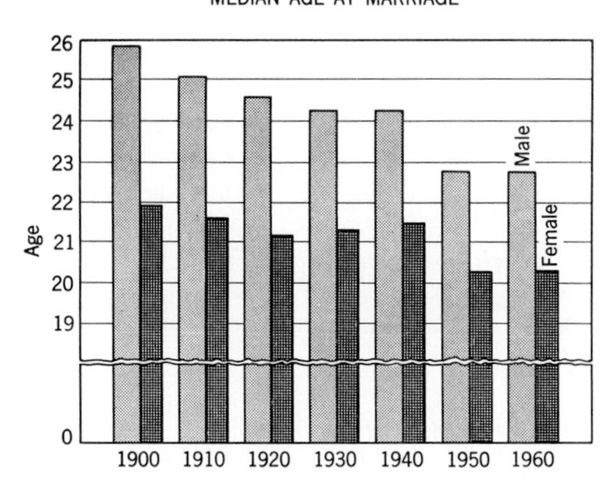

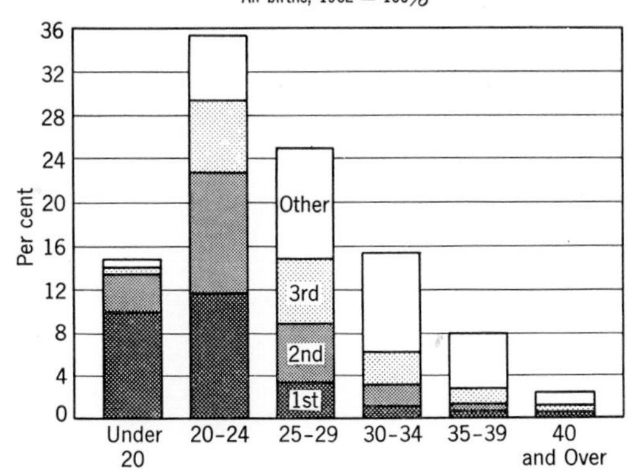

Ages for marriage and motherhood. (Sources: U.S. Department of Commerce, after The National Industrial Conference Board, New York, N.Y.; Office of Vital Statistics, U.S. Department of Health, Education and Welfare, after The National Industrial Conference Board, New York, N.Y.)

Questions for Review and Discussion

1. Why do people buy new clothing? Are their reasons largely emotional or rational? Explain.
2. Summarize the major socioeconomic changes which are occurring in the consumer market and suggest their implications for the fashion business.
3. Do you agree that the "American customer is the real Czar of the (fashion) industry from whose dictum there is no appeal." (from reading "Fashion Is A Hot Tin Roof"). Explain.
4. Do you believe that the fashion industries can halt or reverse the declining trend in consumers clothing expenditures? Defend your opinion.
5. Is clothing "out of fashion" as a status symbol? Why?
6. Do today's customers know more about fashion than did those of ten years ago? Why?
7. Do today's customers have better taste than did those of ten years ago? Explain.
8. Suggest ways in which apparel retailers have adapted or may adapt to the changes taking place in the consumer market. Consider methods of selling, store hours, store locations, services, assortments, etc., etc.
9. Are the majority of apparel purchases that are made by ultimate customers preplanned or are they bought on impulse? Explain.
10. Winston Churchill once said that "We shape our buildings; thereafter, they shape us." By substituting the word *fashion* for *buildings,* does the statement also apply to the fashion business? Why?

Appendix

Fashion Language Guide

ADAPTION. Garment similar to an original couture model, yet having some changes.

AVANT GARDE. In any art, the most daring of the experimentalists; innovation of original and startingly unconventional designs, ideas, or techniques during a particular period.

CAUTION FEE. An admission or entrance fee charged to commercial customers by *Haute Couture* houses.

CHAMBRE SYNDICALE DE LA COUTURE PARISIENNE. French Trade Association which represents the *Haute Couture* houses of Paris.

CHECKED OUT. A style number that sells rapidly (generally refers to retail sales).

CHIC. French word meaning originality and style in dress.

CLASSIC. A particular style that continues in fashion over an extended period of time.

CONTRACTOR. A manufacturing concern which does the sewing for other producers (socalled because this work is done on a contractual arrangement).

COTY FASHION AWARD. Annual awards bestowed on outstanding designers.

THE COUTURE GROUP. New York trade association of higher-priced dress manufacturers.

COUTURIER. (Couturiere-Fem.) French word for designer; usually one who has his or her own dressmaking establishment.

CRAZE. A fad or fashion characterized by much crowd excitement or emotion.

CUSTOM MADE. Made to a customer's special order; cut and fitted to individual measurements.

CUTTING-UP TRADE. That segment of the fashion industries which produce the items of apparel that have to be cut and sewed together, i.e., apparel manufacturers.

DESIGN. An arrangement of parts, form, color, etc., of a style.

FAD. A minor or short-lived fashion.

A FASHION (OR FASHIONS). The prevailing style(s) at any given time. When a style is followed or accepted by many people, it is a fashion.

FASHION. A process of change in the styles of dress that are accepted and followed by a large segment of the public at any given time.

FASHION BULLETIN. Written report on significant fashions prepared by fashion specialists.

FASHION CLINIC. Meeting of a group of persons interested in fashion, under the direction of a fashion authority, for the purpose of presenting and/or discussing significant fashion trends; clinics are usually held at the beginning of new fashion seasons.

FASHION CONSULTANT. A person who gives professional fashion advice or services.

FASHION CYCLE. A term which refers to the rise, popularization, and decline of a fashion. It is usually represented visually by a wavelike curve.

FASHION FORECAST. A prediction as to which fashions and/or styles will be popular during any coming season.

FASHION GROUP. A national noncommercial association of women engaged in the fashion business.

FASHION INTELLECTUAL. A person who is familiar with the past and present developments of the fashion industry and who can interpret events in terms of their impact on the industry as a whole.

(THE) FASHION PRESS. Reporters of fashion news for magazines, newspapers, etc.

FASHION REPORTER. A person who specializes in reporting fashion news for magazines and/or newspapers.

FASHION SHOW OR SHOWING. Formal presentation of a group of styles, often in connection with showing the season's new merchandise.

FASHION TREND. The direction in which fashion is moving.

FORD. A particular style or design that is produced by many different manufacturers at many different price lines.

GARMENT INDUSTRY. Synonym for the apparel industry.

HIGH FASHION. A fashion that has limited acceptance.

HOT NUMBER. A style number that sells quickly and in sizeable quantities.

HAUT COUTURE. The most important dressmaking houses in Paris.

I.L.G.W.U. International Ladies Garment Workers Union.

INSIDE SHOP. An apparel concern which performs all the manufacturing processes on its own premises or in its own plant (as opposed to an outside shop).

KNOCK-OFF. A style which is a copy of a higher-priced style.

LINE. A collection of styles shown by a producer.

LINE-FOR-LINE COPY. Exact copy of a style originated by a foreign couturier.

MASS PRODUCTION. Production of goods in quantity—many at a time as opposed to one at a time.

MODE. Synonym for a fashion.

N.R.M.A. (National Retail Merchants Association.) A trade association of the leading retailers in the United States.

OPENINGS. Fashion showing by apparel producers of new styles at the beginning of a season.

OUTSIDE SHOP. An apparel concern that utilizes contractors to do the sewing and finishing of their garments.

PRET-A-PORTER. (French term meaning literally ready-to-carry.) French ready-to-wear apparel, as distinguished from couture clothes which are custom-made.

PRIMARY MARKET. Producers of the raw materials of fashion such as leathers and fabrics, etc.

READY-TO-WEAR. Apparel which is mass produced as opposed to apparel made to a customer's special order (custom made).

REORDER NUMBER. A style number which continues to be ordered by sellers and consumers.

RESOURCE. A retailer's term for a wholesale supplier.

RUNNER. A style number that continues to sell quickly over a period of time and that is reordered frequently.

SAMPLE. The model or trial garment (may be original in design, a copy or an adaptation) to be shown to the trade.

SECONDARY MARKET. Producers of finished consumer fashion products (dresses, coats, suits, etc.), the cutting-up trade.

SEVENTH AVENUE. An expression used as a synonym for New York City's apparel industry. (In reality, a street on which are located the showrooms of many garment manufacturers.)

SHOWING. See Fashion Showing.

SMART. Having a fashionable appearance.

STYLE (NOUN). A type of product with specific characteristics which distinguish it from another type of the same product.

STYLE (VERB). To give fashion features to an article or group of articles (as to style a line of coats, suits, etc.).

STYLIST. One who advises concerning styles in clothes, furnishing, etc.

STYLE PIRACY. A term used to describe the use of a design without the consent of the originator.

TRIANGLE FIRE. A fire which occurred in the Triangle Shirtwaist factory in 1911 and took 146 lives—it was the turning point in the "sweat shop" era because it awoke the public conscience to the labor conditions in the garment industry.

VENDEUSE. French term meaning saleswoman.

VENDOR. One who sells.

WOMEN'S WEAR DAILY. Trade publication of the women's fashion industries.

General References and Selected Readings

Books

Adams, Walter, *The Structure of American Industry,* New York, Macmillan, 1957.

Alderfer, E. B., and H. E. Michl, *Economics of American Industry,* New York, McGraw-Hill, 1957.

Appel, Joseph H., *Business Biography of John Wanamaker,* New York, Macmillan, 1930.

Arnold, Pauline, and Percival White, *Clothes and Cloth,* New York, Holiday House, 1961.

Baker, H. G., *Rich's of Atlanta: The Story of a Store Since 1867,* Atlanta, Division of Research University of Georgia, 1953.

Ballard. Bettina, *In My Fashion,* Philadelphia, McKay, 1960.

Barker, Clare W., Ira D. Anderson, and J. Donald Butterworth, *Principles of Retailing,* New York, McGraw-Hill, 1956.

Beaton, Cecil W. H., *The Glass of Fashion,* Garden City, N. Y., Doubleday, 1954.

Bell, Quentin, *On Human Finery,* New York, A. A. Wyn, 1949.

Bender, Pearl, *Muffs and Morals,* New York, Morrow, 1954.

Bergler, Edmund, *Fashion and The Unconscious,* New York, R. Brunner, 1953.

Bertin, Celia, *Paris A La Mode,* New York, Harper, 1957.

Boehn, Max von, *Modes and Manners,* Philadelphia, Lippincott, 1932.

Brenner, Barbara, *Careers in Fashion,* New York, Dutton, 1964.

Britt, Steuart Henderson, *The Spenders,* New York, McGraw-Hill, 1960.

Burris-Meyer, Elizabeth, *This is Fashion,* New York and London, Harper, 1943.

Cahill, Jane, *The Backbone of Retailing,* New York, Fairchild, 1960.

Campbell, Persia, *The Consumer Interest,* New York, Harper, 1949.

Case, Margaret, *And The Price is Right,* Cleveland, World, 1958.

Chambers, Bernice, *Fashion Fundamentals,* New York, Prentice-Hall, 1947.

Chambers, Bernice, *Keys to a Fashion Career,* New York and London, McGraw-Hill, 1946.

Chase, Edna W., *Always in Vogue,* Garden City, N. Y., Doubleday, 1954.

Cox, Reavis, *The Marketing of Textiles,* The Textile Foundation, Washington, D.C., 1938.

Crawford, Morris De Camp, *One World of Fashion,* New York, Fairchild, 1946.

Crawford, Morris De Camp, *The Ways of Fashion,* New York, Fairchild, 1948.

Cunningham, Cecil W., *Why Women Wear Clothes,* London, Faber & Faber, 1941.

Curtis, Frieda, *Careers in the World of Fashion,* New York, Women's Press, 1953.

Daché, Lilly, *Talking Through My Hats,* New York, Coward-McCann, 1946.

Dior, Christian, *Christian Dior and I,* New York, Dutton, 1957.

Dior, Christian, *Talking About Fashion,* New York, Putnam, 1954.

Disher, M. L., *American Factory Production of Women's Clothing,* London, Devereaux, 1947.

Drucker, Peter, *America's Next 20 Years,* New York, Harper, 1957.

Duncan, Delbert J., and Charles F. Phillips, *Retailing Principles and Methods,* Homewood, Ill., Richard D. Irwin, 1960.

Emmett, Jueck, *Catalogues and Counters,* Chicago, University of Chicago Press, 1950.

Entenberg, R. D., *The Changing Competitive Position of Department Stores in the United States by Merchandise Lines,* Pittsburgh, University of Pittsburgh Press, 1961.

Epstein, Beryl, *Fashion is Our Business,* Philadelphia, Lippincott, 1945.

Epstein, Beryl, *Young Faces in Fashion,* Philadelphia, Lippincott, 1956.

Fashion Group, *The Making and Makers of Fashion,* New York, The Fashion Group Inc., 1959.

Fashion Group of L.A., *California Fashion Explorers,* Los Angeles, W. Ritchie Press, 1945.

Feldman, Egal, *Fit for Men,* Washington, D.C., Public Affairs Press, 1960.

Ferry, J. W., *A History of the Department Store,* New York, Macmillan, 1960.

Flugel, John C., *The Psychology of Clothes,* London, Hogarth, 1930.

Fortune, *The Changing American Market,* Garden City, N. Y., Hanover House, 1955.

Fortune, *Market of the 60's,* New York, Harper, 1960.

Fried, Eleanor, *Is The Fashion Business Your Business?,* New York, Fairchild, 1958.

Garland, Madge, *Fashion,* England, Penguin, 1962.

Gately, Olive, and The Fashion Group, *Your Future in Fashion,* New York, The Fashion Group through Richards Rosen, 1960.

Glover, John George, and William Cornell, *The Development of American Industries,* New York, Prentice-Hall, 1955.

Gold, Ed., *The Dynamics of Retailing,* New York, Book Division, Fairchild, 1963.

Hahn, Lew, *Stores, Merchants, Customers,* New York, Fairchild, 1952.

Hall, Max, *Made in New York,* Cambridge, Mass., Harvard University Press, 1959.

Hamburger, Estelle, *It's a Woman's Business,* New York, Vanguard, 1939.

Hamilton, D. B., *The Consumer in Our Economy,* Boston, Houghton-Mifflin, 1962.

Hawes, Elizabeth, *Fashion is Spinach,* New York, Random House, 1938.

Herndon, Booton, *Bergdorf's on the Plaza,* New York, Knopf, 1956.

Hurlock, Elizabeth Bergner, *The Psychology of Dress,* New York, The Ronald Press, 1929.

Kaplan, Albert A. and Margaret de Mille, *Careers in Department Store Merchandising,* New York, H. Z. Walck, 1962.

Katona, George, *The Powerful Consumer,* New York, McGraw-Hill, 1960.

Kimbrough, Emily, *Through Charley's Door,* New York, Harper, 1952.

Kohler, Carl, *A History of Costume,* Philadelphia, McKay (N.D.), 1928.

Latour, Anny, *Kings of Fashion,* New York, Coward-McCann, 1958.

Laver, James, *Dress,* London, J. Murray, 1950.

Laver, James, *Taste and Fashion,* New York, Dodd, Mead, 1938.

Levin, Phyllis Lee, *The Wheels of Fashion,* New York, Doubleday, 1965.

Mahoney, Tom, *The Great Merchants,* New York, Harper, 1955.

Mayfield, Frank, *The Department Store Story,* New York, Fairchild, 1949.

McCardell, Claire, *What Shall I Wear?,* New York, Simon and Schuster, 1956.

Merriam, Eve, *Figleaf: The Business of Being in Fashion,* Philadelphia, Lippincott, 1960.

National Retail Merchants Association, *The Buyer's Manual,* New York, National Retail Merchants Association, 1965.

Nystrom, Paul, *Economic Principles of Consumption,* New York, Ronald Press, 1929.

Nystrom, Paul, *Economics of Fashion,* New York, Ronald Press, 1928.

Nystrom, Paul, *Fashion Merchandising,* New York, Ronald Press, 1932.

Ohrbach, Nathan M., *Getting Ahead in Retailing,* New York, McGraw-Hill, 1935.

Packard, Vance, *The Hidden Persuaders,* Philadelphia, David McKay, 1957.

Packard, Vance, *The Status Seekers,* Philadelphia, David McKay, 1959.

Palmer, J. L., *The Origin, Growth, and Transformation of Marshall Field and Company,* New York: Newcomen Society in North America, 1963.

Parsons, Frank, *The Psychology of Fashion,* Garden City, N. Y., Doubleday, 1920.

Phillips, Charles F., and Delbert J. Duncan, *Marketing Principles and Methods,* Homewood, Ill., Richard D. Irwin, fourth edition, 1960.

Pickens, Mary Brooks, *The Fashion Dictionary,* New York, Funk and Wagnalls, 1957.

Pickens, Mary Brooks, and Dora L. Miller, *Dressmakers of France,* New York, Harper, 1956.

Price, Julius, *Dame Fashion,* Paris and London, S. Low, Marston Co., 1913.

Rich, S. A., *Shopping Behavior of Department Store Customers,* Boston, Division of Research, Graduate School of Business Administration, Harvard University, 1963.

Richards, Florence, *The Ready-to-Wear Industry,* New York, Fairchild, 1951.

Robson, R., *The Man-Made Fibers Industry,* London, Macmillan, 1958.

Roshko, Bernard, *The Rag Race,* New York, Funk and Wagnalls, 1962.

Rudofsky, Bernard, *Are Clothes Modern?,* Chicago, P. Theobald, 1947.

Saunders, Edith, *The Age of Worth,* Bloomington, Indiana University Press, 1955.

Sices, Murray, *Seventh Avenue,* New York, Fairchild, 1953.

Snow, Carmel, with Mary Louise Aswell, *The World of Carmel Snow,* New York, McGraw-Hill, 1962.

Spanier, Ginette, *It Isn't All Mink,* New York, Random House, 1959.

Stuart, Jessie, *The American Fashion Industry,* Boston, Simmons College, 1951.

Swinney, John B., *Merchandising of Fashions,* New York, Ronald Press, 1942.

Tolbert, Frank X., "Neiman Marcus, Texas," New York, Holt, 1953.

Vance, Stanley, *American Industries,* Englewood Cliffs, N. J., Prentice-Hall, 1957.

Walton, Frank, *Tomahawks to Textiles: The Fabulous Story of Worth Street,* New York, Appleton-Century-Crofts, 1953.

Walton, Perry, *The Story of Textiles,* Boston, Mass., John S. Lawrence, 1912.

Warburton, Gertrude, and Jane Maxwell, *Fashion For a Living,* New York, McGraw-Hill, 1939.

Wendt, Lloyd, and Herman Kogan, *Give the Lady What She Wants,* Chicago, Rand-McNally, 1952.

Wingate, John W., and Arnold Corbin, *Changing Patterns in Retailing,* Homewood, Ill., R. D. Irwin, 1956.

Wolff, Janet, *What Makes Women Buy,* New York, McGraw-Hill, 1958.

Women's Wear Daily, *Sixty Years of Fashion,* New York, Book Division, Fairchild, 1963.

Young, Agnes (Brooks), *Recurring Cycles of Fashion, 1760–1937,* New York, Harper, 1937.

Business Publications *

GENERAL:

Daily News Record, 7 East 12 Street, New York.

Women's Wear Daily, 7 East 12 Street, New York.

RETAIL MANAGEMENT:

Chain Store Age, 2 Park Avenue, New York.

Stores, 100 West 31 Street, New York.

SPECIALIZED AS TO INDUSTRY OR TRADE:

Boot & Shoe Recorder, Chestnut & 56 Streets, Philadelphia.

Corset & Underwear Review, 111 Fourth Avenue, New York.

Dress & Costume Merchandiser, 230 Park Avenue, New York.

Handbags & Accessories, 111 Fourth Avenue, New York.

Hosiery & Underwear Review, 307 Fifth Avenue, New York.

Jewelers' Circular-Keystone, Chestnut & 56 Streets, Philadelphia.

Lingerie Merchandising, 307 Fifth Avenue, New York.

Trade Associations †

Color Association of the United States, 200 Madison Avenue, New York.

Corset & Brassiere Association of America, 200 Madison Avenue, New York.

*This is a selected list, designed to provide a cross section. For a complete list of business publications in any field, consult Standard Rate & Data Service, Business Publication Section, published monthly at Evanston, Illinois. Copies are usually available in business libraries and in the offices of advertising agencies.

Handkerchief Industry Association, 274 Madison Avenue, New York.

International Council of Shopping Centers, 342 Madison Avenue, New York.

International Silk Association, 185 Madison Avenue, New York.

Irish Linen Guild, 1270 Sixth Avenue, New York.

Jewelry Industry Council, 608 Fifth Avenue, New York.

Knitted Outerwear Foundation, 386 Park Avenue, New York.

National Association of Leather Glove Manufacturers, 52 S. Main Street, Gloversville, N. Y.

National Board of the Coat and Suit Industry, 450 Seventh Avenue, New York.

National Cotton Council of America, 1918 Parkway, Memphis 12, Tenn.

National Millinery Planning Board, 10 East 40 Street, New York.

National Retail Merchants Association, 100 West 31 Street, New York.

National Shoe Manufacturers Association, 342 Madison Avenue, New York.

National Shoe Retailers Association, 274 Madison Avenue, New York.

Popular Priced Dress Manufacturers Group, 1440 Broadway, New York.

Toilet Goods Association, 1270 Avenue of the Americas, New York.

United Better Dress Manufacturers Association, 110 West 40 Street, New York.

Wool Bureau, 360 Lexington Avenue, New York.

†This is a selected list, designed to provide a cross section of the larger, more active associations in the fashion field. For a complete listing consult Directory of National Associations of Businessmen, 1961, by Jay Judkins, Chief, Trade Association Division, United States Department of Commerce, Washington 25, D. C., available at any field office of the U. S. Department of Commerce and on sale at the Government Printing Office, Washington 25, D. C.

Index